Historical and Geographical Influences on Psychopathology

Historical and Geographical Influences on Psychopathology

Edited by

Patricia Cohen
Columbia University College of Physicians & Surgeons
New York State Psychiatric Institute

Cheryl Slomkowski
Columbia University College of Physicians & Surgeons

Lee N. Robins
Washington University School of Medicine

LEA LAWRENCE ERLBAUM ASSOCIATES, PUBLISHERS
1999   Mahwah, New Jersey   London

Lawrence Erlbaum Associates, Inc., Publishers
10 Industrial Avenue
Mahwah, New Jersey 07430

Cover design by Kathryn Houghtaling Lacey

Library of Congress Cataloging-in-Publication Data

Historical and geographical influences on psychopathology / edited by
    Patricia Cohen, Cheryl Slomkowski, Lee N. Robins.
        p.   cm.
    Includes bibliographical references and index.
    ISBN 0-8058-2426-X (hardcover : alk. paper). — ISBN 0-8058-2427-8
(pbk. : alk. paper).
    1. Psychiatric epidemiology.   I. Cohen, Patricia.
II. Slomkowski, Cheryl.   III. Robins, Lee N.
RC455.2.E64H57   1998
616.89—dc21   98-7194
                                                                  CIP

Books published by Lawrence Erlbaum Associates are printed on acid-free paper,
and their bindings are chosen for strength and durability.

Printed in the United States of America
10 9 8 7 6 5 4 3 2 1

Contents

Preface

Historical and geographical perspectives are essential components of a sound understanding of psychopathology and the factors that increase the risk of psychopathology. We can learn a great deal from the study of both uniformities and variations in the incidence and course of disorder and in the apparent causal connections between risks and disorders over time and place. This book results from a meeting of the Society for Life History Research in Psychopathology at which studies focusing on these issues were presented.

We start from the assumption that a deep understanding of the origins of psychopathology and human dysfunction and their course is fundamental to the quest for the good society, and perhaps even to our survival as a species. An important contribution to that understanding may be found in differentials in the distribution of psychopathology over time and place— "where and when," and the translation of these observations into etiologic hypotheses.

- When incidence rates are stable over time and across populations, we are prompted to expect an underlying biological etiology and relatively small environmental impact.
- When a change in incidence rates occurs rapidly within a locale, there is no possibility of a genetic explanation, and we are encouraged to seek, as potential explanations, historical events—whether social or biological—that affected large parts of that population.

- When incidence rates are stable over time but vary across nations or cultural groups, we seek, as risk factors, characteristics those high-rate groups share.
- When incidence rates are similar across nations or cultural groups but prevalence varies, we are pointed toward consideration of different ways in which communities respond to psychopathology, ways that may delay or enhance recovery.

Therefore, specification of the population and historical period to which one's generalizations apply is always prudent and often a useful means of obtaining leverage on theories of etiology and course of disorder. We often pay too little attention to population issues at all, and hardly ever to these broader issues. Describing our samples should be seen as a series of successive approximations to the variables known to be relevant to the prevalence of problems and the varying relationships among predictors and outcome. Such an emphasis is not only relevant to the study of psychopathology, but has been recognized as a critical next step for understanding the epidemiology of diseases in general (Susser & Susser, 1996).

As the studies in this volume well illustrate, comparing prevalences and risk factors across time and place makes use of concepts and methods from history, geography, sociology, anthropology, economics, psychology, social and medical services research, social policy, and psychiatry, as well as epidemiology. Each of these disciplines has much to contribute. The last 15 years or so have seen the emergence of the new multidisciplinary field of developmental psychopathology. As conceptualized by Cicchetti (1990), the union of studies of normal development and psychopathology, long kept separate in both the theories employed and the disciplines from which researchers came, would be synergistic. Simultaneously considering normal development, which constitutes the center of the distribution, and psychopathology, its outermost fringes will be mutually informative. This merging of normal and abnormal development has brought to the attention of developmentalists, clinical psychologists, and psychiatrists this need to clarify when a trait is dimensional, suggesting multifactorial causation, and when there is a sharp point of discontinuity where psychopathology is qualitatively different from the normal, suggesting a single or few causal factors. Such an integration may require collaboration of disciplines such as genetics and sociology. This combined perspective is usefully expanded to explicitly encompass the influences of time and place when examining specific risk factors for the development of psychopathology.

The studies in this volume both illustrate the methods and methodological difficulties involved in such work and provide important insights into the disorders and dysfunctions that they investigate.

REFERENCES

Cicchetti, D. (1990). A historical perspective on the discipline of developmental psychopathology. In J. Rolf, A. Masten, D. Cicchetti, K. Neuchterlein, & S. Weintraub (Eds.), *Risk and protective factors in the development of psychopathology* (pp. 2–28). New York: Cambridge University Press.

Susser, M., & Susser, E. (1996). Choosing a future for epidemiology: II. From black box to Chinese boxes and eco-epidemiology. *American Journal of Public Health, 86,* 674–677.

— Patricia Cohen
— Cheryl Slomkowski
— Lee N. Robins

Chapter 1

Introduction: Time, Place, and Psychopathology

Patricia Cohen
Columbia University College of Physicians & Surgeons
New York State Psychiatric Institute

Cheryl Slomkowski
Columbia University College of Physicians & Surgeons

Lee N. Robins
Washington University School of Medicine

Historical and geographical perspectives can add breadth and validity to our theories about the etiological and course-determining factors in psychopathology. Our initial speculations about causes often apply to members of our own contemporary culture, because that is the population we have usually spent our lives trying to understand. But when we move outside this population, we can perceive the limitations of our theories as our predictions fail. All effects are conditional. Although many of the risks for increased probability of psychopathology may replicate over time and population, there are always circumstances in which their effects are empirically or theoretically absent, particularly when the mechanisms through which their effects operate are neutralized or eliminated. When these mechanisms are identified, we reach a more profound understanding of why, when, and how the geographic, cultural, and historical frames permit, promote, and inhibit the development of psychopathology.

The research reported in this book is interdisciplinary and longitudinal. It compares the prevalence and course of psychopathology between places and over time. In this chapter, we note two major kinds of causal effects that are illuminated in these investigations. First, there are those primarily or solely identifiable at the aggregate level—by looking at group differences or changes over time or place (Diez-Roux, in press). Second, the relationship of risk factors to outcome for individuals may vary over place or era. Investigations at both the aggregate and individual level provide scope for expertise in diverse scientific disciplines. In both kinds of investigations there are serious methodological issues and difficulties, which are briefly reviewed here.

VARIATIONS IN THE PREVALENCE OF PSYCHOPATHOLOGY AND RELATED PHENOMENA OVER TIME AND PLACE

Geographic Differences in the Prevalence of Psychopathology

Psychopathology researchers often focus on individuals, trying to determine why one individual becomes ill and another does not. Predictors on this level may not be useful in accounting for historical and geographical differences. Some important processes and predictors of pathology, such as the differential regional availability of substances to abuse, may not be identified when we conduct studies focusing on individual differences within a region. Lyme disease may provide a useful analogy. Although the spirochete is endemic, the disease has increased substantially over time and varies substantially over geographic areas, in accordance with classic epidemiological mechanisms. Prediction of which residents of a local area will become ill may be only modestly successful, whereas factors such as the size of the tick population and traditions having to do with where and when hunting occurs may effectively explain why areas differ substantially in disease prevalence.

It is traditional in cross-cultural psychiatry to examine variations in the phenomenology of psychopathology across a range of cultures and geographic locations and to test theories about why these variations occur (Murphy & A. H. Leighton, 1965; Price, Shea, & Mookherjee, 1995; Sartorius, Nielsen, & Stromgren, 1989). Studies that explicitly seek sociocultural explanations for geographically distributed rates are particularly valuable. Leighton's pioneering theorizing posited that sociocultural areas vary in the degree to which they provide physical security, ability to secure sexual satisfaction, legitimate ways of expressing hostility, the ability to give and secure love, recognition for achievement, freedom of spontaneous expression, a clear orientation regarding one's place in society and that of others, membership in a definable ethnic group, and a sense of belonging to a moral order and being right in what one does. He proposed that the degree to which an area is deficient will determine its level of psychopathology (A. H. Leighton, 1959). Leighton argued that these deficiencies will be more prevalent in communities with many broken homes, few and weak social organizations, few and weak leaders, few recreational opportunities, high rates of crime and delinquency, and a weak and fragmented network of communications. These patterns, in turn, often follow a recent history of disaster, widespread ill health, extensive poverty, cultural confusion, widespread secularization, extensive migration, and rapid and widespread social change. We would need to study a massive number of communities to validate each of these hypothetical causes of social disorganization and to explore their separate effects on the level of psychopathology. Leighton and colleagues examined several Nova Scotian communities that differed on combinations of these variables (Hughes, Tremblay, Rapoport, & A. H. Leighton, 1960; A. H. Leighton, 1959; D. C. Leighton, Harding, Macklin, Macmillan, & A. H. Leighton, 1963). Psychopathological variations were also found at the neighborhood level (Simcha-Fagan & Schwartz, 1986) and the regional level (Cohen, 1996; Cohen, Nisbett, Bowdle, & Schwarz, 1996) within the relatively homogeneous culture of a single country or ethnic group. Communities, neighborhoods, and regions often differ more in rates of psychopathology than do nations.

In chapter 11, Zoccolillo and colleagues compare national figures attained by similar interviews and sampling methods in different countries with respect to antisocial personality disorder. They find similar rates in nations geographically dispersed but sharing ancestry and traditions (the United States, New Zealand, and Canada) and large differences between countries that differ profoundly in their cultures, even when they are racially similar (e.g., as Taiwan has low rates compared to the three countries with British origins and to other Asian countries, such as South Korea and Hong Kong). These authors point out that examination of rates across countries can reveal risk factors obscured in studies within the relative homogeneity of a single country.

The study reported by Costello, Farmer, and Angold (chapter 12) compares Native American and White samples of children who live in the Appalachian Mountains in the eastern United States. Despite the substantial cultural differences between these groups, the only reliable difference in the prevalence of mental disorders was a higher rate of substance abuse in the Native American children.

Regional differences in prevalence may arise either because of a difference in the incidence of disorder, or a difference in how long an episode of disorder usually lasts. The duration of episodes may be influenced by how medical services are organized. In chapter 14, DeSisto, Harding, and colleagues show a substantial difference in the course of schizophrenia between the two neighboring New England states of Vermont and Maine. They believe the difference stems from the way these states provide treatment. Although both Vermont and Maine had policies favoring deinstitutionalization and regionalization of services between 1945 and 1980, and both initiated new drug and psychosocial treatments and mental health centers, Vermont's programs focused more on rehabilitation, including provision of halfway houses and comprehensive vocational rehabilitation. At follow-up, more of those with a history of schizophrenia in Vermont than in Maine were living independently, in halfway houses, or in boarding homes, and they had spent fewer of the intervening years in hospitals. In addition, more of those formerly hospitalized were working full or part time in Vermont than in Maine.

Historical Changes in Prevalence

Variations in the rate of psychopathology may also occur over time. Such changes may take place as a consequence of social, cultural, or economic change, or in reaction to war or natural disaster. Clausen was a pioneer in this area, with his study culminating in the recent book, *American Lives* (1993). Elder (1974) showed the influence of the timing of the Great Depression and World War II on the lives of the young men he studied. Elder and his colleagues pointed out that the study of developmental psychology has commonly ignored the influence of social history on development, in favor of an individualistic and noncontextualized perspective (Elder, Modell, & Parke, 1993). Bronfrenbrenner argued for an ecological view of development relating development to children's milieux, cultural group, and the historical period into which they are born. He also emphasizes the role of chance in people's lives (Bronfenbrenner, Kessel, Kessen, & White, 1988). Sampson and Laub (1996) examined the impact of a major historical event—a nearly universal military experience for young U.S. men in World War II and their reaping of postservice educational benefits—on their later social mobility and deviance.

The tendency to examine individuals as if there were no significant factors other than their own characteristics and their immediate surround characterizes much research on psychopathology. One exception is chapter 10 by Ullman and Newcomb, who take advantage of an unusual longitudinal data set to assess the impact of a natural disaster on psychopathology rates. Although experiencing an earthquake was sometimes followed by the expected posttraumatic stress disorder, rates of depression and anxiety did not rise and alcohol consumption declined, probably due in part to a decline in alcohol availability. Their analyses show that pre-existing characteristics of the survivors are important moderators of the effects of natural disasters.

A major effort to identify historical changes in the psychopathology of adolescents was undertaken by a consortium of European researchers. In the resulting volume edited by Rutter and Smith (1995), the difficulties in reaching definitive conclusions as to whether or not rates of psychopathology in young people increased over the last two or three generations were well discussed and illustrated. The volume included a review of historical changes in society that might account for such increases, if indeed they exist. Candidate changes that might account for increases in the prevalence of disorders among the young are: a rising standard of living, improvements in health, shifts in the population's age structure, decreasing availability of entry-level employment, a rise in expected years of education, migration, urbanization, decline in the proportion of families with traditional two-parent structure, historical stressors such as war and economic depression, growth of the media and changes in its content, and shifts in values related to morality and individualism. These multiple historical (and geographical) changes cause serious difficulty in identifying the particular clusters of factors that may be accounting for change in the prevalence of psychopathology. Our best test for the validity of hypothesized explanations lies in the successful prediction of increases in psychopathology when the cluster is present. It would also be relevant to show that the same cluster preceded changes in earlier epochs, but unfortunately, reliable measures of rates of psychopathology in the population are relatively recent inventions, making comparisons in rates over time perilous.

In chapter 6, Fombonne reviews the evidence for an historical increase in depression among young adults. He finds the argument for an increase persuasive, although women remain at much greater risk than men. However, he notes that the same increase is occurring in other disorders as well, including antisocial personality disorder. The fact that depression and antisocial personality differ dramatically in their demographic correlates makes their parallel increases puzzling.

In a 20-year longitudinal study, Reinherz and colleagues (chapter 7) report rates of major depression consistent with other reports of a trend toward increased depression in younger age groups. They also show that some risk factors are shared by young men and women, whereas others differ in ways consistent with gender-specific roles in the larger society. These findings on depression may be usefully linked with international trends for adolescent suicide (Diekstra, 1989).

The same behaviors may have different meanings and consequences in different historical times. In chapter 2, McCord examines changes in social conditions that may account for changes in crime rates. This chapter argues that looking over longer periods of history can debunk some misconceptions about the causes of crime. For example, after showing that official crime rates of African Americans have not always been higher than those of Whites, McCord chronicles some social policies that may have contributed to a rise in African American crime rates. Among these were federal loan policies in the 1930s that "redlined" housing based on the ethnic composition of the neighborhood, making it difficult for African Americans to purchase or sell houses they owned. This policy helped to isolate African Americans in urban centers, and thus prevented their living near job sites, which in turn led to the pattern of social disintegration that Leighton found to be associated with psychopathology and crime.

Changes in our understanding of psychopathology and related social phenomena also takes place over historical time, as Robins demonstrates in chapter 3 on conduct disorder. She notes that the disorder has been recognized in the official nosology only since 1968, and has been redifined with every revision of the diagnostic manuals. Nonetheless, there remain a common core of symptoms and stability in their relative frequencies. Like Fombonne, Robins finds evidence that the prevalence of the disorder has been increasing, and asks whether that increase is associated with a change in risk factors or consequences. Surprisingly, she finds no evidence for such changes. The impact of childhood behavior problems on adult adjustment has not been moderated as these behaviors have grown more common.

Such uniformity is not found, however, when the behaviors are tolerated or even admired. Karstedt (chapter 5) describes characteristics of early Nazis revealed in autobiographical accounts from the 1930s as compared to those of the neo-Nazis of the 1980s and 1990s. Although it does not focus on psychopathology, Karstedt provides insights that should broaden our understanding of psychopathology. Karstedt shows that similar kinds of violent and disruptive activities can have different origins and meanings to their perpetrators in eras in which the majority condone the activities, as was the case in the 1930s in Germany, as compared to the current era in which popular opinion strongly favors tolerance. Further, the degree of formal organizational structure associated with these attitudes will influence in which ways hostility will be expressed by young people.

Hodgins and Lalonde (chapter 4) review the scientific literature as well as asylum records and conclude that the association between major mental disorder (schizophrenia, major depression, bipolar disorder) and violence is a relatively new phenomenon, limited to patients born since World War II. These authors attribute the appearance of this association to dissolution of the restrictive environments, close supervision, and punitive restraints typical of mental hospitals before the beginning of the deinstitutionalization movement. They also attribute the violence to increases in alcohol and drug use disorders among persons with major mental illness; increases in the proportion of the mentally ill who have a history of conduct problems before developing mental illness (as demonstrated by Robins); increased exposure to psychoactive drugs in utero; and increased exposure to violent television and movies. These authors also urge specifying the population to which our findings are expected to generalize.

CAUSAL CONNECTIONS WITH INDIVIDUAL
PSYCHOPATHOLOGY OVER TIME AND PLACE

Studies Examining the Stability of Prevalence, Processes, and Causal Links Over Time

One set of questions has to do with the mechanisms of change and continuity over time. Kaplan and Liu (chapter 8) examine similarity in the antisocial character of two generations of females assessed when each generation was in early adolescence. This study of intergenerational transmission of psychopathology is an informative design, although one that requires a long-term investigator commitment. Kaplan and Liu found that first-generation parenting style was related to a history of antisocial behavior in the mother and to antisocial behavior in the offspring. However, their analyses suggest this relationship may be spurious, reflecting only the common influence of maternal psychological distress on both parenting and offspring behavior. These authors note that despite the elegance of their study design, the model they proposed may have been misspecified if the problems in parenting and the antisocial behavior of the daughter had contributed to maternal psychopathology. This causal path could not be ruled out because all three associated variables, parenting quality, daughter's antisocial behavior, and mother's psychopathology, were measured at the same time, making it impossible to determine in what order they had appeared.

In chapter 9, which examines mothers' interaction with toddlers in two generations, Kasen and her colleagues look at changes between generations in the rates of mothers' report of angry temperament in their toddlers and the discipline techniques they use with this age group. Despite an increase in the proportion of children perceived as having angry temperaments, mothers in the more recent generation are less likely to use physical punishment, the technique reserved primarily for toddlers with angry temperaments. Nevertheless, in both generations the risk associated with more power-assertive punishment was apparent. Thus, as in chapter 8, an intergenerational study revealed a complex relationship between parents' style of discipline and the child's behavior.

Studies Examining the Stability of Risk Mechanisms Over Populations

Longitudinal data are particularly useful for identifying causal mechanisms because temporal priority can be established. One of the signs of valid inference from longitudinal data is consistency of the effect over replications that involve changes in measures or populations. Such replications are more convincing than are precise repetitions in the same population because they suggest the mechanisms may be universal, rather than applying only under highly specified conditions. Broadening the diversity of method and setting can save us from "looking more and more at less and less" (Bronfenbrenner, Kessel, Kessen, & White, 1988, p. 1219).

When it is unknown if findings are only locally valid, they have not been adequately specified. Sometimes the limitations in these specifications are as central to our understanding and even to our efforts to intervene to prevent disorders as is the original theory. For example, the finding that early puberty increases girls' participation in delinquent activities or in a diagnosis of conduct disorder holds only in settings in which the girls' behavior and association with other children is not strictly controlled. No such effect is found among girls raised in conservative sects (Magnusson, Stattin, & Allen, 1986); in strict single-gender schools (Caspi, Lynam, Moffitt, & Silva, 1993); and in cultures that fully organize encounters with the opposite gender, including setting the age and rules for dating and marriage (Rutter & Rutter, 1993).

Some of the most interesting and intriguing differences in effects on psychopathology involve demographic subgroups and structural variables. The absence of an effect of poverty on the Appalachian Native American sample of children, despite an effect in the White children living in that area, is reported in chapter 12. This finding is reminiscent of the general absence of a correlation between poverty and psychopathology at a national or regional level, even when the poorest individuals within regions are found to be at excessive risk. The answer to this puzzle may lie in some combination of the role of White parents' psychopathology in accounting for the family's social drift into poverty (Dohrenwend et al., 1992), defective parenting performance, and the effects of a drop in status which disappoints children's expectations and lowers their self-esteem. Together, poor parenting and low self-esteem may lead to symptoms in the child. No similar pattern would be found among Native Americans because they had not experienced or expected less poverty.

Another interesting variation in the effect of risk comes from investigations of psychiatric disorders in the elderly. Studies of samples of older people carried out in the 1950s found and assumed to be natural an increase in demoralization among the elderly, including those who were not overtly physically ill (D. C. Leighton et al., 1963). However, the healthy elderly in the United States are not at higher risk of major depression than are younger people (Robins & Regier, 1991). This change may be a consequence of the much improved financial status of the elderly, as well as their improved physical robustness, functioning, and less social isolation as their contemporaries more often survive into old age.

When processes can be shown to be consistent over time and space, we improve the likelihood that we have identified causal effects. When processes are not consistent, chances are that our theoretical models contain errors, apply only to a limited population, or are incomplete. Farrington and Loeber's study (chapter 13) shows impressive replicability of risk factors for delinquency across two countries in cohorts born about 25 years apart. Despite differences in measurement, each of the sets of variables assessed in common significantly contributed to court appearance for juvenile delinquency in both London and Pittsburgh. This study also brings to the fore the difficulty in determining whether there are real differences in the causal influences on psychopathology in two settings. For example, did parental discipline and the boy's involvement in home activities protect him more from delinquency in London than in Pittsburgh? Or did measurement differences (or simple sampling variation) account for this difference in findings? Again, replication is the critical test, but one particularly hard to achieve when studies are carried out in different times and with different sources providing a measure of outcomes.

Measurement differences were not a problem in the comparison of inner-city areas of concentrated poverty with other urban poor communities in chapter 15 by Gorman-Smith, Tolan, and Henry. This study examined the extent to which the relationship of stress to delinquency was mediated by family variables in each area. Despite comparable levels of measured stress and of most family variables in the two areas in the inner city, the effect of stress on delinquency was not entirely mediated through its effect on family functioning. This study is a good example of the difficulties in testing geographical or historical differences in more complex models. Given the relatively modest prediction of delinquency by these variables, no effort was made to determine whether family variables moderate the effects of stress. Moderation would imply that adaptive family processes could help a child cope with stressors, whereas mediation simply suggests that stress may effect delinquency by interfering with adaptive family processes. Tests of differential moderation (interaction among predictors) in different populations imply three-way interactions, for which large samples or unusually large effects are required. Nevertheless, this study adds to other evidence supporting the presence of large context effects on delinquency (Simcha-Fagan & Schwartz, 1986).

METHODOLOGICAL ISSUES

Measurement

Comparisons across time and place require measures of psychopathology and risk factors that can be applied in diverse settings, different eras, and different populations. Kaplan and Liu remind us of the importance of using the same instruments administered in the same fashion. Robins also notes that it is important for subjects and informants to be at the same developmental stage, lest differences deriving from different accounts of the risk period traversed be misinterpreted as differences due to time or place. Using a single instrument is not a perfect solution because words change their meanings and connotations over time, and equivalence of translations is always a problem in cross-cultural studies. Even if the assessment instrument remains fixed, there can be variations in subjects' readiness to recognize and report their symptoms. Even in Kaplan and Lui's study, where these issues were faced squarely, it was not possible to keep all these elements stable. Even when measures are assessed comparably, it is possible to discern by their correlates that a change in validity or in meaning may have taken place. Perhaps one of the most interesting findings in the Kaplan and Lui study is a change in the relationships among antisocial behaviors over one generation, with a stronger general factor in the more recent generation. Whether this may be due to an increase in the prevalence of these misbehaviors, or in their variance, or may reflect a more fundamental change in the meaning of the measure, has not yet been fully explored.

Separation of Age, Period, and Cohort Effects

Epidemiologists are aware of the difficulty in determining whether findings of divergent histories of psychopathology in persons of different ages are attributable to age at ascertainment (i.e., developmental stage and length of exposure); to birth cohort membership, which could determine factors such as stability of families, size of sibships, and ethnic mixes; or changes in the historical period, such as being a young adult during the Great Depression or a war. Longitudinal data on multiple birth cohorts can assist in this untangling, but there is no statistical method that can solve the problem entirely. Beliefs, however, become firmer as evidence cumulates from studies conducted in different eras. Schaie was one of the first life-span researchers to argue for a consideration of the contextual effect of time in developmental research, and he outlined various research paradigms that could be used: cross-sectional designs, which examine age differences at a single point in time; longitudinal designs, in which maturational stage is confounded with historical or secular trends; and mixes of the two, including cohort-sequential, time-sequential, and cross-sequential designs (see Schaie, 1977, 1994).

Fombonne, in reviewing findings for the secular increase in the rates of depression in the United States, clarifies some of the more common misinterpretations of what may be age, period, or cohort effects. One astute point made in the chapter is that the search for a statistical solution that disentangles age, period, and cohort effects is seductive, but perhaps pointless, for the concept (or scale) of time underlies all of these variables, and "time acts only as a proxy indicator for unmeasured causal influences." Fombonne also suggests that these risk factors or mechanisms can be determined through designs taking advantage of natural experiments. Robins shows that the confounding of age and cohort effects can be reduced by comparing results for the same cohort interviewed at different ages in different studies. Ultimately, only the development and testing of theories about the causal mechanisms underlying the cohort, period, or age effects will provide satisfactory solutions to this conundrum.

Discriminating Change From Sampling Error and Study Design Effects

Rutter and Smith (1995) pointed out how difficult it is to verify changes over time in the prevalence of major depressive disorder, juvenile delinquency, and eating disorders. In addition to changes in assessment methods and conception or definition of the variables, differences in sampling frames and variation in lengths of recall all contribute to uncertainty about interpreting the repeated finding of increasing rates over time.

Limitations on the Number of Settings

Generalization from a sample of individuals to a population is made possible by random selection of sufficient cases. But it is generally not feasible to choose large samples of settings and eras. This makes conclusions much more tentative. For example, in a study of adolescents and young adults, Cairns and Cairns (1994) described in detail the two towns from which their samples were drawn and the time period over which data were collected. Still, with only two sites, it is impossible to decide which of the many differences between the towns are most relevant for determining the life course of the young people who live in them.

Farrington and Loeber have the same problem in comparing London with Pittsburgh. In their conclusion, they discuss the definition of each variable in order to identify potential methodological explanations for discrepancy across the two sites of their study. For example, the measure of father's antisociability in Pittsburgh was based on reported behavior problems, whereas in London it was based on criminal conviction, the greater seriousness of which may have accounted for its better prediction of sons' delinquency.

Despite the methodological advantages of intergenerational studies, the influence of time-varying mechanisms is noted by Kaplan in the discussion of his study. He notes that without the benefit of a cohort-sequential design, it is unclear whether the results of his study are due to intergenerational continuity or sociocultural change. He states that "during periods of social stability, intergenerational transmission becomes a major mechanism for maintaining the stability of attitudes," and during more unrestful times "intergenerational influences may be watered down by the degree to which new attitudes, behaviors, and mores are reinforced in societal contexts."

In view of all of these methodological and conceptual difficulties, it is clear that the task of developing a thorough understanding of the role of historical and geographical context on psychopathology demands further theory development, empirical input, and, particularly, ingenuity in study design. We believe the research reported in this volume usefully contributes to each of these aspects of the work. However, studies contrasting results over time and place have already made an important contribution to genetics.

Contributions of Studies Over Time and Place to Genetics. Family-genetic researchers have begun to seriously consider the implications of cohort effects on psychiatric disorders, such as the notable increase in risk for major depressive disorder since 1960. Given the evidence for cohort effects, it was suggested that genetic studies of affective disorder should focus on siblings and cousins of approximately the same age, from the same birth cohort, and exposed to the same period effects (Todd, Neuman, Geller, Fox, & Hickok, 1993). It also suggests that measuring familial aggregation by the method which corrects for percentage of the risk period lived through needs refinement, so that it reflects the drop in age of onset in recent cohorts. Developmental psychopathologists may need to make "generational" adjustments in their definitions of the clinical phenotype based on cohort effects, such as limiting assessment of addiction in addicted probands' parents to alcoholism, but adding drug addiction to assessment of addiction in siblings (Luthar & Rounsaville, 1993). The argument in studies of affective disorders and drug abuse is not that genetic influences change across generations, but rather that historical changes can lead to an alteration in the phenotype that is observed. These examples serve as concrete reminders of the utility of complex models that attempt to examine the impact of individual and familial risk factors within the context of historical changes in manifestations of psychopathology.

REFERENCES

Bronfenbrenner, U., Kessel, F., Kessen, W., & White, S. (1988). Toward a critical social history of developmental psychology: A propaedeutic discussion. *American Psychologist, 41,* 1216–1230.

Cairns, R. B., & Cairns, B. D. (1994). *Lifelines and risks: Pathways of youth in our time.* New York: Cambridge University Press.

Caspi, A., Lynam, D. R., Moffitt, T. E., & Silva, P. A. (1993). Unraveling girls' delinquency: Biological, dispositional, and contextual contributions to adolescent misbehavior. *Developmental Psychology, 29*, 19–30.

Clausen, J. (1993). *American lives: Looking back at the children of the Great Depression.* New York: The Free Press.

Cohen, D. (1996) Law, social policy, and violence: The impact of regional cultures. *Journal of Personality and Social Psychology, 70*, 961–978.

Cohen, D., Nisbett, R. C., Bowdle, B. F., & Schwarz, N. (1996). Insult, aggression, and the Southern culture of honor: An "experimental ethnography." *Journal of Personality and Social Psychology, 70*, 945–960.

Diekstra, R. F. W. (1989). Suicidal behavior in adolescents and young adults: The international picture. *Crisis, 10*, 16–35.

Diez-Roux, A. (in press). Bringing context back into epidemiology: Variables and fallacies in multilevel analysis. *American Journal of Public Health.*

Dohrenwend, B. P., Levav, I., Shrout, P. E., Schwartz, S., Naveh, G., Link, B. G., Skodal, A. E., & Stueve A. (1992). Socioeconomic status and psychiatric disorders: The causation-selection issue. *Science, 255*, 946–952.

Elder, G. H. (1974). *Children of the Great Depression.* Chicago: University of Chicago Press.

Elder, G. H., Modell, J., & Parke, R. D. (1993). *Children in time and place.* New York: Cambridge University Press.

Hughes, C. C., Tremblay, M., Rapoport, R. N., & Leighton, A. H. (1960). *The people of Cove and Woodlot.* New York: Basic Books.

Leighton, A. H. (1959). *My name is legion.* New York: Basic Books.

Leighton, D. C., Harding, J. S., Macklin, D. B., Macmillan, A. M., & Leighton, A. H. (1963). *The character of danger: Psychiatric symptoms in selected communities.* New York: Basic Books.

Luthar, S. S., & Rounsaville, B. J. (1993). Substance misuse and comorbid psychopathology in a high-risk group: A study of siblings of cocaine misusers. *International Journal of the Addictions, 28*, 415–434.

Magnusson, D., Stattin, H., & Allen, V. L. (1986). Differential maturation among girls and its relation to social adjustment: a longitudinal perspective. In P. B. Baltes, D. Featherman, & R. M. Lerner (Eds.), *Life-span development* (Vol. 7, pp. 136–172). New York: Academic Press.

Murphy, J. S., & Leighton, A. H. (1965). *Approaches to cross-cultural psychiatry.* Ithaca, NY: Cornell University Press.

Price, R. K., Shea, B. M., & Mookherjee, H. N. (Eds.). (1995). *Social psychiatry across cultures: Studies from North America, Europe, Asia, and Africa.* New York: Plenum.

Robins, L. N., & Regier, D. A. (Eds.). (1991). *Psychiatric disorders in America.* New York: The Free Press.

Rutter, M., & Rutter, M. (1993). *Developing minds: Challenge and continuity across the life span.* London: Penguin Books.

Rutter, M., & Smith, D. J. (Eds.). (1995). *Psychosocial disorders in young people: Time trends and their causes.* New York: Wiley.

Sampson, R. J., & Laub, J. H. (1996). Socioeconomic achievement in the life course of disadvantaged men: Military service as a turning point, circa 1940–1965. *American Sociological Review, 61*, 347–367.

Sartorius, N., Nielsen, J. A., & Stromgren, E. (1989). Changes in frequency of mental disorder of time: Results of repeated surveys of mental disorders in the general population. *Acta Psychiatrica Scandinavica, 79*, Supplement 248.

Schaie, K. W. (1977). Quasi-experimental research designs in the psychology of aging. In J. E. Birren & K. W. Schaie (Eds.), *Handbook of the psychology of aging* (pp. 39–68). New York: Van Nostrand Reinhold.

Schaie, K. W. (1994). Developmental designs revisited. In S. H. Cohen & H. W. Reese (Eds.), *Life-span developmental psychology: Methodological contributions* (pp. 45–65). Hillsdale, NJ: Lawrence Erlbaum Associates.

Simcha-Fagan, O., & Schwartz, J. E. (1986). Neighborhood and delinquency: An assessment of contextual effects. *Criminology, 24*, 667–703.

Todd, R., Neuman, R., Geller, B., Fox, L., & Hickok, J. (1993). Genetic studies of affective disorders: Should we be starting with childhood onset probands? *Journal of the American Academy of Child and Adolescent Psychiatry, 32*, 1164–1171.

Part I

THE IMPACT OF HISTORY

Chapter 2

Crime: Taking an Historical Perspective

Joan McCord
Temple University

This chapter uses an historical approach to challenge current causal theories of crime and to expand perspectives on crime to include events indirectly related to risk conditions. I consider three commonly accepted theories about causes of crime and then direct attention to the process of urban isolation that has led to high rates of violence in U.S. cities. I show how taking an historical approach can correct current theory or deepen understanding of criminogenic processes. Before turning to these topics, I discuss two sources of data about crime rates and their biases.

CRIME RATES AS A SOURCE OF DATA

Many researchers rely on crime rates to posit and to check hypotheses about causes of crime. These rates are designed to take account of differences in population and number of crimes committed. Generally, they are computed using decennial census figures in the denominator and annual data in the numerator. Rate differences reflect population changes and shifts in the numbers of crimes committed. Thus, for example, declining crime rates can be expected between the years when a census is taken if the population increases—and rates will rise if population declines. Crime rates provide rough pictures of trends through time and across cultures.

Although crime rates purport to provide an objective measure of change, they depend on how society evaluates victims. Killings of Mexican Americans, Native Americans, African Americans, Mormons, and Asian Americans were not counted as criminal acts at various periods in U.S. history (Frantz, 1969; Hershberg, 1973; Hofstadter, 1970; Hollon, 1974; Lane, 1976). Although common in urban centers, infanticide and drunken violence were disregarded during much of the 19th century (Gurr, 1979; Lane, 1980, 1986; Wade, 1972). Lane (1979) discovered that in Philadelphia, fewer than one half of those indicted for homicide were convicted. He explained: "Juries, especially early in the period, were usually quite tolerant of assaultive behavior and were always greatly influenced by moral or social rather than purely legal considerations" (p. 66). Describing working-class life during the mid-19th century, Gorn (1986) postulated: "Men tolerated violence—created violence—because high death rates, horrible accidents, and senseless acts of brutality were a psychological burden that only stoicism or bravado helped lighten" (p. 144).

Crime rates also depend on the methods for collecting information about intentional injury. Since 1933, the Federal Bureau of Investigation (FBI) has been collecting information about local crimes from police departments around the country. The FBI converts the data to crime rates and publishes them under the title "Uniform Crime Reports" (UCR). The FBI Index counts murder and non-negligent manslaughter, forcible rape, robbery, and aggravated assault as violent crimes.

The UCRs capture only part of the crime picture, a part reflecting social and political reality as well as popular beliefs about police efficacy and proper behavior (Black, 1970; Chaiken, 1978; Nagin, 1978; Seidman & Couzens, 1974). The police exercise discretion in terms of the calls to which they respond, what they report to their own offices, and how local data are reported to the federal government. Also, victims and observers vary in the degree to which they seek official police assistance for crime control. People who have little confidence in the government are unlikely to report crimes and, if they do, may find the police unwilling to make an official record of the report.

To overcome these sources of bias, in 1965–1966, The National Opinion Research Center undertook a study of households to determine the feasibility of gathering data on crimes from victims and other members of their households. They asked 10,000 randomly selected adult informants whether they or any other member of the household had been victims of a variety of crimes, using definitions based on those used for the UCRs. Victims' reports uncovered approximately twice as much forcible rape, robbery, and aggravated assault as was reported to police (Ennis, 1967). Since 1973, the federal government has collected information about victimization through household surveys in order to measure crimes not reported to the police. These surveys inquire about crimes committed against respondents over the age of 11.

The two federal sources of data yield different pictures of crime rates. The UCR excludes crimes not reported to police; the victim surveys omit homicides and crimes against children. Both, however, were used in support of the hypothesis that industrialization and urbanization contribute to violence.

INDUSTRIALIZATION AND URBANIZATION
AS CAUSES OF CRIME

Rates for violent crimes reported to the FBI began an almost constant, jagged rise as the United States industrialized for World War II, and the rise continued through 1992 (Maguire & Pastore, 1994; National Commission on the Causes and Prevention of Violence, 1969). Over most of this period, rates of violence were higher in urban than in suburban or rural areas. In 1992, for example, there were approximately 871 violent crimes known to the police per 100,000 people living in large cities, whereas in smaller cities the rate was 486, and in rural areas the violent crime rate was 220 per 100,000 (Flanagan & Maguire, 1992). Although they fail to show increasing violence, victim reports do show higher rates of violent crimes in urban than in suburban or nonmetropolitan areas (Bureau of Justice Statistics, 1994). Rates of violent crime are correlated with city size (U.S. Department of Justice, 1991).

Increasing rates of violent crime coincided, during most of this period, with urban growth and industrialization. This coincidence, coupled with increases in violent crimes reported by industrializing countries in many other parts of the world, seems to support the hypothesis that violence could be attributed to urbanization or industrialization (Buendia, 1989).

Park (1925/1967) argued that one of the most important effects of city growth is the substitution of secondary relationships for primary ones. This substitution, according to the argument, produces a breakdown of social controls that contributes to demoralization, crime, and vice. Echoing de Tocqueville (1835/1961), Park wrote: "Under these circumstances the individual's status is determined to a considerable degree by conventional signs—by fashion and 'front'—and the art of life is largely reduced to skating on thin surfaces and a scrupulous study of style and manners" (p. 40). Style and manners, in turn, appear to link violence with urban living in what Anderson (1990) described in terms of street wisdom.

Nevertheless, historical data suggest that the hypothesis is wrong. After a careful reconstruction of crime rates for England between 1200 and 1970, Gurr (1989a) concluded that rates of violent crime were at least 10 times higher in medieval England than in the 20th century. Since the Middle Ages, crime rates in the Netherlands and in Germany, too, show that rural societies tended to be more violent than urban ones (Diederiks, 1996; Johnson, 1996; Johnson & Monkkonen, 1996).

Gurr (1989a) summarized evidence regarding violence during the 19th and 20th centuries: "We can be reasonably confident that assaults, like murder, became less common during most of this period but increased after about 1950" (p. 34). Despite urbanization, rates of violent crimes declined in France and Great Britain as well as in the United States during the late 19th century (Lane, 1989; Lodhi & Tilly, 1973; Monkkonen, 1981).

Between 1830 and 1860, crime rates among Whites in largely rural South Carolina were several times those of urbanized, industrialized Massachusetts, belying "any notion of rural tranquility" (Hindus, 1980, p. 77). As Butterfield (1995) noted, "This goes against a central theorem of modern criminology, which predicts higher homicide rates in densely populated urban regions, where crowding and anonymity break down traditional social ties and values" (p. 8).

Gurr (1981) suggested that the long-term decline in rates of violence should be attributed to changing values of social and intellectual elites. Lane (1968) attributed the decline to urban-industrial growth itself, noting that city living and industrial employment require cooperation and self-discipline.

Contrary to a large body of sociological theorizing, the longer historical perspective provides grounds for believing that urbanization and industrialization contributed to regularizing life, forcing coordination and cooperation. Lane (1969) concluded that urbanization resulted in a "settling, literally a civilizing, effect on the population involved" (p. 469). In the rural United States, he noted, no built-in checks restricted fits of violence or bouts of drunkenness.

ETHNIC FACTORS AS CAUSE OF CRIME

A second set of hypotheses that deserves reconsideration on historical evidence rests on the high rates of violent crimes committed by African Americans. Although hypotheses related to race vary in detail, they amount to a claim that some criminogenic features linked with being African American (or Hispanic) are biologically transmitted. Yet, during the 19th and first half of the 20th centuries other ethnic groups were more violent than African Americans—who were more likely to be victims than perpetrators of violence (Butterfield, 1995; Haller, 1973; Hollon, 1974; Lane, 1986; Spear, 1967). Much of the violence against African Americans was not counted as criminal. In South Carolina Hindus (1980) wrote, "wanton killing of slaves" became illegal only in 1821, and even after that time, "if a slave was found off the plantation and refused to submit to investigation, any white had the right to kill him summarily" (pp. 132–133).

The institution of slavery could not have been maintained without at least a threat of violence. Capital punishments were dispensed against African Americans for behavior constituting nothing worse than a misdemeanor when performed by Whites (Blassingame, 1979; Hindus, 1980). But violence against African Americans was certainly not restricted to maintaining slaves or controlling their behavior. Wade (1972) reflected: "Emancipation freed the Negro from bondage, but it did not grant him either equality or immunity from white aggression" (p. 483).

African Americans, Catholics, Irish, Mormons, and foreigners were among the targeted victims of urban mobs. Between 1834 and 1860, serious urban riots occurred in New York, Philadelphia, Boston, Cincinnati, St. Louis, Louisville, and Vicksburg. Describing conditions for free African Americans in the 1850s, Bennett (1962/1993) wrote: "Most free blacks at this juncture lived along the docks and wharves and in alleys. Wherever they lived, people wanted them to go away ... Time and time again, immigrants, fresh from the boats, cracked their skulls and burned their homes and churches" (p. 181). In antebellum Philadelphia, wrote Hershberg (1973), "some blacks were killed, many beaten, and others run out of town" (p. 113). Five major anti-Black riots punctuated life in ghetto areas of Philadelphia between 1829 and 1849 (Johnson, 1973).

In New York during April 1863, "longshoremen's attempts to enforce a standard wage rate and an 'all-white' rule on the docks led to a protracted binge of racial violence that spread into surrounding tenements. For three days mobs of Irish longshoremen beat up black men found working along the docks and fought Metropolitan Police who attempted to save several blacks who defended themselves against lynching" (Bernstein, 1990, p. 120). Intimidation of and assault against Blacks was routine in New York City, where the draft riots of July 1863 accelerated violence against them (Asbury, 1927; Bernstein, 1990). Blacks were killed or driven from their homes and dragged through the streets, their houses destroyed and neighborhoods burned. Anti-Black riots in Memphis and New Orleans during 1866 resulted in many deaths and the destruction of schools and churches (Quarles, 1964; Wade, 1972). Within 10 years after the Civil War, freed slaves in the south were victims of almost 80 riots by Whites (Gurr, 1989b). The Ku Klux Klan, organized for the purposes of reducing the political power of Blacks "by stealth and murder, ... by the braining of the baby in its mother's arms, the slaying of the husband at his wife's feet, the raping of the wife before her husband's eyes," held its first national meeting in 1867 (Bennett, 1962/1993, p. 231). During the Reconstruction period, Black leaders were killed or run out of state.

According to Schlesinger (1933): "In the period 1882–1898 over sixteen hundred recorded lynchings, mainly of blacks, took place in the former slave states ... the victims suspected of rape or attempted rape formed but a minority of the whole number murdered" (p. 383). By 1951, at least 3,400 African Americans had been lynched (Gurr, 1989b). In Chicago between 1917 and 1921, there were 58 racially inspired bombings (Spear, 1967). Threats and bombings were used to chase African Americans away from their homes if Whites claimed the neighborhood. Spear (1967) wrote that African American tenants on one Chicago street received a letter saying: "We are going to BLOW these FLATS TO HELL and if you don't want to go with them you had better move at once" (p. 211).

After World War I and again after World War II, Blacks faced violence as they attempted to maintain or find legal employment. They faced violence when they bought homes in neighborhoods that Whites designated off limits to them. During the 1950s, they faced violence in exercising their legal rights to education in public schools.

A historical perspective shows that although African Americans currently account for a disproportionate amount of reported violence, they have not always been more violent than Whites. This fact makes dubious a claim that racial differences in violence are attributable to racially linked, genetic factors.

ROLE STRAIN AS CAUSE OF CRIME

Current research identifies the late teenage years as the age for greatest serious criminal behavior risk (Elliott, Huizinga, & Menard, 1989; Farrington, 1986a; Greenberg, 1985; Snyder & Aixkmuns, 1995). Because role changes occur around the age of 17, some attributed the phenomenon to leaving school or tensions related to taking on new, adult responsibilities. Such theories depend either on finding consistency through time in the age of greatest risk for crime or on linking criminal activity to changing ages of role transitions.

Some shifts in crime rates would be expected as a consequence of changes in public attitudes. If crime rates were solely reflecting public attitudes, criminal behavior should not (of course) be considered to represent role strain. Crime rates reflect behavior as well as attitudes toward that behavior, and the question to be addressed is whether criminal behavior is a reflection of role strain.

The Cambridge–Somerville Youth Study provided an opportunity to study age of first offense among men in two generations. The sample was selected during the 1930s as part of a project to study youth and prevent delinquency (McCord, 1992). Between 1939 and 1943, all of the study families lived in congested areas near Boston, Massachusetts. The study site had high crime rates, but the director wanted to avoid stigmatizing boys in the program, so both "good" and "bad" boys were included. The original sample included more than one boy from some families. To avoid bias due to inclusion of these families, I used only one (randomly selected) son from these families. The sample was further restricted by eliminating those lacking information about their natural parents ($N = 61$), those who were over age 10 when the data were first collected ($N = 36$), and those for whom the father's date of birth was not ascertained ($N = 9$). The remaining 376 fathers and sons provided data to assess the age of highest risk for crime across time.

To make comparisons across different historical periods, I divided the sample close to the median for fathers' birthdates. The oldest cohort consisted of 186 fathers born between 1872 and 1896 (M and median = 1890). The second included 190 fathers born between 1897 and 1913 (M = 1902, median = 1901). The third cohort comprised the sons of these two cohorts, divided according to their fathers' dates of birth. Sons of the first were born between 1926 and 1934 (M = 1929, median = 1928). Sons of the second were born between 1926 and 1933 (M and median = 1929). Thus, the sons did not differ in terms of temporal contexts.

The two cohorts of fathers resembled one another in the proportions living in transitional areas: Sixty-eight percent of the first and 67% of the second cohort lived in factory-dominated parts of their communities. They resembled one another, too, in terms of the proportions who lived with their wives at least until their sons had reached the age of 16 (68% of the older cohort and 67% of the younger one).

Almost one half of the sons in each cohort were middle children (48% and 49%, respectively), although sons of the first cohort were more likely to be the youngest (47% vs. 21%) and sons of the second cohort were more likely to be the oldest child in the family (6% vs. 30%). A higher proportion of the older cohort were immigrants: 68% compared with 36% [$X^2(1) = 37.18$, $p < .00$]. The older cohort also had larger families, with a mean of six children compared with a mean of four among the younger cohort [$t(332.1) = 7.28$, $p < .00$]. The older cohort, too, were more likely employed as unskilled workers: 61% compared with 49% [$X^2(1) = 5.24$, $p < .05$]. They were also less likely to be regularly employed: 41% compared with 52% [$X^2(1) = 4.30$, $p < .05$].

A two-generation comparison was valuable for differentiating effects of temporal contexts from biocultural effects. (See McCord, 1995, for a more complete description of cohort differences.) Differences between the cohorts of fathers that were based on cultural or biological factors would also be expected to differentiate the two sets of sons. Differences resulting from temporal contexts would not occur between the two sets of sons.

Assessment of crime relied on official records. Police and court records for fathers' criminal behavior and sons' juvenile criminality were collected in 1948. Data about the sons' criminal behaviors were gathered again in

1979 from probation departments in Massachusetts and in states to which the men migrated. This information was combined with the earlier records. Of course, official records did not include all crimes committed by these men (Murphy, Shirley, & Witmer, 1946). On the other hand, official records appear to identify those who commit serious crimes and those who frequently break the law (Elliott & Ageton, 1980; Farrington, 1979; Hindelang, Hirschi, & Weis, 1979; Morash, 1984; Reiss & Rhodes, 1961). Official criminal records do not report the same types of behavior through time. In Massachusetts, offenses against morality that dominated 17th- and 18-century criminal cases "were not pursued as vigorously in the nineteenth century . . . There was a gradual shift from crime as sin to crime as theft" (Hindus, 1980, p. 69). Serious criminal behavior, however, seems to have been less subject to definitional changes than were the more common crimes against public order (Lane, 1967).

To minimize confusing changes in definitions of crime with changes in behavior of criminals, crimes that appear on the FBI Index for serious street crimes were used to study changes across cohorts. These analyses focus on age for committing felonious crimes against persons and property. The analyses do not indicate a first age for troublesome behavior. Boys convicted for serious crimes have typically been in trouble with the police for less serious behavior (Farrington, 1986b; Lahey & Loeber, 1994; LeBlanc, 1990).

Among the older cohort, 29 fathers had been convicted of at least one FBI Index felony; among the younger cohort, 41 fathers had such convictions. Marked differences appeared in the ages at the time of their first convictions. The first cohort of fathers was about 10 years older than were the second cohort when first convicted for a felony: 38.2 years $(SD = 7.8)$ versus 27.2 years $(SD = 9.6; t(68) = 5.10, p = .00)$. Sons of the first cohort averaged age 17.9 $(SD = 7.7)$ and sons of the second cohort averaged age 16.9 $(SD = 6.8)$, a difference that was not statistically significant. Each of the cohorts of fathers were older than their sons at the time of first conviction for a felony $(p < .00)$.

To understand whether changes in keeping criminal records accounted for all the differences among cohorts, I looked at ages of last felony convictions. Fathers of the first cohort continued to be convicted for felonies through 1945, after the youngest cohort had begun to be convicted. Cohort comparisons for age at time of convictions are shown in Fig. 2.1.

Differences were slightly smaller for last convictions than for first convictions, although the first cohort of fathers committed their last felonies when they were approximately 8 years older than the second cohort [40.8 compared with 32.4; $t(68) = 3.85, p < .00$]. The younger fathers committed their last felonies when they were approximately 9 years older than their own sons [$t(97) = 4.77, p < .00$], who were only 6 months younger than

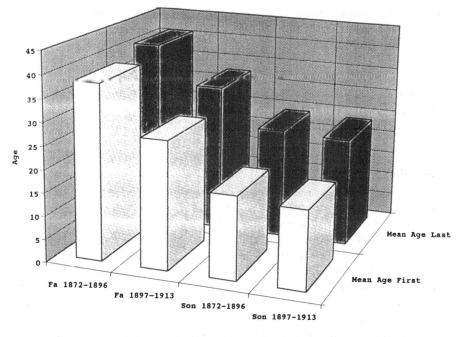

FIG. 2.1.   Cohorts and age of serious crimes.

the sons of the first cohort when they were last convicted for a felony. The similarity in patterns found for age at first and last conviction suggests that temporal contexts affect patterns of criminal behavior and, further, that role transitions are only accidentally linked with high risk for criminality.

To eliminate the possibility that these conclusions rest on a bias created through immigration, with immigrants having committed their youthful crimes before arriving in the United States, analyses were repeated after deleting immigrants and their sons. The age differences remained: The older cohort of fathers ($N = 11$) was about 10 years older than the younger cohort ($N = 31$) at the time when they committed their first Index crimes: 37.2 years ($SD = 10.0$) versus 26.6 years [$SD = 9.4$; $t(40) = 3.15$, $p < .00$]. Sons of the first cohort averaged age 18.4 ($SD = 8.5$) and sons of the second cohort averaged age 17.9 ($SD = 7.7$), a difference that was not statistically significant.

It could be argued that the shift in age at first conviction represented increased police vigilance. If increased police vigilance accounted for earlier age of first convictions for Index crimes, a parallel shift would be expected in the number of convictions. The conviction rates, however, differed little. The mean number of convictions among the 60 nonimmigrants in the older cohort of fathers was 3.4 ($SD = 7.4$) and among the 121 nonimmigrants in the younger cohort of fathers it was 3.8 ($SD = 9.8$).

Sons of the older cohort were convicted a mean of 2.8 (SD = 4.8) times
and sons of the younger cohort were convicted a mean of 3.8 (SD = 11.7)
times, a difference that was not statistically significant.

The shift in age for first committing serious crimes seems not to be an
artifact of policing practices or of immigration. Nor have the age of men at
the time of transition to adult roles been declining (Modell, 1989). These
data suggest that a theory depending on teenage phenomena—whether
biological or related to role transitions—rests on weak foundations.

THE PROCESS OF URBAN ISOLATION

As noted in the introduction, the second way in which historical approaches
contribute to understanding crime is by enlarging the set of events considered causally relevant to producing antisocial behavior. Over the last
several decades, crime statistics have shown urban centers to be areas of
particularly high risk for violence, with African Americans at particularly
high risk, both as perpetrators and as victims. In 1989, the rate of court
cases for African American youths was greater than four times the rate for
Caucasions (Butts & Conners-Beatty, 1993).

According to figures from the Center for Disease Control, homicide
rates for 1989–1990 show that African American males were nearly eight
times as likely as White males, and African American females were nearly
five times as likely as White females to die as victims of intentional violence
(Fingerhut, 1993). The victim survey of 1992 showed that African Americans were approximately 69% more likely than Whites to be victims of
violent crimes. Furthermore, about three out of four of the White teenage
victims were attacked by White offenders and about four out of five of the
Black teenage victims were attacked by Black offenders (Whitaker &
Bastian, 1991).

Policies that brought African Americans to the cities and isolated them
there without legitimate opportunities for success should be considered
as part of the causal stream fertilizing the high rates of crime in U.S. cities.
These policies can be traced to the ways in which government supported
migration to the outskirts of cities. During 1800–1850, cities were walking
size. Living in the center was desirable, and therefore the poor and Blacks
typically lived on the periphery, in "suburbs," among distasteful businesses
such as slaughterhouses and tanneries (Jackson, 1985; Wade, 1964). During
1850–1900, mass transportation facilitated industrial centralization and promoted residential migration to the outskirts (Warner, 1962/1978; Yancey,
Ericksen, & Juliani, 1976). Bands of wanderers and crowded conditions
for workers contributed to urban disorganization (Lane, 1986). As the city
became less comfortable, romantic notions about country life promoted

the building of a new type of suburb where wealthy families could escape the turmoil of city living. The middle classes followed the wealthy, although their homes were closer to the center of the city and built on smaller plots. These new suburbs were racially and economically segregated (Barth, 1980; Sugrue, 1993; Ward, 1971, Warner, 1962/1978).

Shortly after the turn of the century, private automobiles began to replace public transportation. The Federal Highway Act of 1916 dedicated public funds to constructing roads on which private automobiles could travel to and around the suburbs. By 1929, every state had a gasoline tax dedicated to construction of highways. These highways promoted use of private automobiles and trucks at the expense of public transportation and railroad hauling (Jackson, 1985). Without low-cost public transportation, the poor were locked into living within walking distance of potential employment.

As the wealthy migrated to the suburbs, their older urban houses became commercial properties or multiple-family dwellings for the millions of European immigrants who arrived in the United States and settled in cities (Johnson, 1973; Sugrue, 1993; Warner, 1962/1978; Yancey et al., 1976). White immigrants were given preference over Black workers, even in the skilled jobs for which Blacks had already been trained (Axinn & Levin, 1975; Bennett, 1962/1993; Hershberg, Burstein, Ericksen, Greenberg, & Yancey, 1979; Lane, 1986; Quarles, 1964; Ward, 1971). Blacks were constrained to employment in the least skilled occupations (Horton, 1993; Lane, 1986).

Most unions refused to admit African Americans (Massey & Denton, 1993; Quarles, 1964). Often unable to obtain work on a regular basis, African Americans were used by employers as strike breakers (Horton, 1993; Lane, 1986; Massey & Denton, 1993; Olzak, 1989; Quarles, 1964; Spear, 1967), further fueling racial tensions. Between 1895 and 1916, African Americans were repeatedly hired as strike breakers in New York. They were hired as strike breakers for the steel mills of Pittsburgh in 1875, 1888, 1892, and 1909. Both Blacks and Polish immigrants were strike breakers in the Chicago stockyards during 1904 and 1905. When the strikes ended, although the Polish immigrants kept their jobs most of the Blacks were fired (Spear, 1967; Trotter, 1993).

In 1900, 80% to 90% of African Americans lived in the rural south. Until 1910, they migrated only gradually to cities in the north and midwest, typically in search of better opportunities (Myrdal, 1944; Spear, 1967). After the Civil War, "Black Codes" had restricted the movement of African Americans in the south (Bennett, 1962/1993; Quarles, 1964; Robinson, 1993). But crises in the cotton industry, brought about by the boll weevil spoiling crops at the turn of the century and a drop in cotton prices, made farm hands expendable (Spear, 1967).

Foreign immigration into the United States came to a halt with World War I. The labor shortage led northern industrialists to recruit southern

African Americans as replacement workers, offering them free transportation and high wages. "Northern fever swept through the South in 1915 and 1916 much as America fever had infected much of Europe throughout the nineteenth century," wrote Spear (1967, p. 133).

The northern migration of African Americans brought about strenuous and often violent resistance to integrated housing. Forced to live in designated and often dilapidated urban neighborhoods, Blacks were unable to reap the fruits of their labor with homes for their families or education for their children (Quarles, 1964; Wade, 1972). Although settlement houses were dedicated to helping immigrants resettle in the urban United States, they deserted communities as African Americans migrated to the cities (Lasch-Quinn, 1993). Those few able to afford comfortable housing found themselves subjected to violence when persuasion, blacklisting, and boycotting failed to convince them to live in designated African American neighborhoods (Horton, 1993; Quarles, 1964; Spear, 1967; Wade, 1972).

Federal loan policies, too, were central to segregation of housing. On June 13, 1933, Franklin D. Roosevelt signed a law creating the Home Owners' Loan Corporation. This law enabled home buyers to borrow money insured by the federal government. Because the risk was reduced, interest rates could be low. Using standardized and discriminatory appraisal policies, the Home Owners' Loan Corporation trained appraisers in every U.S. city with a population greater than 25,000. Racial and ethnic characteristics of neighborhoods were among the criteria used for these assessments (Bartelt, 1993; Jackson, 1985; Quarles, 1964).

Neighborhoods with African American residents were never given a rating above the fourth from highest (Jackson, 1985). The practice of downgrading housing with reference to ethnic composition of the neighborhood, known as "red lining," continued until 1975. Negative attitudes toward urban life were reflected in the appraisers' judgments, making it difficult to receive approval for a loan on urban property. Therefore, government loans distributed benefits to the middle class and encouraged their migration to the suburbs.

During the 1940s, guidelines from the Home Owners' Loan Corporation were transferred to the Federal Housing Authority. After World War II, federally guaranteed loans made it cheaper to own tract housing than to rent. These loans could not be used for construction that would change a neighborhood's *character*, a term used to refer to racial composition as well as land use (Adams et al., 1991; Bartelt, 1993; Jackson, 1985). Thus, African Americans were precluded from taking advantage of postwar building and job opportunities in the suburbs.

Restrictive covenants confined African Americans to areas in which the schools were poor, the roads badly maintained, and public services inferior. Although powerless to change the situation, in 1944, the Mayor's Committee of Chicago went on record in opposition to "conspiracies known as restrictive covenants" (Drake & Cayton, 1945/1962, p. 212). The Shelley vs. Kraemer decision rendered these covenants illegal in 1948, but gentlemen's agreements among realtors and mortgage policies by banks perpetuated practices that restricted ownership of most housing to Whites (Sugrue, 1993). Although the Civil Rights Act of 1968 banned discrimination in the sale or rental of housing, violations are rarely prosecuted. Landlords elevated rents for African American tenants trapped by housing restrictions, and grocery store owners raised their prices in African American neighborhoods (Quarles, 1964; Robinson, 1993).

In addition to receiving low-cost loans to build their homes in suburbs, the middle class and wealthy received tax deductions for interest on their home mortgages. This income subsidy for shelter was not available to urban renters. Availability of electricity, highway construction, and plentiful inexpensive land contributed to an exodus of industries from cities. Such federal programs as the Rural Electrification Administration and Tennessee Valley Authority spread electricity throughout the United States. The Federal Interstate Highway Act of 1956 assured funds for interstate highways (Sugrue, 1993). In the suburbs, inexpensive single-story industrial structures could be surrounded by parking lots. Suburban factories favored by tax laws allowing accelerated depreciation for new constructions further encouraged abandonment of older urban buildings (Adams et al., 1991; Robinson, 1993). Shopping malls and other services followed industries to the suburbs, carrying with them many of the jobs suitable for unskilled workers. The urban poor, without transportation, could not compete for these jobs. Although in 1950, about 70% of both Black and White men between the ages of 16 and 24 were employed, by 1983–1985, young White men were about 2.5 times as likely to have a job as were young Black men (Jaynes & Williams, 1989).

Zoning restrictions further contributed to the separation of the social classes. These restrictions stipulated the size of land parcels and the placement of houses, minimum floor areas, and allowable dwelling uses. They effectively produced affluent sanctuaries from which the poor and African Americans were excluded as residents. By 1970, over 80% of African Americans lived in urban areas (Roof, 1979). Yet by 1970, relocation and transformation of industries removed most of the job opportunities for African Americans. Robinson (1993) described the situation: "Jobs in the central city, mostly white-collar, were taken by whites driving in from suburban homes, financed by federally secured mortgages, over federally built roads" (p. 303). Housing segregation interacted with the policy of local taxes to exacerbate the struggles of urban residents. Prosperous suburbs could incorporate separately and devote few community resources to welfare. Taxes could be low and dedicated to such benefits as education and public lands. Low taxes attracted businesses, further reducing the tax base for urban areas.

A policy of heavy reliance on local taxes left those least able to pay for them most responsible for supporting welfare, police, and urban services. Low income contributed to increased demand for public housing, health care, and social services. Increased taxes became necessary to provide these services, and increased taxes induced the middle class and affluent to migrate out of the cities—leaving the cities with even higher proportions of low-income residents.

During the period of rapid construction of the suburbs, public housing was largely restricted to already congested urban areas. In the United States, public housing required local authorization, which enabled residents to decide what kind of housing, if any, to permit in their neighborhoods. The very poor were encouraged to remain in congested areas by legislative tactics that permitted public housing as replacement only for existing slum dwellings. In 1980, public housing constituted about 1% of the U.S. housing market. By way of comparison, public housing constituted about 46% of the housing market in England and Wales and 37% of the housing market in France (Jackson, 1985).

Federal highway construction, loan policies favoring new buildings rather than renovations, and mortgage deductions for home ownership encouraged White migration into the suburbs. Federal taxing policies with investment credits and accelerated depreciation encouraged industrial movement away from cities. The suburban combination of housing and industry led to decentralization of shopping and service facilities along with the jobs such facilities require.

As a result of housing segregation, denigration of public transportation, and the movement of industries to the suburbs, the uneducated are separated from locations where they might obtain employment (Kasarda, 1989, 1992; Lichter, 1988; Wilson, 1991). This separation deprives the uneducated of legal means for self-support. Having a job creates what Wilson (1991) referred to as a "coherent organization of the present" (p. 10). Having a job provides a framework for eating, sleeping, and arranging activities. If Lane (1986) was correct about the civilizing influences of industrial employment, long-standing joblessness contributes to reduced inhibitions against personal displays of violence.

An historic perspective shows how social policies isolated poor African Americans in inner cities, depriving them of opportunities for advancement through legitimate labor. It shows that government policies granted benefits to the economically better off. And it suggests that government policies contributed to the isolation and unemployment of urban poor. The isolated, poor, unjustly treated population who have little grounds for attachment to a social order from which they are excluded are at high risk for criminal actions.

SUMMARY

I argued that taking an historical approach broadens the ability to challenge and correct current causal theories of crime. I showed that neither industrialization nor urbanization could be important criminogenic forces. I demonstrated that high rates of violent crime among African Americans are too transient to support genetic theories. And I introduced data to suggest that changing ages for criminal behavior undermine theories attributing crime to adolescent role transitions. I used an historical approach to lay the ground for urging that reduction in serious urban crime depends on taking into account the residue of older social policies and the results of current ones.

REFERENCES

Adams, C., Bartelt, D., Elesh, D., Goldstein, I., Kleniewski, N., & Yancey, W. (1991). *Philadelphia: Neighborhoods, division, and conflict in a postindustrial city.* Philadelphia, PA: Temple University Press.

Anderson, E. (1990). *Streetwise.* Chicago: Chicago University Press.

Asbury, H. (1927). *The gangs of New York: An informal history of the underworld.* New York: Knopf.

Axinn, J., & Levin, H. (1975). *Social welfare: A history of the American response to need.* New York: Dodd, Mead.

Bartelt, D. W. (1993). Housing the "underclass." In M. B. Katz (Ed.), *The "underclass" debate* (pp. 118–160). Princeton, NJ: Princeton University Press.

Barth, G. (1980). *City people: The rise of modern city culture in nineteenth-century America.* New York: Oxford University Press.

Bennett, L. B., Jr. (1993). *Before the Mayflower: A history of Black America* (6th ed.). New York: Penguin. (Original work published 1962)

Bernstein, I. (1990). *The New York City draft riots.* New York: Oxford University Press.

Black, D. J. (1970). Production of crime rates. *American Sociological Review, 35,* 733–748.

Blassingame, J. W. (1979). *The slave community: Plantation life in the antebellum south.* New York: Oxford University Press.

Buendia, H. G. (Ed.). (1989). *Urban crime: Global trends and policies.* Hong Kong: The United Nations University.

Bureau of Justice Statistics. (1994). *Criminal victimization in the United States, 1992.* Washington, DC: U.S. Department of Justice.

Butterfield, F. (1995). *All God's children.* New York: Knopf.

Butts, J. A., & Conners-Beatty, D. J. (1993). *The Juvenile Court's response to violent offenders: 1985–1989.* Washington, DC: U.S. Department of Justice.

Chaiken, J. M. (1978). What is known about deterrent effects of police activities. In J. A. Cramer (Ed.), *Preventing crime* (pp. 109–135). Beverly Hills, CA: Sage.

Diederiks, H. (1996). Urban and rural criminal justice and criminality in the Netherlands since the late Middle Ages: Some observations. In E. A. Johnson & E. H. Monkkonen (Eds.), *The civilization of crime: Violence in town and country since the Middle Ages* (pp. 153–164). Urbana: University of Illinois Press.

Drake, S. C., & Cayton, H. R. (1962). *Black metropolis: A study of Negro life in a northern city.* New York: Harper & Row. (Original work published 1945)

Elliott, D. S., & Ageton, S. S. (1980). Reconciling race and class differences in self-reported and official estimates of delinquency. *American Sociological Review, 45,* 95–110.

Elliott, D. S., Huizinga, D., & Menard, S. (1989). *Multiple problem youth: Delinquency, substance use and mental health problems.* New York: Springer-Verlag.

Ennis, P. H. (1967). *Criminal victimization in the United States: A report of a national survey.* Washington, DC: U.S. Government Printing Office.

Farrington, D. P. (1979). Environmental stress, delinquent behavior, and convictions. In I. G. Sarason & C. D. Spielberger (Eds.), *Stress and anxiety* (Vol. 6, pp. 93–106). New York: Wiley.

Farrington, D. P. (1986a). Age and crime. In N. Morris & M. Tonry (Eds.), *Crime and justice* (Vol. 7, pp. 189–250). Chicago: University of Chicago Press.

Farrington, D. P. (1986b). Stepping stones to adult criminal careers. In D. Olweus, J. Block, & M. Radke-Yarrow (Eds.), *Development of antisocial and prosocial behavior* (pp. 359–384). New York: Academic Press.

Fingerhut, L. A. (1993). The impact of homicide on life chances: International, intranational and demographic comparisons. In C. R. Block & R. L. Block (Eds.), *Questions and answers in lethal and non-lethal violence 1993.* Washington, DC: National Institute of Justice.

Flanagan, T. J., & Maguire, K. (Eds.). (1992). *Sourcebook of criminal justice statistics 1991: U.S. Department of Justice, Bureau of Justice Statistics.* Washington, DC: U.S. Government Printing Office.

Frantz, J. B. (1969). The frontier tradition: An invitation to violence. In H. D. Graham & T. R. Gurr (Eds.), *Violence in America* (pp. 127–154). New York: Bantam Books.

Gorn, E. J. (1986). *The manly art: Bare-knuckle prize fighting in America.* Ithaca, NY: Cornell University Press.

Greenberg, D. F. (1985). Age, crime, and social explanation. *American Journal of Sociology, 91,* 1–21.

Gurr, T. R. (1979). On the history of violent crime in Europe and America. In H. D. Graham & T. R. Gurr (Eds.), *Violence in America: Historical and comparative perspectives* (pp. 353–374). Beverly Hills, CA: Sage.

Gurr, T. R. (1981). Historical trends in violent crimes: A critical review of the evidence. In M. Tonry & N. Morris (Eds.), *Crime and justice* (Vol. 3, pp. 295–353). Chicago: University of Chicago Press.

Gurr, T. R. (1989a). Historical trends in violent crime: Europe and the United States. In T. R. Gurr (Ed.), *Violence in America: Vol. 1. The history of crime* (pp. 21–54). Newbury Park, CA: Sage.

Gurr, T. R. (1989b). The history of protest, rebellion, and reform in America: An overview. In T. R. Gurr (Ed.), *Violence in America: Vol. 2. Protest, rebellion, reform* (pp. 11–22). Newbury Park, CA: Sage.

Haller, M. H. (1973). Recurring themes. In A. F. Davis & M. H. Haller (Eds.), *The peoples of Philadelphia: A history of ethnic groups and lower-class life, 1790–1940* (pp. 277–290). Philadelphia: Temple University Press.

Hershberg, T. (1973). Free blacks in antebellum Philadelphia. In A. F. Davis & M. H. Haller (Eds.), *The peoples of Philadelphia* (pp. 111–134). Philadelphia: Temple University Press.

Hershberg, T., Burstein, A., Ericksen, E., Greenberg, S., & Yancey, W. (1979). A tale of three cities: Blacks and immigrants in Philadelphia, 1850–1880 and 1970. *The Annals of the*

American Academy of Political and Social Science: Race and Residence in American Cities, 441, 55–81.

Hindelang, M. J., Hirschi, T., & Weis, J. G. (1979). Correlates of delinquency: The illusion of discrepancy between self-report and official measures. *American Sociological Review, 44*, 995–1014.

Hindus, M. S. (1980). *Prison and plantation: Crime, justice, and authority in Massachusetts and South Carolina, 1767–1878*. Chapel Hill: University of North Carolina Press.

Hofstadter, R. (1970). Reflections on violence in the United States. In R. Hofstadter & M. Wallace (Eds.), *American violence: A documentary history* (pp. 3–43). New York: Vintage Books.

Hollon, W. E. (1974). *Frontier violence: Another look*. New York: Oxford University Press.

Horton, J. O. (1993). *Free people of color: Inside the African American community*. Washington, DC: Smithsonian Institution Press.

Jackson, K. T. (1985). *Crabgrass frontier: The suburbanization of the United States*. New York: Oxford University Press.

Jaynes, G. D., & Williams, R. M., Jr. (Eds.). (1989). *A common destiny—Blacks and American society, by The Committee on the Status of Black Americans*. Washington, DC: National Academy Press.

Johnson, D. R. (1973). Crime patterns in Philadelphia, 1840–1870. In A. F. Davis & M. H. Haller (Eds.), *The peoples of Philadelphia* (pp. 89–110). Philadelphia: Temple University Press.

Johnson, E. A. (1996). Urban and rural crime in Germany, 1871–1914. In E. A. Johnson & E. H. Monkkonen (Eds.), *The civilization of crime: Violence in town and country since the Middle Ages* (pp. 217–257). Urbana: University of Illinois Press.

Johnson, E. A., & Monkkonen, E. H. (1996). Introduction. In E. A. Johnson & E. H. Monkkonen (Eds.), *The civilization of crime: Violence in town and country since the Middle Ages* (pp. 1–13). Urbana: University of Illinois Press.

Kasarda, J. D. (1989). Urban industrial transition and the underclass. *The Annals: The Ghetto Underclass: Social Science Perspectives, 501*, 26–47.

Kasarda, J. D. (1992). The severely distressed in economically transforming cities. In A. V. Harrell & G. E. Peterson (Eds.), *Drugs, crime and social isolation* (pp. 45–98). Washington, DC: The Urban Institute Press.

Lahey, B. B., & Loeber, R. (1994). Framework for a development model of oppositional defiant disorder and conduct disorder. In D. K. Routh (Ed.), *Disruptive behavior in childhood* (pp. 285–314). New York: Plenum.

Lane, R. (1967). *Policing the city: Boston 1822–1885*. Cambridge, MA: Harvard University Press.

Lane, R. (1968). Crime and criminal statistics in nineteenth-century Massachusetts. *Journal of Social History, 2*, 156–163.

Lane, R. (1969). Urbanization and criminal violence in the 19th century: Massachusetts as a test case. In H. D. Graham & T. R. Gurr (Eds.), *Violence in America* (pp. 468–484). New York: Bantam.

Lane, R. (1976). Criminal violence in America: The first hundred years. *The Annals of the American Academy of Political and Social Science, 423*, 1–13.

Lane, R. (1979). *Violent death in the city*. Cambridge, MA: Harvard University Press.

Lane, R. (1980). Urban homicide in the nineteenth century: Some lessons for the twentieth. In J. A. Inciardi & C. E. Faupel (Eds.), *History and crime: Implications for criminal justice policy* (pp. 91–110). Beverly Hills, CA: Sage.

Lane, R. (1986). *Roots of violence in Black Philadelphia 1860–1900*. Cambridge, MA: Harvard University Press.

Lane, R. (1989). On the social meaning of homicide trends in America. In T. R. Gurr (Ed.), *Violence in America: Vol. 1. The history of crime* (pp. 55–79). Newbury Park, CA: Sage.

Lasch-Quinn, E. (1993). *Black neighbors*. Chapel Hill: University of North Carolina Press.

LeBlanc, M. (1990). Two processes of the development of persistent offending: Activation and escalation. In L. N. Robins & M. Rutter (Eds.), *Straight and devious pathways from childhood to adulthood* (pp. 82–100). Cambridge, England: Cambridge University Press.

Lichter, D. T. (1988). Racial differences in underemployment in American cities. *American Journal of Sociology, 93*(4), 771–792.

Lodhi, A. Q., & Tilly, C. (1973). Urbanization, crime, and collective violence in 19th century France. *American Journal of Sociology, 79*(2), 296–318.

Maguire, K., & Pastore, A. L. (Eds.). (1994). *Sourcebook of criminal justice statistics—1993: U.S. Department of Justice, Bureau of Justice Statistics.* Washington, DC: U.S. Government Printing Office.

Massey, D. S., & Denton, N. A. (1993). *American apartheid: Segregation and the making of the underclass.* Cambridge, MA: Harvard University Press.

McCord, J. (1992). The Cambridge–Somerville Study: A pioneering longitudinal–experimental study of delinquency prevention. In J. McCord & R. E. Tremblay (Eds.), *Preventing antisocial behavior: Interventions from birth through adolescence* (pp. 196–206). New York: Guilford Press.

McCord, J. (1995). Ethnicity, acculturation, and opportunities: A study of two generations. In D. F. Hawkins (Ed.), *Ethnicity, race and crime: Perspectives across time and place* (pp. 69–81). Albany: State University of New York Press.

Modell, J. (1989). *Into one's own: From youth to adulthood in the United States 1920–1975.* Berkeley: University of California Press.

Monkkonen, E. H. (1981). *Police in urban America 1860–1920.* New York: Cambridge University Press.

Morash, M. (1984). Establishment of a juvenile police record: The influence of individual and peer group characteristics. *Criminology, 22,* 97–111.

Murphy, F. J., Shirley, M. M., & Witmer, H. L. (1946). The incidence of hidden delinquency. *American Journal of Orthopsychiatry, 16,* 686–696.

Myrdal, G. (1944). *An American dilemma: The Negro problem and modern democracy* (Vol. 1). New York: Harper & Row.

Nagin, D. (1978). General deterrence: A review of the empirical evidence. In A. Blumstein, J. Cohen, & D. Nagin (Eds.), *Deterrence and incapacitation: Estimating the effects of criminal sanctions on crime rates* (pp. 95–139). Washington, DC: National Academy of Sciences.

National Commission on the Causes and Prevention of Violence. (1969). *To establish justice, to insure domestic tranquility: Final report of the National Commission on the Causes and Prevention of Violence.* Washington, DC: U.S. Government Printing Office.

Olzak, S. (1989). Labor unrest, immigration, and ethnic conflict in urban America, 1880–1914. *American Journal of Sociology, 94*(6), 1303–1333.

Park, R. E. (1967). *The city.* Chicago: University of Chicago Press. (Original work published 1925)

Quarles, B. (1964). *The Negro in the making of America.* New York: Collier Books.

Reiss, A. J., Jr., & Rhodes, A. L. (1961). Delinquency and class structure. *American Sociological Review, 26*(5), 720–732.

Robinson, C. D. (1993). The production of black violence in Chicago. In D. F. Greenberg (Ed.), *Crime and capitalism: Readings in Marxist criminology* (pp. 279–333). Philadelphia, PA: Temple University Press.

Roof, W. C. (1979). Race and residence: The shifting basis of American race relations. *Annals of the American Academy of Political and Social Science, 441,* 1–12.

Schlesinger, A. M. (1933). *The rise of the city 1878–1898.* Chicago: Quadrangle Books.

Seidman, D., & Couzens, M. (1974). Getting the crime rate down: Political pressure and crime reporting. *Law & Society, 10,* 457–493.

Snyder, H. N., & Aixkmuns, M. (1995). *Juvenile offenders and victims: A national report.* Washington, DC: Office of Juvenile Justice and Delinquency Prevention.

Spear, A. H. (1967). *Black Chicago: The making of a Negro ghetto 1890–1920*. Chicago: The University of Chicago Press.

Sugrue, T. J. (1993). The structures of urban poverty: The reorganization of space and work in three periods of American history. In M. B. Katz (Ed.), *The "underclass" debate* (pp. 85–117). Princeton, NJ: Princeton University Press.

Tocqueville, A. de (1961). *Democracy in America* (Vol. I). New York: Schocken Books. (Original work published 1835)

Trotter, J. W., Jr. (1993). Blacks in the urban North: The "underclass question" in historical perspective. In M. B. Katz (Ed.), *The "underclass" debate* (pp. 55–84). Princeton, NJ: Princeton University Press.

U.S. Department of Justice. (1991). *Crime in the United States 1990*. Washington, DC: U.S. Government Printing Office.

Wade, R. C. (1964). *Slavery in the cities: The South 1820–1860*. New York: Oxford University Press.

Wade, R. C. (1972). Violence in the cities. In K. T. Jackson & S. K. Schultz (Eds.), *Cities in American history* (pp. 475–491). New York: Knopf.

Ward, D. (1971). *Cities and immigrants*. New York: Oxford University Press.

Warner, S. B., Jr. (1978). *Streetcar suburbs: The process of growth in Boston, 1870–1900*. Cambridge, MA: Harvard University Press. (Original work published 1962)

Whitaker, C. J., & Bastian, L. D. (1991). *Teenage victims: A National Crime Survey report*. Washington, DC: U.S. Department of Justice.

Wilson, W. J. (1991). Studying inner-city social dislocations: The challenge of public agenda research—1990 Presidential Address. *American Sociological Review, 56*(2), 1–14.

Yancey, W. L., Ericksen, E. P., & Juliani, R. N. (1976). Emergent ethnicity: A review and reformulation. *American Sociological Review, 41*(3), 391–403.

Chapter 3

A 70-Year History of Conduct Disorder: Variations in Definition, Prevalence, and Correlates

Lee N. Robins
Washington University

This chapter reports on variation over time and place in the prevalence of, risk factors for, and consequences of conduct disorder. Our ability to draw correct conclusions about these variations depends on conduct disorder being a valid syndrome, whether it was reliably measured in representative samples in different eras and cultures, and whether its correlates can be interpreted as its causes or consequences. Conduct disorder has been studied more than any other childhood psychiatric disorder. Yet, systematic studies assessing its prevalence, risk factors, and consequences are scarce, relatively new, and have methodological problems.

For many years, there was no official definition of the disorder. Its first official definition appeared in 1974 in the World Health Organization's glossary for mental disorders in the *International Classification of Diseases* (*8th ed.* [*ICD–8*]). No childhood disorders appeared in the American Psychiatric Association's earliest *Diagnostic and Statistical Manual of Mental Disorders* (*DSM*) published in 1952. In its second edition, *DSM–II* (1968), the closest equivalent to conduct disorder was a combination of three diagnoses: runaway reaction, unsocialized aggressive reaction, and group delinquent reaction.

It was not until *DSM–III* (American Psychiatric Association, 1980) that specific criteria for conduct disorder appeared in the official diagnostic nomenclature (Table 3.1). The criteria became more detailed in subsequent editions, *DSM–III–R* (American Psychiatric Association, 1987) and *DSM–IV* (American Psychiatric Association, 1994). In each edition ap-

TABLE 3.1

How Criteria for Conduct Disorder Have Changed Over Time

	DSM-IV	DSM-III-R	DSM-III[a]	Runaway Reaction	Unsocialized Aggressive	Group Delinquency
					II	
No. of SX	15	13	15	3	9	3
7 *Aggression*						
Bullies	X	-	-	-	X	-
Fights	X	X	(Assault)	-	X	-
Weapon	X	X	-	-	-	-
Physical cruelty						
People	X	X	-	-	-	-
Animals	X	X	-	-	-	-
Robbed	X	X	X	-	-	-
Rape	X	X	X	-	-	-
2 *Vandalism symptoms*						
Fire setting	X	X	X	-	-	-
Other vandalism	X	X	X	-	X	-
3 *Deceit or theft*						
Break-in	X	X	X	-	-	-
Lie	X	X	X	-	X	-
Steal	X	X	X	X	X	X

	Aggressive Nonsocialized	Nonaggressive Nonsocialized	Aggressive Socialized	Nonaggressive Socialized
3 Violation of rules				
Out late	X	-	X	X
Runaway	X	X	X	-
Truant	X	X	X	X
1 Substance abuse	-	X	-	-
5 Unsocialized				
No lasting friendship	X	X	-	-
No altruism	X	X	-	-
No guilt	X	X	-	-
Blames others	X	X	-	-
No concern for others	X	X	-	-
3 Verbal bad behavior				
Quarrelsome	X	-	X	-
Verbal aggression	X	-	X	-
Tantrums	X	-	X	-

[a]4 Categories: Aggressive Nonsocialized, Nonaggressive Nonsocialized, Aggressive Socialized, Nonaggressive Socialized.

peared the symptoms of physical aggression, stealing, breaking and entering, rape, lying, firesetting, vandalism, running away, and truancy. These also appeared in *ICD–10*, and might therefore be seen as the core symptoms of conduct disorder. However, if one asks what symptoms have been mentioned in every edition of *DSM* and of *ICD* glossaries since 1974 (World Health Organization, 1974, 1993), there are only two: physical aggression and stealing.

There are other striking trends in the changes in criteria since 1974. The symptoms of early substance use and early sexual intercourse were dropped after *DSM–III*, although the text of *DSM–IV* noted their association with conduct disorder. The distinction between socialized and unsocialized conduct disorder, initially used by Hewitt and Jenkins (1946) to describe delinquents and appearing in both *DSM–III* and *ICD–9*, was dropped in *DSM–IV*, but persisted in *ICD–10* as a possible subdivision, along with specifiers regarding whether problems occur only in the family, presence of hyperactivity or emotional disturbance, and severity. Verbal aggression was removed from the criteria and became a symptom of a separate disorder: oppositional defiant disorder. The symptom of physical aggression was subdivided and expanded since *DSM–III*. The result of these changes was an increased "masculinization" of the disorder, because aggressive girls use verbal abuse more than physical fighting. The nature of their sexual deviance is early and promiscuous intercourse, rather than initiating rape. Evidence that these changes excluded girls from the diagnosis of conduct disorder was provided by a study in Quebec, which followed girls from kindergarten through age 10. Those identified by parents or teachers in kindergarten as antisocial were seven times as likely to be diagnosed with conduct disorder at age 10 by *DSM–III* as by *DSM–III–R* criteria (Zoccolillo, Tremblay, & Vitaro, 1996).

In *ICD–10*, conduct disorder includes the 8 symptoms of *DSM–IV* oppositional defiant disorder as well as the 15 *DSM–IV* symptoms of conduct disorder. However, an *ICD–10* conduct disorder diagnosis requires at least 3 of the DSM–IV conduct disorder symptoms, whereas a diagnosis of oppositional defiant disorder allows no more than 2 of these 15 symptoms. Thus, although the presentation differs in the two manuals, they end with identically diagnosed cases.

In the absence of published criteria, studies of misbehavior before 1968 used official delinquency records (Glueck & Glueck, 1950; Shaw & McKay, 1942; Stott, 1959; West & Farrington, 1977), aggression, or behaviors that could have been grounds for defining a child as delinquent if the child had appeared in Juvenile Court (Nye & Short, 1957; Robins, 1966). As Hewitt and Jenkins (1946), Reiss (1986), and Moffitt, Caspi, Dickson, Silva, and Stanton (1996) noted, not all delinquents have a history of the broad picture of antisocial behavior required for a diagnosis of conduct disorder. This is particularly the case for children who are arrested only as a member of a group charged with a crime. However, by definition, they were all seen in juvenile court, whereas many children with conduct disorder were not. Because children with no prior arrest history who commit minor offenses are often simply warned or taken home by the police rather than being booked as delinquent, official delinquents probably have committed more thefts and acts of vandalism than have other children with these symptoms. So we cannot assume delinquency is equivalent to a diagnosis of conduct disorder, although the two are certainly correlated. Some delinquents would not meet the criteria, and those who would are likely to be more serious cases than are a general population sample of children with conduct disorder.

It is difficult to tell whether cases in early studies making specific diagnoses of conduct disorder (Hagnell, 1966; Rutter, Cox, Tupling, Berger, & Yule, 1975) would meet current criteria. In precomputer days, studies often had clinicians assign diagnoses without recording the number of symptoms, which specific symptoms were present, or the duration of the syndrome. Post hoc diagnosis became possible in more recent studies, even when categorical diagnosis was not done or did not follow algorithms prescribed in the official manuals, because individual symptoms were entered into computer programs and could be combined to test whether diagnostic criteria in the official nomenclature were met.

A second impediment to both early and recent studies of conduct disorder was uncertainty about who is the best informant and, if there are multiple informants, whether to accept positive symptoms from all or require agreement between them. Even after specific behaviors were designated as symptoms of conduct disorder, children were rarely asked to report them. Children were considered unable to give reliable information, and instead parents, teachers, or both were selected as informants. However, children turned out to be adequate reporters of the behaviors used to assess conduct disorder. A community study of psychiatric disorders in children (Jensen et al., 1995) found conduct disorder the most reliably assessed disorder for both parents ($\kappa = .66$) and children ($\kappa = .60$). Offord, Alder, and Boyle (1986) found children reported more antisocial behavior than did their parents or teachers, whereas parents and teachers seldom agreed.

Oddly, although there was reluctance to ask children about their symptoms, studies of delinquency were asking them to report their delinquent behavior. When their responses were compared with official records (Gibson, Morrison, & West, 1970; Huizinga & Elliott, 1986), children were found to report most of the offenses in official records plus others that presumably did not result in a police record. The high rates of self-reported delinquency show that children are usually willing to admit to acts that are socially disapproved. The high rate of subject retention in panel studies in which children were repeatedly asked about their delinquent acts showed that a third impediment, the belief that asking about illegal behavior would threaten future cooperation in longitudinal studies, was probably unfounded (Wadsworth, 1979).

Of course, like adults, children are not completely reliable informants about psychiatric symptoms. However, questions about illegal behaviors are answered more reliably than are questions about internal states, such as depression and anxiety. Answers about behaviors are probably more reliable than answers about subjective states because the questions are a better match for the contents of the respondents' memory bank. Children can easily say whether they have stolen, truanted, or started a fight, because this is the way such events are stored in memory. They may be unable to decide whether they felt sad for most of the day on most days over a 2-week period, as required when they are to be evaluated for meeting criteria for a depressed mood. When children or adults are asked to construct an answer from their memories of dysphoric feelings, which they have never thought of in terms of duration or the number of consecutive days affected, it is not surprising that they are apt to reach a different conclusion when asked to repeat that construction some days later.

Whether or not specific symptoms are recorded, the diagnosis of conduct disorder can be tested for reliability by seeing whether the same diagnosis is made when the interview is repeated at another time, and for validity by seeing whether the study diagnosis agrees with medical records or an expert clinician's opinion. Although such tests evaluate the interview, they do not validate the syndrome. Only after studies began recording data on individual symptoms was it possible to test the validity of the syndrome with Cronbach's alpha or GOM analysis, which show whether the symptoms are highly intercorrelated, or to learn whether symptoms appear in a regular order. The conduct disorder syndrome passed all such tests handily. High correlations among the symptoms, the regularity of progression from fighting and stealing to running away, and the strong association between a count of symptoms with demographic characteristics and family type (Moffitt, 1996) argue for the reality of the syndrome. Thus, the first requirement for a valid comparison across time and place is met by current criteria. However, these tests do not tell us whether the description of the syndrome is complete. It may be that some of the associated descriptive features mentioned in *DSM–IV*, such as lack of empathy, misperceiving others as hostile, temper tantrums, early sexual behavior, and early substance use, would pass the same tests the official symptoms have and should therefore be considered symptoms in their own right, as many of them were in past editions.

Given the recency of a detailed description of the syndrome in standard nomenclatures and the disagreements between the U.S. (*DSM*) and International (*ICD*) nomenclatures until 1994, it is no wonder that there are few studies from different eras and in different places that have sufficient consistency of measuring instruments to be sure that conclusions about historical and geographical variation are justified. But inconsistency in diagnostic criteria is not the only problem. Cross-epoch and cross-cultural comparisons suffer because respondents in different eras and cultures may not be equally willing to participate in assessments of their behaviors, nor equally frank when they do. It is difficult to assess whether differences in rates are true differences or are explained by differences between populations in their views of the value and legitimacy of survey research.

An additional source of unintended methodological variation results from changes in meaning, tone, and understandability in the course of translation of the interviews. The last 20 years have seen the translation into many languages of two U.S. instruments, the Child Behavior Check List (CBCL), designed for assessing children's problem behaviors and other symptoms and characteristics (Achenbach & Edelbrock, 1981), and the Diagnostic Interview Schedule (DIS; Robins, Cottler, Bucholz, & Compton, 1996; Robins, Helzer, Cottler, & Goldring, 1989; Robins, Helzer, Croughan, Williams, & Spitzer, 1981), designed for assessing adults. The CBCL does not make the diagnosis of conduct disorder, but its Delinquent Behavior scale (Verhulst, Eussen, Berden, Sanders-Woudstra, vam der Ende, 1993) comes close to including the *DSM–IV* and *ICD–10* criteria, and was shown to strongly correlate with a *DSM–III–R* diagnosis of conduct disorder (Kasius, Ferdinand, van den Berg, & Verhulst, 1997). The CBCL was modified to serve as a diagnostic instrument for a study of children in Ontario (Offord, Alder, & Boyle, 1986). The DIS, originally written for the Epidemiologic Catchment Area (ECA) project carried out in five areas of the United States, was translated for studies in many countries. Although designed to assess adult disorders, the DIS is able to approximate the diagnosis of *DSM–IV* and *ICD–10* conduct disorder because three conduct problems before age 15 were required as the childhood precursor of adult antisocial personality. Although these translations may not be perfect, translation of a single instrument guarantees that the same topics are covered and that they are scored identically, so that interpretation of the diagnostic criteria is standardized across studies.

PREVALENCE OVER TIME AND PLACE

Interpreting differences in prevalence between studies done at different times and places as indicating truly different rates may not be justified. This is because of the slow development of standard criteria for conduct disorder as the basis for survey instruments suitable for administration to general population samples, the avoidance of interviews with children, and the uncertainties of translation.

Differences in subjects' ages also cause lack of comparability across studies. Conduct problems often become evident when a child entering school does not accept direction from the teacher. The variety of behavior problems increases as the child grows and gains freedom to go where there is no direct supervision by parent or teacher. Thus, the likelihood of meeting criteria increases with age until late adolescence, whether lifetime or cross-sectional criteria are used. As a result, studies of young children provide lower rates than do studies of adolescents or of adults asked for retrospective reports of earlier behavior. Because we do not know the precise increments with age, comparing studies of children of different ages does not permit concluding that differences in their prevalences are explained by time or place unless the younger sample has a higher rate of conduct disorder.

Retrospective reports by adults have two important drawbacks. As they age, sample members may increasingly forget behavior problems they had as children, and cases are likely to be missing from the sample because conduct disorder is associated with premature deaths by non-natural means (suicide, accident, homicide). Thus, the prevalence of conduct disorder may be underestimated, particularly in older sample members.

Studies of adults do, however, have three important advantages: All subjects have passed through the risk period for conduct disorder; when the age range is broad, changes in prevalence over time can be estimated from rates in respondents of different ages, who were children in different historical periods; and a uniform definition of conduct disorder is applied to these different historical periods. Thus, a single study can provide information about changes in prevalence over time, without being hampered by variations in criteria over the time periods covered.

Table 3.2 lists studies providing estimates of the prevalence of conduct disorder in nonclinical samples of children with a median age of less than 15. (Omitted is a study in the Netherlands that used the CBCL, but set an arbitrary cutoff point for a symptom count that would create a predetermined prevalence rate of 10%, rather than applying a priori criteria. Also omitted are studies that provided rates for "disruptive disorders" or combined oppositional disorder and conduct disorder, without providing rates for conduct disorder alone [Bird et al., 1994; Brown, Lewisohn, Seeley, & Wagner, 1996]). These studies used data collected over a 30-year period, and studied children in Sweden, England, Canada, China, and the United States. There seems no obvious pattern by either time or place. The lack of pattern could mean that rates are similar across time and place, or it may be that the

TABLE 3.2
Conduct Disorder Assessed in Studies of Children
Whose Average Age Was Below 15

Year to Which DX[a] Applies	Age Dxed[a]	Location	Prevalence		
			M %	F %	TOTAL %
1965	7–18	STOCKHOLM[b]	8		5
1970	10–11	ISLE OF WIGHT[c]			4
1975	10–11	INNER LONDON[d]			8
1983	4–16	ONTARIO[e]	9		5
1983	11–13	BEIJING[c]	11		7
1985	9–18	NEW YORK STATE[g]			9
1994	4–11	CANADA[h]	11		10
1994	9–17	4 U.S. SITES[i]			6
1995	9, 11, 13	NORTH CAROLINA[j]	5	1	3[a]

[a]Criteria met in last 3 months. [b]Hodgins, 1994. [c]Rutter et al., 1970. [d]Rutter et al., 1975. [e]Offord et al., 1986. [f]Ekblad, 1990. [g]Cohen et al., 1993. [h]Offord & Lipman, n.d. [i]Shaffer et al., 1996. [j]Costello, 1996.

rates are not comparable because the children were different ages, methods of sampling varied, a variety of instruments were used—including in one case (Stockholm) records rather than interviews or questionnaires, and one (NC) required that criteria be met in the last 3 months.

The picture is clearer when we look at results for cohorts born in different eras who were all adult or late adolescents at the time of assessment (Table 3.3). New Zealand rates (Dunedin and Christchurch) appear to be somewhat lower than rates in the United States and Australia. And in the United States and Australia there seems to be a strong cohort effect, with the later born cohorts having much higher rates than the earlier cohorts. The two adult U.S. studies and the Australian study produced similar results, even though the samples and data collection methods were quite different. The ECA was not limited to persons residing in households, whereas the National Comorbidity Study (NCS; Kessler et al., 1997) was, perhaps explaining its somewhat lower rate. The ECA and NCS samples were scientifically selected random samples of households, and for the ECA only, of institutions. The Australian sample was a large sample of twins recruited in a variety of ways—from school records, by advertising, and by other means. The ECA and NCS were first attempts at contacting the selected sample members and were face-to-face interviews. The Australian study was conducted by telephone with persons who had responded to previous mailed questionnaires. As a result, the Australian study, although done at the same time as the NCS, lacked a young cohort, because

TABLE 3.3
Conduct Disorder as Assessed by Symptoms
Before 15 Recalled by Adults and Older Adolescents

Year Birth Cohort Passed Age 15	Study	Prevalence		
		M %	F %	TOTAL %
1922	5 US AREAS[a]	6	0	3
1937	AUSTRALIA[b]	7	0	4
1942	5 US AREAS[a]	9	0	5
1957	AUSTRALIA[b]	14	2	7
1964	NCS US[c]	13	3	8
1966	5 US AREAS[a]	19	4	11
1967	AUSTRALIA[b]	15	2	9
1974	NCS US[c] NATION[a]	18	3	10
1975	AUSTRALIA[b]	22	5	14
1975	5 US AREAS[a]	26	10	18
1987	DUNEDIN[d]	13		
1990	CHRISTCHURCH[e]			11

[a]ECA, Robins et al., 1991. [b]Australia, Slutke et al. (in press). [c]NCS, Kessler et al., 1997. [d]Moffitt et al., 1996. [e]Fergusson et al., 1993.

all had to have been 18 or older at the time of the first mailed questionnaire in 1980, just about the time that the ECA began. What did unite the three were the questions used. All were based on questions written for the ECA, and the wording varied little across the studies. Recruitment success was also similar across studies.

Figure 3.1 shows prevalence rates for the three adult retrospective studies arranged to show time effects more clearly. Each cohort is placed at the year in which its median member passed age 15. Because the two U.S. studies were carried out at different times, and the Australian study, although performed about the same time as the NCS, had a different age range (29 to 96, rather than 15 to 54), combining the studies unlinks year of birth from age at interview, and thus unlinks cohort of birth from the length of recall demanded and from the length of time at risk of premature death. That is, a respondent aged 35 in the ECA study passed age 15 the same year a respondent aged 47 did in the NCS, and the NCS respondent therefore had survived an additional 12 years and was 12 years farther from the period he or she was asked to recall, although the two respondents belonged to the same birth cohort. Figure 3.1 shows that there was an increase in prevalence over time that cannot be explained simply by the fact that recall of childhood behaviors demands longer survival and recall over more years from earlier cohorts than from more recent ones.

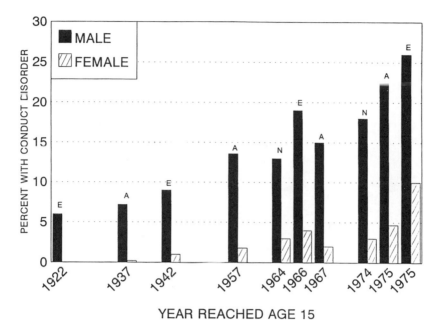

FIG. 3.1. Retrospective studies of conduct disorder before age 15, by birth cohort (U.S. ECA [E], U.S. NCS [N], and Australia [A]).

CORRELATES OF CONDUCT DISORDER OVER TIME AND PLACE

Correlates of conduct disorder are of special interest when they can be considered as possible risk factors, and can encourage interventions to modify them or to prevent the occurrence of conduct disorder. However, because conduct symptoms begin early in life, it is difficult to establish whether the correlates that were not present at birth preceded the disorder. This is a particular problem with parent–child interactions, including expression of affection, supervision, and disciplinary practices, which can be influenced not only by the parents' values, skills, and personality, but also by the parents' response once a child becomes disobedient and hostile. A similar limitation exists in interpreting the child's school failure or association with a deviant peer group as causal, because these may also result from the disorder rather than causing it.

A look at changes in prevalence over time and place already gave us two correlates of conduct disorder: belonging to a later born cohort (which may be partly confounded with better recall and lower mortality), and being male. These correlates appear consistently across cultures and studies. They apply to conduct disorder as a whole and to each of its symptoms (Fig. 3.2).

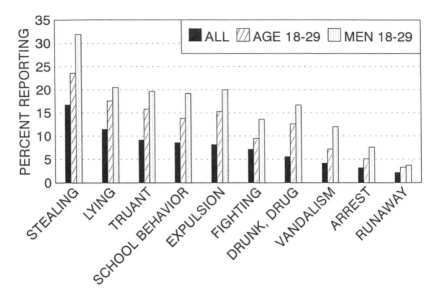

FIG. 3.2. Recall of child conduct problems by ECA sample.

The smallest cohort differences are found in fighting and running away from home. The smallest sex differences occur in lying and running away. Running away is the rarest of the conduct symptoms and the last to appear. It is also the best predictor of the presence of each of the other symptoms, suggesting that it is the most serious and most prototypic of all conduct disorder symptoms.

The only potential risk factor (other than cohort and sex) routinely available in retrospective studies that with certainty predates onset of the disorder is ethnicity. Ethnicity was not found to be related to prevalence of conduct disorder in the ECA, but it was related to conduct disorder in inner London.

Studies of children often explore family size and type, parental disciplinary practices, socioeconomic status, neighborhood, peer group, IQ, and preschool temperament and behavior as possible causal factors. Each was found to be correlated with conduct disorder in more than one study, and there are virtually no negative results. Thus, we know that conduct problems occur disproportionately in poor families with unconventional structures—the child is illegitimate or one of an unusually large sibship; there is no father in the home, or the father suffers from substance abuse or antisocial behavior; parents are negligent or abusive toward this child or toward each other. The consistency of these findings argues for a causal role for the family, but does not tell us how its effects come about.

The strong association of family factors with conduct disorder is consistent with at least three causal paradigms: a learning paradigm (imitation of parental behavior), a stunting paradigm (failure of parents to provide the ingredients necessary to normal moral development—predictability, love, rewards for good behavior, support, education), and a genetic paradigm (inheritance of the parents' traits). The genetic paradigm has been or is being tested in a variety of studies of adoptees and twins being done in Denmark, Australia, England, and in the United States in Minneapolis, Missouri, Virginia, and among U.S. veterans (Brennan & Mednick, 1993; Eaves et al., in press; Lyons et al., 1995; Maughan & Pickles, 1990; Slutske et al., 1997). Each study thus far found a genetic effect on measures of conduct problems, but they also found substantial additional effects of the home environment. So the genetic studies have not ruled out the learning or stunting paradigms.

Children with conduct disorder were often already difficult as infants and toddlers. Traditionally, behavior in this early period was interpreted as an expression of inborn personality traits, rather than as a product of the environment. This view was supported by large differences between siblings who presumably experienced similar early environments. Although parents may treat each of their children differently, those differences may be responses to differences between babies as well as changes in the parents' own situation. Conduct problems are often (but not uniformly) preceded by a history of attention problems or hyperactivity, and slightly low IQ. These, too, are thought to be largely genetic in origin. Coincident with the appearance of conduct problems, affected children often associate with an antisocial peer group and begin sexual activity and substance use unusually early. They are often punished harshly or unsupervised by their parents. These correlates may be causal, but they might also be consequences of the conduct problems.

To my knowledge, the possibility that the size of the genetic contribution might vary by time and place has not been investigated systematically, although such variation is plausible. The size of the genetic contribution varies inversely with the heterogeneity of environments—appearing larger in homogeneous environments, smaller in heterogeneous ones. Comparisons across time and place could test this hypothesis.

Selecting which environmental elements to study as possibly causal is puzzling. We are overwhelmed by the variety of associated environmental variables consistently identified in studies in different eras and different places. The standard approach is to try to identify environmental factors that preceded the first conduct problem in order to satisfy the requirement that a cause must precede its effect. But later environmental events cannot be ruled out as causes, because they may sustain already existing conduct problems or serve as catalysts for diversification into additional types of behavior problems. But how are environmental events subsequent to the first symptom to be distinguished from the effects of conduct disorder?

Many events could be either. Harsh parental disciplinary practices, lack of school success, an antisocial peer group, and early exposure to sex, alcohol, and other drugs might be mechanisms through which inadequate parents, a disorganized neighborhood, or a poorly run school increases the risk of conduct problems. But it seems equally likely that these events could be consequences of the child's conduct symptoms—or be symptoms belonging in the syndrome but not included in the current nomenclature. The very strength of the correlation between such events and conduct disorder argues for the plausibility of a reciprocal pattern, in which the child born into a poorly functioning family living in a crime-ridden neighborhood will attend an inferior school, where interactions with a deviant peer group can maintain and contribute to his or her behavior problems, which result in his or her inadequate parents disciplining and supervising him or her even more poorly than they would a more tractable child. The poor discipline leads to estrangement from the parents and selection of equally rebellious peers as companions. We do not, at present, have analytic procedures that can divide correlations into causal and consequential portions, and portions accounted for by common antecedents.

CONSEQUENCES OF CONDUCT DISORDER

There is an abundant literature on the later outcomes for children with conduct disorder in studies of adults that include a retrospective history of conduct problems and in follow-up studies of children into late adolescence or adulthood. Both types of studies provide information about current marital status, occupation, substance abuse, mental disorders, and criminal history. Follow-up studies were carried out in several countries: the United States, New Zealand, England, the Netherlands, Sweden. Some of the major studies are ordered by publication date in Table 3.4. They begin in 1940 and continue to the present.

All studies show powerful effects of conduct disorder on adverse outcomes. Effects are found not only with respect to outcomes that can easily be understood as resulting from continuing antisocial behavior (e.g., arrests, job loss, divorce) but also with respect to events to which adult behavior problems seem to make little direct contribution (being robbed, being assigned to combat roles in the military, losing a parent through death). It is particularly interesting, in light of an increase in the prevalence of conduct disorder, to ask what effect this increase has had on the probability of adverse adult outcomes.

Decreased continuity of antisocial behavior from childhood into adult life is one possible result of an increased rate of conduct disorder. It has been known for a long time that aggressive behavior in childhood is re-

TABLE 3.4

Prospective Studies of Conduct Disordered Children as Adults

Massachusetts	Glueck, S., & Glueck, E.: *Juvenile Delinquents Grown Up*	1940
	Unraveling Juvenile Delinquency	1950
Sweden	Ahnsjo, S.: *Delinquency in Girls and Its Prognosis*	1941
Sweden	Otterstrom, E.: *Delinquency and Children From Bad Homes*	1946
United States	Morris, H. H., et al.: *Aggressive Behavior Disorders of Childhood: A Follow-Up Study*	1951
Minnesota	Roff, M. E.: *Relationship Between Pre-Service Factors and Psychoneurosis During Military Duty*	1957
Massachusetts	McCord, W., & McCord, J.: *Origins of Crime*	1959
	Origins of Alcoholism	1960
St. Louis	Robins, L.: *Deviant Children Grown Up*	1966
St. Louis	Robins, L.: *The Adult Psychiatric Status of Black Schoolboys*	1971
London	Farrington, D.: *Longterm Criminal Outcomes of Hyperactivity*	1990
London	Quinton, D., & Rutter, M.: *Continuities in Psychiatric Disorders From Childhood to Adulthood in Children of Psychiatric Patients*	1990
Sweden	Magnusson, D., & Bergman, L.: *A Pattern Approach to the Studies of Pathways From Childhood to Adulthood*	1990
England	Zoccolillo, M.: *The Outcome of Childhood Conduct Disorder: Implications for Defining Adult Personality Disorder and Conduct Disorder*	1992
Netherlands	Ferdinand, R. F., & Verhulst, F.: *Continuity and Change of Self-Reported Problem Behaviors From Adolescence Into Young Adulthood*	1995

markably stable over time. And recent studies, like the early ones, find conduct disorder the most stable form of child psychopathology. The Gluecks (1968) found that many juvenile delinquents were convicted of adult crimes, and Verhulst, Eussen, Berden, Sanders-Woudstra, and vam der Ende (1993) replicated the finding of many earlier studies that there is more continuity for externalizing than for internalizing disorders. There are no studies that fail to find continuity, including studies in which conduct problems were measured prior to school age (White, Moffitt, Earls, Robins, & Silva, 1990).

Finding that substantial stability of conduct problems has continued does not necessarily mean that conduct disorder is as likely as ever to be followed by the pervasive and diverse adult antisocial behavior warranting a diagnosis of antisocial personality disorder. However, the likelihood that a child with conduct disorder will qualify for an antisocial personality diagnosis after age 18 is reasonably consistent across different eras—varying between 25% and 40% of conduct-disordered children being diagnosable as adult antisocial personalities (Robins, 1966; Robins, Tipp, & Przybeck, 1991; Zoccolillo, Pickles, Quinton, & Rutter, 1992). Using data from the ECA, we tested the hypothesis that conduct symptoms would be less predictive of adult antisocial behavior in young people than in older people because they were more common among the young. We found no change over time (Table 3.5). The proportion who developed the adult syndrome of antisocial personality among those who had any specific conduct problem was the same for the youngest cohort as for the total sample. The higher rate of antisocial personality in the young was entirely explained by their having had more conduct problems as children.

Follow-up studies of delinquents (Glueck & Glueck, 1968; Sampson & Laub, 1993), of children referred to psychiatric care because of antisocial behavior (Robins, 1966), and of antisocial children in inner-city areas (Farrington, 1989) showed many adverse outcomes in addition to the symptoms of antisocial personality. They include an elevated death rate from nonnatural deaths (homicide, accidental death, and suicide), high arrest rates, high rates of marital disruption, of sexual promiscuity, of friendlessness, of offspring with conduct disorder. The psychiatric syndromes particularly common in addition to antisocial personality are alcohol dependence and drug abuse or dependence (Kessler et al., 1997; Robins et al., 1991). Women with a history of conduct disorder also have increased rates of depression and anxiety. Even when there is insufficient continuity of antisocial behavior to merit a diagnosis of antisocial personality, most children with conduct disorder develop substance abuse, a psychiatric disorder, or have some adverse adult outcomes. This wide variety of adverse adult

TABLE 3.5
Are Younger Subjects Less Likely to Qualify for Antisocial Personality
Than Older Ones With the Same Number or Type of Conduct Problems?
(ECA, 1980–1985)

	Percent With Antisocial Personality	
	All Adults	Those Under 45
Total Population	2.6	3.8
Total qualifying as children:		
3+ behaviors	26	28
Exactly 3	18	19
4 or 5	26	29
6+	46	47
With specific child behaviors (whether or not 3+ in all):		
Runaway	29	31
Delinquent	25	26
Vandal	21	23
Substance use	18	18
Fight	17	20
Expelled, suspended	16	16
Truant	16	17
Lying	13	15
Stealing	11	13

outcomes consistently found in studies whose subjects grew up in different eras means that as behaviors qualifying a child for conduct disorder become more common, they do not become less ominous.

The stability over time in the strength of the association between conduct symptoms before age 15 and adult consequences suggests that the widely lamented increase in adult crime, poor work histories, and marital instability among adults might be largely explained by the increase in behavior problems in childhood. It does not imply that intervention with adults is useless, however. Successful treatment of medical disorders seldom requires eliminating their cause, and the same is probably true of social pathology. However, it does suggest that successful early intervention to prevent or treat conduct disorder can be expected to have important benefits for children and the adults they become.

A promising place to start would be in preventing or interrupting truancy and running away from home. Although early and recent studies agree that the number of conduct symptoms is a better predictor of adult outcomes than is any individual symptom, these two symptoms appear to be the only ones that increase the likelihood of antisocial personality after controlling for the total number of symptoms. This finding was repeated in studies conducted 25 years apart (Robins, 1966; Robins et al., 1991).

CONCLUSIONS

The study of variation in the prevalence of conduct disorder over time and place suffered from a lack of specific criteria in the early days of research into child mental health and delinquency, by frequent changes in the official criteria, by past avoidance of direct interviewing of children, and by missed opportunities to follow until the end of adolescence those children still at risk of developing the disorder at the time of the initial survey so that all studies would cover the complete risk period. Despite these handicaps, there is reasonably convincing evidence that the rate of conduct disorder in the Western world has been increasing over the last 70 years. We do not know whether this is a worldwide phenomena.

This increase has been matched by an increase in a host of adult problems that may be consequences of the increase in conduct disorder—arrests, violence, marital instability, promiscuity, substance abuse, depression, youthful suicides, and parenting a new generation of children with conduct disorder. We need to investigate further to what extent these increases in adult behavior problems are reflections of the rise in conduct disorder and to what extent both are products of the same social changes. It will be useful to partial out the contribution of genetic factors to child and adult behaviors when seeking effects of social changes. Participants in interventions that appear to successfully treat conduct disorder should have high priority for long-term follow-up to learn whether the results persist through early adulthood.

We observe the increase in conduct disorder, but are not sure of the reasons for it. Studies explaining change in rates require designs dating onset of risk factors and symptoms, developing methods for demonstrating effects on persistence and proliferation of symptoms and on their initiation, and testing alternative causal pathways simultaneously. A start was made in current genetic studies that distinguish shared and unique environmental factors, but the task remains challenging.

Although levels of conduct disorder change over time and probably vary from one culture to another, its predictors and outcomes seem remarkably similar across time and place. Existing research allows certain conclusions: All cultures in which conduct disorders were investigated provide recognizable examples of the disorder. Prevalences appear to have been on the increase for the last 50 years in industrialized countries. We do not know if this is also the case in developing countries. Rates are much higher in males than females, and in families that are stressed by conflict, poverty, and characteristic psychiatric disorder in the parents—antisocial personality and alcoholism. Many children with this disorder will go on to develop serious adult antisocial behavior, and those who do not are likely to develop substance abuse and other psychiatric syndromes. Although we cannot be sure that these correlates of conduct disorder in childhood and adulthood are uniform across all eras and all cultures, there is no evidence suggesting serious exceptions, nor have the consequences become less serious as prevalence has risen. Thus, conduct disorder has a long history as a most important public health concern. The current picture warrants our increasing commitment to discover ways of preventing and treating this disorder wherever it appears.

REFERENCES

Achenbach, T. M., & Edelbrock, C. S. (1981). Behavioral problems and competencies reported by parents of normal and disturbed children aged four through sixteen. *Monographs of the Society for Research in Child Development, 46,* Serial No. 188.

American Psychiatric Association. (1952). *Diagnostic and statistical manual: Mental disorders.* Washington, DC: Author.

American Psychiatric Association. (1968). *Diagnostic and statistical manual of mental disorder* (2nd ed.). Washington, DC: Author.

American Psychiatric Association. (1980). *Diagnostic and statistical manual of mental disorders* (3rd ed.). Washington, DC: Author.

American Psychiatric Association. (1987). *Diagnostic and statistical manual of mental disorders* (3rd rev. ed.). Washington, DC: Author.

American Psychiatric Association. (1994). *Diagnostic and statistical manual of mental disorders* (4th ed.). Washington, DC: Author.

Bird, H., Canino, G., Rubio-Stipec, M., Gould, M. S., Ribera, J., Sesman, M., Woodbury, M., Huertas-Goldman, S., Pagan, A., & Sanchez-LaCay, A. (1994). Estimates of the prevalence of childhood maladjustment in a community survey in Puerto Rico. *Archives of General Psychiatry, 45*, 1120–1126.

Brennan, P. A., & Mednick, S. A. (1993). Genetic perspectives on crime. *Acta Psychiatrica Scandinavica, 370*, 19–26.

Brown, R. A., Lewisohn, P. M., Seeley, J. R., & Wagner, E. F. (1996). Cigarette smoking, major depression and other psychiatric disorders among adolescents. *Journal of American Child Adolescent Psychiatry, 35*, 1602–1610.

Eaves, L. J., Silberg, J. L., Meyer, J. M., Maas, H. H., Simonoff, E., & Pickles, A. (in press). Genetics and developmental psychopathology: 2. The main effects of genes and environment on behavioral problems in the Virginia Twin Study of Adolescent Behavioral Development. *Journal of Child Psychology and Psychiatry.*

Farrington, D. (1989). Long-term prediction of offending and other life outcomes. In H. Wegener et al. (Eds.), *Criminal behavior and the justice system.* London: Springer-Verlag.

Gibson, H. B., Morrison, S., & West, D. J. (1970). The confession of known offences in response to a self-reported delinquency schedule. *British Journal of Criminology, 10*, 227–280.

Glueck, S., & Glueck, E. (1950). *Unravelling juvenile delinquency.* New York: The Common Wealth Fund.

Glueck, S., & Glueck, E. (1968). *Delinquents and nondelinquents in perspective.* Cambridge, MA: Harvard University Press.

Hagnell, O. (1966). *A prospective study of the incidence of mental disorder.* Stockhom: Svenska Bokforlaget.

Hewitt, L. E., & Jenkins, R. L. (1946). *Fundamental patterns of maladjustment: The dynamics of their origin.* Springfield: State of Illinois.

Huizinga, D., & Elliott, D. S. (1986). Reassessing the reliability of self-report delinquency measures. *Journal of Quantitative Criminology, 2*, 293–327.

Jensen, P., Roper, M., Fisher, P., Piancentini, J., Canino, G., Richters, J., Rubio-Stipec, M., Dulcan, M., Goodman, S., & Davies, M. (1995). Test-retest reliability of the Diagnostic Interview Schedule for Children (DISC 2.1). *Archives of General Psychiatry, 52*, 61–71.

Kasius, M. C., Ferdinand, R. F., van den Berg, H., & Verhulst, F. C. (1997). Associations between different diagnostic approaches for child and adolescent psychopathology. *Journal of Child Psychology and Psychiatry, 38*, 625–644.

Kessler, R. C., Anthony, J. C., Blazer, D., Bromet, E., Eaton, W. W., Kindler, K., Swartz, M., Wittchen, H. U., & Zhao, S. (1997). The US National Comorbidity Survey: Overview and future directions. *Epidemiologia e Psichiatria Sociale, 6*, 4–16.

Lyons, M. J., True, W., Eisen, S., Goldberg, J., Meyer, J. M., Faraone, S. V., Eaves, L. J., & Tsuang, M. T. (1995). Differential heritability of adult and juvenile antisocial traits. *Archives of General Psychiatry, 52*, 906–915.

Maughan, B., & Pickles, A. (1990). Adopted and illegitimate children growing up. In L. N. Robins & M. R. Rutter (Eds.), *Straight and devious pathways from childhood to adulthood* (pp. 36–61). New York: Cambridge University Press.

Moffitt, T. E. (1996). Measuring children's antisocial behaviors. *Journal of the American Medical Association, 275*, 403–404.

Moffitt, T., Caspi, A., Dickson, N., Silva, P., & Stanton, W. (1996). Childhood-onset versus adolescent-onset antisocial conduct problems in males: Natural history from ages 3 to 18 years. *Development and Psychopathology, 8*, 399–424.

Nye, F. I., & Short, J. F., Jr. (1957). Scaling delinquent behavior. *American Sociological Review, 22*, 326–331.

Offord, D. R., Alder, R. J., & Boyle, M. H. (1986). Prevalence and sociodemographic correlates of conduct disorder. *American Journal of Social Psychiatry, 4,* 272–278.

Reiss, A. J., Jr. (1986). Co-offender influences on criminal careers. In A. Blumstein, J. Cohen, J. A. Roth, & C. A. Visher (Eds.), *Criminal careers and "career criminals"* (Vol. 2, pp. 121–160). Washington, DC: National Academy Press.

Robins, L. (1966). *Deviant children grown up: A sociological and psychiatric study of sociopathic personality.* Baltimore: Williams & Wilkins.

Robins, L. N., Cottler, L., Bucholz, K., & Compton, W. (1996). *The Diagnostic Interview Schedule, Version IV.* St. Louis: Authors.

Robins, L. N., Helzer, J. E., Cottler, L., & Goldring, E. (1989). *The Diagnostic Interview Schedule, Version III-R.* St. Louis: Authors.

Robins, L. N., Helzer, J. E., Croughan, J. L., Williams, J. B. W., & Spitzer, R. L. (1981). *The NIMH Diagnostic Interview Schedule, Version III.* (HSS) ADM–T–42–3 (5–81, 8–81). Washington, DC: Public Health Service.

Robins, L. N., Tipp, J., & Przybeck, T. (1991). Antisocial personality. In L. N. Robins & D. Regier (Eds.), *Psychiatric disorders in America* (pp. 258–290). New York: The Free Press.

Rutter, M., Cox, A., Tupling, C., Berger, M., & Yule, W. (1975). Attainment and adjustment in two geographical areas: I. The prevalence of psychiatric disorder. *British Journal of Psychiatry, 126,* 493–509.

Sampson, R. J., & Laub, J. H. (1993). *Crime in the making.* Cambridge, MA: Harvard University Press.

Shaw, C. R., & McKay, H. D. (1942). *Juvenile delinquency and urban areas.* Chicago: University of Chicago Press.

Slutske, W. S., Heath, A. C., Dinwiddie, S. H., Madden, P. A. F., Bucholz, K. K., Dunne, M. P., Statham, D. J., & Martin, N. G. (1997). Modeling genetic and environmental influences in the etiology of conduct disorder. *Journal of Abnormal Psychology, 106,* 266–279.

Stott, D. H. (1959). Delinquency. *Advancement of Science, 61,* 497–505.

Verhulst, F. C., Eussen, M. L., Berden, G. F., Sanders-Woudstra, J., & vam der Ende, J. (1993). Pathways of problem behaviors from childhood to adolescence. *Journal of the American Academy of Child and Adolescent Psychiatry, 32,* 388–396.

Wadsworth, M. (1979). *Roots of delinquency.* Oxford, England: Martin Robertson.

West, D. J., & Farrington, D. P. (1977). *The delinquent way of life.* London: Heinemann.

White, J. L., Moffitt, T. E., Earls, F., Robins, L., & Silva, P. A. (1990). How early can we tell? Predictors of childhood conduct disorder and adolescent delinquency. *Criminology, 28,* 507–533.

World Health Organization. (1974). *Glossary of mental disorders and guide to their classification for use in conjunction with the International Classification of Diseases, 8th revision.* Geneva: Author.

World Health Organization. (1978). *Mental disorders: Glossary and guide to their classification in accordance with the ninth revision of the International Classification of Diseases.* Geneva: Author.

World Health Organization. (1993). *The ICD-10 classification of mental and behavioural disorders.* Geneva: Author.

Zoccolillo, M., Pickles, A., Quinton, D., & Rutter, M. (1992). The outcome of childhood conduct disorder: Implications for defining adult personality disorder and conduct disorder. *Psychological Medicine, 22*(4), 971–986.

Zoccolillo, M., Tremblay, R., & Vitaro, F. (1996). DSM-III-R and DSM-III criteria for conduct disorder in preadolescent girls: Specific but insensitive. *Journal of the American Academy of Child and Adolescent Psychiatry, 35,* 461–470.

Chapter 4

Major Mental Disorders and Crime: Changes Over Time?

Sheilagh Hodgins
Nathalie Lalonde
Université de Montréal

Since the 1960s compelling evidence has indicated that persons who suffer from major mental disorders (schizophrenia, major depression, bipolar disorder) are more likely than are non-disordered persons to commit crimes and to perpetrate violence. It is not clear, however, whether this is a new phenomenon, or whether persons with major disorders always behaved in this manner and it was only first documented in the 1960s.

Yet, it is important to know if the criminality and violence perpetrated by individuals who suffer from major mental disorders today differs from the behavior of similarly afflicted individuals who lived in the past. The answer to this question has important implications for the development of strategies to prevent criminality, and for advancing our understanding of the nature and etiology of the major mental disorders. We want to discover what factors increase and what factors decrease criminal behavior. If there has been no change since the mid-1960s in the frequency and severity of aggressive and criminal behavior among persons with major mental disorders, then various types of treatment and management do not impact these behaviors. Alternatively, if such behaviors have increased in frequency and severity in this population, two explanations are possible: Current treatment and management of persons with major mental disorders create a situation in which these persons are likely to behave aggressively or illegally, or persons born since World War II who have developed major mental disorders are more prone to aggressive and illegal behaviors than were earlier generations of persons suffering from the same disorders.

Although many authors assumed that the policy of deinstitutionalization led to criminality among persons suffering from major mental disorders, few examined the impact of this policy in the context of other changes occurring at approximately the same time. It is important to attempt to discover if the implementation of the policy of deinstitutionalization was associated with an increase in criminality among persons suffering from major mental disorders. If so, we must identify what aspects of the policy of deinstitutionalization are associated with criminality and violence; is it a lack of supervision, noncompliance with medications, relatively easy access to firearms, alcohol, and other drugs, or the combination of all of these factors? The policy of deinstitutionalization was implemented in a context of a number of other changes, such as the introduction of new medications, modifications in criteria for involuntary hospitalization and patients' rights, which impacted persons suffering from these disorders, and mental health professionals and government agencies responsible for administering mental health services. Did these changes lead to a situation in which persons with major mental disorders were committing crimes or violence? Are persons with these disorders more likely to behave aggressively or illegally now than in the past?

This chapter is divided into three sections. The first reviews the evidence that has accumulated since the mid-1960s on the relation between the major mental disorders and crime and violence. The next section describes our attempts to discover if this is a new phenomenon. Two time periods are examined: from 1900 to the beginning of the implementation of the policy of deinstitutionalization, and the years during which this policy was being implemented. The last section presents possible explanations of the changes in the behavior of persons with major mental disorders during this century.

RECENT EVIDENCE ON THE ASSOCIATION BETWEEN MAJOR MENTAL DISORDER AND CRIME

Three types of investigations addressed the relation between the major mental disorders and crime: follow-up studies of psychiatric patients discharged to the community, studies of the prevalence of the major mental disorders among convicted offenders, and investigations of unselected birth cohorts comparing the prevalence of criminality between persons with major disorders and those with no disorders.

Studies of Psychiatric Patients Discharged to the Community

In the 1960s and 1970s many follow-up studies were conducted in the United States in which the criminal activity of persons who had been discharged from psychiatric wards was compared to that of persons living in the communities surrounding the hospitals (Durbin, Pasewark, & Albers, 1977; Giovanni & Gurel, 1967; Rappeport & Lassen, 1965, 1966; Sosowsky, 1974, 1978, 1980; Steadman, Cocozza, & Melick, 1978; Zitrin, Hardesty, Burdock, & Drossman, 1976). Each of these investigations documented higher rates of criminality among the former patients than among the non-disordered population in the community where the patients lived. However, because of the methodology of these studies, the information they provide on the criminality of persons suffering from major mental disorders is limited. For example, diagnoses of the discharged patients were often not reported, and it is likely that the samples were not comparable with respect to the proportions of subjects with various diagnoses. Subject attrition was relatively high, and in many instances, criminal records were available for only one state (for a further discussion, see Hodgins, 1993).

Four recent investigations overcame these problems. Lindqvist and Allebeck (1990) followed all inpatients in Stockholm County with a diagnosis of schizophrenia who were born between 1920 and 1959 and discharged in 1971. Patients were rediagnosed by an independent clinician, using *DSM–III* criteria, and 85% (644) met the criteria for schizophrenia. These 644 patients were then followed for 14 years. The relative risk of a criminal offense among these schizophrenics as compared to the general Swedish population was 1.2 for the men and 2.2 for the women. However, the schizophrenics "committed four times as many violent offenses as the general population" (pp. 346–347).

In a carefully designed investigation, Link, Andrews, and Cullen (1992) examined the criminality of psychiatric patients compared to subjects who lived in the same neighborhood of New York but who had never received any mental health treatment. Four groups were followed: (a) patients who received psychiatric treatment for the first time in the year preceding the study, (b) patients who were in treatment during the previous year and once before, (c) former patients who received no treatment in the previous year, and (d) a community sample with no history of psychiatric treatment. Among the patients, 34% received a diagnosis of major depression, 19% schizophrenia, 10% another psychotic disorder, and 37% another mental disorder. Although 6.7% of the community cohorts and 6% of the first contact patients had been arrested, 12.1% of the repeat treatment patients and 11.7% of the former patients had been arrested. The arrests of the patients were more likely to have been for felonies and for violent acts than were the arrests of the subjects in the community sample.

A recent investigation followed patients who had been consecutively admitted to psychiatric wards in three different U.S. cities. All patients were included in the study except those with a primary diagnosis of mental retardation. During the 2 months prior to admission, 34.8% of the women and 39% of the men reported at least one violent incident. During the 2 months after discharge, 32.8% of the women and 22.4% of the men reported behaving violently at least once (Steadman et al., 1993). The rate of violence increased by 25.6% when the information from the collaterals was combined with self-report data from the patients (Steadman et al., 1994).

A follow-up study of all 281 males released from forensic hospitals in Finland over a 14-year period revealed that the patients were 300 times more likely than the males in the general population to commit a homicide during the first year in the community. During a follow-up period averaging 7.8 years, the risk of committing a homicide for the discharged male patients was 53 times that for the general Finnish male population (Tiihonen, Hakola, Eronen, Vartianen & Ryynänen, 1996).

Studies of the Mental Health of Offenders

Looking at the same problem from the opposite point of view are the studies of mental disorder among convicted offenders. Recent studies of representative samples of U.S. jail inmates (Teplin, 1990; Teplin, Abram, & McClelland, in press), U.S. prison inmates (Collins & Schlenger, 1983; Daniel, Robins, Reid, & Wilfey, 1988; Hyde & Seiter, 1987; Neighbors et al., 1987), and Canadian penitentiary inmates (Hodgins & Côté, 1990) have revealed higher prevalence rates of mental disorders within these facilities, and particularly of the major disorders, than in the general population. In this latter investigation, we were able to confirm that in the large majority of cases the major mental disorder was present before incarceration.[1] These investigations all employed the same diagnostic criteria, and standardized, reliable, and valid diagnostic instruments. These same instruments were used to examine the prevalence of mental disorders in the general population and, consequently, comparisons between the prevalence of disorders among inmates and in the general population can be made with some confidence.

In addition to these studies, four investigations suggest that the prevalence of the major disorders is even higher among homicide offenders. Most investigations of homicide offenders include only compilations of the psychiatric and psychological evaluations conducted at the request of the court. Such samples are biased and represent only a small proportion of homicide offenders. In Scandinavia, persons accused of homicide undergo an intensive psychiatric, psychological, and social assessment. The accused are usually hospitalized for several weeks in order to complete the evaluation, and family members, friends, employers, and witnesses to the crime

---

[1]Evidence on the etiologies of the three major mental disorders suggests that although the stress of incarceration may trigger an acute episode, it would not "cause" the disorder in a nonvulnerable individual (for further discussion, see Hodgins, 1995b, 1996).

are interviewed. Several mental health professionals contribute to the determination of the diagnoses and the assessment and conclusions are reviewed by senior forensic psychiatrists. A study of all homicide offenders in Copenhagen over a 25-year period revealed that 20% of the men and 44% of the women were diagnosed psychotic (Gottlieb, Gabrielsen, & Kramp, 1987). A similar investigation was conducted in northern Sweden between 1970 and 1981 (Lindqvist, 1986). Of the 64 individuals who were convicted of committing a homicide, 34 (53%) were found to suffer from a major mental disorder. Eronen, Tiihonen, and Hakola (1996) studied each of the 1,423 homicide offenders in Finland over a 12-year period. Schizophrenia was found to be much more prevalent among the homicide offenders than in the general population, matched for gender. The odds of a man with schizophrenia and no secondary diagnoses of alcoholism committing a homicide was found to be 6.4 times higher than for a man with no disorder. Similarly, among women suffering from schizophrenia and no secondary alcoholism, the risk of committing a homicide was 5.3 times greater than that for a woman with no disorder.

This overrepresentation of persons suffering from major mental disorders among homicide offenders is also evident in Canada. Here, there are four possible outcomes of a homicide: (a) the perpetrator is not identified, (b) the perpetrator commits suicide immediately after committing the homicide, (c) the perpetrator is found not guilty by reason of insanity or not responsible because of mental disorder, or (d) the perpetrator is convicted and incarcerated. In Côté and Hodgins (1992) a representative sample of incarcerated homicide offenders was diagnosed and 35% met the criteria for a major mental disorder. Those excused because of mental disorder suffered from a major mental disorder (Hodgins & Webster, 1992), and we assume that many of those who commit suicide also suffer from a major affective disorder. These findings suggest an association between the major mental disorders and homicide.

Studies of the Prevalence of Criminality in Unselected Birth Cohorts

The Scandinavian countries have registers of all of their residents allowing the identification of birth cohorts (e.g., all persons born in a designated area in a specified time period), documenting all admissions to all psychiatric wards, and documenting all police contacts and court convictions. Information from these registers was used to examine the prevalence of criminality among persons with major mental disorders who were hospitalized as compared to that among persons never admitted to a psychiatric ward. In considering the findings from these investigations, it is important to understand the methodology. At the end of the follow-up period, the subjects who were admitted to a psychiatric ward were classified by principal discharge diagnosis and usually a hierarchy of diagnoses is constructed. The comparison group included all subjects who were never admitted to a psychiatric ward. The criminal convictions for subjects in each group are then examined. Consequently, the timing of the convictions and the onset of the disorder were not taken into account. If the subject was admitted to a psychiatric ward with a diagnosis of a major disorder at any time before the end of the follow-up period, he or she was classified in the major mental disorder group. If this subject was convicted of a crime, he or she was counted as a person with major mental disorder who had committed a crime. The crime could have been committed before or after the onset of the disorder.

In 1975, Ortmann (1981) examined the criminality of all persons born in Copenhagen in 1953. Although the subjects were only 23 years of age, he found more of those who had been admitted to a psychiatric ward with a diagnosis of a major mental disorder (as compared to subjects who had never been admitted) had been registered for a criminal offense. As admissions to hospitals were independent of court judgments, and central registers recorded all admissions to psychiatric wards and all crimes, this first epidemiological investigation of an entire birth cohort suggested an association between the major disorders and criminality.

An investigation of an unselected birth cohort composed of all 15,117 persons born in Stockholm in 1953 and still living there in 1963 showed that subjects who develop major mental disorders are at significantly increased risk for criminality as compared to non-disordered persons. Among the male subjects, 31.7%[2] of those with no mental disorder and no retardation as compared to 50% of those who developed major disorders were registered for a criminal offense by the age of 30. Among the female subjects, 5.8% of the non-disordered women as compared to 19% of those who developed major mental disorders were registered for a criminal offense by age 30. Both the men and the women who developed major disorders were found to be at even greater risk for violent crimes than for nonviolent crimes. The offenders with major mental disorders committed, on average, as many or more offenses as did the non-disordered offenders. They committed all types of crimes. Examination of the ages when subjects began offending suggests that there are two groups among these mentally disordered offenders: one group who began offending when they are young, before the symptoms of the major mental disorder would be evident; and a second group composed of those who began offending as adults (Hodgins, 1992). These findings were replicated with a much larger Danish birth cohort composed of 324,401

---

[2]This figure may appear to be high. But in Stockholm at this time, this number of males in the general population were held responsible for a criminal act.

persons followed to age 43 (Hodgins, Mednick, Brennan, Schulsinger, & Engberg, 1996). Although the prevalence rates of criminality for both non-disordered and disordered subjects differ in each country, the increased risk among persons suffering from the major mental disorders is also evident in the Danish cohort. Also similar is the finding that offenders with major mental disorders commit, on average, as many or more offenses than the non-disordered offenders. Two other birth cohort studies, one conducted in Finland (Tiihonen, Isohanni, Koiranen, Moring, & Rantakallio, 1997) and the other in Israel (Link, 1996), also found higher rates of criminality among persons who develop major mental disorders than among persons without such disorders.

Conclusion

Three types of investigations compared the prevalence of criminality and violence among persons suffering from major mental disorders and those with no disorders: follow-up studies of patients with major mental disorders discharged from psychiatric wards to the community, investigations of the mental health of representative samples of incarcerated offenders, and three studies of unselected birth cohorts. All three types of investigations indicate that persons suffering from one or other of these three disorders are more likely than non-disordered persons to commit crimes and to perpetrate acts of violence. In addition to the increased risk of criminal convictions, analyses of retrospective self-report data (Link et al., 1992; Steadman & Felson, 1984; Swanson & Holzer, 1991; Swanson, Holzer, Ganju, & Jono, 1990) and of reports of the behavior of patients in the days preceding admission to a psychiatric ward (for a review, see Hodgins, 1993) suggest an increased risk of aggressive behavior among persons with major mental disorders.

IS VIOLENCE AMONG THOSE WITH MAJOR MENTAL ILLNESS NEW?

We set out to investigate whether or not the criminality and violence observed among persons suffering from major mental disorders since the 1960s is a new phenomenon. Do people with these disorders behave differently now than in the past? In order to answer our question we divided the past into two time periods, before and after the policy of deinstitutionalization had been implemented and neuroleptic medications were widely used. It seemed reasonable to presume that the answer to our question might differ for these two time periods when individuals suffering from mental disorders were subjected to dissimilar treatments. We also attempted to look separately at official criminality (offenses prosecuted in criminal court) and at aggressive or violent behavior that did not lead to criminal prosecution.

What Is the Record Prior to Deinstitutionalization?

In order to gather information on persons who suffered from major mental disorders in the period before deinstitutionalization, we examined all available documents, records, and reports from the largest "asylum" in Québec. This hospital is located on the southeast tip of the island on which the city of Montréal is situated. Physically, it was, and still is, a beautiful place. Large, elegant gray limestone buildings face out over green (or white depending on the season) lawns that slope gradually down to the river. Behind was a large farm and gardens. The grounds and buildings constituted a separate municipality with its own fire and police services. From the turn of the century, the population of the hospital continued to grow, from 1,543 in 1895 to 3,144 in 1918, to 6,158 in 1955. In the annual report of 1895–1896, it was noted by the government inspectors that not even 20% of the Québec population enjoyed the comforts of the patients at the asylum. Like most hospitals in Québec at this time, it was run by an order of nuns, the Soeurs de la Providence. The available data indicate that this was not an isolated, backwoods institution. In the 1920s and 1930s, it won prizes from both the American Psychiatric Association and the American College of Physicians and Surgeons in recognition of the treatments provided.

Our objective was to consult records and reports at the hospital in an effort to document: (a) the proportion of offenders with major mental disorders who were transferred for treatment;[3] (b) the rates of aggressive behavior of patients suffering from major mental disorders, and (c) the proportions of patients with these disorders who were admitted to the hospital because of aggressive behavior. After consulting with the librarians and historians responsible for the hospital records, we were surprised to learn that only the official statistical reports compiled annually for the government remained. Even some of these reports have vanished. However, from 1895 to 1960, most were available.

Our next surprise was to note that up until 1905 the reports were compiled by the "Inspector of Prisons and Asylums." One government agency was responsible for both asylums and prisons, and both types of

---

[3]Although other Canadian provinces had established special institutions for the criminally insane as early as 1857, in Québec a secure psychiatric hospital was opened only in the 1970s. Here, there continues to be a tradition of treating patients found not guilty by reason of insanity in general hospitals, with only a proportion being sent to the secure facility (Hodgins, 1993; Hodgins & Webster, 1992).

institutions were inspected by the same person. The available statistics for the entire period include information on admissions, discharges, deaths, diagnoses, treatments, transfers, and physical disorders and treatments.

Premature Death

At the turn of the century, 10% of the patients in the asylum died each year, principally from infectious diseases. The percentage of patients who died each year declined from 1900 to 1950. Although it is known that before the discovery of antibiotics, individuals housed in large institutions were at increased risk of developing infectious diseases (which were often fatal), the high death rate needs to be considered in light of two lines of evidence. First, epidemiological studies continue to demonstrate that persons who develop major mental disorders are at increased risk for premature death as compared to individuals who do not suffer from these mental disorders. Most of these deaths are due to disease, not suicide, at least in the case of schizophrenia (see, e.g., Baldwin, 1979) and bipolar disorder (Goodwin & Jamison, 1990). Second, there is some evidence that individuals who are both antisocial and have a major mental disorder may be at even higher risk for premature death than are other persons with the same major mental disorder. This latter finding makes some sense, as it is known that males with conduct disorder are at increased risk for premature death (Hodgins, 1994), and that individuals who have both a major disorder and who behave in an antisocial manner are much more likely to put themselves in life-threatening situations than are other patients who may be more withdrawn or isolated. Regardless of the cause of death, if it is true that antisocial individuals with major mental disorders die earlier than do non-antisocial patients with the same disorders, then the analysis of their antisocial behavior must take their shorter life spans into account.[4]

Major Mental Disorders Among Offenders

The annual reports of the asylum we studied documented a small number of transfers, each year, from prisons to hospital and vice-versa. For example, in 1918, 15% of the patients had a criminal record for either violent or nonviolent offenses. We could find no studies of the mental health of

---

[4]This is a difficult problem to overcome in follow-up studies of discharged patients. In most countries, an individual's criminal record is destroyed at the time of death. Consequently, former patients most likely to have committed crimes are dropped at the end of the follow-up period when the criminal records are collected. Unfortunately, most follow-up studies of former patients do not ever document the death rates of subjects. As a result, they may present an inaccurate picture of criminal activity among patients who are discharged to the community.

offenders before 1969 when Guze, Goodwin, and Crane reported on a follow-up of 209 male felons. Rates of the major disorders in this sample did not exceed rates for the general population. A similar study of female felons (Cloninger & Guze, 1973) came to the same conclusion. Roth and Ervin (1971) examined treatment records of a sample of federal prisoners,[5] and concluded that only 5% presented a psychotic disorder. These findings, and the lack of studies, are not surprising. Correctional facilities of this period did not provide mental health care (see, e.g., Roth, 1986). Even today, individuals with major mental disorders are often tried in criminal court and incarcerated without ever being identified as suffering from a mental disorder. In fact, in Hodgins and Côté (1993) we showed that the criminal records of offenders with major mental disorders are similar to those of non-disordered offenders. Consequently, officials in the criminal justice system who rely on such records would be unlikely to identify the offender who suffers from a major mental disorder. In light of these findings, the small number of individuals transferred from the criminal courts and the prisons to the asylum at this period in history does not allow us to conclude that individuals suffering from major mental disorders were not committing crimes.

Aggressive and Violent Behavior Among Patients

For the entire time period studied, in none of the records of the asylum could we find any mention of aggressive behavior, reasons for the use of restraints, or reasons for the use of isolation cells. However, we know from documents describing the buildings and equipment that both restraints and isolation cells existed. The absence of even one mention of aggressive behavior over all of these years and for this large number of patients perplexed us until we began to study the treatments provided to patients. In the 1920s and 1930s, these included infection by injection with malaria and treatment with quinine to reduce delusions;[6] physical constraints; being tied in a hammock in a hot bath with a bag of ice on the head; being wrapped in hot sheets; Scottish showers alternating hot and cold water; injection of turpentine to create an abscess that would lead to infection and fever (the abscess was broken, the fever subsided and so supposedly did the depressive symptoms); taking blood intravenously and reinjecting it intramuscularly; provoking seizures by insulin, and later by electric shock; lobotomy; and finally, the isolation cells.

---

[5]In the United States, prisoners in federal prisons have been convicted of breaking federal laws. They tend to be more white collar than blue collar prisoners.

[6]Although this was the accepted treatment for neurosyphilis at the time, the records of the hospital noted that it was used to reduce delusions.

Stepping back and looking at the information available for this period, what becomes apparent is that the entire hospital was organized to manage the patients. Our impression is that the staff expected the patients to behave in an aggressive or violent manner and that the hospital provided the means to prevent and to control these behaviors. The treatments, it could be argued, caused pain and could have been used as punishments for unacceptable behavior, or as deterrents to show other patients what would happen if they misbehaved. What is clear is that the staff had at their disposal numerous methods to control agitated or aggressive patients, with, to our knowledge, no limits on their power and authority to use these methods. We can find no evidence that the staff were limited, in any way, in their use of these various forms of control.

The only evidence we could find about the reasons why certain of these procedures were used came from a book titled *Les Fous Crient au Secours*[7] (Pagé, 1961), which was written by a former patient. The author described finding the isolation cells he was not supposed to see. The attendant informed him that the man he saw in one of these cells was being punished for having hit one of the nuns. He had been in the cell, at that time, for 16 months and 17 days and as far as was known had been fed only bread and water.

Scientific Knowledge of Mental Disorder and Crime at the Time

We can find no studies of the proportions of persons with major mental disorders who committed crimes before the 1950s. We can find no systematic studies of aggressive behavior or violence among these persons. We can find many descriptions of spectacular cases of violence perpetrated by mentally disordered persons, but these do not address the issue of whether or not individuals with major mental disorders are at increased risk for criminality or violence as compared to non-disordered persons. However, our impression is that in the latter part of the 19th century psychiatrists thought that the major disorders were associated with an increased risk of violence. For example, in an important psychiatric textbook, *Insanity and Its Treatment*, published in 1871, G. Fielding Blandford (1871/1976), an eminent British psychiatrist, stated: "We may roughly class insane acts under two heads—those which affect the person or property of the patient, and those which affect other persons or property of others . . . while under the second we find homicide, arson, rape, and acts of violence or mischief of innumerable kinds" (p. 175). In his textbook, Blandford distinguished between patients suffering from what we call today the major disorders,

---

[7]The English translation of this title is *The Crazies Call for Help*.

and mental retardation, epilepsy, and psychopathy or antisocial personality disorder. He noted: "Homicide may be perpetrated without any impulse or delusion by a patient enraged at being restrained, simply to free himself from detention. Many of the attacks to which attendants are subject are of this nature" (p. 186). These citations, and Blandford's book, give the impression (but provide no data) that much violence was observed among persons suffering from major mental disorders.

Although writers in the 1800s and early 1900s seemed to suggest that patients suffering from dementia praecox were at increased risk to kill, this notion disappeared as dynamically oriented thinking became predominate in the 1930s. Colaizzi (1989) concluded that "Anglo-American medical writers of the 'teens and 'twenties believed that insane homicide was positively associated with the peculiar disordered thought processes of dementia praecox" (p. 106); "the certain connection between schizophrenia and dangerousness soon became less apparent in the widely used textbooks [of the 1930s]" (p. 107). However, empirical data from the period indicate that an association did (and does) exist. In 1935, Strecker and Ebaugh, in their textbook of psychiatry, described their own study of 200 cases of schizophrenia. They noted that only 20 were actively homicidal. In an investigation of persons with schizophrenia at the turn of the century in rural Sweden, it was reported that high rates of alcoholism and "psychopathy" were found among their relatives (Lindelius, 1970). In 1937, Bender noted the high rate of delinquency among children of women who suffered from schizophrenia. The following year, Kallmann (1938) found high rates of criminality among his schizophrenic subjects and their children. As noted earlier, subsequent, methodologically rigorous investigations confirmed these observations (e.g., Kay, 1990; Silverton, 1985).

Rabkin (1979) described four follow-up studies conducted between 1922 and 1955 of patients discharged from psychiatric hospitals. In 1922, the superintendent of the Middletown State Homeopathic Hospital examined the criminal records of 1,000 (mainly female) patients who were discharged during the previous 10 years. Rabkin noted that although almost 25% of the patients were involved in conflicts serious enough to be brought to the attention of hospital staff, only 12 were arrested. During the follow-up period, the hospital staff could involuntarily rehospitalize patients at any time. In 1938, Pollock published a study of all patients discharged during 1937 from psychiatric hospitals in New York state. The study was conducted in response to the "frequently made charge that the paroling of mental patients by State hospitals is a dangerous procedure" (Pollock, p. 236, cited in Rabkin, p. 10). Arrest rates were very low. Cohen and Freeman (1945) published a similar study again in reaction to public resistance to discharging patients from state hospitals in Connecticut. Again, they found low arrest rates. For our purposes, the most serious limitation of these investigations is the lack of information on the diagnoses of those who were arrested. The report suggests that most of those who committed crimes suffered from what would today be called *personality disorders* and *substance use disorders*. The most complete and rigorous of the investigations of this period was that of Brill and Malzberg (1962), who examined arrest rates of 10,247 men discharged from psychiatric hospitals in New York state during fiscal 1947. In the 5½ years following discharge, arrest rates for felonies for the patients were higher and overall arrest rates lower than in the general population. "Rearrested patients were over-represented in the diagnostic categories of alcoholism, drug abuse, and psychopathic personality and significantly under-represented among the major functional psychiatric disorders" (p. 12). As noted by Rabkin, "The preceding four studies . . . together constitute the foundation for psychiatric reassurances that former mental patients are no threat or danger to their neighbors" (p. 12). However, these investigations did not test whether or not patients with major mental disorders committed crimes once released to the community, because few would have ever been released. Furthermore, these studies described the careful selection of those who were discharged, and the willingness and authority of hospitals to readmit patients who were misbehaving or found to be difficult by their families, the police, or the community. This is a very different situation than that which developed in the 1960s.

Conclusion

From the turn of the century until the policy of deinstitutionalization was implemented, we can find no evidence indicating that persons suffering from major mental disorders were more likely to be convicted of criminal offenses than were non-disordered persons. Further, there is no evidence that significant numbers of incarcerated offenders suffered from major mental disorders. Three studies of the criminality of discharged patients, some of whom may have been suffering from major mental disorders, did document lower arrest rates for the former patients than for the general population. However, those few who were discharged were carefully selected and were subject to involuntarily rehospitalization at any time.

We can find no adequate data to indicate whether or not persons with major mental disorders were more likely than others to behave aggressively or violently. The fact that they were hospitalized for most, if not all, of their adult lives in institutions in which staff could use any number of physical and biological controls on their behavior could be interpreted as suggesting that many did behave aggressively or at least in a threatening manner. Alternatively, it could be argued that these institutions and their means of control were a response to the severe and chronic symptoms presented by these persons. The writings of psychiatrists at the time would, we think, tend to favor the first explanation. However, these individuals would have been called upon to examine and to treat those among the mentally disordered who had committed crimes or atrocious acts of violence, and their impressions may be biased. The only rigorous findings are those few indicating increased rates of criminality among persons suffering from schizophrenia and their biological relatives. The whole matter is further complicated by the possibility that individuals who are antisocial and who suffer from a major mental disorder die at a much earlier age than do non-antisocial persons with the same disorders.

AFTER DEINSTITUTIONALIZATION, WERE PERSONS WHO SUFFER FROM MAJOR MENTAL DISORDERS AT INCREASED RISK FOR CRIMINALITY OR VIOLENCE?

Transfer of Care to the Community

In the United States, the policy of deinstitutionalization was implemented in two phases: From 1955 to 1965, there was a 15% reduction in the number of state psychiatric hospital patients, and from 1965 to 1980 a further reduction of 71%. The first phase involved discharging patients who had spent many years in institutions and treating newly admitted patients for only short periods of time. During this phase, patients could be easily readmitted, and the asylums essentially provided back-up services for the new community treatment programs. During the second phase, however, the asylums stopped readmitting former patients and admitting new patients. Morrissey and Goldman (1986) stated that the demarcation between these two phases can be located in the late 1960s. The policy of deinstitutionalization was defined and implemented in similar ways in Canada (see, e.g., Barnes & Toews, 1983).

A number of events were occurring at the same time, and they may have had an impact on the criminality and violence of the mentally disordered. The community treatment programs were understandably more interested in treating new patients rather than those who had spent years in the asylums. According to Morrissey and Goldman, early on there was some unheeded concern that patients were being transferred from the "back wards to the back alleys" (p. 21), indicating that the former asylum patients were not receiving adequate or appropriate care. It is clear, however, that the problem with the new community treatment programs was more profound than simply their biased selection of patients. In retrospect, we can see that the empirical data on which the community treatment programs rested were inadequate. The movement toward community care was not based on empirical data demonstrating the superiority of this form of treatment over that provided by the asylums (for reviews, see Hodgins & Gaston, 1987a, 1987b). Rather, the movement was bolstered by the belief that the new medications would eliminate the symptoms of the major mental disorders, and by the descriptions of the deplorable conditions discovered in many asylums. We now know that these programs were overwhelmed by the number of patients requiring care, that some proportion of persons with major mental disorders refused care, that services were not diversified to meet the needs of different types of patients, and that staff were not trained to diagnose nor to treat patients with substance abuse comorbid with a major disorder.

Other factors impacting this situation were court-ordered closing of asylums or orders to invest huge sums of money to bring these institutions up to certain standards. In Québec, after *Les Fous Crient au Secours* was published, the government conducted an investigation of the hospital we studied. The deplorable conditions and treatment of the patients were made public and the government took over the management and financing of the hospital promising reforms.

Requests to the Courts for Discharge

Not surprisingly, given the ethos of the time, several cases were taken to court in the United States in an effort to obtain discharges for patients held in institutions for the criminally insane. Baxstrom was serving a sentence in a New York State prison. During his prison stay, he was transferred to a state hospital. When he had served his sentence, he was further detained in the hospital on a civil commitment warrant. In 1966, he convinced the U.S. Supreme Court to discharge him and 966 other persons with similar status to civil hospitals where they were to be assessed and discharged to the community if they did not meet the criteria for civil commitment. In 1971, the Dixon case led to a similar reassessment of 586 patients from an institution for the criminally insane in Pennsylvania. As a result of the assessments, approximately 50% of the Baxstrom patients (Steadman & Cocozza, 1974) and 65% of the Dixon patients were discharged (Thornberry & Jacoby, 1979). In other words, even after long periods of hospitalization (and supposedly treatment), large proportions of these patients who had a history of criminality were considered a danger to society and consequently held in hospitals under civil commitment warrants. Those who were discharged were extensively studied. Thornberry and Jacoby, who studied the Dixon cohort, reported the following:

> The general recidivism rate of the Dixon patients, 23.7 percent, is also quite similar to the rate for the Baxstrom patients. Among this sample of ninety-eight criminally insane patients released from civil mental hospitals in New

York State, 20.4 percent were rearrested after a follow-up period that extended for a maximum of four years (Steadman & Cocozza, 1974, p. 139). Thus neither the Dixon nor Baxstrom patients, mentally ill offenders who had experienced long-term hospitalization and who were predicted at security hospitals to be dangerous after release, were more likely to be arrested than comparable members of a national sample of paroled, non-mentally ill offenders. (p. 185)

The conclusions of these two investigations added to the growing concern that mentally ill persons were being abused by professionals and being unnecessarily and unfairly confined to institutions with deplorable conditions that provided little care. The results of these investigations were interpreted as proof that mental health professionals could not predict dangerousness; that is, they could not accurately identify the patient who is likely to behave aggressively or violently if discharged to the community. According to the authors and to many commentaries at the time and currently, these investigations show that mental health professionals overpredict violence among patients and thereby unnecessarily and unfairly deprive them of their liberty. These findings contributed to the movement to reduce the authority of mental health professionals to involuntarily hospitalize patients whether using civil or criminal legislation (see, e.g. the description by Abramson, 1972, of the reasons why California increased the strictness of their civil commitment legislation). At the same time, legislation spelling out patients' rights, including their right to refuse treatment, became more and more prevalent.

Looking back, the data from the studies of the Baxstrom and the Dixon cases can be interpreted differently. After lengthy hospital stays in which clinicians had more than adequate time to observe these individuals, and after careful assessments conducted under the scrutiny of the courts, about 20% of those who were discharged committed new offenses. The data from the follow-up studies of the Baxstom and Dixon cohorts could be interpreted as indicating that even among carefully assessed and older subjects who suffered from major mental disorders, criminal activity is relatively common. In hindsight, other findings were also available as the policy of deinstitutionalization was being implemented to indicate that significant numbers of individuals who suffered from major mental disorders were committing crimes.

Consequences of Closing Beds and Transferring Care
to the Community

In what turned out to be a prophetic study, Grunberg, Klinger, and Grumet (1977) examined homicide offenders in Albany County, New York, comparing two time periods: 1963 to1969, when institutional care was available;

and 1970 to 1975, after the new community mental health center opened. Even in this short period of time, they observed an increase in the proportion of homicides committed by mentally disordered (principally schizophrenic) subjects. In their paper they referred to another psychiatrist (Virkunnen from Finland) who also noted the disproportionate amount of violence perpetrated by persons suffering from schizophrenia.

Follow-up studies of patients discharged from asylums continued to be published as in the earlier period. In 1965 and 1966, Rappeport and Lassen published studies of Maryland patients who were discharged between 1947 and 1957. They reported that more of the former patients than the general Maryland population were arrested for violent crimes. The authors noted that the largest proportions of arrestees were those with diagnoses of alcohol abuse and schizophrenia. Giovanni and Gurel (1967) published a study of 1,142 males suffering from schizophrenia who were discharged from 12 Veterans Administration hospitals in the United States. During the 4-year follow-up period, the annual rate of homicide for the schizophrenic men was 0.99 as compared to 0.05 for the general male population, whereas the annual rate for burglary was 0.65 for the schizophrenic men and 5.1 for the general population. Sosowsky (1974) examined former inpatients and outpatients in California hospitals, and showed their disproportionate involvement in violent crimes committed in 1971. Until Rabkin's literature review was published in 1979, similar findings continued to accumulate. At this time she concluded that "Since 1965, eight American studies including nine samples were designed to contribute further empirical evidence to the question of the dangerousness of discharged mental patients. Each study found that arrest or conviction rates of former mental patients equalled or exceeded those of the general population in at least some crime categories when patients were considered as a homogeneous group" (p. 13). However, she noted that before 1965, data indicated that discharged patients committed fewer crimes than did the general population.

By the early 1970s, psychiatrists who worked in jails were reporting increases in the numbers of arrestees with serious mental disorders (see, e.g., Allodi, Robertson, & Kedward, 1974). Although the clinicians responsible for these programs continued to insist that there was an increase in the numbers of arrestees who suffered from major mental disorders, academic researchers pointed out possible biases in these perceptions. Counting cases referred for treatment did not provide robust data documenting an increase in arrest rates of mentally disordered persons. Police have discretionary powers and could divert mentally ill persons to hospitals rather than charging them. At the time, many jurisdictions did not have adequate data to examine whether there was an increase in the numbers of persons being found unfit to stand trial and not guilty by reason of insanity.

Conclusion

Figure 4.1 presents a resume of changes occurring in the period in which the policy of deinstitutionalization was implemented. On the left of the figure are the only data we know of that document criminality among patients with major mental disorders over time. The data are drawn from the twin registry at the Maudsley Hospital in London. Although the sample is not large (N = 490) and is biased (all twins, one of whom was treated for a major mental disorder), the findings clearly demonstrate that from 1948 through 1988 the proportion of patients with a criminal record increased. On the right of the figure, other changes are presented that we (and others) suggest have affected persons suffering from major mental disorders.

There is evidence that following deinstitutionalization, persons with major mental illness were more likely to be arrested for crimes, and particularly for crimes of violence. Civil commitment legislation and patient rights were strengthened during this time making it difficult to involuntarily hospitalize patients. The adequacy of care and the compliance of patients with the new forms of treatment were quickly called into question. Nevertheless, during this period patients often received little or no community care; probably there was less after-care than previously or currently. For example, we examined a cohort composed of all the persons found not guilty by reason of insanity in Québec between 1973 and 1975 (Hodgins & Hébert, 1984; Hodgins, Hébert, & Baraldi, 1986). Almost 50% of these patients received no follow-up care after discharge. Today, it is unlikely this could occur. In a similar study in some of the same institutions all but a few of the patients discharged between 1988 and 1992 received follow-up care (Hodgins, Toupin, Fiset, & Moisan, 1995).

WHAT FACTORS ARE ASSOCIATED WITH THE INCREASE IN CRIMINALITY AND VIOLENCE AMONG PERSONS SUFFERING FROM MAJOR MENTAL DISORDERS?

The principal difference in the two eras already described is the intensity and quality of supervision of persons suffering from major mental disorders. Before deinstitutionalization, individuals with these disorders were feared by the community and most spent their adult lives within asylums. Even if they were discharged, which was unlikely, they could be readily rehospitalized, even against their wishes. From what we can understand of the period, often the family or police or community at large demanded readmission as a result of difficulties experienced with the patient. Today,

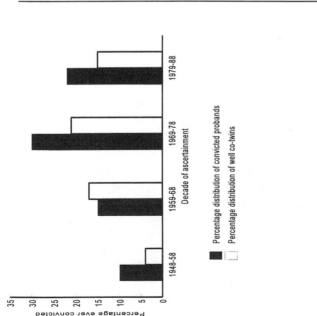

CO-OCCURRING EVENTS

- 1955 - 1980
  FEWER AND FEWER HOSPITAL BEDS

- 1948 →
  SHORTER HOSPITAL STAYS

- 1970s - early 1980s
  NOT MUCH AFTER-CARE (ROOMING-HOUSES)

- Late 1970s - Beginning 1980s
  ECONOMIC RECESSION OR ECONOMIC RESTRAINT
  ASSOCIATED WITH LACK OF FUNDING FOR
  COMMUNITY AFTER CARE

- 1966, 1969, 1974, 1976
  COURT-ORDERED EXAMINATIONS AND RELEASE OF
  LONG-TERM SO-CALLED "DANGEROUS PATIENTS"

- Late 1960s and 1970s
  TIGHTENING OF CIVIL COMMITMENT PROCEDURES

- 1970s
  INCREASE IN PATIENTS' RIGHTS
  (ESPECIALLY TO REFUSE TREATMENT)

Percentage distribution of convicted probands
Percentage distribution of well co-twins

FIG. 4.1. Percentage distribution of convicted probands and well co-twins, 1948–1988. From Coid, Lewis, and Reveley (1993). Copyright © 1993 by Royal College of Psychiatrists. Reprinted by permission.

with much more stringent rules for involuntary commitment and substantial patient rights to refuse treatment, it is very difficult in most jurisdictions to hospitalize a patient against his or her wishes. The limited number of available psychiatric beds and policies dictating short hospital stays further constrain the use of hospitals to treat persons with major mental disorders. Many of these persons refuse out-patient treatment, accept parts of it, or accept it sporadically. This lack of supervision and care of the severely disordered was empirically examined, and its impact on serious violence noted immediately (see, e.g., the study of homicide offenders in the 5 years preceding and succeeding the setting up of community mental health services in Albany). Still, the current mental health system was not organized to take account of the consistent findings linking inadequate care and supervision to increased violent behavior among persons with major disorders.

In the early follow-up studies of the criminality of discharged patients, the authors noted the disproportionate numbers of offenders who had comorbid substance abuse problems. All investigations to date confirmed that alcohol and drug use increase the risk of criminal and violent behavior among both men and women who suffer from major mental disorders. However, as noted elsewhere (Hodgins, 1993, 1994), alcohol and drug use do not explain away the criminality and violence of persons with major disorders. As with non-disordered persons, substance abuse increases the likelihood of criminal behavior. Whether or not the various drugs increase the likelihood of criminality and violence to the same extent for persons suffering from each of the major disorders as compared to those with no disorders is not presently known (see, e.g., Beaudoin, Hodgins, & Lavoie, 1993). However, it appears that persons with major disorders are more likely than non-disordered persons to develop alcohol and drug use disorders (Anthony & Helzer, 1991; Helzer, Burnam, & McEvoy, 1991; Hodgins, 1994). Brill and Malzberg (1962) noted that patients who had a history of criminal behavior before being admitted to a psychiatric hospital were more likely to commit offenses after discharge than were other patients. Subsequent investigations confirmed that after the policy of deinstitutionalization was implemented, the proportion of patients with prior criminal records who were admitted to hospitals increased (for reviews, see Monahan & Steadman, 1983; Rabkin, 1979). More recent investigations showed that there are antisocial boys and adolescents who develop major mental disorders at the end of adolescence or in early adulthood (Hodgins, 1995a; Robins, Tipp, & Przbeck, 1991). They differ from other men and women with major disorders who commit crimes in that they demonstrate a stable pattern of antisocial behavior from a young age, long before the symptoms of the major disorder is apparent (for a further discussion, see Hodgins, Côté, & Toupin, 1998; Hodgins, Toupin, & Côté, 1996). There may be an increase in the numbers of such men. Two other lines of evidence support this contention: (a) Epidemiological data that the proportion of subjects reporting three or more symptoms of antisocial behavior in childhood has increased across cohorts born later in this century (Robins et al., 1991), and (b) high comorbidity exists between conduct disorder and the major disorders. Investigations of children at risk for schizophrenia identified a subgroup who are characterized by aggressive behaviour (Cannon, Mednick, & Parnas, 1990; Silverton, 1985). Epidemiological studies of childhood mental disorders are currently documenting high rates of comorbidity for affective disorders and conduct disorders, and one prospective study showed that conduct disorder preceded the development of bipolar disorder in a proportion of boys. In other words, if there are more antisocial children, there will be more antisocial young adults who develop major mental disorders (Angold & Costello, 1993; Carlson & Weintraub, 1993).

A factor that has not been investigated, but which may be associated with the criminality and violence of persons with major mental disorders, is obstetrical complications. If there were an increase in criminality or violence among persons with major mental disorders since the early 1960s, it may be because these persons were injured during fetal development (see, e.g., Raine, Brennan, & Mednick, 1994). The studies of birth cohorts, incarcerated offenders, and former patients described in the first part of this chapter include subjects with major mental disorders whose mothers may have taken alcohol or drugs, or who may have been given neuroleptic medications or electroconvulsive therapy (ECT) during their pregnancies. It is now known that any of these may structurally alter the developing fetal brain (McNeil, 1988). Persons at genetic risk for a major mental disorder may also be at increased risk for central nervous system (CNS) damage resulting from pregnancy and birth complications (Brennan, Mednick, & Jacobsen, 1995; Mednick, Cannon, Barr, & LaFosse, 1991; Torrey, Bowler, Taylor, & Gottesman, 1994). It is possible that pregnancy and birth complications occurring to fetuses at risk for a major mental disorder may lead to damage that increases the risk of eventual antisocial or violent behavior. More precautions are now taken with pregnant women than in the past. If possible, women with schizophrenia and major depression are withdrawn from medications during pregnancy. However, women with bipolar disorder usually continue to take medications during the second and third trimesters of pregnancy (Goodwin & Jamison, 1990), and may be given ECT (Miller, 1994). Such treatments may place their offspring at risk.

Another factor that is often proposed to account for the increase in violence is the effect of violent television and movies. Longitudinal investigations conducted in different countries concur in demonstrating that more aggressive (than nonaggressive) children watch violent television programs. Low socioeconomic status, low IQ, and mother working outside the home are factors that were found to be correlated with this increased viewing of violence (Huesmann & Eron, 1986), as is the fact that most of these aggressive children grow up to be aggressive adults. Children who are at genetic risk for one of the major mental disorders may be susceptible to modeling what they see on television or in the movies. However, the two birth cohorts we studied, both of which provided evidence that proportionately more of those with major mental disorders than those with no disorders committed crimes and violence, were not exposed to violent television or movies. When they were growing up there was little television, and none of it was violent. It was not customary at the time for families to go to movies, except for special children's films. However, if as noted previously there are more antisocial children, some of whom will develop major mental disorders in adulthood, violence on television and in the movies may be acting to consolidate or reinforce their aggressive behavior. Consequently, given the consistent results of the effects of violent film on aggressive behavior, this factor merits, in our opinion, further testing.

These factors can be combined into a parsimonious, although at this point speculative, hypothesis to explain the increased criminality and violence of those with major disorders. We propose that there are two types of offenders who suffer from major mental disorders. The first, those who commit crimes or violence in response to delusions or hallucinations, have not proportionately increased in numbers. But as they can more easily obtain firearms and alcohol and drugs than in the past, as many of them refuse to take medications to control their symptoms, and as their symptomatology and behavior is not supervised, more of them commit crimes presently than was the case when they were institutionalized for life. The second type of offender with major mental disorders may be more prevalent now than in the past. It is hypothesized that obstetrical complications of fetuses that are genetically vulnerable to major mental disorders may alter CNS functioning rendering the individual more likely to develop a stable pattern of aggressive and antisocial behavior across his/her lifespan.

SUMMARY

Evidence has accumulated since the mid-1960s indicating that persons who suffer from major mental disorders are more likely than persons with no disorder to commit crimes and crimes of violence. We examined both the scientific literature and the records of an asylum from 1895 through 1960 in an effort to understand if the behavior of persons with major mental disorders changed over time. In the early 1900s, scientific texts mentioned violence perpetrated by persons suffering from what we now call the major mental disorders. However, there were few studies during this period that examined the frequency of such behavior in this population. Persons with major disorders spent their lives within asylums where staff exercised enormous control over their behavior.

In the records of the asylum we found no mention of aggressive behavior. This is hard to interpret, given the intensity of social control within the institution. Once the asylums were closed or drastically reduced in size, however, empirical data indicated that, very quickly, significant proportions of individuals suffering from major mental disorders were committing crimes and crimes of violence. Although the lack of adequate services and appropriate treatment for this population is clearly associated with their criminal behavior, persons with major mental disorders born since World War II may be more prone to illegal behaviors than were previous generations who suffered from the same disorders.

ACKNOWLEDGMENTS

This work was carried out with a grant to Hodgins from the Social Sciences and Humanities Research Council, and a grant from the Fonds pour la Formation des Chercheurs et l'Aide à la Recherche to cover expenses for Lalonde.

REFERENCES

Abramson, M. F. (1972). The criminalization of mentally disordered behavior: Possible side-effect of a new mental health law. *Hospital & Community Psychiatry, 23,* 101–105.

Allodi, F. A., Robertson, M., & Kedward, H. B. (1974). *Insane but guilty: Psychiatric patients in jail.* Paper presented at the annual meeting of the Canadian Psychiatric Association, Ottawa.

Angold, A., & Costello, E. J. (1993). Depressive comorbidity in children and adolescents: Empirical, theoretical, and methodological issues. *American Journal of Psychiatry, 150,* 1779–1791.

Anthony, J. C., & Kelzer, J. E. (1991). Syndromes of drug abuse and dependence. In L. N. Robins & D. A. Regier (Eds.), *Psychiatric disorders in America* (pp. 81–115). New York: The Free Press.

Baldwin, J. A. (1979). Schizophrenia and physical disease. *Psychological Medicine, 9,* 611–618.

Barnes, G. E., & Toews, J. (1983). Deinstitutionalization of chronic mental patients in the Canadian context. *Canadian Psychology, 24,* 22–36.

Beaudoin, M. N., Hodgins, S., & Lavoie, F. (1993). Homicide, schizophrenia and substance abuse or dependency. *Canadian Journal of Psychiatry, 38,* 1–7.

Bender, L. (1937). Behavior problems in the children of psychotic and criminal parents. *Genetic Psychology Monographs, 19,* 229–339.

Blandford, G. F. (1976). *Insanity and its treatment.* New York: Arno Press. (Original work published 1871)

Brennan, P. A., Mednick, S. A., & Jacobsen, B. (1995). Assessing the role of genetics in crime using adoption cohorts. In *Genetics of criminal and antisocial behaviour* (pp. 115–128). Chichester, England: Wiley.

Brill, H., & Malzberg, B. (1962). Statistical report on the arrest record of male ex-patients released from New York State Mental Hospitals during the period 1946–48. In *Criminal Acts of Ex-Mental Hospital Patients* (Suppl. No. 153). Washington, DC: American Psychiatric Association Mental Hospital Service.

Carlson, G. A., & Weintraub, S. (1993). Childhood behavior problems and bipolar disorder—Relationship or coincidence? *Journal of Affective Disorders, 28,* 143–153.

Cloninger, C. R., & Guze, S. B. (1973). Psychiatric disorders and criminal recidivism. *Archives of General Psychiatry, 29,* 266–269.

Coid, B., Lewis, S. W., & Reveley, A. M. (1993). A twin study of psychosis and criminality. *British Journal of Psychiatry, 162,* 87–92.

Collins, J. J., & Schlenger, W. E. (1983). *The prevalence of psychiatric disorder among admissions to prison.* Paper presented at the 35th annual meeting of the American Society of Criminology, Denver.

Côté, G., & Hodgins, S. (1992). The prevalence of major mental disorders among homicide offenders. *International Journal of Law and Psychiatry, 15,* 89–99.

Cannon, T. D., Mednick, S., & Parnas, J. (1990). Antecedents of predominantly negative and predominantly positive symptom schizophrenia in a high risk population. *Archives of General Psychiatry, 47,* 622–632.

Colaizzi, J. (1989). *Homicidal insanity, 1800–1985* (L. D. Stephen, Ed.). Tuscalloosa and London: The University of Alabama Press.

Daniel, A. E., Robins, A. J., Reid, J. C., & Wilfley, D. E. (1988). Lifetime and six-month prevalence of psychiatric disorders among sentenced female offenders. *Bulletin of the American Academy Psychiatry and the Law, 16,* 333–342.

Durbin, J. R., Pasewark, R. A., & Albers, D. (1977). Criminality and mental illness: A study of current arrest rates in a rural state. *American Journal of Psychiatry, 134,* 80–83.

Eronen, M., Tiihonen, J., & Hakola, P. (1996). Schizophrenia and homicidal behavior. *Schizophrenia Bulletin, 22,* 83–90.

Giovanni, J. M., & Gurel, L. (1967). Socially disruptive behaviour of ex-mental patients. *Archives of General Psychiatry, 17,* 146–153.

Goodwin, F. D., & Jamison, K. R. (1990). *Manic-depressive illness.* New York: Oxford University Press.

Gottlieb, P., Gabrielsen, G., & Kramp, P. (1987). Psychotic homicides in Copenhagen from 1959 to 1983. *Acta Psychiatrica Scandinavica, 76,* 285–292.

Grunberg, F., Klinger, B. I., & Grumet, B. R. (1977). Homicide and deinstitutionalization of the mentally ill. *American Journal of Psychiatry, 134,* 685–687.

Helzer, J. E., Burnam, A., & McEvoy, L. T. (1991). Alcohol abuse and dependence. In L. N. Robins & D. A. Regier (Eds.), *Psychiatric disorders in America* (pp. 81–115). New York: The Free Press.

Hodgins, S. (1992). Mental disorder, intellectual deficiency and crime: Evidence from a birth cohort. *Archives of General Psychiatry, 49,* 476–483.

Hodgins, S. (1993). The criminality of mentally disordered persons. In S. Hodgins (Ed.), *Mental disorder and crime* (pp. 1–21). Newbury Park, CA: Sage.

Hodgins, S. (1994). Letter to the editor. *Archives of General Psychiatry, 51,* 71–72.

Hodgins, S. (1995a). Major mental disorder and crime: An overview. *Psychology, Crime and Law, 2,* 5–17.

Hodgins, S. (1995b). *Une recension des écrits portant sur les facteurs de risque des troubles mentaux graves.* Report commissioned by the Conseil Québécois de la Recherche Sociale.

Hodgins, S. (1996). The major mental disorders: New evidence requires new policy and practice. *Canadian Psychology, 37,* 95–111.

Hodgins, S., & Côté, G. (1990). The prevalence of mental disorders among penitentiary inmates. *Canada's Mental Health, 38*, 1–5.

Hodgins, S., & Côté, G. (1993). The criminality of mentally disordered offenders. *Criminal Justice and Behavior, 28*, 115–129.

Hodgins, S., Côté, G., & Toupin, J. (1998). Major mental disorders and crime: An etiological hypothesis. In D. J. Cooke, A. Forth, & R. D. Hare (Eds.), *Psychopathy, theory, research and implications for society* (pp. 231–256). Dordrecht, The Netherlands: Kluwer.

Hodgins, S., & Gaston, L. (1987a). Composantes d'efficacité des programmes de traitement communautaires destinés aux personnes souffrant de désordres mentaux. *Santé Mentale au Québec, 12*, 124–134.

Hodgins, S., & Gaston, L. (1987b). Les programmes communautaires pour patients chroniques: L'élaboration d'un cadre conceptuel. *Santé Mentale au Canada, 35*, 7–10.

Hodgins, S., & Hébert, J. (1984). Une étude de relance auprès de malades mentaux ayant commis des actes criminels. *Revue Canadienne de Psychiatrie, 29*, 669–675.

Hodgins, S., Hébert, J., & Baraldi, R. (1986). Women declared insane: A follow-up study. *International Journal of Law and Psychiatry, 8*, 203–216.

Hodgins, S., Mednick, S. A., Brennan, P., Schulsinger, F., & Engberg, M. (1996). Mental disorder and crime: Evidence from a birth cohort. *Archives of General Psychiatry, 53*, 489–496.

Hodgins, S., Toupin, J., & Côté, G. (1996). Schizophrenia and antisocial personality disorder: A criminal combination. In L. B. Schlesinger (Ed.), *Explorations in criminal psychopathology: Clinical syndromes with forensic implication* (pp. 217–237). Springfield, IL: Charles C. Thomas.

Hodgins, S., Toupin, J., Fiset, S., & Moisan, D. (1995). *Une comparaison des soins externes offerts aux patients souffrant de troubles mentaux graves pendant 24 mois suite à leur sortie d'un centre hospitalier.* Report commissioned by the Conseil Québécois pour la Recherche Sociale, Quebec, Quebec.

Hodgins, S., & Webster, C. D. (1992). *The Canadian data base: Patients held on Lieutenant-Governors' Warrants.* Ottawa: Department of Justice of Canada.

Huesmann, L. R., & Eron, L. D. (1986). The development of aggression in American children as a consequence of television violence viewing. In L. R. Huesmann & L. D. Eron (Eds.), *Television and the aggressive child: A cross-national comparison* (pp. 45–80). Hillsdale, NJ: Lawrence Erlbaum Associates.

Hyde, P. S., & Seiter, R. P. (1987). *The prevalence of mental illness among inmates in the Ohio prison system.* The Department of Mental Health and the Ohio Departments of Rehabilitation and Correction. Interdepartmental Planning and Oversight Committee for Psychiatric Services to Corrections, Columbus, Ohio.

Kallmann, F. J. (1938). *The genetics of schizophrenia.* New York: Augustin.

Kay, S. R. (1990). Significance of the positive–negative distinction in schizophrenia. *Schizophrenia Bulletin, 16*, 635–652.

Lindelius, R. (Ed.). (1970). A study of schizophrenia: A clinical, prognostic, and family investigation. *Acta Psychiatrica Scandinavica* (Suppl. 216), 1–125.

Lindqvist, P. (1986). Criminal homicide in northern Sweden 1970–1981: Alcohol intoxication, alcohol abuse and mental disease. *International Journal of Law and Psychiatry, 8*, 19–37.

Lindqvist, P., & Allebeck, P. (1990). Schizophrenia and assaultive behaviour: The role of alcohol and drug abuse. *Acta Psychiatrica Scandinavica, 82*, 191–195.

Link, B. G. (1996). *Mental illness and violence: Epidemiological evidence from Israel.* Paper presented at the annual meeting of the American Association for the Advancement of Science, Baltimore.

Link, B. G., Andrews, H., & Cullen, F. T. (1992). The violent and illegal behaviour of mental patients reconsidered. *American Sociological Review, 57*, 275–292.

McNeil, T. F. (1988). Epidemiology: Obstetric factors and perinatal injuries. In M. T. Tsuang & J. C. Simpson (Eds.), *Handbook of schizophrenia: Vol. 3. Nosology, epidemiology and genetics of schizophrenia* (pp. 319–344). Amsterdam: Elsevier.

Mednick, S. A., Cannon, T. D., Barr, C. E., & LaFosse, J. M. (1991). *Developmental neuropathology of schizophrenia. Series A: Life sciences* (Vol. 17). New York: Plenum.

Miller, L. J. (1994). Use of electroconvulsive therapy during pregnancy. *Hospital and Community Psychiatry, 45,* 444–450.

Monahan, J., & Steadman, H. J. (1983). Crime and mental disorder: An epidemiological approach. In M. Tonry & R. Morris (Eds.), *Crimes and justice: An annual review of research* (Vol. 4, pp. 145–189). Chicago: University of Chicago Press.

Morrissey, J. P., & Goldman, H. H. (1986). Care and treatment of the mentally ill in the United States: Historical developments and reforms. *The Annals of the American Academy of Political and Social Science, 484,* 12–27.

Neighbors, H. W., Williams, D. H., Gunnings, T. S., Lipscomb, W. D., Broman, C., & Lepkowski, J. (1987). *The prevalence of mental disorder in Michigan prisons.* Final report submitted to the Michigan Department of Corrections, Lansing.

Ortmann, J. (1981). Psykisk ofvigelse og kriminel adfaerd en under sogelse af 11533 maend fodt i 1953 i det metropolitane omrade kobenhaun. *Forksningsrapport, 17,* 1–53.

Pagé, J.-C. (1961). *Les fous crient au secours.* Montréal: Éditions du Jour.

Rabkin, J. G. (1979). Criminal behavior of discharged mental patients: A critical appraisal of the research. *Psychological Bulletin, 86,* 1–27.

Raine, A., Brennan, P., & Mednick, S. A. (1994). Birth complications combined with early maternal rejection at age 1 year predispose to violence crime at age 18 years. *Archives of General Psychiatry, 51,* 984–988.

Rappeport, J. R., & Lassen, G. (1965). Dangerousness arrest rate comparisons of discharged patients and the general population. *American Journal of Psychiatry, 121,* 776–783.

Rappeport, J. R., & Lassen, G. (1966). The dangerousness of female patients. A comparison of the arrest rate of discharged psychiatric patients and the general population. *American Journal of Psychiatry, 123,* 413–419.

Robins, L. N., Tipp, J., & Przbeck, T. (1991). Antisocial personality. In L. Robins & D. A. Regier (Eds.), *Psychiatric disorders in America* (pp. 258–290). New York: The Free Press.

Roth, L. H. (1986). Correctional psychiatry. In W. J. Curran, A. L. McGarry, & S. A. Shah (Eds.), *Forensic psychiatry and psychology* (pp. 429–468). Philadelphia: F. A. Davis.

Roth, L. H., & Ervin, F. R. (1971). Psychiatric care of federal prisoners. *American Journal of Psychiatry, 128,* 424–430.

Silverton, L. (1985). *Crime and the schizophrenia spectrum: A study of two Danish cohorts.* Unpublished doctoral thesis, University of Southern California, Los Angeles.

Sosowsky, L. (1974). Violence and the mentally ill. In *Putting state mental hospitals out of business—The community approach to treating mental illness in San Mateo County* (pp. 17–33). Berkeley: University of California Graduate School of Public Policy.

Sosowsky, L. (1978). Crime and violence among mental patients reconsidered in view of the new legal relationship between the state and the mentally ill. *American Journal of Psychiatry, 135,* 33–42.

Sosowsky, L. (1980). Explaining the increased arrest rate among mental patients: A cautionary note. *American Journal of Psychiatry, 137,* 1602–1605.

Steadman, H. J., & Cocozza, J. J. (1974). *Careers of the criminally insane.* Lexington, MA: Lexington Books, D. C. Heath.

Steadman, H. J., Cocozza, J. J., & Melick, M. E. (1978). Explaining the increased arrest rate among mental patients: The changing clientele of state hospitals. *American Journal of Psychiatry, 135,* 816–820.

Steadman, H. J., & Felson, R. B. (1984). Self-reports of violence. Ex-mental patients, ex-offenders, and the general population. *Criminology, 22,* 321–342.

Steadman, H. J., Monahan, J., Robbins, P. A., Applebaum, P., Grisso, T., Klassen, D., Mulvey, E., & Roth, L. (1993). From dangerousness to risk assessment: Implications for appropriate research stategies. In S. Hodgins (Ed.), *Mental disorder and crime* (pp. 22–39). Newbury Park, CA: Sage.

Steadman, H. J., Monahan, J., Applebaum, P. S., Grisso, T., Mulvey, E., Roth, L. H., Robbins, P. A., & Klassen, D. (1994). Designing a new generation of risk assessment research. In J. Monahan & H. J. Steadman (Eds.), *Violence and mental disorder: Developments in risk assessment* (pp. 297–318). Chicago: The University of Chicago Press.

Strecker, E. A., & Ebaugh, F. G. (1935). *Practical clinical psychiatry.* Philadelphia.

Swanson, J. W., & Holzer, C. E. (1991). Violence and ECA data: Letter to the editor. *Hospital and Community Psychiatry, 42,* 954–955.

Swanson, J. W., Holzer, C. E., Ganju, V. K., & Jono, R. T. (1990). Violence and psychiatric disorder in the community: Evidence from the epidemiologic catchment area surveys. *Hospital and Community Psychiatry, 41,* 761–770.

Thornberry, T. P., & Jacoby, J. E. (1979). *The criminally insane: A community follow-up of mentally ill offenders.* Chicago: University of Chicago Press.

Tiihonen, J., Hakola, P., Eronen, M., Vartianen, H., & Ryynänen, O.-P. (1996). Risk of homicidal behaviour among discharged forensic psychiatric patients. *Forensic Science International, 79,* 123–129.

Tiihonen, J., Isohanni, M., Koiranen, M., Moring, J., & Rantakallio, P. (1997). Specific mental disorders and criminality: The 1966 Northern Finland birth cohort. *American Journal of Psychiatry, 154,* 840–845.

Teplin, L. A. (1990). The prevalence of severe mental disorder among male urban jail detainees. *American Journal of Public Health, 80,* 663–669.

Teplin, L. A., Abram, K. M., & McClelland, G. M. (1996). The prevalence of psychiatric disorder among incarcerated women: I. Pretrial jail detainees. *Archives of General Psychiatry, 53,* 505–512.

Torrey, E. F., Bowler, A. E., Taylor, E. H., & Gottesman, I. I. (1994). *Schizophrenia and manic depressive disorder.* New York: Basic Books.

Zitrin, A., Hardesty, A. S., Burdock, E. T., & Drossman, A. K. (1976). Crime and violence among mental patients. *American Journal of Psychiatry, 133,* 142–149.

Chapter 5

Early Nazis 1923–1933—Neo-Nazis 1980–1995: A Comparison of the Life Histories of Two Generations of German Right-Wing Extremists

Susanne Karstedt
University of Bielefeld

CONTINUITY OR CHANGE IN GERMAN RIGHT-WING EXTREMISM?

The recent wave of right-wing extremist activities, violent assaults against foreigners, and anti-Semitism has shocked Germany and the world. This wave seems to be part of a general increase in xenophobic attitudes and right-wing extremism that has affected many Western European countries since 1990 (Alber, 1995; Björgo & Witte, 1993; Merkl & Weinberg, 1993; Wiegand, 1992, 1993). But its history sets Germany apart. The question of continuity and change in German right-wing extremism has become a *leitmotif* of research in this area since its beginning in the 1980s.

How can this question be reasonably asked today, and answered by scientific research? The simple explanation that National Socialist ideology was handed down through the generations is unlikely. There is no indication of a widespread survival of National Socialist ideology in the population of the Federal Republic of Germany (FRG). Rather, such positions have continously decreased since 1949. Right-wing extremist parties have mobilized no more than a small margin of the population. Democratic values and institutions are nearly unanimously supported, as they are elsewhere in Western Europe. Nationalism is less prominent in the FRG than in other European countries (Scheuch, 1990, 1991). The proportion of ethnocentrist or xenophobic views does not differ from other nations in the European Union (Eurobarometer, 1989). If continuity in the sense of tradition is ruled out, common sociopolitical and economic causal factors have to be considered. Despite the socioeconomic crisis in Germany today, even the most critical observer will find little similarity with the economic and political crisis of the late Weimar Republic when the National Socialist German Workers Party (NSDAP, Nazis) rose to power (Alber, 1991; Scheuch, 1988). The intensity of political strife and hostility of political factions was incomparably greater than in the FRG, where the spectrum of political orientations and actions is situated more in the center, compared to other European countries (Barnes, Kaase, et al., 1979; Inglehart, 1989; Klages, Hippler, & Herbert, 1992; Scheuch, 1990).

An alternative hypothesis lies in the German authoritarian national or modal character and the specific culture that shapes it. Does it still make Germans susceptible to right-wing extremist ideologies and parties (Inkeles & Levinson, 1968; Scheuch, 1991)? Today, young Germans are mostly less authoritarian than comparable groups in other nations (e.g., the United States; Lederer & Kindervater, 1995a, 1995b), and family patterns and educational styles in Germany do not differ from those in other Western democracies (Scheuch, 1991).

This study begins with the basic assumption that guided the research of the psychiatrist Henry V. Dicks (1972) on National Socialism with German prisoners of war as early as 1944, namely that ". . . collective behavior cannot be fully understood except by reference to its social matrix in space and time; but the great currents of group and mass action remain enigmatic if we exclude from their study the influence of the strivings and roles of individual actors—leaders and led" (p. 17). It approaches the "German enigma" on the level of individual actors by comparing the life courses of two generations of German right-wing extremists: Early Nazis who joined the NSDAP between 1923 and 1933, and right-wing extremists (neo-Nazis) between 1980 and 1995. Both generations were in the marginal situation of an emerging and still small political movement and its supporting network. From this perspective, the problem of continuity and change is reduced to two questions. Are there factors common to the life courses of both generations that are related to right-wing extremist ideology and political action despite the decisively different social contexts? Or do their characteristics and circumstances suggest that the right-wing extremists of the 1980s and 1990s are quite different in character, with only certain rudiments of ideological convictions in common with the early members of the NSDAP?

The study is a secondary analysis of published reports. For the early Nazis, it relies mostly on autobiographical accounts collected by the Chicago researcher Theodore Abel in 1934 (1938/1986) and coded by Merkl (1970a, 1970b). The material on neo-Nazis was generated in a variety of studies, covering the time from 1980 to 1995. Both generations include a considerable group of violent activists who are also contrasted with the not-violent members of each cohort.

The comparison begins with two theories of the rise of National Socialism and the erection of a totalitarian state. These are the theory of authoritarianism and the authoritarian personality (Adorno, Frenkel-Brunswick, Levinson, & Sanford, 1950), and the theory that explains the rise of National Socialism by social degradation and downward mobility, especially of the middle classes (Lipset, 1963). In addition, the study examines theories of social and political movements that stress the role of mobilizing factors (organizations, networks) instead of social deprivation and strain as causes of the emergence of political movements. From these theories the variables for the individual-level analysis of the life histories are selected as providing links to the social matrix of the two generations of Nazis.

This study does not explicitly consider psychopathology. Although psychopathology was prominent in explanations of the Nazi movement and state during and after World War II (Dicks, 1950; Gilbert, 1950; Kelley, 1946; Winnicott, 1950), subsequently it has been largely rejected for several reasons. First, it implies the presence of collective psychopathology or paranoid culture (Dicks, 1972). Abel (1938/1945), who collected these biographies of the early Nazis, rejected any psychopathological explanation of National Socialism on the basis of his research. Second, research on German prisoners of war during and after World War II found few and mostly small correlations between adherence to Nazi ideology, authoritarianism, and personality variables, including several that indicated psychopathological personality traits (Ansbacher, 1948; Dicks, 1950, 1972). Third, although collective psychopathology was proposed as an explanation of atrocities, "licenced mass murder" (Dicks, 1972), and the Holocaust (Alexander, 1948; Gilbert, 1950), mostly ordinary men committed the atrocities (Arendt, 1965; Browning, 1992), who easily slipped back into normal life after the war. A psychopathological explanation has been mostly abandoned from the analysis of genocide in general and for the specific case of Germany (Charny, 1984; Dimsdale, 1980; Staub, 1989).

THEORETICAL APPROACHES: AUTHORITARIANISM AND THE AUTHORITARIAN PERSONALITY

The concept of the authoritarian personality was the most influential and dominant paradigm after World War II.[1] It was based on the theory that specific childrearing practices had produced personalities susceptible to

---

[1]The most influential studies were Schaffner (1948), McGranahan (1946), McGranahan and Janowitz (1946), and Rodnick (1948). Early critics of the concept especially with regard to re-education policies included Becker (1951); for an evaluation of the impact of the concept, see Füssl (1994), Inkeles and Levinson (1968), and Loewenberg (1971, 1975); for critical assessment, see Christie and Jahoda (1954) and Stone, Lederer, and Christie (1993).

right-wing extremist and Nazi ideology, who readily submitted to the totalitarian Nazi regime. Three concepts broadly defined authoritarianism as (a) receptiveness to prejudice and aggression toward those weaker than oneself, especially ethnic minorities; (b) readiness to subordinate oneself to those more powerful (authoritarian submission); and (c) conventionalism (Altemeyer, 1988; Hopf, 1993a, 1993b). Authoritarianism is still a strong predictor of right-wing attitudes, support of right-wing extremist politicians and groups, racism, and racist violence (Heitmeyer, Collmann, Conrads, et al., 1995; Oesterreich, 1993).

The relation between parenting patterns and authoritarianism was a seminal aspect of the theory. Strict, disciplinarian upbringing by a distant, dominating father should produce high authoritarians. When most families correspond to this pattern, the modal or national character should be authoritarian (Inkeles & Levinson, 1968). This crucial link between family and authoritarianism was not confirmed in more recent research, especially because childrearing styles have changed dramatically in all Western industrialized countries since World War II. Recent studies found that authoritarians came nearly equally from affectionate and reciprocal families, from protective and controlling families, and from cold and rejecting families (Berger & Schmidt, 1995; Hoffmeister & Sill, 1992).

Other approaches define authoritarianism as a reaction tendency in situations of uncertainty and insecurity, following a line of argument developed as early as 1941 by Fromm. The concept of a situational, authoritarian reaction describes behavior in critical, anxiety-arousing situation as well as the development of an authoritarian personality. This personality is characterized by a readiness to adhere and submit to groups and institutions that provide security in a situation of crisis (Oesterreich, 1993; Rokeach, 1960). High levels of protective control in parenting tend to foster these authoritarian reactions in critical, anxiety-arousing situations (Berger & Schmidt, 1995; Hoffmeister & Sill, 1992; Lederer & Kindervater, 1995b). In an analogous way, the break-down of an authoritarian or totalitarian state is hypothesized to expose its citizens to situations of high insecurity that may induce widespread authoritarian reactions (Herrmann & Schmidt, 1995).

Finally, authoritarianism may be simply defined as the organizing principle of a set of attitudes and prejudices (Altemeyer, 1988; Rokeach, 1960). Like other belief systems (Converse, 1964), it is adopted from a variety of influences: parents, peers, teachers and schools, as well as one's own experiences (Altemeyer, 1988). From these conceptual approaches the following variables were selected for comparison of early and neo-Nazis:

1. Attitudes: authoritarianism, ethnocentrism, anti-Semitism; insecurity and group conformity.

2. Family situation and upbringing: structure of the family (incomplete families); family patterns and educational style; family ideology, especially authoritarianism and prejudice.

STATUS DEGRADATION AND DOWNWARD MOBILITY

National Socialism has been characterized as the extremist movement of the middle class (Lipset, 1963). From this perspective, the right-wing movements in Europe during the 1920s and 1930s are defined as a collective anomic reaction to a deep social, political, and economic crisis that had caused downward mobility, status degradation, and economic insecurity on a large scale (Hobsbawm, 1994; Kornhauser, 1959). This explanation has reappeared in research on the recent wave of right-wing extremism. Experiences of crises, insecurity, and individualization (the lack of social networks and support to manage the impact of such crises) are seen as causal factors for right-wing extremism and ethnocentrist violence (Heitmeyer, 1987, 1991; Heitmeyer et al., 1995). Low levels of education, dropping out of school or jobs, and unemployment result in degradation and downward mobility. Juveniles and young adults are then susceptible to authoritarian, racist, and ethnocentrist orientations and actions. These biographical factors enhance their readiness to join right-wing groups, and to take part in violent actions, mostly against foreigners.

This theoretical approach contributes the following variables to the analysis:

3. Social status: social and economic status of the family (father); level of education, occupational career and own status.
4. Degradation and downward mobility: school/ job problems (dropping out); unemployment.

MOBILIZING FACTORS

The above strain model of social movements (Smelser, 1962) was recently challenged by new theories that center on the process of mobilization (Zald & McCarthy, 1979, 1987). According to these theorists, social and economic deprivation and strain is not directly transferred into political orientations and actions. Instead, the supply and availability of mobilizing factors transform private troubles into public issues and political action (Mills, 1972). Mobilizing factors include ideological patterns that give individual problems a particular framing (Snow & Benford, 1988; Snow, Burke-Rochford, & Worden, 1986); links between these frames and attitudes and opinions that are generally held by the population (frame alignment); and an opportunity structure consisting of a network of groups and organizations that serve as a seedbed for the social-political movement.

This framework adds two categories of explanatory variables: those related to the process of political socialization (5,6), and those reflecting the process of mobilization (7,8):

5. Core ideological patterns: adoption of right-wing extremist ideology; anti-democratic attitudes; specific Nazi ideology; prejudice.
6. Socializing agents: the impact of parents, schools, and peers on the formation of right-wing extremist ideology.
7. Contacts and networks: membership in youth groups, peer groups and affiliation to right-wing youth subcultures.
8. Affiliation to right-wing extremism: membership in right-wing extremists groups and parties; type of activities (violent/nonviolent).

For ease of presentation in this chapter, groups will be referred to as *early* and *neo-Nazis*, despite the variation in the explicit self-identification with the Nazi party or Nazi ideology.

EARLY NAZIS

In 1934, Abel collected more than 600 autobiographical accounts from members of the NSDAP, who had joined the party before 1933. The collection was organized as a competition. The participants were asked to give an "exact and detailed account of their life course especially after World War I, and to write especially about their family life, school education, economic conditions, membership in organizations, participation in the Hitler Movement and important experiences, thoughts and feelings about the events and developments of the post-war period" (Merkl, 1970a, p. 495). Because Abel relied on the party organization for the collection of the autobiographies, specific biases cannot be excluded and should be considered possible. The party hierarchy may have selected participants or censored the accounts to present a more positive image of the New Germany and its rulers to the public in the United States. According to Merkl (1975), this bias may not be great, because the autobiographies contain many hate speeches and stories of discrimination, anti-Semitism, atrocities, and violence. Apparently the authors of the biographies felt justified rather than embarrassed by their beliefs and activities after the victory of their cause in 1933.

The biographies well represent the age and occupations of the NSDAP membership before 1930. Compared to the 1933 party statistics, the Abel respondents were older, more were white-collar workers, and they had more education. It may be that these differences were explained by the need to be able to express themselves in writing (Merkl, 1970a, 1975). Six percent were women. When they joined the party, most were under 30 years old (about 75% before 1925, about 66% between 1925 and 1928). Their violent activities increased continuously between 1925 and 1933, as did the violence of the movement (Merkl, 1975).

Merkl (1970a, 1970b, 1975, 1980) conducted a quantitative reanalysis of the autobiographies. In addition, he tried to trace the post-1933 careers of the early NSDAP members. Merkl used a coding scheme of 77 variables, selected to evaluate the theory of the authoritarian personality and the theory of social degradation and downward mobility. In his original analysis, Abel (1938/1986) did not refer to childhood experiences of his subjects. Recent research suggests that people typically retrospectively rate their childhood educational experiences as having been more strict and disciplinarian than they were in fact, perhaps influenced by the profound change toward more permissive styles over this century (Reuband, 1988, 1992). Merkl, classifying the material in the context of the less authoritarian standards of the 1970s, may have overrated the authoritarianism of family patterns.

An additional set of 61 similar life histories were written in 1936 by pre-1933 NSDAP members, including 21 SS officers (Dicks, 1972). They were written for the party archives in order to provide a history of the time before Hitler came to power. No information is available regarding how the writers were selected.

NEO-NAZIS

Surveys of the general population in the 1980s and 1990s included 194 right-wing activists among 16- to 25-year-olds (Noelle-Neumann & Ring, 1984) and 121 and 45 right-wing supporters among 14- to 25-year-old students (Förster, Friedrich, Müller, & Schubarth, 1993; Oesterreich, 1991). These surveys permit comparison of these right-wing youths to other members of the same age groups.

From police and court files, studies of 1398 suspects of right-wing offenses (Willems et al., 1993), 794 proceedings and 624 offenders (Kalinowsky, 1990), 163 youthful offenders (Stöss, 1984), and 116 violent offenders (Heitmeyer & Müller, 1995) were examined. Results of qualitative interviews with 32 members of right-wing organizations (Hennig, 1982), 20 juvenile pro-Nazi protesters (Stöss, 1984), and 45 violent offenders (Heitmeyer & Müller, 1995) were also reported in these analyses.

The neo-Nazis were younger than the early Nazis studied. Several of the studies were conducted in schools and vocational training, and thus respondents were mostly 15 to 25 years old. Three quarters of the suspects and sentenced offenders were under age 21 (Willems et al., 1993). About one half of the sentenced right-wing offenders during the 1980s were in this age group, a proportion that increased during the decade (Kalinowsky, 1990). Almost all subjects were men. Most studies were restricted to the former FRG. Some recent studies (Förster et al., 1993; Heitmeyer & Müller, 1995; Oesterreich, 1993) included subjects from former East Germany.

FINDINGS

Ideological Orientation, Prejudice, and Authoritarianism

The essential elements of right-wing extremist ideology are political authoritarianism and antidemocratic orientation. The leadership principle and the idea of a national community of the people (*solidarische Volksgemeinschaft*, Hennig, 1984, p. 159), from which social and political conflicts are eliminated by submission of individual interests to the common good of the nation, are prominent Nazi elements of political authoritarianism. This in-group orientation is linked to ethnocentrism and racist prejudice (Lederer & Schmidt, 1995; Noelle-Neumann & Ring, 1984; Oesterreich, 1993).

The position of right-wing extremism within public opinion today is decisively different from the 1920s. Public opinion during the Weimar Republic strongly rejected democracy. This is confirmed by retrospective data in 1951, when a majority of the older generation preferred one-party systems or a strong leader at the top, and gave bottom ratings to the Weimar democracy (Noelle & Neumann, 1974; Zinnecker, 1985b). The success of the Nazis in elections between 1930 and 1933 confirm public support (Childers, 1986).

Neutral or positive evaluations of National Socialism have steadily declined since the 1950s (Geißler & Delitz, 1981). The neo-Nazis of the 1980s lived in an environment characterized by the nearly unanimous adoption of democratic values, muted nationalism, and disapproval of overt Nazi ideology. In 1985, young people and the generation of their parents both disapproved of the Nazis, and defined Nazis mainly by dictatorship, totalitarianism, racism, and the Holocaust (Zinnecker, 1985b). In general the neo-Nazis accept a positive view of democracy (Heitmeyer et al., 1995; Heitmeyer & Müller, 1995; Noelle-Neumann & Ring, 1984), but they have at their disposal a pool of traditional Nazi slogans and symbols.

The level of political knowledge was rated as astonishingly poor for the early NSDAP-members (Merkl, 1975). For neo-Nazis, several studies similarly describe low levels of knowledge among those who were involved in

TABLE 5.1

Ideological Themes and Orientations of Early and Neo-Nazis

| | Early Nazis[a] | 1980/1990 16- to 25-Year-Olds[b] | |
| | Total Group | 16- to 25-Year-Olds | Right-Wing Activists |
Beliefs			
Anti-Semitism	14%	3%	18%
Romantic-nationalistic, German race, culture	6%	4%	42%
Nationalistic-patriotic/revanchism	28%	22%	58%
Social solidarity, community of people	57%	10%	32%
Führer cult	17%	2%	21%
No specific ideology	3%		

Note. These proportions are not strictly comparable because the older sample was assigned to one main theme only.
[a]Merkl (1975, p. 493). [b]Noelle-Neumann & Ring (1984, pp. 60, 69–72, 183).

violent actions against foreigners (Heitmeyer & Müller, 1995; Willems et al., 1993), and those who scored high on ethnocentrism and hostile attitudes toward foreigners (Fend, 1994). In Table 5.1, the main ideological themes of both generations are compared. The early Nazis show a surprisingly small proportion of dominant anti-Semitic and xenophobic attitudes. In fact, anti-Semitism played no important role in the propaganda campaigns of the NSDAP during its rise to power in the Weimar Republic (Childers, 1983; Hamilton, 1982; Paul, 1990; Winkler, 1985). The ideological pattern was largely defined by nationalist, revanchist attitudes (concerns about revenge for Germany's loss of status and power), anti-leftist orientation, and adherence to the Volksgemeinschaft, the "solidarity of the (German) people." Dicks' study yielded similar results. One quarter named anti-Semitism as a dominant motivation, whereas revanchist, anti-Marxist attitudes, and generalized hate against Germany's enemies prevailed. The 21 SS-men were also more overtly concerned with left-wing enemies, and "an identification of all such enemies with the 'Jewish world conspiracy' was latent" (Dicks, 1972, p. 80).

The relative weight of the different ideological themes was similar among the neo-Nazis:[2] Nationalism and social solidarism (Volksgemeinschaft) were ranked first and second. Leadership cult and anti-Semitism were more important for the early Nazis, whereas ethnocentrism was more important for the neo-Nazis. Compared to other 16- to 25-year-olds, neo-Nazis differ most in overtly National Socialist elements: anti-Semitism and racism, na-

---

[2]To this purpose, a rank order was computed; the computation was based on the proportion of strong consent to one item in relation to the respective proportions of all five items of the study by Noelle-Neumann and Ring (multiple response).

tionalism, and an in-group and leadership (Führer) orientation. Their theme of social solidarism has more support in the general population of young people. Hennig (1984) found the leader principle and social solidarity to be dominant themes of right-wing organizations.

As shown in Table 5.2, 43% of the biographies of the early Nazis reflected ethnocentrism as related to Germany's defeat in World War I and the so-called "humiliation of Versailles." Such ethnocentrism was directed mainly against foreign nations, and less against ethnic groups within Germany. Such nations were seen as part of an international conspiracy, for which Jews and Marxists were often thought to be responsible. Anti-Semitism was a latent but integral part of their ethnocentrist pattern (see Dicks, 1972). Ethnocentrism is a dominant characteristic of the neo-Nazis (Stöss, 1984). It is focused on foreigners (asylum-seekers and immigrant workers) who live in Germany. There is public support for this view, especially with regard to asylum-seekers (Ohlemacher, 1994). The majority of supporters of right-wing groups strongly assent to various xenophobic statements (Förster et al., 1993). Nearly two thirds of right-wing activists belong to a group which they describe as mainly against foreigners (6% total sample; Noelle-Neumann & Ring, 1984).

Table 5.3 shows that the pattern of authoritarian attitudes is similar between early and neo-Nazis. Both generations rejected democracy, were preoccupied with law and order, and adhered to the leadership principle. This led to considerable opposition to current authorities in both generations. Among the neo-Nazis, hard-core right-wing extremists were significantly more venturesome, self-assertive and prone to argue with authorities (Hopf, Rieker, & Sanden-Marcus, 1995; Oesterreich, 1993). Thus the attitude toward authorities is contrary to the classic sense of the authoritarian personality (cf. Hopf, Rieker, & Sanden-Marcus, 1995), both for the young right-wing radicals and for the early Nazis.

TABLE 5.2
Ethnocentric Beliefs of Early and Neo-Nazis

Beliefs	Early Nazis	1980/1990 16- to 25-Year-Olds	
	Total Group[a]	16- to 25-Year-Olds	Right-Wing Activists
Ethnocentrism, any object	43%		
Anti-alien views	19%	4%	42%[b]
Ethnic, racial superiority	10%	5%	>50%[c]
International threat	14%	Not noted	
No specific ethnocentrism	57%		

Note. Merkl has assigned individuals only to the dominant theme.
[a]Merkl (1975, p. 517). [b]Noelle-Neumann & Ring (1984, p. 72). [c]Förster et al. (1993, pp. 106, 111).

TABLE 5.3
Attitudes Toward Authority and Authoritarianism

Early Nazis[a]		Persons Age 16–25 in 1980s[b]	
	%	Activists % Strongly Agree	Total Sample % Strongly Agree
Against multiparty state and divisive groups	42	Parties and unions cause damage to the public good[c]	52	16
		One strong party that represents the interests of all	32	10
Leadership cult, Hitler cult, strongly anti-democratic	16	Pro Führer	21	2
Pro-leader and police authority, order and cleanliness	25	If we had work camps law and order would be no problem	24	3
		For law and order	73	45
Disrespectful toward police, government authority	17	Often argues with teachers	56	31
		Problems with police	13	7

[a]Merkl (1975, p. 490). [b]Noelle-Neumann & Ring (1984, except c). [c]SINUS (1981).

Childhood Settings: The Impact of Family Settings and Ideological Orientation

Family discipline patterns changed considerably over this century. Retrospective surveys reveal a continous and profound increase in child autonomy and decrease in strictness and discipline both at home and in educational settings. Table 5.4 shows that despite having lived in more authoritarian and disciplinarian times, many of the early Nazis did not grow up in authoritarian families. Almost as many grew up in relatively liberal or permissive homes as in homes with a strict disciplinarian style.Those who came from poor and economically deprived homes in the rural and urban underclasses normally experienced less authoritarian styles than did those from the middle classes (Blinkert, 1976; Peukert, 1986). Thus, the upbringing of the early Nazis was probably not more authoritarian than was typical of the period.

When the neo-Nazis grew up, authoritarian patterns in families belonged mostly to the past, and were experienced by only a minority of children and adolescents in Germany (Reuband, 1988, 1992; Zinnecker, 1985a). The neo-Nazis came from more authoritarian, disciplinarian homes than did their peers. They had significantly less autonomy, were often reprimanded, and frequently experienced corporal punishment. They reported

TABLE 5.4
Childhood Setting of Early and Neo-Nazis

Early Nazis[a]	%	Persons Age 16 to 25 in 1980s[b]	Activists %	Total Sample %
Economically secure, unconstrained	26	Unconstrained childhood	28	52
Economically secure, sheltered	20	Happy childhood	37	56
Strict discipline	9	Not allowed to contradict father	29	21
		Often reprimanded	23	12
		Corporal punishment[c]	frequent	
		Authoritarian father[c]	high proportion	
Orphan, personally deprived	13	Parents divorced	16	10
Large family in poverty/poor farm family/other deprivation	32	Enough money as a child	11	23
		Parents had financial problems	30	22

[a]Merkl (1975, p. 291). [b]Noelle-Neumann & Ring (1984, pp. 119–120, except c). [c]Stöss (1984, p. 181).

less happy childhoods, perhaps because of family economic problems or divorce. One third of sentenced right-wing offenders (violent and nonviolent) grew up in broken or single parent homes (Kalinowsky, 1990). Within the affluent and more liberal environment of Western Germany since the 1960s, neo-Nazis have experienced an unusual share of social, economic, and personal deprivation. For the early Nazis, no comparable data are available to decide whether they were disproportionately hit by personal or economic deprivation. However, one quarter reported extreme difficulties in their families, caused by the loss of a parent, other personal distress in the family, or severe economic problems.

The relationship between rearing and ideological orientation can be examined only for the early Nazis. Anti-Semitism was most frequent in the group who had experienced an economically secure and permissive childhood, probably in middle-class (bourgeois) homes. Those who grew up in poverty came from the traditionally less anti-Semitic working class (Peukert, 1984). The more authoritarian family pattern—sheltered and disciplinarian—is related to a combination of ethnocentrism and political revanchism. It produced high proportions of political authoritarians and antidemocrats, but significantly fewer anti-Semites (Merkl, 1975). These results suggest differentiation between two processes: educational patterns on the one hand and the transmission of family political attitudes on the other. Bourgeois homes that allowed for a secure and permissive childhood did not raise authoritarian personalities, but did transmit anti-Semitism. By comparing those who experienced either a strict authoritarian style or came from incomplete families, we find that both produced authoritarian submission and hostile attitudes against existing authorities. Both types of homes produced offspring given to verbal aggression against ethnic and social minorities (Merkl, 1975). In the neo-Nazis, both experiences and feelings of insecurity within the incomplete family and rejecting and disciplinarian family styles were related to right-wing extremism and particularly to authoritarian aggression (Hopf et al., 1995).

The political orientation of parents was conservative in both generations. Right-wing extremism rarely develops in total opposition to the parents' orientation. Most of the early Nazis came from a nationalist, conservative background: 56% from nationalist or militarist homes, 12% from explicitly *völkisch* (ethnocentric) and anti-Semitic ones. Adherents to the strongest party in Germany before and after World War I, the Social Democrats, were underrepresented (5.2%). Conflicts with fathers were rarely reported (2%; Merkl, 1975). Thus, we conclude that the family setting determined the direction of prejudices. *Völkisch* homes produced the largest share of ardent anti-Semites. The militarist authoritarian homes mainly produced ethnocentrist and xenophobic attitudes toward those perceived to be Germany's enemies.

The neo-Nazis came mostly from conservative homes (Bundesministerium des Innern, 1982; Hennig, 1984; Willems et al., 1993). They more
often agreed with the political opinions of their parents (38%) than their
peers (30%), but their extreme political opinions caused less agreement
with family than observed for right-wing conservatives in general (46%;
Noelle-Neumann & Ring, 1984). Extreme right-wing and xenophobic attitudes, especially when combined with a readiness for violence against
foreigners, were significantly more likely to have come from political groups
and parties than from parents (Heitmeyer et al., 1995). Consequently, this
group often reported conflicts with their parents (Hopf et al., 1995).

Experiences of Downward Mobility and Degradation

The Nazi movement has been characterized as a revolt of the lower middle
classes, those most severely hit by the Great Depression (Lipset, 1963). A
lower middle class background is overrepresented in the NSDAP before
and after 1930, and in the Abel sample. Nearly one half (44%) were in
the same social position as their fathers, downward mobility was experienced by a minority (13%), and 38% had gained a higher status than their
fathers (Merkl, 1975). The upwardly mobile group included migrants from
rural areas to the cities who had profited from the speed of industrialization
and economic expansion in Germany before World War I. The early Nazis
who wrote these autobiographies had more education than did the majority
of their peers. Three quarters (73%) had completed 8 years of schooling,
15% had finished secondary levels (10 years of schooling), and 12% had
passed the university entrance examination (*Abitur*; 12 years of schooling).
The respective proportions in the 1926 population were 86%, 3%, and
11% (Götz von Olenhusen, 1987). Another 20% may be assumed to have
been privileged, as they did not start occupational life before they were
17 years old. One quarter started working early and mostly without any
professional training (Merkl, 1975). One quarter experienced interrup-
tions of their occupational careers before 1928, had lost their jobs or their
businesses, or had other economic difficulties that were not directly caused
by the war. Another one quarter was hit by the Great Depression between
1928 and 1933; these were mostly the youngest members of the Abel sample
who began their occupational life in a badly deteriorated labor market.
However, one half of the Abel sample had a normal occupational career.

Compared to their peers, the young neo-Nazis came disproportionately
from homes where the parents had little education (Oesterreich, 1993).
The sentenced right-wing offenders had a more differentiated background:
professionals and entrepreneurs (9%), independent businessmen (21%),
white-collar employees in higher positions (15%), white-collar employees
in lower positions and skilled workers (42%), and unskilled workers (11%;

Kalinowsky, 1990). Because of their younger age, downward mobility is not easily detectable in the new generation. All studies agree on significantly lower levels of education, a higher proportion of school dropouts, more in training positions, and more working at an early age, compared to their respective age group (Kalinowsky, 1990, Noelle-Neumann & Ring, 1984, Oesterreich, 1993). Sentenced right-wing offenders are obviously at risk of downward mobility. Only one half of this group (47%) was stable in their economic position, and 48% were downwardly mobile or unemployed before their trial (Kalinowsky, 1990). In contrast to the early Nazis, none of the neo-Nazis were upwardly mobile. They had not participated in the vastly expanded system of general and higher education since the 1960s, and thus belonged to the risk groups within the labor market. They most closely resembled the youngest members of the early Nazi group, those hit by the Great Depression. The whole Abel sample in contrast can be characterized as modestly upwardly mobile at the start. The early Nazis experienced economic crises and downward mobility at a later stage in their life courses than did the neo-Nazis.

Networks of Political Mobilization: Schools, Peers, and Political Groups

Schools in imperial Germany and during the Weimar Republic are held responsible for the transmission of authoritarian attitudes, national arrogance, and anti-Semitic and ethnocentric prejudice. Their ideological position, of course, reflected the society in which they were embedded (Merkl, 1975). The early Nazis attributed a decisive impact on the development of their political orientations to schools and teachers. The nationalistic patriotic atmosphere in schools nourished revanchist, nationalist attitudes and an orientation toward the "community of the people"; the *völkisch* school environment instilled anti-Semitism and hostility against foreigners and the "political enemy" (Merkl, 1975). Those who later had positions in the SA or SS came from this background especially often. Schools today are the dominant source of information on National Socialism and the Holocaust for the young generation (Zinnecker, 1985b). The young right-wing extremists experience considerably more conflicts with teachers (56%; 31% total sample; Noelle-Neumann & Ring, 1984). They are conscious of their minority position and develop their political opinions in arguments with teachers or in defiance of them (Bundesministerium des Innern, 1982; Hennig, 1984). Of the sentenced right-wing offenders, 27% stressed their independent position and ideological foundation (Kalinowsky, 1990).

The youth of the Weimar Republic have been portrayed as the most political generation of the 1900s because of an extremely high rate of membership in organized and politically oriented youth groups (Jaide, 1988). At the end of the Weimar Republic about 5 million youths under 25 years of age were organized in about 100 organizations (excluding athletic organizations; Mogge, 1985). In 1930, about 300,000 youths belonged to right-wing paramilitary and quasimilitary organizations (Stachura, 1975).

In Western Germany, membership in right-wing organizations declined from about 60,000 in 1959 to 20,000 in 1976 (Geissler & Delitz, 1981). Since then, the proportion of young people (under 25 years) within these organizations increased considerably as the organizations have become more militant (Bundesministerium des Innern, 1982). Right-wing organizations today form a network of small organizations. In 1994, 82 right-wing extremist organizations existed in Germany with about 56,500 members, about 10% of whom are rated as militant right-wing extremists (Bundesministerium der Justiz, 1995).

Table 5.5 demonstrates these differences in the process of mobilization in both generations. More than one half of the early Nazis entered right-wing organizations through youth groups, and 23% belonged to a para- or quasimilitary youth organization. Later in their careers, more than one half became members in one of the right-wing paramilitary organizations: One third of these members joined organizations that were founded after World War I in times of civil strife (Vigilants, Free Corps); 30% belonged to influential veteran organizations. These early Nazis show the impact of a well-organized and quasimilitary network of right-wing organizations, ending in NSDAP membership.

Organized right-wing extremism is much less important in the careers of the neo-Nazis. Table 5.5 shows the organizational affiliation for three different groups: right-wing activitists, sentenced right-wing offenders, and

TABLE 5.5
Organizational Membership of Early and Neo-Nazis

	Early Nazis[a]	Neo-Nazis		
		Activists[b]	Sentenced Offenders[c]	Violent Offenders[d]
Paramilitary, quasimilitary	23%	9%	—	—
NSDAP organizations;				
right-wing parties & org.	12%	50%	7%	—
(Neo)-Nazi groups, right-wing				
extremist groups	22%	41%	38%	25%
Informal (peer) right-wing group	—	—	4%	57%
Other groups or organizations	13%	—	—	10%
No group association	30%	—	51%	8%

[a]Merkl (1975, p. 238). [b]Bundesministerium des Innern (1982, p. 16). [c]Kalinowsky (1990, p. 53). [d]Willems et al. (1993, p. 127).

suspects who were involved in violent actions against foreigners. Right-wing activists had the highest proportion (28%) of engagement in strictly political organizations, but most were connected with small right-wing groups (41% in neo-Nazi groups). A few (9%) belonged to militant groups. Some of these neo-Nazi groups have been prohibited and membership is consequently a criminal offense. The periphery of the right-wing network—Skinhead and other peer groups—is the seedbed for involvement in violence against foreigners. According to court files, there are links between these informal groups and organized right-wing groups (Bergmann & Erb, 1994). Thus, the lack of a network of organized right-wing groups is compensated for by a variety of personal and group contacts: With peer groups with strong antiforeigner orientation (59%, 6% total sample), with other right-wing students (42%, 5% total sample), with World War II Nazi figures (31%, total sample 5%), with members of a right-wing party (56%, total sample 3%), and with former politically prominent Nazis (21%, total sample 2%; Noelle-Neumann & Ring, 1984). Of sentenced right-wing offenders, 40% had been recruited by personal contacts (Kalinowsky, 1990).

VIOLENCE AND RIGHT-WING EXTREMISM

In this section I compare characteristics of those early and neo-Nazis who participated in violent actions with those who did not. The societal setting for early and neo-Nazis was very different, with much stronger public and institutional support for the early Nazis. As a consequence, personal selection factors, such as family background and one's own achievements and problems, were probably less influential on the decision to become an early Nazi. Nazi party members had a broad range of motivations for joining. Once in the party, they could choose among a range of activities. Those who were strongly motivated by anger, the tendency to blame others, and revenge were more likely to choose violent activities. Violent activities also appealed to those trained in violent activities in paramilitary organizations.

The neo-Nazis, in contrast, were virtually all in rebellion against the nearly universal views of their society, and thus may be classified as marginal, regardless of the nature of their participation. The actual activities they carried out may have depended on the particular group of peers with whom they happened to associate. The structure of these peer networks was quite informal.

Therefore, we may anticipate that for most comparisons, the violent and nonviolent neo-Nazis will be less easily discriminated than the violent and nonviolent early Nazis. When society is organized to promote right-wing beliefs and actions in schools and socially sanctioned organizations, as was the case in Germany in the 1920s and early 1930s, most members of these organizations will not have an unusual proclivity to violence. However, persons who are violence-prone will find such organizations a convenient framework and source of support for their deviant behavior.

A Definition of Violent Activities

Right-wing violence is not limited to political violence in the narrow sense of planned acts of terrorism, militant actions, or violence during demonstrations. It includes violence against ethnic minorities, against the homeless and disabled, against homosexuals, and against Jews. The militancy of right-wing extremists during the Weimar Republic and of the Nazis "brown column" is reflected in widespread involvement in violent actions among the early Nazis. Nearly one half (43%) were engaged in violent activities during the first phases of their careers, 28% in partisan political violence and street fighting, and 15% in paramilitary organizations during civil strife. When they finally entered the NSDAP, 44% took part in violent actions on behalf of the party (Merkl, 1970b). They were involved in all of the types of violent actions by which the NSDAP terrorized its political enemies or particular groups of the population: streetfighting; attacks on meetings, institutions, or facilities of other parties; and assaults on individuals. Before 1933, violence was nearly exclusively directed against political enemies rather than against Jews. Because most of the violent actions were committed by groups and organized by the party, the extent of individual involvement cannot be exactly defined. Merkl classified violent early Nazis into three types: streetfighters, the most violent group (56%); fighter-proselytizers (44%), who engaged in propaganda activities as well as fighting; and individual provocateurs. The nonviolent group consists of members only, those who took part in nonviolent demonstrations, and proselytizers, whose activities were mostly restricted to propaganda (Merkl, 1975).

Three studies of neo-Nazis relied mostly on officially registered violence with right-wing connotations. Kalinowsky (1990) included right-wing extremists who had participated in violent terrorist and militant actions as well as preparations for such activities. The nonviolent group consisted mostly of agitators, who participated in activities similar to those of the corresponding group of early Nazis. The study by Willems, Eckert, Würtz, and Steinmetz (1993) included suspects and sentenced offenders who committed violent ethnocentrist offenses against foreigners. The offenses ranged from disturbance of peace (the largest group, including 30% of all offenses) to homicide. These offenses included illegal demonstrations, attacking or insulting foreigners, or brawls, and are most similar to the activities of street fighters among the early Nazis. Heitmeyer and Müller (1995) studied two groups involved in violent actions that were right-wing or antiforeigner: officially registered and sentenced offenders, and persons contacted through penal institutions and youth authorities.

Contrasts Between Violent and Nonviolent Groups

In the early Nazi group as well as in the neo-Nazi group, the violent were younger than the nonviolent (Kalinowsky, 1990; Merkl, 1975).

Social Origin and Childhood Setting. The violent early Nazis included substantial proportions of both downwardly and upwardly mobile individuals. The youngest group, which was the most intensely involved in violence, came mainly from a working-class background. The neo-Nazi youth also came mostly from lower-class backgrounds, especially those who committed violent offenses against foreigners (Willems, 1996). Among right-wing sentenced neo-Nazi offenders, no class difference between the violent and the nonviolent group was found (Kalinowsky, 1990). Since NS-propaganda is illegal in the FRG, among those convicted, the violent and nonviolent are all members of a more homogenous politically deviant group.

The violent groups of both generations came disproportionately from incomplete families and broken homes. One quarter of the violent early Nazis had grown up in incomplete families in contrast to 13% of the entire group. In the younger generation, the difference was less marked among sentenced right-wing offenders for reasons already mentioned, with broken families in both groups exceeding rates for age-peers. Evidence for disintegration was found in as many as 80% of the families of offenders who were involved in violence against foreigners (Heitmeyer & Müller, 1995).

Both generations of violent extremists disproportionately experienced strict, disciplinarian, and authoritarian parenting patterns (Heitmeyer & Müller, 1995; Willems et al., 1993). In both generations the violent groups reported more conflicts with their parents and problems at home over a variety of issues, not only over their right-wing affiliation and offenses. Offenders who were sentenced for violence against foreigners experienced strong pressure toward achievement at home, along with a significant lack of adequate problem-solving strategies and poor communication with their parents.

Education and Occupational Career. Although the violent group of early Nazis were mostly young, they had not profited from the expansion of general and higher education: A disproportionate number had left school early to enter the labor market. The youngest, who were most directly and intensely involved in violence, were disproportionately hit by unemployment and downward mobility since 1930. The fighter–proselytizers, who engaged in violent actions only sporadically, were more often upwardly mobile. However, even this group was significantly affected by the economic crises before and after 1928. Violent members experienced more problems in their occupational careers, and were more frequently downwardly mobile than were the nonviolent.

For the neo-Nazis, evidence of downward mobility and social degradation began with their educational histories. Again, the difference between
the violent and nonviolent group among sentenced offenders was not
marked (Kalinowsky, 1990). In this group as a whole, there was a high
proportion with school dropout and low educational attainment. Problems
with achievement continued when they started work: They had high proportions of unskilled or semiskilled workers and unemployment. Low social
status characterized both the violent and the nonviolent.

Affiliation With Right-Wing Organizations and Mobilization. The violent
group among the early Nazis was disproportionately those who were affiliated with paramilitary organizations early in their careers. These organizations served them as training grounds for violent political actions before
they joined the party. Another substantial group joined the NSDAP late—
mostly after 1930—and immediately became involved in violent actions.
They were mostly recruited by friends who were already participating in
the violent activities of the NSDAP. These recruits were the youngest and
most intensely involved in violence.

Only a minority of the violent group of the 1980s were affiliated with
right-wing political organizations. Violent sentenced offenders were more
likely to have been recruited through personal networks. Compared to
nonviolent agitators, they belonged less frequently to organized right-wing
extremist and more frequently to loosely coupled "other groups" (Kalinowsky, 1990). They came from the subcultural periphery of the right-wing
network (e.g., Skinhead groups), or were integrated into peer groups with
racist orientations. The differences between the two generations in the
mobilizing environment account for the differences in types of violent acts
that they committed. Violence of the early Nazis was organized, directed
and channeled by the party. The violent offenses of the new generation
are more spontaneous, very rarely organized, situational, and expressive-
hedonistic (Heitmeyer & Müller, 1995; Willems et al., 1993).

Ideological Orientation and Targets of Violence. In both generations, the
level of ideological orientation and knowledge was lower in the violent group
than the nonviolent (Kalinowsky, 1990). Those who committed violent
offenses against foreigners were usually rated as either having no ideological
orientation at all (44%) or as simple fellow travellers (38%; Heitmeyer &
Müller, 1995). Among the early Nazis, the context of violent actions accounts
for the differences in ideological orientation between the violent and the
nonviolent group. These differences may result from processes of self-selec-
tion or from adaptions to the situation of violence. During its rise to power,
the Nazi political movement was directed against leading left-wing parties,
the Communists and the Social Democratic Party. The majority of the violent

early NSDAP members were motivated by antileftist sentiments (Dicks, 1972; Merkl, 1970). They legitimated their actions by perceived provocations from the political enemy, the "Reds." Some of them had been involved in fighting against occupying forces during the early 1920s. This experience had shaped their marked nationalism, ethnocentrism, and xenophobia. Those most intensely involved in violence were less anti-Semitic than were the nonviolent. Dicks' (1972) study on early Nazis yields identical results; "old fighters," who later become SS-men, were concerned with the enemy on the left, and showed nearly no anti-Semitism at this time.

For the young generation, the analysis must be restricted to those who committed violent offenses against foreigners. Ethnocentrism and xenophobia were the predominant ideological orientations of this group. But these views were far from being coherent or even reflective (Willems et al., 1993). Only one half of the group (53%) interviewed by Heitmeyer and Müller (1995) showed a marked hostility against foreigners, whereas 24% had a pluralistic orientation and another 22% were only partially hostile. Other components of right-wing ideology seemed to be adopted as fragments only. Democracy was nearly unanimously endorsed. Although 30% rejected historical National Socialism, 57% had a more qualified position, which is regarded as characteristic of right-wing extremism (Hennig, 1993). For 30%, aggression and violence were at the center of a generally deviant lifestyle (Heitmeyer & Müller, 1995). Fragments of right-wing ideology, the use of Nazi symbols, or ethnocentrist slogans served as a backdrop for violence of a mostly expressive-hedonistic type committed as a member of a group of aggressive and delinquent peers.

Authoritarianism, Group Conformity, and Violence. The pattern of attitudes that are related to violence in both generations have much in common. They deviate from the authoritarian syndrome of submission to the powerful and aggression against the weak that is assumed to be linked to right-wing extremist violence. The violent early Nazis were disproportionately hostile antiauthoritarians. Their violence was not directed against a group whom they perceived as weaker, but rather as threatening political enemies of equal or even superior strength. Many of the violent Nazis who joined the party during the last phase before the seizure of power had a record of previous convictions, often unrelated to political activities; this indicates a considerable lack of conformity and compliance (Merkl, 1975). On the other hand, they disproportionately adhered to the *Führer-cult* and cherished comradeship and group life (Merkl, 1975). Life in the party compensated them for the insecurity that they had experienced as a consequence of unemployment and social degradation. The most violent were characterized as "very insecure, self-pitying respondents (who) had a great desire to merge their individuality with the movement" (p. 394). Dicks

(1972) found the same pattern for the violent group in his sample, particularly among the 21 SS-men. The intense hostility of the violent street fighters, their degrading and debasing attitudes toward their political enemies, the total lack of regret and the sadistic component that is found in their reports, in contrast to the nonviolent groups, indicate severe deficiencies in prosocial, empathizing behavior (Merkl, 1975).

The violence of the right-wing extremists of the 1980s against foreigners was throughout characterized as expressive-hedonistic. It typically began spontaneously in groups, and alcohol consumption was often involved (Heitmeyer & Müller, 1995; Willems et al., 1993). The use of Nazi symbols by these groups was often provocative (Kalinowsky, 1990) or motivated by antiauthoritarian attitudes (Heitmeyer & Müller, 1995; Willems et al., 1993). Most of the suspects and offenders, as well as the sentenced violent right-wing extremists, have previous convictions and official registrations unrelated to political activities, that indicate a high degree of deviant behavior (Heitmeyer & Müller, 1995; Kalinowsky, 1990; Willems et al., 1993).

Careers of Violent Early NSDAP-Members in the Nazi State

Violent early Nazis disproportionately later entered the SS, the Gestapo, and the SD. In these organizations, they occupied only lower positions, whereas the nonviolent and mostly anti-Semitic groups with higher levels of education and a middle class background rose in the party and state hierarchy (Merkl, 1970a). Similar findings were reported by Dicks (1972): 40% of the SS-men were intensely engaged in violence before 1933. Both studies converge in giving evidence of a specific combination of factors that predestined the violent group for these positions, and that diverted their violence from their former hate targets (Marxists, Reds) to Jews and the civilian population of the occupied countries. These included (a) the need to conform to a group and comply with the orders of a leader; (b) debasing, degrading, and dehumanizing their "enemies"; (c) a total lack of empathy combined with sadistic components of their violent behavior; and (d) early and continuous experiences with organized violence in paramilitary organizations and in the NSDAP.

Discussion: Similarities and Differences, Continuity and Change

The comparison of two generations of right-wing extremists reveals a number of similarities between their life courses. These similarities are more marked in the less heterogeneous group of violent extremists in both generations. On the other hand, the comparison points to differences that can be linked to structural conditions of the social and political environment. The National Socialist movement grew within an opportunity structure that provided it with (a) public support of its right-wing causes in families and schools, (b) a large mobilizing network of legal right-wing organizations and supporters, and (c) an extended network of legal right-wing paramilitary organizations that served as a seedbed especially for violence. The right-wing extremists in the FRG between 1980 and 1995 are far from operating within such a favorable environment: (a) Right-wing extremist and particularly National Socialist ideology mobilize only minorities and lack public support, (b) the network of legal right-wing organizations is very small, and (c) right-wing propaganda activities are criminalized to a considerable degree.

Both movements basically consist of two groups: one that is ideologically dominated, and one for whom participation in violent action is central. The differences in the opportunity structure account for the specific composition of the new right-wing extremism and its internal structure in contrast to the NSDAP between 1923 and 1933. Criminalization of Nazi propaganda blurs the line between the ideologically motivated and the violent right-wing extremists. Both groups differ less with regard to symptoms of social disintegration. The violent group, particularly those who commit offenses against foreigners, are much less integrated into an organized right-wing center, but come from the loosely coupled periphery of subcultural peer groups. In contrast, the NSDAP integrated and used the violent groups directly for the purpose of the party.

The differences in opportunity structure and internal organization of right-wing extremism largely account for differences between the generations:

1. Central ideological themes vary according to public support. For the early NSDAP members, anticommunist and nationalist-revanchist orientations were prevalent. The new generation adheres more to democratic values; ethnocentrism has emerged as a dominant theme that can command considerable public support.

2. From 1980 to 1995, right-wing extremism remains marginal. This accounts for social marginalization and its concentration in those experiencing social deprivation. They come from incomplete families, have experienced family problems and social degradation during their early school careers. Higher educational levels, more upwardly mobile persons, and experiences of social disintegration mainly only after entering their occupational careers indicate a higher degree of social integration for the early NSDAP members.

3. Violent actions in both groups vary according to their context. Those of the early NSDAP members were targeted, directed and organized by the party. In contrast, the recent violent actions against foreigners were more spontaneous, expressive, and less directed by a specific ideology.

Social degradation and downward mobility were linked to right-wing extremism in both generations. These processes are more distinctly visible in the life courses of the later generation, where they started at an earlier age. This is not necessarily an artifact following from their younger age. They might be younger than the early NSDAP members because at present decisive processes of social placement are mostly located within the educational system. In both generations, the violent groups were significantly more affected by social degradation than were the nonviolent groups or right-wing extremists in general. The prevalence of family problems might have caused or contributed to the processes of downward mobility in the violent groups of both generations.

Authoritarian attitudes were found in both generations. Although the young generation adopted democratic institutions and values, political authoritarianism has not changed its importance for right-wing extremist ideology. But both generations deviate from the classic type of the authoritarian personality in important aspects. The core assumptions of the theory about a causal link between authoritarian education, authoritarian personality traits, and right-wing extremism cannot be confirmed for either generation.

In both generations, particularly for the violent groups, relatively high proportions of hostile antiauthoritarian attitudes, nonconformity and a lack of compliance are found. For the later right-wing extremists, self-assertiveness and conflicts with parents and teachers indicate an even higher share of such attitudes. Right-wing movements, during their early stages and political struggle, attract persons with a high degree of political authoritarianism, but they appeal less to the conventionalism and conformity of "authoritarian personalities." The relationship between authoritarian *political attitudes* and authoritarian *personality traits* is not confirmed for either generation.

For neither generation was a causal link found between authoritarian family styles and right-wing extremism. The early NSDAP members did not grow up in obviously more authoritarian homes than their contemporaries. The recent generation had a considerably higher share of authoritarian homes, but only a minority had this risk factor. The lack of a direct relationship between anti-Semitism, ethnocentrism, and authoritarian styles of education for the early NSDAP members suggests that the ideological orientation in the parental home and its social class affiliation had a decisive impact on the formation of authoritarian prejudice, but the parents' degree of authoritarianism toward their child did not. There might be an additive or interactive influence between authoritarian styles and the transmission of right-wing authoritarian attitudes by the parents in particular social class settings (e.g., middle or educated class; *Bildungsbürgertum*), but a direct causal impact is not supported (see Altemeyer, 1988).

In both generations, a considerable proportion had grown up in incomplete homes, particularly in the later generation. This and the later crises during educational and occupational careers contribute to the combined pattern of personal insecurity and high conformity toward the group that prevailed in both generations. Experiences and feelings of insecurity are not a specifically modern precondition of right-wing extremism, as was recently postulated (Heitmeyer, 1987, 1991). They had a decisive role for the membership of the early National Socialist movement as well. The authoritarian reaction toward biographical crises seems to have resulted in affiliation with a right-wing extremist movement and authoritarian submission to its leaders and groups in both generations.

The violent right-wing extremists of both generations were disproportionately raised in authoritarian homes and in incomplete ones. The impact of broken homes on aggressive and violent behavior in general, as well as of cold, rejecting, and punishing patterns of parenting is sufficiently documented by empirical research (Albrecht et al., 1991; Loeber & Dishion, 1984; McCord, 1979, 1983, 1986, 1995). Both incomplete family structure and harsh parenting patterns further violent behavior in general, but a distinct relationship to right-wing extremist violence in particular remains highly doubtful.

The violent groups in both generations have more in common than do the nonviolent ones. Their life courses indicate those patterns of problem behavior and maladaption that are found for violent offenders in general. More than nonviolent right-wing extremists, they were brought up in a way that furthers violent behavior of all kinds. Those in the later generation who committed violent offenses against foreigners have all the characteristics that are found for young violent offenders in general (Schumann, 1993). Therefore it can be assumed that a considerable proportion of the violent right-wing extremists in both generations are recruited from this group. This is in addition supported by the fact that violence seems to be a predominant motive for their joining a right-wing extremist movement or group.

Locating the life courses of two generations of right-wing extremists within the social matrix of their time indicates both continuity and change in German right-wing extremism. Continuity is found in causal factors that are decisive on the road to right-wing extremism, for the individual as well as society. Change over time is accounted for by differences in the internal structure, composition, and success of right-wing extremism from 1923 to 1933 and from 1980 to 1995, as well as by differences in those who are attracted to it, including experiences of insecurity in the family and in adult life; experiences of social degradation and downward mobility as a result of personal, economic and social crises; the availability of a mobilizing network; and general support in public opinion.

The present perspective on right-wing extremism in Germany and the National Socialist movement was predominantly shaped by the totalitarian Nazi state, World War II, and the Holocaust. Continuity between what was called the "National Socialist Revolution" and the Nazi regime seems to be more limited than is assumed from this perspective. Certainly, individual careers of early NSDAP members, and especially of the violent group, continued in the Nazi state. But a considerable ideological reorientation and a retargeting of violence took place after the National Socialists seized power, and prepared for the war and the Holocaust. Absolute submission to the Nazi regime, and willingly following its brutal orders might well be explained by a theory of the authoritarian personality, but that theory fails when the rise of right-wing extremist movements is analyzed.

REFERENCES

Abel, T. (1945). Is a psychiatric interpretation of the German enigma necessary? *American Sociological Review, 10*, 457–464.

Abel, T. (1986). *Why Hitler came into power.* Cambridge: Harvard University Press. (Original work published 1938)

Adorno, T. W., Frenkel-Brunswick, E., Levinson, D. J., & Sanford, R. N. (1950). *The authoritarian personality.* New York: Harper.

Alber, J. (1991). Continuity and change in German social structure. Why Bonn is not Weimar. In U. Hoffmann-Lange (Ed.), *Social and political structures in West Germany: From authoritarianism to postindustrial democracy* (pp. 15–42). Boulder, CO: Westview.

Alber, J. (1995). Zur Erklärung von Ausländerfeindlichkeit in Deutschland. In E. Mochmann & U. Gerhard (Eds.), *Gewalt in Deutschland. Soziale Befunde und Deutungslinien* (pp. 39–78). Munich: Oldenbourg.

Albrecht, G., Howe, C.-W., & Wolterhoff, J. (1991). Familienstruktur und Delinquenz. *Soziale Probleme, 2*, 107–156.

Alexander, L. (1948). Sociopsychologic structure of the SS. Psychiatric report of the Nuremberg Trials for war crimes. *Archives of Neurology and Psychiatry, 1948*, 622–634.

Altemeyer, B. (1988). *Enemies of freedom. Understanding right-wing authoritarianism.* San Francisco: Jossey-Bass.

Ansbacher, H. L. (1948). Attitudes of German prisoners of war: A study of the dynamics of National-Socialistic followership. *Psychological Monographs, 62* (Serial No. 288).

Arendt, H. (1965). *Eichmann in Jerusalem. Ein Bericht von der Banalität des Bösen.* Munich: Piper.

Barnes, S. H., & Kaase, M. et al. (Eds.). (1979). *Political action. Mass participation in five western democracies.* Beverly Hills, CA: Sage.

Becker, H. (1951). German families today. In H. J. Morgenthau (Ed.), *Germany and the future of Europe* (pp. 12–24). Chicago: University of Chicago Press.

Berger, M., & Schmidt, P. (1995). Familienstruktur, Elternwahrnehmung und Autoritarismus. In G. Lederer & P. Schmidt (Eds.), *Autoritarismus und Gesellschaft. Trendanalysen und vergleichende Jugenduntersuchungen 1945–1993* (pp. 337–354). Opladen: Leske & Budrich.

Bergmann, W., & Erb, R. (1994). Kaderparteien, Bewegung, kollektive Episode oder was? Probleme der soziologischen Kategorisierung des modernen Rechtsextremismus. *Forschungsjournal Neue Soziale Bewegungen, 7*, 36–34.

Björgo, T., & Witte, R. (Eds.). (1993). *Racist violence in Europe.* New York: St. Martin's Press.

Blinkert, B. (1976). Autoritarismus, Desorientierung und soziale Schicht. *Soziale Welt, 27,* 166–179.

Browning, C. R. (1992). *Ordinary men: Reserve Police Battalion 101 and the final solution in Poland.* New York: HarperCollins.

Bundesministerium des Innern. (1982). *Neonazistische Militanz und Rechtsextremismus unter Jugendlichen.* Stuttgart: Kohlhammer

Bundesministerium der Justiz. (1995). *Bekämpfung rechtsextremistischer, insbesondere fremdenfeindlicher und antisemitischer Bestrebungen in der Bundesrepublik Deutschland.* Bonn: Bundesministerium der Justiz.

Charny, J. W. (Ed.). (1984). *Toward the understanding and prevention of genocide.* Proceedings of the International Conference on the Holocaust and Genocide. Boulder, CO: Westview.

Childers, T. (1983). *The Nazi voter.* Chapel Hill: University of North Carolina Press.

Childers, T. (1986). *The formation of the Nazi constituency 1919–1933.* London: Croom Helm.

Christie, R., & Jahoda, M. (Eds.). (1954). *Studies in the scope and method of "The Authoritarian Personality": Continuities in social research.* Glencoe, IL: The Free Press.

Converse, P. H. (1964). The nature of belief systems in mass publics. In E. Apter (Ed.), *Ideology and discontent* (pp. 206–261). New York: Free Press.

Dicks, H. V. (1950). Personality traits and National Socialist ideology. A war-time study of German prisoners of war. *Human Relations, 3,* 111–154.

Dicks, H. V. (1972). *Licensed mass murder. A socio-psychological study of some SS killers.* London: Sussex University Press.

Dimsdale, J. E. (Ed.). (1980). *Survivors, victims and perpetrators. Essays on the Nazi Holocaust.* Washington, DC: Hemisphere.

Eurobarometer. (1989). *Rassismus und Ausländerfeindlichkeit* (Commission of the EU, Ed.). Brussels: General Director Information, Communication, Culture.

Fend, H. (1994). Ausländerfeindlich-nationalistische Weltbilder und Aggressionsbereitschaft bei Jugendlichen in Deutschland und der Schweiz—kontextuelle und personale Antecedensbedingungen. *Zeitschrift für Sozialisationsforschung und Erziehungssoziologie, 14,* 131–162.

Förster, P., Friedrich, W., Müller, H., & Schubarth, W. (1993). *Jugend Ost. Zwischen Hoffnung und Gewalt.* Opladen: Leske & Budrich.

Fromm, E. (1941). *Escape from freedom.* New York: Holt, Rinehart & Winston.

Füssl, K.-H. (1994). *Die Umerziehung der Deutschen. Jugend und Schule unter den Siegermächten des Zweiten Weltkriegs 1945–1955.* Munich: Schöningh.

Geißler, R., & Delitz, J. (1981). *Junge Deutsche und Hitler. Eine empirische Studie zur historisch-politischen Sozialisation.* Stuttgart: Klett.

Gilbert, S. M. (1950). *The psychology of dictatorship. Based on the examination of the leaders of Nazi Germany.* New York: Ronald.

Götz von Olenhusen, I. (1987). Die Krise der jungen Generation und der Aufstieg des Nationalsozialismus. In U. Herrmann (Ed.), *Neue Erziehung—neue Menschen. Ansätze zur Erziehungs- und Bildungsreform in Deutschland zwischen Kaiserreich und Diktatur* (pp. 260–278). Weinheim: Beltz.

Hagan, J., Merkens, H., & Boehnke, K. (1995). Delinquency and disdain. Social capital and the control of right-wing extremism among East and West Berlin youth. *American Journal of Sociology, 100,* 1028–1052.

Hamilton, R. F. (1982). *Who voted for Hitler?* Princeton: Princeton University Press.

Heitmeyer, W. (1987). *Rechtsextremistische Orientierungen bei Jugendlichen.* Weinheim: Juventa.

Heitmeyer, W. (1991). Individualisierungsprozesse und Folgen für die politische Sozialisation von Jugendlichen. Ein Zuwachs an politischer Paralysierung und Macchiavellismus? In W. Heitmeyer & J. Jacobi (Eds.), *Politische Sozialisation und Individualisierung* (pp. 15–34). Weinheim: Juventa.

Heitmeyer, W., Collmann, B., Conrads, J., et al. (1995). *Gewalt. Schattenseiten der Individualisierung bei Jugendlichen aus unterschiedlichen Milieus.* Weinheim: Juventa.

Heitmeyer, W., & Müller, J. (1995). *Fremdenfeindliche Gewalt junger Menschen. Biographische Hintergründe, soziale Situationskontexte und die Bedeutung strafrechtlicher Sanktionen* (Bundesministerium der Justiz, Ed.). Bad Godesberg: Forum.

Hennig, E. (1982). Neonazistische Militanz und Rechtsextremismus unter Jugendlichen. *Aus Politik und Zeitgeschichte, B23,* 23–37.

Hennig, E. (1984). Wie wird man rechtsextremer Jugendlicher in der Bundesrepublik. In Bundeszentrale für politische Bildung (Eds.), *Extremismus und Schule. Daten, Analysen und Arbeitshilfen zum politischen Rechts- und Linksextremismus* (pp. 151–170). Bonn: Bundeszentrale für politische Bildung.

Hennig, E. (1993). Neonazistische Militanz und fremdenfeindliche Lebensformen in der "alten" und "neuen" Bundesrepublik Deutschland. In H. U. Otto & R. Merten (Eds.), *Rechtsradikale Gewalt im vereinigten Deutschland. Jugend im gesellschaftlichen Umbruch* (pp. 64–79). Bonn: Bundeszentrale für politische Bildung.

Herrmann, A., & Schmidt, P. (1995). Autoritarismus, Anomie, Ethnozentrismus. In G. Lederer & P. Schmidt (Eds.), *Autoritarismus und Gesellschaft. Trendanalysen und vergleichende Jugenduntersuchungen 1945–1993* (pp. 287–319). Opladen: Leske & Budrich.

Hobsbawm, E. (1994). *Age of extremes. The short twentieth century 1914–1991.* London: Michael Joseph.

Hoffmeister, D., & Sill, O. (1992). *Zwischen Aufstieg und Ausstieg. Autoritäre Einstellungsmuster bei Jugendlichen / jungen Erwachsenen.* Opladen: Leske & Budrich.

Hopf, C. (1993a). Authoritarians and their families: Qualitative studies on the origins of authoritarian dispositions. In W. F. Stone, G. Lederer, & R. Christie (Eds.), *Strength and weakness. The authoritarian personality today* (pp. 119–143). New York: Springer.

Hopf, C. (1993b). Rechtsextremismus und Beziehungserfahrungen. *Zeitschrift für Soziologie, 22,* 449–463.

Hopf, C., Rieker, P., & Sanden-Marcus, M. (1995). *Familie und Rechtsextremismus. Familiale Sozialisation und rechtsextreme Orientierungen junger Männer.* Weinheim: Juventa.

Inglehart, R. (1989). *Kultureller Umbruch. Wertwandel in der westlichen Welt.* Frankfurt a.M.: Campus.

Inkeles, A., & Levinson, D. J. (1968). National character. The study of modal personality and sociocultural systems. In G. Lindzey & E. Aaronson (Eds.), *Handbook of social psychology* (2nd ed., pp. 418–506). Reading, MA: Addison-Wesley.

Jaide, W. (1988). *Generationen eines Jahrhunderts. Wechsel der Jugendgenerationen im Jahrhunderttrend. Zur Sozialgeschichte der Jugend in Deutschland 1871–1985.* Opladen: Leske & Budrich.

Kalinowsky, H. H. (1990). *Rechtsextremismus und Strafrechtspflege. Eine Analyse von Strafverfahren wegen mutmaßlicher rechtsextremistischer Aktivitäten und Erscheinungen* (3rd. ed.). (Bundesministerium der Justiz, Ed.). Bonn: Bundesminister der Justiz.

Kelley, D. M. (1946). Preliminary studies of the Rorschach records of the Nazi war criminals. *Rorschach Research Exchange, 10,* 45–48.

Klages, H., Hippler, H.-J., & Herbert, W. (1992). *Werte und Wandel. Ergebnisse und Methoden einer Forschungstradition.* Frankfurt a.M.: Campus.

Kornhauser, W. (1959). *The politics of mass society.* Glencoe, IL: The Free Press.

Lederer, G., & Kindervater, A. (1995). Wandel des Autoritarismus unter Jugendlichen in den USA. In G. Lederer & P. Schmidt (Eds.), *Autoritarismus und Gesellschaft. Trendanalysen und vergleichende Jugenduntersuchungen 1945–1993* (pp. 86–101). Opladen: Leske & Budrich.

Lederer, G., & Schmidt, P. (Eds.). (1995). *Autoritarismus und Gesellschaft. Trendanalysen und vergleichende Jugenduntersuchungen 1945–1993.* Opladen: Leske & Budrich.

Lipset, S. M. (1963). *Political man. The social bases of politics.* Garden City, NY: Anchor.

Loeber, R., & Dishion, T. J. (1984). Boys who fight at home and school: Family conditions influencing cross-setting consistency. *Journal of Consulting and Clinical Psychology, 52,* 759–768.

Loewenberg, P. (1971). The psychohistorical origins of the Nazi youth cohort. *American Historical Review, 76,* 1457–1502.

Loewenberg, P. (1975). Psychohistorical perspectives on modern German history. *Journal of Modern History, 47,* 229–279.

McCord, J. (1979). Some child-rearing antecedents of criminal behavior in adult men. *Journal of Personality and Social Psychology, 37*, 1477–1486.

McCord, J. (1983). A longitudinal study of aggression and antisocial behavior. In K. Teilmann van Dusen & S. A. Mednick (Eds.), *Prospective studies of crime and delinquency* (pp. 269–275). Boston: Kluwer-Nijhoff.

McCord, J. (1986). Instigation and insulation: How families affect antisocial aggression. In A. Olweus, J. Block, & M. Radke-Yarrow (Eds.), *Development of antisocial and prosocial behavior* (pp. 343–357). Orlando: Academic Press.

McCord, J. (Ed.). (1995). *Coercion and punishment in long-term perspectives.* Cambridge: Cambridge University Press.

McGranahan, D. V. (1946). A comparison of social attitudes among American and German youth. *Journal of Abnormal and Social Psychology, 41*, 245–257.

McGranahan, D. V., & Janowitz, M. (1946). Studies of German youth. *Journal of Abnormal and Social Psychology, 41*, 3–14.

Merkl, P. H. (1970a). Die alten Kämpfer der NSDAP. *Sozialwissenschaftliches Jahrbuch für Politik, 2*, 495–517.

Merkl, P. H. (1970b). *To be a political soldier of Adolf Hitler. Extremist recruitment in the pre-1933 NSDAP.* Munich: International Political Science Association, World Congress.

Merkl, P. H. (1975). *Political violence under the Swastika. 581 Early Nazis.* Princeton, NJ: Princeton University Press.

Merkl, P. H. (1980). Zur quantitativen Analyse von Lebensläufen "Alter Kämpfer". In R. Mann (Ed.), *Die Nationalsozialisten. Analysen faschistischer Bewegungen* (pp. 67–83). Stuttgart: Klett-Cotta.

Merkl, P. H., & Weinberg, L. (Eds.). (1993). *Encounters with the contemporary radical right.* Boulder, CO: Westview Press.

Mills, C. W. (1972). The big city: Private troubles and public issues. In C. W. Mills (Ed.), *Power, politics and people. The collected essays of C. W. Mills* (pp. 395–404). London: Oxford University Press.

Mogge, W. (1985). Wandervogel, Freideutsche Jugend und Bünde. Zum Jugendbild der bürgerlichen Jugendbewegung. In T. Koebner, R.-P. Janz, & F. Trommler (Eds.), *"Mit uns zieht die neue Zeit." Der Mythos Jugend* (pp. 174–198). Frankfurt a.M.: Suhrkamp.

Noelle, E., & Neumann, P. (Eds.). (1974). *Jahrbuch der öffentlichen Meinung 1968–1973.* Allensbach: Verlag für Demoskopie.

Noelle-Neumann, E., & Ring, E. (1984). *Das Extremismus-Potential unter jungen Leuten in der Bundesrepublik Deutschland.* Allensbach: Institut für Demoskopie.

Oesterreich, D. (1993). *Autoritäre Persönlichkeit und Gesellschaftsordnung.* Weinheim: Juventa.

Ohlemacher, T. (1994). Public opinion and violence against foreigners in the reunified Germany. *Zeitschrift für Soziologie, 23*, 222–236.

Paul, G. (1990). *Aufstand der Bilder. Die NS-Propaganda vor 1933.* Bonn: Dietz Nachf.

Peukert, D. (1984). Arbeiterschaft und Nationalsozialismus. In L. Niethammer (Ed.), *Die Menschen machen ihre Geschichte nicht aus freien Stücken, aber sie machen sie selbst. Einladung zu einer Geschichte des Volkes in NRW* (pp. 159–163). Bonn: Dietz Nachf.

Peukert, D. (1986). Alltagsleben und Generationserfahrungen von Jugendlichen in der Zwischenkriegszeit. In D. Dowe (Ed.), *Jugendprotest und Generationskonflikte in Europa im 20. Jahrhundert* (pp. 139–150). Bonn: Verlag Neue Gesellschaft.

Reuband, K.-H. (1988). Von äußerer Verhaltenskonformität zu selbständigem Handeln. Über die Bedeutung kultureller und struktureller Einflüsse für den Wandel in den Erziehungszielen und Sozialisationsinhalten. In H. O. Luthe & H. Meulemann (Eds.), *Wertwandel—Fakten oder Fiktion. Bestandsaufnahmen und Diagnosen aus kultursoziologischer Sicht* (pp. 73–97). Frankfurt a.M.: Campus.

Reuband, K.-H. (1992). Veränderungen in den familialen Lebensbedingungen Jugendlicher seit der Jahrhundertwende. Eine Analyse auf der Basis retrospektiver Daten. *Zeitschrift für Sozialisationsforschung und Erziehungssoziologie, 12*, 99–113.

Rodnick, D. (1948). *Postwar Germans. An anthropologist's account.* New Haven: Yale University Press.

Rokeach, M. (1960). *The open and closed mind.* New York: Basic Books.

Schaffner, B. (1948). *Father Land. A study of authoritarianism in the German family.* New York: Columbia University Press.

Scheuch, E. K. (1988). Continuity and change in German social structure. *Historical Social Research, 46,* 31–121.

Scheuch, E. K. (1990). Die Suche nach der Besonderheit der heutigen Deutschen. *Kölner Zeitschrift für Soziologie und Sozialpsychologie, 42,* 734–752.

Scheuch, E. K., & Scheuch, U. (1991). *Wie deutsch sind die Deutschen.* Bergisch-Gladbach: Lübbe.

Schumann, K. F. (1993). Schutz der Ausländer vor rechtsradikaler Gewalt durch Instrumente des Strafrechts. *Strafverteidiger, 6,* 324–330.

Smelser, N. J. (1962). *Theory of collective behavior.* London: Routledge.

Snow, D. A., Burke Rochford, E., Jr., & Worden, St. K. (1986). Frame alignment and mobilization. *American Sociological Review, 51,* 464–481.

Snow, D. A., & Benford, R. D. (1988). Ideology, frame resonance and participant mobilization. In B. Klandermans, H. Kriesi, & S. Tarrow (Eds.), *International social movement research* (Vol. 1, pp. 197–217). Greenwich, CT: JAI Press.

Stachura, P. D. (1975). *Nazi youth in the Weimar Republic* (Introduction by P. H. Merkl). Santa Barbara, CA: Clio Books.

Staub, E. (1989). *The roots of evil. The origin of genocide and other group violence.* Cambridge: Cambridge University Press.

Stöss, R. (1984). Pronazistisches Protestverhalten in der Schule. Ursachen und Ausmaß. In Bundeszentrale für politische Bildung (Ed.), *Extremismus und Schule* (pp. 171–194). Bonn: Bundeszentrale für politische Bildung.

Stone, W. F., Lederer, G., & Christie, R. (Eds.). (1993). *Strength and weakness. The authoritarian personality today.* New York: Springer.

Wiegand, E. (1992). Zunahme der Ausländerfeindlichkeit? Einstellungen zu Fremden in Deutschland und Europa. *ZUMA-Nachrichten, 16*(31), 1–35.

Wiegand, E. (1993). Ausländerfeindlichkeit in der Festung Europa. *Informationsdienst Soziale Indikatoren, ZUMA,* No. 9. Mannheim.

Willems, H., Eckert, R., Würtz, S., & Steinmetz, L. (1993). *Fremdenfeindliche Gewalt. Einstellungen, Täter, Konflikteskalation.* Opladen: Leske & Budrich.

Willems, H. (1996). Kollektive Gewalt gegen Fremde. Entwickelt sich eine soziale Bewegung von Rechts? In H.-G. Heiland & C. Lüdemann (Eds.), *Soziologische Dimensionen des Rechtsextremismus* (pp. 27–56). Opladen: Westdeutscher Verlag.

Winkler, H. A. (1985). Die deutsche Gesellschaft der Weimarer Republik und der Antisemitismus. In B. Martin & E. Schulin (Eds.), *Die Juden als Minderheit in der Geschichte* (pp. 271–289). Munich: dtv.

Winnicott, D. W. (1950). Some thoughts on the meaning of the word democracy. *Human Relations, 3,* 175–183.

Zald, M. N., & McCarthy, J. D. (Eds.). (1979). *The dynamics of social movements.* Cambridge, MA: Winthrop.

Zald, M. N., & McCarthy, J. D. (Eds.). (1987). *Social movements in an organizational society. Collected essays.* New Brunswick, NJ: Transaction.

Zinnecker, J. (1985a). Kindheit, Erziehung, Familie. In A. Fischer, W. Fuchs, & J. Zinnecker (Eds.), *Jugendliche und Erwachsene '85: Generationen im Vergleich* (Ed. by Jugendwerk der Deutschen Shell; pp. 97–292). Opladen: Leske & Budrich.

Zinnecker, J. (1985b). Politik, Parteien, Nationalsozialismus. In A. Fischer, W. Fuchs, & J. Zinnecker (Eds.), *Jugendliche und Erwachsene '85: Generationen im Vergleich* (Ed. by Jugendwerk der Deutschen Shell; pp. 321–408). Opladen: Leske & Budrich.

Chapter 6

Time Trends in
Affective Disorders

Eric Fombonne
University of London

Several reports suggested that rates of depressive disorders are increasing (Cross National Collaborative Group, 1992; Fombonne, 1994; Klerman, 1988; Klerman & Weissman, 1989). This increase may lead to the identification of psychosocial causal mechanisms explaining these time trends. The main goals of this chapter are to critically review empirical evidence of a secular increase in the incidence of depressive conditions and to discuss interpretation problems in the available published studies. I do not address the issue of possible mechanisms underlying time trends in depressive conditions that are discussed elsewhere (Fombonne, 1995).

DEFINITIONS

Because the term *depression* is used with different meanings in the literature, all of them being relevant to this review, three levels of definition are used here. *Depressed mood or affect* refers to a state of dysphoria occurring frequently in the course of normal development. Depressed mood is part of a broader set of negative feelings and can be distinguished from normal feelings of sadness, from demoralization, and from other negative affects such as anxiety. *Depressive syndrome* refers to a constellation of observable symptoms (of which depressed mood is only one component) such as tearfulness, irritability, death thoughts, loss of appetite, disturbances of sleep, lack of energy, and so on, which tend to cluster together. At the individual level, a depressive syndrome is recognized when the behavioral characteristics reach a given threshold signaling a significant deviation from the individual's usual state. *Depressive disorders* correspond to psychiatric diagnoses of depression as defined in *ICD–10* (World Health Organization, 1992) or *DSM–III–R* and *DSM–IV* (American Psychiatric Association, 1987, 1994). In essence, they consist in the clustering of depressive symptoms in a given individual, with two additional features: The cluster of symptoms lasts for some time (duration criterion), and it impinges on the subject's adaptive functioning (impairment criterion). Several divisions of depressive disorders exist in current psychiatric classifications. In this review, we are mostly concerned with those depressive disorders that do not form part of a bipolar disorder.

It is assumed that developmental pathways exist that sequentially link these three constructs in the course of normal and pathological development, although little is actually known of the rates and patterns of these transitions. Thus, depressed mood is reported in over one third of community samples of adolescents (Petersen et al., 1993) whereas prevalence rates of depressive disorders fluctuate around 1% for children and 3% to 4% for adolescents (Fombonne, 1998). Important methodological differences exist across studies according to the particular operationalization of depressive phenomena used, which jeopardizes efforts to compare results across datasets. For example, depressed mood is a construct typically employed in developmental research and is closely associated with specific measurement (self-report questionnaires) and design approaches (longitudinal studies of community samples of adolescents). Depressive syndrome is linked with a dimensional approach to psychopathology reliant on factor analytic and other multivariate approaches to measurement. By contrast, most data on categorically defined depressive disorder come from interview-based studies of either psychiatric patient samples or cross-sectional studies of adult populations. Thus, the need to retain these different levels of definition of depressive conditions was obvious in order to review evidence as completely as possible. The term *depressive conditions* or *phenomena* is used whenever more than one level of definition will be implied.

TYPES, STRENGTHS, AND LIMITATIONS
OF DATA SOURCES

Rates of other behavior problems such as crime, delinquency, or drug use, can be monitored over time by consulting routine reports summarizing arrest records. No such surveillance system exists that would allow for a monitoring of the incidence of depressive conditions over significant periods of time. In the few countries where longitudinal studies of birth cohorts or repeated health surveys were conducted, measures of depression or of mental health were generally not included. As a consequence, most of the relevant datasets were generated after 1970, and indeed during the last 15 years for the vast majority of them. Thus, ideal designs to examine secular trends, namely *prospective follow-up studies* of multiple birth cohorts, are rarely used; such designs are optimal because they allow for an unbiased estimation of age of onset and incidence rate.

The data available for an examination of secular changes come mostly either from large *community surveys* of psychiatric disorders or from *family studies* of affective disorders. In such studies, cross-sectional data are collected at a single point of time. The present and past occurrence of depressive disorder in each subject is established, and the age at first onset when appropriate. Then, data are treated as if they were derived from a prospective study starting from birth, using age at first onset or age at interview as a survival time.

Health statistics routinely collected in modern countries could also be informative, although only indirectly. Hospital statistics could theoretically provide evidence of an increase in the number of psychiatric hospitalizations over time in relation with depressive disorders. However, such data are sparse, and any trend would be extremely difficult to interpret as evidence of an actual increase in the incidence of depressive conditions, because it would not be possible to gauge how much of this increase would reflect a better detection or acceptance of depression, easier access to hospital care, the availability of new and more efficacious treatments, or changes in diagnostic practices.

Although suicides do not occur necessarily as a consequence of depressive disorders, suicide occurs with a variety of depressive conditions. Thus, if there has been a secular increase in rates of depression, then trends in suicide rates should at least not contradict that trend. Changes over time in the strength of the relationship between suicide and depression would be crucial to detect.

EVIDENCE OF AN INCREASED INCIDENCE OF DEPRESSIVE CONDITIONS

During the last 10 years, several studies provided continuing support to the hypothesis of a recent increase in the rates of depressive disorders (Klerman, 1988; Klerman & Weissman, 1989).

Family Studies

Evidence of a secular trend stemmed originally from two large family genetic studies. In the first study, 2,289 first degree relatives of 523 depressed probands were studied in five sites of the National Institutes of

Mental Health (NIMH) research program on the psychobiology of depression (Klerman et al., 1985). Findings suggested increasing rates of depressive disorders among successive birth cohorts throughout the century. The data also indicated an earlier age of onset in the most recent birth cohorts and a persistence of the female preponderance, although a trend was noted towards a less pronounced sex differential in recent birth cohorts. However, a more recent investigation of the same data confirmed the continuing gender difference in rates of depressive disorders (Leon, Klerman, & Wickramaratne, 1993). In a second family genetic study, 823 first degree relatives of bipolar and schizoaffective probands were examined (Gershon, Hamovit, Guroff, & Nurnberger, 1987). The age-corrected lifetime prevalence of any affective disorder was 21.7% for the pre-1940 birth cohorts as compared to 40.6% in the post-1940 cohorts and, using actuarial life-table analysis, a significant difference was found between the two corresponding cumulative hazard functions.

Three recent family data sets yielded similar results. A 6-year follow-up of 965 relatives who were unaffected at entry into the study indicated an increased incidence of new onset depressive disorders in the younger cohort (less than 40 years) who had rates three times as high as did the oldest cohort (Coryell, Endicott, & Keller, 1992). In this study, of course, it is impossible to separate cohort from age effects; nevertheless, this study has the advantage of a prospective design. In a family study of prepubertal depressed children, the effect of birth cohort on the cumulative risk of becoming depressed was examined among the 86 siblings of the probands and the 77 siblings of control subjects (Ryan et al., 1992). Younger siblings of the depressed children had significantly higher rates of depressive disorders. Younger siblings of both groups also had higher lifetime rates of all psychiatric disorders; however, the increase in depression for the younger siblings of the depressed children was higher than the increase in other disorders in this group. Finally, a third family data set from Germany produced similar evidence in a sample of adults (Maier, Hallmayer, Lichtermann, Philipp, & Klinger, 1991).

Community Studies

Strikingly consistent evidence has come from the various studies of large community samples conducted recently throughout different countries with precise sampling methodologies, comparable diagnostic definitions, and use of standardized diagnostic interviews of known reliability and validity. The Epidemiologic Catchment Area (ECA) study provided several leads to the question (Robins, Locke, & Regier, 1991). These findings were based on self-reported lifetime onset (incidence) dates of selected disorders. The prevalence estimates based on these data are thus not confounded with the duration of disorders, although they underestimate the lifetime morbid risk because of forgetting. Assuming that psychiatric disorders are not strongly associated with increased mortality and that recall of past episodes remains constant throughout the life span, lifetime prevalence rates should increase with age because the time at risk augments. One surprising finding was that the lifetime rate of any disorder declined with age, with lower rates being found among the elderly (Robins, Locke, & Regier, 1991). This pattern of decreasing lifetime rate with age was particularly pronounced for affective disorders. Thus, for men and women, respectively, the lifetime rates were 6.4% and 10.6% for the 18- to 29-year-olds, 6.6% and 15.3% for the 30- to 44-year-olds, declined thereafter to 3.6% and 9.3% in the 45 to 64 age group and fell to 1.6% and 3.3% among those over age 65 (Weissman et al., 1991). These results were found across the five study sites, and reflected, at least in part, a younger mean age of onset. Graphical displays of the results indicate that, at any age, the youngest birth cohorts that have completed the period at risk have higher rates of disorders than do the older cohorts, and they also show a progressively earlier age of onset. Figure 6.1 provides a display of the graphical appearance of findings in the ECA and similar studies.

Similar results were obtained in three other North American studies. Lifetime rates of self-reported major depression declined in the oldest age groups in a community sample of Canadian adults; however, no clear pattern in rates could be observed before age 55 (Bland, Orn, & Newman, 1988). Another study of community samples of adults using diagnostic interviews and criteria different from those of the ECA study led to con-

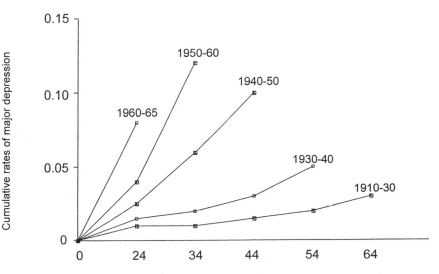

FIG. 6.1. Lifetime prevalence rates of depression according to birth cohort (hypothetical data from a cross-sectional survey).

vergent results, thus ruling out the specific diagnostic instrument used in previous studies as the source of a major artifactual effect (Lewinsohn, Rohde, Seeley, & Fischer, 1993). In this study, measures of current mood state, memory ability, social desirability, and self-labeling were available. The authors were therefore able to assess, and eventually partial out, the effect of these potential artifacts on what they called the *depression epidemic*. Significant differences between survival curves were found for six birth cohorts for both sexes, the more recent ones experiencing a higher risk of major depressive episode at a younger age. Among the four potentially confounding factors, three were significantly related to the number of past episodes of depressive disorders reported by the subjects, although the magnitudes of these associations were quite small. When their effect was controlled for, they appeared to exert little or no influence on these trends, either independently or in combination. Moreover, whereas the oldest cohort of their adolescent subsample, born between 1968 and 1971, had a higher lifetime rate than did the youngest cohort (1972–1974) due to their increased time at risk, the cumulative probability of major depressive disorder by age 16 was already significantly higher in the youngest birth cohort, thus suggesting that the trend toward an earlier age of onset could be detected even between two fairly recent birth cohorts. Finally, in the National Comorbidity Survey (NCS) of a nationally representative sample of more than 8,000 American adults, lifetime and 12-month prevalence rates of major depression were again found to decline with age (Kessler, McGonagle, Swartz, Blazer, & Nelson, 1993).

Some consistent conclusions were reached in the long-term prospective Lundby study in Sweden (Hagnell, Lanke, Rorsman, & Ojesjö, 1982). Diagnostic assessments were based on a more classical clinical approach and, due to the true prospective design of the study, age standardized incidence rates could be computed for each sex over a 25-year period, from 1947 to 1972. Rates increased in the most recent period for depressive disorders associated with mild or medium impairment, but *not* for the more severe psychotic type of depression. Again, an elevated incidence rate was noticed among 20- to 39-year-old subjects, with a sharper rise for men than for women. The possibility of a progressive leveling off of sex differences was also suggested in a community study conducted in New Zealand on a sample of roughly 1,500 adults and calibrated on the ECA methods (Joyce, Oakley-Browne, Wells, Bushnell, & Hornblow, 1990; Oakley-Browne, Joyce, Wells, Bushnell, & Hornblow, 1989; Wells, Bushnell, Hornblow, Joyce, & Oakley-Browne, 1989). Survival analyses showed a progressively increasing cumulative risk by birth cohort for major depression in both sexes. In addition, an earlier age of onset, and higher six month prevalence rates in men than in women were found in the youngest birth cohort (5.5% vs. 3.5%). Finally, using a different diagnostic procedure, lower lifetime rate of depression were reported by those older than 50 years in a community sample of 790 adults of south east London (Bebbington, Katz, McGuffin, Tennant, & Hurry, 1989).

In contrast, four other major community surveys, using a methodology similar to that of ECA and two other datasets, failed to document an increase in the lifetime prevalence of affective disorder among the youngest birth cohorts. In a nationwide survey of mental disorders of 5,100 rural and urban Koreans between the ages of 18 and 65 (Lee et al., 1987), no significant association of age group with lifetime prevalence rates of major depression was found. However, the highest rate for affective disorders was found in the 18- to 24-year-old urban group. Failure to reach a significant age trend may simply have reflected the lack of power of the study due to the relatively limited subsample sizes and to the low base rate of the disorder (3.3% averaged across age groups). Similarly, in the Mexican-American subsample of the Los Angeles site of the ECA study, the age-specific prevalence of major depressive episode was roughly equal in the younger and the older age groups in both sexes (Karno et al., 1987). The lifetime rate in the youngest non-Hispanic American Whites was more than twice as high as that of the young Hispanic American subsample, and their rate was also two to three times higher than that of the oldest White age group. Another community study, again drawing upon the ECA methodology, was conducted in Puerto Rico in a representative sample of 1,513 adults (Canino et al., 1987). A continuous increase with age in the lifetime prevalence rates of major depressive episodes, and of affective disorders in general, was found. A survey of 7,229 Hong Kong residents found rates of major depression to be low at all ages in both genders and no age effect could be detected (Chen et al., 1993).

In a prospective Canadian study, age-specific prevalence rates for depression were not found to vary according to birth cohorts. This negative finding in a sample of older adults may have reflected the absence of recent birth cohorts in the study (Murphy, Sobol, Neff, Olivier, & Leighton, 1984). These data from Nova Scotia also suggest that sex differences in rates of depression may have declined, especially in middle age.

Another prospective study including three waves of data collection (1965, 1974, and 1983) in Alameda County, California (Roberts, Lee, & Roberts, 1991), found that rates of current depression remained consistently higher in those born before 1912 than among the more recently born U.S. citizens. Current depression rates increased during the mid-1970s for all subjects born between 1913 and 1948, but in 1983 prevalence rates declined to the levels of 1965. The data suggested that the elevated rates among old subjects reflected a cohort rather than an age effect, with oldest cohorts being at increased risk. Similar findings were reported in another longitudinal investigation of a U.S. adult sample where oldest cohorts also reported higher levels of depressive symptoms (Srole & Fischer, 1980). Findings from selected community surveys are summarized in Table 6.1.

TABLE 6.1
Lifetime Rates of Major Depression According to Birth Cohorts: Results From Selected Cross-Sectional Surveys

Author	Country	Sample Size	Measures	Gender	\<-- Age Specific Rates --\>					
					18–24	25–34	35–44	45–54	55–64	65+
1. Bland et al., 1988	Canada (Edmonton)	3,258	*DSM–II/DIS*	MF	6.0	11.5	8.5	12.0	7.6	4.1
2. Kessler et al., 1993	U.S. (NCS Survey)	8,098	*DSM–III–R/* UM CIDI		*15–24*	*25–34*	*35–44*	*45+*		
				M	11.0	13.1	14.7	11.8		
				F	20.8	19.4	23.8	21.8		
3. Weissman et al., 1991	U.S. (ECA 5 sites)	19,182	*DSM–III/DIS*		*18–29*		*30–44*	*45–64*		*65+*
				MF	6.7		9.5	5.0		2.0
4. Wells et al., 1989	New Zealand (Christchurch)	1,498	*DSM–III/DIS*		*18–24*	*25–44*		*45–64*		
				MF	9.7	15.1		10.8		
5. Wittchen et al., 1992	Germany (Munich)	1,366	*DSM–III/DIS*		*18–24*	*25–44*		*45–64*		
				MF		10.6		8.61		
6. Chen et al., 1993	Hong Kong (Shatin)	7,229	*DSM–III/DIS*		*18–24*	*25–44*		*45–65*		
				M	2.26	1.27		0.71		
				F	1.54	2.82		1.91		
7. Lee et al., 1987	Korea (Nationwide)	5,100	*DSM–III/DIS*		*18–39*			*40+*		
				MF rural	2.69			3.89		
				MF urban	3.76			3.54		
8. Karno et al., 1987	U.S. (LA Mexican American)	1,243	*DSM–III/DIS*	M	4.0			3.4		
				(White rates)	(8.7)			(3.6)		
				F	6.1			6.5		
				(White rates)	(15.3)			(5.2)		
9. Canino et al., 1987	Puerto Rico	1,513	*DSM–III/DIS*		*18–24*	*25–44*		*45–64*		
				MF	3.6	4.7		5.1		

Multinational Comparisons

The findings on temporal trends in nine community samples and three family studies that used similar diagnostic criteria and psychiatric interviews were recently reevaluated (Cross National Collaborative Group, 1992). In addition to the already cited databases, new data from one German family study (Maier et al., 1991) and from recent community surveys conducted in Italy (Faravelli, Guerrini, Aiazzi, Incerpi, & Pallanti, 1990), Germany (Wittchen, Esau, von Zerssen, Krieg, & Zaudig, 1992), France (Lépine et al., 1989), Lebanon (Karam, Barakeh, & Karam, 1991) and Taïwan (Hwu, Yeh, & Chang, 1989) were included (for a summary, see Cross National Collaborative Group, 1992), for a sample of more than 43,000 subjects. Using a sophisticated statistical modeling technique, the authors found in every dataset a significant "drift" in rates of depression over time, that is, a regular linear increase in the incidence of depressive disorders cutting across generations, historical periods, and cultural boundaries. The range and magnitude of the drift parameter did not differ between family and community samples. They further identified specific cohort and period effects in some, but not all, sites. None of the family datasets exhibited such nonlinear period or cohort effects, a finding that, according to the authors, could be suggestive either of less sensitivity to environmental factors of depressive disorders occurring in genetically loaded families or of an instrumentation effect (because the psychiatric interview used in these studies, Schedule for Affective Disorders and Schizophrenia [SADS] differed from that (Diagnostic Interview Schedule [DIS] used in the community surveys). In spite of the statistical power provided by such a large sample, results were not provided separately by gender. Although the authors alluded to possible analytical and statistical differences, no explanation was provided for the absence of a period effect in data where it had been described in prior reports including the family studies and Puerto Rican and Mexican-American surveys. The difficulties in distinguishing among period, cohort, and age effects are, of course, legendary (see the introductory chapter to this volume) but this undiscussed discrepancy leaves doubt as to the meaning of this statistical estimate and detracts from the persuasiveness of the overall findings. Little attempt was made to relate these effects to other explanatory factors.

TRENDS IN SUICIDAL BEHAVIORS

Suicide rates have been rising progressively in the youngest birth cohorts in several countries, especially in males, with a pronounced trend to a marked increase of suicides among youth (Brent, Perper, & Allman, 1987;

Diekstra, Kienhorst, & de Wilde, 1995; Holinger & Offer, 1991; Lester, 1991; McClure, 1984; McIntosh, 1991; Shaffer, 1988). These data are relevant for the study of depressive disorders for several reasons.

First, retrospective studies of adult suicides show a high rate of depression preceding the suicidal act (Barraclough, Bunch, Nelson, & Sainsbury, 1974). Among suicidal adolescents too, affective disorders are frequently found with or without comorbid disorders (Brent et al., 1994; Shaffer et al., 1996). In the New York study of completed suicides (Shaffer et al., 1996), major depression was found to be the second strongest predictor of suicide after prior attempt. Similarly, in five recent psychological autopsies of adolescent suicides (Brent et al., 1988; Marttunen, Aro, Henriksson, & Lönnqvist, 1991; Rich, Young, & Fowler, 1986; Runeson, 1989; Shafii, Carrigan, Whittinghill, & Derrick, 1985), the median rates of major depression and affective disorders were 24% and 52%, respectively. In a Finnish study (Marttunen et al., 1991), 40% of the 53 adolescent suicides had depressive disorder as a principal diagnosis, and 64% had depressive syndromes. Unfortunately, we lack data on temporal changes in the proportion of adolescent suicides attributable to depressive conditions. The most informative study on this issue is an investigation of suicidal behavior falling short of completed suicide. Studying 1,313 male adolescents who had attended a London hospital over a 21-year period, Fombonne (in press) found a secular increase in suicidal behavior. These behaviors were associated with both depression and substance abuse, especially alcohol abuse (Fombonne, in press). However, rather than being linked to increased rates of depression, the increase in suicidal behaviors was attributed to increased rates of alcohol abuse. This study provides the first findings, using individual level data, on the role of psychiatric disorders in the secular increase of suicidal behaviors among adolescents. To what extent its results will extend to completed suicide and to adolescents in the general population remains, however, to be tested.

Secondly, although data are relatively scarce, follow-up studies of adolescents show that, in keeping with the excess suicide risk found among adults with affective disorders, adolescent clients of psychiatrists have a higher risk of suicide than do adult clients, whether they present with general psychological dysfunction or with specific affective disorders (Harrington, Fudge, Rutter, Pickles, & Hill, 1990; Harrington, Rutter, & Fombonne, 1996; Kovacs & Puig-Antich, 1991; Rao, Weissman, Martin, & Hammond, 1993; Rao et al., 1995).

Third, comparison of psychological autopsies in two series of adult male suicides, studied 25 years apart, suggests that depressive disorders, especially in conjunction with other psychiatric diagnoses and alcohol abuse, are found with higher proportions among the young subjects of the most recent sample (Carlson, Rich, Grayson, & Fowler, 1991). These findings are consistent with those reported by Fombonne (in press) in a clinical sample of referred adolescents in London.

Overall, these findings shed only partial light on the actual relation between adolescent suicide and depressive phenomena, and further research is needed in order to gauge to what extent secular trends in suicide rates could be explained by similar temporal changes in depressive conditions. As it stands, the available evidence indicates that trends in suicide rates, regarded as proxy epidemiological indicators of depressive conditions, provide indirect but additional support to the findings from family and community studies of depression.

REPEATED CROSS-SECTIONAL SURVEYS
OF DEFINED POPULATIONS

Two repeat surveys of large representative samples of 7- to 16-year-old U.S. children were conducted over a 13-year interval with identical instruments, allowing for a fine-tuned analysis of trends in problem behaviors in a multicohort sample (Achenbach & Howell, 1993). In the more recent survey, parents, and especially teachers, reported more depressed mood as measured by a single item, although the absolute magnitude of the increase remained modest. Increases were also found for depressive syndromes. However, suggesting that these trends were not specific to depressive phenomena, these findings were paralleled by increases in many other kinds of behavior problems and syndromes, in particular those reflecting disruptive behaviors.

Also relevant to the study of changes over time are two repeat cross-sectional surveys of mental health carried out in 1957 and 1976 on representative samples of over 2,200 U.S. adults (Gurin, Veroff, & Feld, 1960; Veroff, Douvan, & Kulka, 1981; Veroff, Kulka, & Douvan, 1981). The strength of these two household surveys lies in the rigor of sampling and in the close comparability of the interview schedules used 19 years apart. In the more recent survey, fewer young adult respondents reported feelings of happiness and high morale, and more reported worries and anxiety. Although the focus was on general feelings of well-being and not on depression, results suggested that these changes not only reflected cultural shifts but were largely accounted for by new patterns of orientation toward work, family life, and self-definition emerging among the youngest generation (Veroff, Douvan, & Kulka, 1981). Relevant to this discussion are also the findings by Rodgers (1982) who reviewed 15 surveys of national U.S. samples (N > 28,000). Data were collected by personal interview. In all but one survey, levels of reported happiness declined from the late 1950s up to the early 1970s and subsequently increased, a trend more pronounced among young respondents. Whereas differences between the constructs measured in these surveys should be borne in mind, their results run parallel to those of psychiatric surveys.

HOSPITAL STATISTICS

Three hospital datasets were used to examine temporal trends in depressive conditions. The first study has provided diagnostic data on more than 62,000 admissions to a university hospital in Zürich from 1920 to 1982 (Angst, 1985). The frequency of the diagnosed depression before 1950 was constantly below 2%, but rose to 5% or more subsequently. Because these data have been cited as evidence of an increased proportion of depressed patients in treatment settings (Klerman & Weissman, 1989), a critical examination of them is necessary. Diagnoses were obtained retrospectively from hospital records, using unspecified diagnostic criteria. Admissions for depression increased, at first moderately with the introduction of the electro-convulsive therapy, with the introduction of neuroleptic drugs between 1940 and the late 1950s, and even more steeply in the following years with the advent of specifically antidepressant drugs. In addition, both depression and mania showed the same increase over the last three decades, suggesting that selection factors or changes in diagnostic habits may have operated to produce an artifactual increase in the incidence of depressive disorders when estimated from admission data. Moreover, data were not analyzed separately for first psychiatric admissions only and could therefore reflect higher readmission rates for depressive disorders in more recent years. This study illustrates the caution necessary when hospital statistics are used to examine long-term trends in psychiatric or other disorders.

A second dataset provided information on more than 6,000 children and adolescents (8- to 18-year-olds) attending the child psychiatry department of the Maudsley Hospital in London, during the period from 1970 to 1990 (Fombonne, in press). Although the frequency of suicidal behaviors increased during that period, no increase was found for depressive phenomena. Because these data derived from the routinely completed item sheets of a tertiary referral center and because the time span encompassed is somewhat limited, these negative findings should be regarded in the context of their limitations. A third study examined secular changes in the age of onset of major depression and dysthymia of 92 children referred for psychiatric services in Pittsburgh between 1978 and 1987 (Kovacs & Gatsonis, 1994). As for adult studies, this sample of patients born after the mid-1960s showed a trend towards an earlier age of onset. This finding was interpreted as pointing toward an increased vulnerability to affective disorders among young children. Further replications are needed, however, owing to the selected nature and limited size of this sample.

METHODOLOGICAL AND ANALYTICAL PROBLEMS

In the ECA study, the finding of lower lifetime prevalence rates of psychiatric disorders among the oldest groups led to the systematic search for possible artifacts at the origin of the results. However, the findings were robust when various strategies were implemented to control for factors such as the attribution of psychiatric symptoms to physical illness, the dismissal of symptoms with low associated impairment, or mild cognitive impairment (Robins, Locke, & Regier, 1991).

Memory Artifacts

The most obvious alternative explanation of lower rates in the elderly is that they may have forgotten past episodes of disorder due to a longer time interval since onset. Simulation studies show that small but constant forgetting rates over time could create a spurious pattern of rates across birth cohorts comparable to that actually obtained with many datasets (Giuffra & Risch, 1994). Other studies showed that the test–retest reliability of lifetime rates decreases with time and that recent episodes of depression increase recall of past episodes (Aneshensel, Estrada, Hansell, & Clark, 1987; Prusoff, Merikangas, & Weissman, 1988). Because current rates of depressive disorders are lower among oldest respondents, they have a diminished likelihood of a recent depressive episode and thus are less likely to recall past episodes. This hypothesis is also supported by the analysis of Simon and VonKorff (1992) who showed that, at all ages, age of reported onset clustered in the 10 years prior to interview. Although this explanation has face validity, it does not account for the fact that the inverse correlation of lifetime rates of any psychiatric disorders with age was observed among the White subjects and not among the Black subjects (Robins, Locke, & Regier, 1991). Although rates of other psychiatric disorders among Black Americans did not decrease with age in general, their lifetime rates for affective disorders exhibited a pattern similar to other groups, with an increase in age-specific incidence in the youngest age groups. This suggests a relative specificity of this age-related phenomenon for depressive disorders.

In order to further examine whether apparent secular trends could be the result of age-related forgetting of earlier episodes, lifetime diagnoses were reevaluated by interviewers blind to the original assessments among 1,684 first-degree relatives of a family study, after a 6-year interval (Warshaw, Klerman, & Lavori, 1991a). A large number (37%) of diagnoses of depression disappeared on the second interview; however, age was not related to the amount of change. More recent episodes were more likely to be forgotten than older ones, and age of first onset showed high stability. In another test–retest study, older respondents were even found to decrease self-reported ages of first onset at reinterview (Farrer, Florio, Bruce, Leaf, & Weissman, 1989). These latter results make it unlikely that artifactual period effects would arise as a function of age-related systematic errors in reporting the age of first onset. If memory effects are major artifacts, they should apply to rates of affective disorders for every dataset. Results from the Puerto Rican study ran in the opposite direction (Canino et al., 1987). The decline with age of lifetime rates of depression was perceptible in studies where analyses were restricted to relatively recent birth cohorts (Bland et al., 1988; Joyce et al., 1990; Lavori et al., 1987). Findings in the prospective Lundby study (Hagnell et al., 1982) and the prospective follow-up sample of Coryell et al., (1992) could not be due to artifacts of recall. In the same vein, converging results from adolescent and children samples (Kovacs & Gatsonis, 1994; Lewinsohn et al., 1993; Ryan et al., 1992) argue against the possibility that artifactual memory effects could have by themselves produced such findings. It is, however, noteworthy that the magnitude of the findings is much less pronounced in prospective studies as compared to retrospective assessments derived from cross-sectional surveys.

Instrumentation

The accuracy of lifetime estimates obtained with psychiatric diagnostic interviews such as the DIS in the ECA-type studies was questioned (Parker, 1987). As suggested in the retest study (Warshaw et al., 1991a), the test–retest stability of lifetime rates is far from satisfactory and, in particular, low consistency in reports was found for depressive disorders (Anthony et al., 1985; Bromet, Dunn, Connell, Dew, & Schulberg, 1986; Helzer et al., 1985). The detailed examination of the sources of disagreement (clinical vs. community sample, lay vs. clinical interviewers) falls outside our objectives. Even though the absolute validity of lifetime rates is questionable due to measurement error, there is no suggestion that *trends* in rates could be a by-product of improper instrumentation. As imperfect as these instruments may be, we would need to postulate that their properties vary as a linear function of the age of the interviewees in order for the DIS to account for the trends in lifetime rates. There is no obvious plausible reason, and indeed no evidence, to hypothesize that interviews would operate differentially in the 30 to 39 and 40 to 49 age groups, for example. Furthermore, the increase in rates for recent birth cohorts was found in studies using other research instruments (Bebbington et al., 1989; Gershon et al., 1987; Klerman et al., 1985; Lavori et al., 1987; Lewinsohn et al., 1993; Maier et al., 1991; Ryan et al., 1992) or a clinical diagnosis (Hagnell et al., 1982). In the recent NCS study (Kessler et al., 1993), the structured diagnostic interview (Composite International Diagnostic Interview; CIDI) was purposefully modified to facilitate recall of past episodes, yet the results were in line with the ECA findings. The increases in levels of depressed mood reported by multi-informant assessments in Achenbach and Howell (1993) also support the convergent validity of the results and argue against a simple artifact of self-report measures.

SUBSTANTIVE EXPLANATIONS OF SECULAR TRENDS

Psychological Mindedness

Differences in the psychological mindedness of younger and older subjects and in the way they label depressive descriptions was proposed as an explanation of secular increases in rates. On presentation with case vignettes portraying major depression, older subjects were less likely to recognize these descriptions as an emotional or psychological problem (Hasin & Link, 1988). Veroff, Kulka, and Douvan's work (1981) suggests that the youngest generation relies less on classical role standards and more on self-expression as a basis of self-definition; these changes were paralleled by increased psychological orientation and help-seeking behaviors oriented toward mental health experts in the context of problems among young adults. However, no association was found between age and labeling in other studies (Lewinsohn et al., 1993; Robins, Locke, & Regier, 1991), although the former study is limited to adolescents. Because the decrease in lifetime rates is manifest during midlife years, it is unlikely to account entirely for the findings. Nevertheless, the data clearly suggest that differential psychological orientation can be a significant factor in the secular increase among the young.

Institutionalization

It is theoretically possible that higher rates of depression among the young occur because the older persons with early onset depression are more likely to be institutionalized, and thus are not in general population surveys. However, this is unlikely to be a plausible explanation of the findings because depressive disorders rarely lead to long-term hospitalization in psychiatric institutions. In addition, the last two decades have witnessed the development of efficient treatment methods, a fact that, taken in conjunction with a general trend in occidental countries to close down psychiatric beds in favor of outpatient care runs against this possibility. In the psychiatric facility sample of the ECA study, the rate of major depression was not significantly different from that of the main sample (Weissman et al., 1991). Simon and VonKorff (1992) calculated that rates of institutionalization for 70-year-old women with a history of depression would have to be 16 times higher than those of younger persons to explain the age trends in the ECA data.

Differential Migration and Selective Mortality

Other explanations of the apparent cohort effect such as differential migration or selective mortality are also not easily supported. Urban rural differences are not unequivocal for depressive disorders, and other migration effects that may influence inclusion in study samples are also unclear. An explanation based on selective mortality would have to assume implausibly enormous differences in magnitude by age group. Simon and VonKorff (1992) have estimated that, even with conservative assumptions, aggregate mortality rates for 40-year-old women with an history of depression should be eight times higher than in the general population in order to account for their findings. Yet studies of increases in mortality rates among community residents with affective disorders have shown relative lower risks, not in excess of 2 (Murphy, Monson, Olivier, Sobol, & Leighton, 1987).

The Issue of Specificity

One important question raised by these reports is that of specificity. To what extent is the increase in rates of psychiatric disorders confined to depressive conditions? Alternatively, does this increase reflect a general trend for psychiatric dysfunction to be more prevalent now? Using the ECA data, separate analyses of manic disorders produced the same results of a higher prevalence among recent birth cohorts (Lasch, Weissman, Wickramaratne, & Bruce, 1990), suggesting that the whole range of affective disorders is concerned, as already found in one family study (Gershon et al., 1987). Examination of the same ECA data also indicated that rates of nonaffective psychiatric disorders were higher in the youngest than the oldest cohorts, as was particularly shown for antisocial personality (Robins, Tipp, & Przybeck, 1991).

Few studies reported simultaneously on trends for several psychiatric disorders. The recent reanalysis of ECA data by Simon and VonKorff (1992) showed that prevalence rates of depression, panic disorder and schizophrenia exhibited a six- to eight-fold increase among subjects between the ages of 36 and 45 as compared to those over 65 years, whereas similar but less dramatic findings applied to alcohol use and phobia. These trends in nonaffective disorders were not attributable to comorbidity with depression because the patterns remained unchanged after exclusion of comorbid cases (Simon & VonKorff, 1992). They further reported analyses of lifetime rates for individual psychiatric symptoms and found that lifetime rates again peaked among the youngest cohorts for almost all of them, with roughly a twofold increase in rates of reported symptoms of depression, schizophrenia, and alcohol use among youngest respondents compared to oldest subjects, and nearly a threefold increment for symptoms of mania. This uniform pattern applying both to psychiatric symptoms and disorders with different epidemiological correlates provides evidence for a lack of specificity of the findings and suggests either a general increase in psychological dysfunction over the last decades or, alternatively, pervasive methodological bias. The latter explanation is less likely to account entirely for this pattern, in view of similar findings stemming from two repeat cross-sectional surveys of U.S. children and adolescents using different measurement approaches (Achenbach & Howell, 1993).

Finally, any artifact of measurement of lifetime diagnoses in the epidemiological studies reviewed here does not explain the temporal trends in the suicide rates mentioned previously. Although suicide can occur in psychiatric disorders other than depression, the proportion of depressive syndromes and disorders found among suicidal youth is high and some evidence suggests this proportion has increased over time. Thus, the finding of increased suicide rates among youth gives indirect support to the increase in depression; certainly, it does not invalidate it.

Age, Period, or Cohort Effects?

Interpretation of time trends is far from easy. As for suicide rates (Newman & Dyck, 1988), temporal trends may reflect age, period, or cohort effects, and their interactions. Changes in rates of disorders over time may reflect variations in the age structure of the population under study when the incidence of the disorder varies with age (age effect), a historical increase of incidence as in epidemics and other historical events (period effect), or an increased vulnerability of groups of subjects who have shared a common experience, in particular as they were born from the same generation (cohort effect). Although they appear conceptually different, these three effects incorporate time as a common scale, though their measurements proceed from different origins. Thus, one difficulty in disentangling these effects lies in their interdependence so that any one effect may always be expressed as a function of the two others (i.e., age = period − cohort). The fundamental statistical difficulty is to obtain independent estimates of the three effects. Because there exists no unique solution, several combinations of parameter estimates will provide comparable fitted rates in modeling techniques. Attempts have been made to solve this problem of identifiability but caution is needed on the underlying mathematical assumptions lest they lack biological plausibility (Clayton & Schifflers, 1987; Holford, 1992).

For example, although time-dependent variables should be treated as continuous variables, a common practice is to create time intervals and age groupings where the exact relationship between the variables no longer holds true (Clayton & Hill, 1993). Changes in birth rates may mimic cohort effects and lead to spurious increases in rates of disorder (see Clayton & Schifflers, 1987). The problem can be further complicated when groupings of unequal width are used, as is usually done for the extreme of the age distributions to compensate for lower sample sizes. Although these potential statistical artifacts are recognized, little attention has been paid to them in the psychiatric literature. For example, examination of the robustness of the findings within and across datasets for different age and time groupings would be easy to perform, but no attempt has been made in that direction. Only one study used year of birth as a continuous variable to test for "cohort" effects (Ryan et al., 1992). However, as recognized by the authors, cohort and period effects were indistinguishable and the statistical analysis was based on another strong, and indeed unrealistic, mathematical assumption of a constant multiplicative annual increment of the risk across the study period. Moreover, the value of estimated effects based on this small sample (26 cases of depression out of a sample of 163 siblings) were higher than those from larger family datasets and, again, this calls for prudence in the use and interpretation of statistical models.

As far as temporal trends in depression are concerned, the findings are sparse and contradictory. A large dataset analyzed by Wickramaratne et al. (1989) suggests that a sharp increase in the risk of depression applies to the cohort of women born between 1935 and 1945, and to that of men born between 1935 and 1954. In addition, the authors identified a period effect between 1960 and 1980 for both sexes. These results were established on the White subsample of the ECA study, and they are somewhat at variance with the age and period effects described by Lavori et al. (1987), with those of Gershon et al. (1987) who suggest a single post-1940s birth cohort effect, and with those of Warshaw et al. (1991b) which indicate a period effect starting in the mid-1960s and an age period interaction for both sexes. In a recent reanalysis of some of these data using different statistical approaches (Cross National Collaborative Group, 1992), the period effects found by Lavori et al. (1987) and Warshaw et al. (1991b) were not replicated, reflecting the vulnerability of these separations of age period cohort effects to the model assumptions. In the follow-up of unaffected relatives from a family study (Coryell et al., 1992), the study design ruled out a period effect, at least for these particular years, but age and cohort effects could not be distinguished. One interesting finding of the study of Lewinsohn et al. (1993) was also that the relapse rate was significantly higher for the more recent birth cohorts. Insofar as relapse is independent of the particular time period, this result argues for a true cohort effect. In general, when a study investigation is confined to a single period, age and cohort are completely confounded.

There is no emerging pattern in the available analyses, and the preliminary results from U.S. datasets clearly warrant replication. The findings of the recent international collaborative study (Cross National Collaborative Group, 1992) appear to support the notion of temporal increases in rates of depressive disorders. However, the relative lack of specificity of the findings and the inconsistencies with other studies strongly suggest that statistical artifacts may at least partially account for the results. A more stringent test of the statistical solution found could have been performed using the large ECA sample to replicate the results across the five U.S. sites included within this study. Using this natural experiment where homogeneity of instrumentation, sampling, and background characteristics would have been relatively high, a more robust test of the validity of the linear and nonlinear period and cohort effects parameters could be provided.

Beyond the still imperfect development of sophisticated modeling techniques and computer technologies, the pursuit of a statistical solution to the age period cohort analysis appears also pointless. All these variables have time as a common scale, and time cannot be an explanatory variable. Time only acts as a proxy indicator for unmeasured causal influences that may be pinpointed using natural experiments, where one variable is allowed to fluctuate with the others fixed. There also seems to exist an unrecognized assumption that rising rates of depression reflect a single underlying mechanism, whereas it is more likely that a mixture of processes operate, thereby rendering more precarious the attempt to identify a unique solution. Thus, the regular linear increase in rates of depressive disorders, distinct from cohort and period effects, found recently in 12 contrasted samples is in itself unlikely to have any meaningful biological, psychopathological, or social interpretability. This lack of plausibility cautions against the use of statistical models alone.

CONCLUSION

The evidence thus far is in favor of an increase in depression in the most recent birth cohorts. Convergent findings from a wide array of studies conducted with various designs, in different countries, and with heterogeneous measures argue for the validity of this finding. However, the actual magnitude of this secular change is unknown and most probably small because there is also evidence that a sizeable portion of the reported increase is in fact due to artifacts and study methods effects. Furthermore, the extent to which this increased incidence applies specifically, or more specifically, to depressive phenomena remains to be established. Although one study provided some evidence on specific effects (Ryan et al., 1992), other findings suggest that other psychiatric disorders, be they affective (Lasch et al., 1990) or not (Robins, Locke, & Regier, 1991; Robins, Tipp, & Przybeck, 1991), exhibited the same recent trends. Reports that could *simultaneously* assess trends of a range of problem behaviors (Achenbach & Howell, 1993) or of psychiatric disorders (Simon & VonKorff, 1992) do not argue strongly for the specificity of the increase in depressive conditions. The current evidence still suggests that women of all ages and cohorts are at greater risk of depression than men (Leon et al., 1993) but some data point toward a trend for a closing of the gender difference in the incidence of depressive disorders for the youngest birth cohorts (Weissman et al., 1993).

The epidemiological investigations of these secular trends are somewhat disappointing in that no clear theory has emerged as to the nature of the factor(s) responsible for these changes. The negative findings in three studies (Canino et al., 1987; Karno et al., 1987; Lee et al., 1987) suggest that broad cultural and societal differences are implicated and that less affluent and more traditional populations are relatively protected. Conversely, the increased incidence in the Lundby study corresponded to a period of economic transformation and social changes (migration toward the city, more employment in the services); the authors conveyed their impression of a link between the two phenomena but were unable to empirically examine such a connection (Hagnell et al., 1982). In the same vein, attempts were made to relate fluctuations in rates of depressive disorders in a Lebanese sample to periods of war and political instability (Cross National Collaborative Group, 1992). This association, hypothesized in the smallest and most atypical sample of this collaborative investigation, measured with an instrument where low test–retest reliability had been reported particularly for dating past events (Karam et al., 1991), and with no control of selection factors such as differential migration or mortality, should be viewed so far as highly speculative. A more informative analysis of the five ECA sites, capitalizing on diverging trends over time in some subsamples (i.e., Hispanic-American and White subsamples in Los Angeles) and on the availability in all ECA sites of indices of social and economic indicators may yet be performed. Changes have occurred in the biological, developmental, familial, and social context of adolescence that provide clues as to candidate mechanisms that could explain such time trends (Fombonne, 1995). Further research relying on prospective longitudinal designs and more sophisticated measurement strategies is however needed to develop and test models that may account for the development of depressive conditions among young people. It would also appear useful for future projects surveying the health of various populations regularly to include a systematic measure of depression as a sensitive indicator of mental health.

REFERENCES

Achenbach, T. M., & Howell, C. T. (1993). Are American children's problems getting worse? A 13-year comparison. *Journal of the American Academy of Child and Adolescent Psychiatry, 32*(6), 1145–1154.

American Psychiatric Association. (1987). *Diagnostic and statistical manual of mental disorders—DSM-III-R* (3rd rev. ed.). Washington, DC: Author.

American Psychiatric Association. (1994). *Diagnostic and statistical manual of mental disorders—DSM-IV* (4th ed.). Washington, DC: Author.

Aneshensel, C. S., Estrada, A. L., Hansell, M. J., & Clark, V. A. (1987). Social psychological aspects of reporting behavior: Lifetime depressive episode reports. *Journal of Health and Social Behavior, 28*, 232–246.

Angst, J. (1985). Switch from depression to mania—A record study over decades between 1920–1982. *Psychopathology, 18*, 140–154.

Anthony, J. C., Folstein, M., Romanoski, A. J., Von Korff, M. R., Nestadt, G. R., Chahal, R., Merchant, R., Brown, C. H., Shapiro, S., Kramer, M., & Gruenberg, E. M. (1985). Comparison of the lay Diagnostic Interview Schedule and a standardized psychiatric diagnosis. *Archives of General Psychiatry, 42*, 667–675.

Barraclough, B. M., Bunch, J., Nelson, B., & Sainsbury, P. (1974). A hundred cases of suicide: Clinical aspects. *British Journal of Psychiatry, 125*, 355–373.

Bebbington, P., Katz, R., McGuffin, P., Tennant, C., & Hurry, J. (1989). The risk of minor depression before age 65: Results from a community survey. *Psychological Medicine, 19*, 393–400.

Bland, R. C., Orn, H., & Newman, S. C. (1988). Lifetime prevalence of psychiatric disorders in Edmonton. *Acta Psychiatrica Scandinavica (Suppl. 338), 77*, 24–32.

Brent, D. A., Perper, J. A., & Allman, C. J. (1987). Alcohol, firearms, and suicide among youth: Temporal trends in Allegheny County, Pennsylvania, 1960 to 1983. *Journal of the American Medical Association, 257*, 3369–3372.

Brent, D. A., Perper, J. A., Goldstein, C. E., Kolko, D. J., Allan, M. J., Allman, C. J., & Zelenak, J. P. (1988). Risk factors for adolescent suicide: A comparison of adolescent suicide victims with suicidal inpatients. *Archives of General Psychiatry, 45*, 581–588.

Brent, D. A., Perper, J. A., Moritz, G., Baugher, M., Schweers, J., & Roth, C. (1994). Suicide in affectively ill adolescents: A case-control study. *Journal of Affective Disorders, 31*, 193–202.

Bromet, E. J., Dunn, L. O., Connell, M. M., Dew, M. A., & Schulberg, H. C. (1986). Long-term reliability of diagnosing lifetime major depression in a community sample. *Archives of General Psychiatry, 43*, 435–440.

Canino, G. J., Bird, H. R., Shrout, P. E., Rubio-Stipec, M., Bravo, M., Martinez, R., Sesman, M., & Guevara, L. M. (1987). The prevalence of specific psychiatric disorders in Puerto Rico. *Archives of General Psychiatry, 44*, 727–735.

Carlson, G. A., Rich, C. L., Grayson, P., & Fowler, R. C. (1991). Secular trends in psychiatric diagnoses of suicide victims. *Journal of Affective Disorders, 21*, 127–132.

Chen, C. N., Wong, J., Lee, N., Chan-Ho, M.-W., Tak-Fai, Lau J., & Fung, M. (1993). The Shatin community mental health survey in Hong Kong: II. Major findings. *Archives of General Psychiatry, 50,* 125–133.

Clayton, D., & Hills, M. (1993). *Statistical models in epidemiology.* Oxford, England: Oxford University Press.

Clayton, D., & Schifflers, E. (1987). Models for temporal variation in cancer rates: II. Age-period-cohort models. *Statistics in Medicine, 6,* 469–481.

Coryell, W., Endicott, J., & Keller, M. (1992). Major depression in a nonclinical sample: Demographic and clinical risk factors for first onset. *Archives of General Psychiatry, 49,* 117–125.

Cross National Collaborative Group. (1992). The changing rate of major depression: Cross-national comparisons. *Journal of the American Medical Association, 268,* 3098–3105.

Diekstra, R., Kienhorst, C., & de Wilde, E. (1995). Suicide and suicidal behaviours among adolescents. In M. Rutter & D. Smith (Eds.), *Psychosocial disorders in young people: Time trends and their causes* (pp. 686–781). Chichester, England: Wiley.

Faravelli, C., Guerrini, D., Aiazzi, L., Incerpi, G., & Pallanti, S. (1990). Epidemiology of mood disorders: A community survey in Florence. *Journal of Affective Disorders, 20,* 135–141.

Farrer, L. A., Florio, L. P., Bruce, M. L., Leaf, P. J., & Weissman, M. M. (1989). Reliability of self-reported age at onset of major depression. *Journal of Psychiatric Research, 23,* 35–47.

Fombonne, E. (1994). Increased rates of depression: Update of epidemiological findings and analytical problems. *Acta Psychiatrica Scandinavica, 90,* 145–156.

Fombonne, E. (1995). Depressive disorders: Time trends and possible explanatory mechanisms. In M. Rutter & D. Smith (Eds.), *Psychosocial disorders in young people: Time trends and their causes* (pp. 544–615). Chichester, England: Wiley.

Fombonne, E. (1998). The management of depression in children and adolescents. In S. Checkley (Ed.), *The management of depression* (pp. 345–363). Oxford, England: Blackwell Science.

Fombonne, E. (in press). Suicidal behaviours in vulnerable male adolescents: Time trends and their correlates *British Journal of Psychiatry.*

Gershon, E. S., Hamovit, J. H., Guroff, J. J., & Nurnberger, J. I. (1987). Birth-cohort changes in manic and depressive disorders in relatives of bipolar and schizoaffective affective patients. *Archives of General Psychiatry, 44,* 314–319.

Giuffra, L. A., & Risch N. (1994). Diminished recall and the cohort effect of major depression: A simulation study. *Psychological Medicine, 24,* 375–383.

Gurin, G., Veroff, J., & Feld, S. C. (1960). *Americans view their mental health.* New York: Basic Books.

Hagnell, O., Lanke, J., Rorsman, B., & Ojesjö, L. (1982). Are we entering an age of melancholy? Depressive illnesses in a prospective epidemiological study over 25 years: The Lundby study, Sweden. *Psychological Medicine, 12,* 279–289.

Harrington, R., Fudge, H., Rutter, M., Pickles, A., & Hill, J. (1990). Adult outcomes of childhood and adolescent depression: I. Psychiatric status. *Archives of General Psychiatry, 47,* 465–473.

Harrington, R., Rutter, M., & Fombonne, E. (1996). Developmental pathways in depression: Multiple meanings antecedents and endpoints. *Development and Psychopathology, 8,* 601–616.

Hasin, D., & Link, B. (1988). Age and recognition of depression: Implications for a cohort effect in major depression. *Psychological Medicine, 18,* 683–688.

Helzer, J. E., Robins, L. N., McEvoy, L. T., Spitznagel, E. L., Stoltzman, R. K., Farmer, A., & Brockington, I. F. (1985). A comparison of clinical and diagnostic interview schedule diagnoses. *Archives of General Psychiatry, 42,* 657–666.

Holford, T. R. (1992). Analysing the temporal effects of age, period and cohort. *Statistical Methods in Medical Research, 1,* 317–337.

Holinger, P. C., & Offer, D. (1991). Sociodemographic, epidemiologic, and individual attributes. In L. Davidson & M. Linnoila (Eds), *Risk factors for youth suicide* (pp. 3–17). New York: Hemisphere Publishing.

Hwu, H.-G., Yeh, E.-K., & Chang, L.-Y. (1989). Prevalence of psychiatric disorders in Taiwan defined by the Chinese Diagnostic Interview Schedule. *Acta Psychiatrica Scandinavica, 79,* 136–147.

Joyce, P. R., Oakley-Browne, M. A., Wells, J. E., Bushnell, J. A., & Hornblow, A. R. (1990). Birth cohort trends in major depression: Increasing rates and earlier onset in New Zealand. *Journal of Affective Disorders, 18,* 83–89.

Karam, E. G., Barakeh, M., & Karam, A. N. (1991). The Arabic diagnostic interview schedule. *Revue Médicale Libanaise, 3,* 28–30.

Karno, M., Hough, R. L., Burnam, M. A., Escobar, J. I., Timbers, D. M., Santana, F., & Boyd, J. H. (1987). Lifetime prevalence of specific psychiatric disorders among Mexican Americans and non-Hispanic Whites in Los Angeles. *Archives of General Psychiatry, 44,* 695–701.

Kessler, R. C., McGonagle, K. A., Swartz, M., Blazer, D. G., & Nelson, C. B. (1993). Sex and depression in the National Comorbidity Survey: I. Lifetime prevalence, chronicity and recurrence. *Journal of Affective Disorders, 29,* 85–96.

Klerman, G. L. (1988). The current age of youthful melancholia: Evidence for increase in depression among adolescents and young adults. *British Journal of Psychiatry, 152,* 4–14.

Klerman, G. L., Lavori, P. W., Rice, J., Reich, T., Endicott, J., Andreasen, N. C., Keller, M. B., & Hirschfield, R. M. A. (1985). Birth-cohort trends in rates of major depressive disorder among relatives of patients with affective disorder. *Archives of General Psychiatry, 42,* 689–693.

Klerman, G. L., & Weissman, M. M. (1989). Increasing rates of depression. *Journal of American Medical Association, 261,* 2229–2235.

Kovacs, M., & Gatsonis, C. (1994). Secular trends in age at onset of major depressive disorder in a clinical sample of children. *Journal of Psychiatric Research, 28,* 319–329.

Kovacs, M., & Puig-Antich, J. (1991). "Major psychiatric disorders" as risk factors in youth suicide. In L. Davidson & M. Linnoila (Eds.), *Risk factors in youth suicide* (pp. 127–143). New York: Hemisphere Publishing.

Lasch, K., Weissman, M., Wickramaratne, P., & Bruce, M. L. (1990). Birth-cohort changes in the rates of mania. *Psychiatry Research, 33,* 31–37.

Lavori, P. W., Klerman, G L., Keller, M. B., Reich, T., Rice J., & Endicott J. (1987). Age-period-cohort analysis of secular trends in onset of major depression: Findings in siblings of patients with major affective disorder. *Journal of Psychiatric Research, 21*(1), 23–35.

Lee, C. K., Kwak, Y. S., Rhee, H., Kim, Y. S., Han, J. H., Choi, J. O., & Lee, Y. H. (1987). The nationwide epidemiological study of mental disorders in Korea. *Journal of Korean Medical Sciences, 2,* 19–34.

Leon, A. C., Klerman, G. L., & Wickramaratne, P. (1993). Continuing female predominance in depressive illness. *American Journal of Public Health, 83*(5), 754–757.

Lépine, J.-P., Lellouch, J., Lovell, A., Teherani, M., Ha, C., Verdier-Taillefer, M.-H., Rambourg, N., & Lempérière, T. (1989). Anxiety and depressive disorders in a French population: Methodology and preliminary results. *Psychiatrie et Psychobiologie, 4,* 267–274.

Lester, D. (1991). Suicide across the life span. A look at international trends. In A. A. Leenaars (Ed.), *Life span perspectives of suicide: Time-lines in the suicide process* (pp. 71–80). New York: Plenum Press.

Lewinsohn, P. M., Rohde, P., Seeley, J. R., & Fischer, S. A. (1993). Age-cohort changes in the lifetime occurrence of depression and other mental disorders. *Journal of Abnormal Psychology, 102*(1), 110–120.

Maier, W., Hallmayer, J., Lichtermann, Philipp, M., & Klingler, T. (1991). The impact of the endogenous subtype on the familial aggregation of unipolar depression. *European Archives of Psychiatry and Clinical Neurosciences, 240,* 355–362.

Marttunen, M. J., Aro, H. M., Henriksson, M. M., & Lönnqvist, J. K. (1991). Mental disorders in adolescent suicide: *DSM–III–R* axes I and II diagnoses in suicides among 13- to 19-year-olds in Finland. *Archives of General Psychiatry, 48,* 834–839.

McClure, G. M. G. (1984). Recent trends in suicide amongst the young. *British Journal of Psychiatry, 144,* 134–138.

McIntosh, J. (1991). Epidemiology of suicide in the United States. In A. A. Leenaars (Ed.), *Life span perspectives of suicide: Time-lines in the suicide process* (pp. 55–69). New York: Plenum Press.

Murphy, J. M., Monson, R. R., Olivier, D. C., Sobol, A. M., & Leighton, A. H. (1987). Mortality risk and psychiatric disorders: Results of a general population survey. *Archives of General Psychiatry, 44,* 473–480.

Murphy, J. M., Sobol, A. M., Neff, R. K., Olivier, D. C., & Leighton, A. H. (1984). Stability of prevalence: Depression and anxiety disorders. *Archives of General Psychiatry, 41,* 990–997.

Newman, S. C., & Dyck, R. J. (1988). On the age-period-cohort analysis of suicide rates. *Psychological Medicine, 18,* 677–681.

Oakley-Browne, M. A., Joyce, P. R., Wells, J. E., Bushnell, J. A., & Hornblow, A. R. (1989). Christchurch psychiatric epidemiology study: Part II. Six month and other period prevalences of specific psychiatric disorders. *Australian and New Zealand Journal of Psychiatry, 23,* 327–340.

Parker, G. (1987). Are the lifetime prevalence estimates in the ECA study accurate? *Psychological Medicine, 17,* 275–282.

Petersen, A. C., Compass, B., Brooks-Gunn, J., Stemmler, M., Ey, S., & Grant, K. (1993). Depression in adolescence. *American Psychologist, 48,* 155–168.

Prusoff, B. A., Merikangas, K. R., & Weissman, M. M. (1988). Lifetime prevalence and age of onset: Recall 4 years later. *Journal of Psychiatric Research, 22,* 107–117.

Rao, U., Ryan, N. D., Birmaher, B., Dahl, R. E., Williamson, D. E., Kaufman, J., Rao, R., & Nelson, B. (1995). Unipolar depression in adolescence: Clinical outcome in adulthood. *Journal of the American Academy of Child and Adolescent Psychiatry, 34,* 566–578.

Rao, U., Weissman, M. M., Martin, J. A., & Hammond, R. W. (1993). Childhood depression and risk of suicide: A preliminary report of a longitudinal study. *Journal of the American Academy of Child and Adolescent Psychiatry, 32,* 21–27.

Rich, C. L., Young, D., & Fowler, R. C. (1986). San Diego suicide study: I. Young versus old subjects. *Archives of General Psychiatry, 43,* 577–582.

Roberts, R. E., Lee, E. S., & Roberts, C. R. (1991). Changes in prevalence of depressive symptoms in Alameda County. *Journal of Aging and Health, 3,* 66–86.

Robins, L. N., Helzer, J. E., Weissman, M. M., Orvaschel, H., Gruenberg, E., Burke, J. D., & Regier, D. A. (1984). Lifetime prevalence of specific psychiatric disorders in three sites. *Archives of General Psychiatry, 41,* 949–958.

Robins, L. N., Locke, B. Z., & Regier, D. A. (1991). An overview of psychiatric disorders in America. In L. N. Robins & D. A. Regier (Eds.), *Psychiatric disorders in America: The Epidemiologic Catchment Area study* (pp. 328–366). New York: The Free Press.

Robins, L. N., Tipp, J., & Przybeck, T. (1991). Antisocial personality. In L. N. Robins & D. A. Regier (Eds.), *Psychiatric disorders in America: The Epidemiologic Catchment Area study* (pp. 258–290). New York: The Free Press.

Rodgers, W. (1982). Trends in reported happiness within demographically defined subgroups, 1957–78. *Social Forces, 60*(3), 826–842.

Runeson, B. (1989). Mental disorders in youth suicide: *DSM–III–R* axes I and II. *Acta Psychiatrica Scandinavica, 79,* 490–497.

Ryan, N. D., Williamson, D. E., Iyengar, S., Orvaschel, H., Reich,T., Dahl, R. E., & Puig-Antich, J. (1992). A secular increase in child and adolescent onset affective disorder. *Journal of the American Academy of Child and Adolescent Psychiatry, 31,* 600–605.

Shaffer, D. (1988). The epidemiology of teen suicide: An examination of risk factors. *Journal of Clinical Psychiatry (Suppl. 9)*, *49*, 36–41.

Shaffer, D., Gould, M. S., Fisher, P., Trautman, P., Moreau, D., Kleinman, M., & Flory, M. (1996). Psychiatric diagnosis in child and adolescent suicide. *Archives of General Psychiatry, 53*, 339–348.

Shafii, M., Carrigan, S., Whittinghil, J. R., & Derrick, A. (1985). Psychological autopsy of completed suicide in children and adolescents. *American Journal of Psychiatry, 142*, 1061–1064.

Simon, G. E., & VonKorff, M. (1992). Reevaluation of secular trends in depression rates. *American Journal of Epidemiology, 135*, 1411–1422.

Srole, L., & Fischer, A. K. (1980). The Midtown Manhattan longitudinal study vs. "the Mental Paradise Lost" doctrine. *Archives of General Psychiatry, 37*, 209–221.

Veroff, J., Douvan, E., & Kulka, R. (1981). *The inner American*. New York: Basic Books.

Veroff, J., Kulka, R. A., & Douvan, E. (1981). *Mental health in America: Patterns of help-seeking from 1957 to 1976*. New York: Basic Books.

Warshaw, M. G., Klerman, G. L., & Lavori, P. W. (1991a). Are secular trends in major depression an artifact of recall? *Journal of Psychiatric Research, 25*, 141–151.

Warshaw, M. G., Klerman, G. L., & Lavori, P. W. (1991b). The use of conditional probabilities to examine age-period-cohort data: Further evidence for a period effect in major depressive disorder. *Journal of Affective Disorders, 23*, 119–129.

Weissman, M. M., Bland, R., Joyce, P. R., Newman, S., Wells, J. E., & Wittchen, H.-U. (1993). Sex differences in rates of depression: Cross-national perspectives. *Journal of Affective Disorders, 29*, 77–84.

Weissman, M., Livingston, Bruce M., Leaf, P. J., Florio, L. P., & Holzer, C. (1991). Affective disorders. In L. N. Robins & D. A. Regier (Eds.), *Psychiatric disorders in America: The Epidemiologic Catchment Area study* (pp. 53–80). New York: The Free Press.

Wells, J. E., Bushnell, J. A., Hornblow, A. R., Joyce, P. R., & Oakley-Browne, M. A. (1989). Christchurch psychiatric epidemiology study: Part I. Methodology and lifetime prevalence for specific psychiatric disorders. *Australian and New Zealand Journal of Psychiatry, 23*, 315–326.

Wickramaratne, P. J., Weissman, M. M., Leaf, P. J., & Holford, T. R. (1989). Age, period and cohort effects on the risk of major depression: Results from five United States communities. *Journal of Clinical Epidemiology, 42*, 333–343.

Wittchen, H. U., Esau, C. A., von Zerssen, D., Krieg, J. D., & Zaudig, M. (1992). Lifetime and six-month prevalence of mental disorders in the Munich follow-up study. *European Archives of Psychiatry Clinical Sciences, 241*, 273–282.

World Health Organization. (1992). *The ICD-10 classification of mental and behavioural disorders: Clinical description and diagnostic guidelines*. Geneva: Author.

Chapter 7

Coming of Age in the 1990s: Influences of Contemporary Stressors on Major Depression in Young Adults

Helen Z. Reinherz
Rose M. Giaconia
Michelle S. Wasserman
Amy B. Silverman
Lisa Burton
Simmons College

The study discussed in this chapter was designed to assess the relationship of contemporary stressors to the course, onset, and impact of major depression in a community population of young adults. This research focus is particularly compelling because the traditional stressors of entrance into adult responsibilities are augmented by the rapidly changing social and economic context of the 1990s. Many recent studies emphasized the vulnerability of contemporary young adults to the onset of psychiatric disorder (Christie et al., 1988, Giaconia et al., 1994). Additionally, the young adult period also represents a time when existing disorders originating in childhood and adolescence may continue (American Psychiatric Association, 1994).

Major depression has been identified as a disorder that presents a greater risk for the current generation of young adults compared to previous generations (Burke, Burke, Rae, & Regier, 1991; Blazer, Kessler, McGonagle, & Swartz, 1994). In addition to reflecting secular trends in the increased prevalence of depression in younger age groups (Robins, Locke, & Regier, 1991), these findings may also represent the higher levels of stress experienced by contemporary 18- to 25-year-olds (Mirowsky & Ross, 1992). For the young adult coming of age in the 1990s, there are several emerging contemporary social and economic stressors that may impede the achievement of expected developmental goals and result in social and occupational impairment. Such failure to meet societal and personal expectations also increases the risk for psychiatric disorders (Dohrenwend, 1974; Fiske & Chiriboga, 1990; Paykel, 1984; Rabkin & Struening, 1976; Rutter & Rutter, 1993).

The role of psychosocial stressors in the onset and course of psychiatric disorder was examined extensively (Dohrenwend, 1974; Fiske & Chiriboga, 1990; Paykel, 1984; Rabkin & Struening, 1976). The reciprocal relationship between vulnerability and stress was likened by Fiske and Chiriboga (1990) to a type of camel's back syndrome. The accumulation of stressors tends to accentuate pre-existing personality characteristics and vulnerabilities and may lead to a condition where a new stressor will precipitate a potentiated reaction (Coyne & Whiffen, 1995; Elder & Caspi, 1990; Hammen, 1991). These links between stressful life events and onset of depression were consistently reported in recent studies (Brown, Bifulco, & Harris, 1987; Dohrenwend, Shrout, Link, Skodol, & Stueve, 1995; Lewinsohn, Gotlib, & Seeley, 1995; Monroe & Depue, 1991; Potthoff, Holohand, & Joiner, 1995). In addition, negative life events were also associated with higher risk of relapse (Hooley, Orley, & Teasdale, 1986; Lewinsohn, Clarke, Seeley, & Rohde, 1994; Swindle, Cronkite, & Moos, 1989).

CONTEMPORARY YOUNG ADULT STRESSORS

Although the transition to adulthood can present major challenges, there is reason to believe that the current social environment confronting today's young adults contains special challenges. In a recent volume, Cote and Allahar (1996) described the unique external influences of the 1990s and portrayed today's young adults as a disenfranchised, economically manipulated group. Among the negative forces described are increased exposure to violence and "higher levels of un-and-underemployment, epidemic levels of suicide . . . all part of the same problem that leaves many young people aimlessly groping to come of age in the 1990's" (Cote & Allahar, 1996).

The completion of formal schooling and entrance into the workforce mark the end of the transition from youth to adulthood (Starr, 1986). For both contemporary men and women, work constitutes a powerful source of both satisfaction and stress (Rutter & Rutter, 1993). Because one's job is a major component of self-identity in today's society (Everly & Smith, 1987), dissatisfaction with unemployment may have a profound effect. People who are dissatisfied with their jobs have lower self-esteem, are more depressed, feel more hopeless, and rate their life satisfaction lower than those content with their work (Winefield, Winefield, Tiggemann, & Goldney, 1991). Unemployed young adults are three to six times more likely than employed young adults to experience a psychiatric disorder (Bland, Stebelsky, Orn, & Newman, 1988; Finlay-Jones & Eckhardt, 1984; Zales, 1985). Frequent job changes, termination, quitting a job without having another one, and frequent absences or tardiness from work are all significantly related to a lifetime diagnosis of one or more psychiatric disorders (Bland et al., 1988). Because unemployment tends to make people more vulnerable to the effects of other stressful life events, the risk for depression is greatest when unemployment coincides with other stressors (Rutter & Rutter, 1993).

Inability to complete an educational program also may have serious consequences for a young adult. Results of the Epidemiologic Catchment Area (ECA) study suggest that both high school and college dropouts are at greater risk than graduates for psychiatric disorder (Helzer, Burnham, & McEvoy, 1991; Karno & Golding, 1991; Robins, Tipp, & Przybeck, 1991). Young adults who fail to meet their own educational goals as well as those placed on them by familial and societal expectations, are faced with increasing levels of stress as they struggle to find a place for themselves within the framework of society.

Separating from parents and establishing intimate relationships of one's own are major tasks necessary for the young adult. Conflict between family of origin and the young adult often arises regarding the optimal time for leaving the parents' home (Goldscheider & Goldscheider, 1993). Conflicts arise not only when young adults want an independent residence before their parents feel it is appropriate, but also when they find they are compelled to return to live with parents due to contemporary economic pressures (Schnaiberg & Goldenberg, 1989). Trying to forge their own identity is particularly difficult for young adults forced back into their childhood living environment.

Among the primary developmental tasks of young adulthood is the establishing of intimate relationships. The inability to achieve such relationships or the severing of close personal ties present stressors for young adults. Valentiner, Holohan, and Moos (1994) noted that the ending of a romantic relationship was cited as one of the most important problems experienced in the past year by college students.

The current research was designed to examine the links between depression in a community population of young adults and current young adult stressors. The specific aims of the study were to (a) determine the prevalence, onset, and severity of major depression in a community population of young adults (age 21); (b) examine relationships between the stressors of young adulthood and major depression; and (c) identify the recency of mental health services received by young adults with major depression.

METHOD

Sample

The 375 young adults were participants in an ongoing longitudinal study that began in 1977 when they entered kindergarten in one public school system in a predominantly working class community in the northeast

United States. Additional data collection waves, using multiple informants (subjects, parents, teachers), occurred in 1981 (age 9), 1987 (age 15), 1990 (age 18), and 1993–1994 (age 21). This report focuses on data collected at ages 18 and 21. Between 1977 and 1994, attrition occurred primarily in the early grades when students transferred from the public school system to parochial and private schools. Nonetheless, more than 72% of those who continued in the public school system through Grade 3 remained in the study at age 21. Analyses at each major data collection wave verified that those who continued to participate did not differ from nonparticipants on any key demographic, academic, behavioral, or emotional factors (Reinherz, Giaconia, Lefkowitz, Pakiz, & Frost, 1993).

When last interviewed in 1993–1994, the sample of young adults included 188 males and 187 females, 92% whom were 21 years old. Parents (usually mothers) of these 375 young adults were also interviewed in 1994 and provided information about the young adult's functioning. Almost all (98%) of the participants were White and the socioeconomic status (SES) of their households throughout childhood and adolescence was predominantly working or lower middle class.

At 21, almost all of the young adults (97.6%) had completed at least a high-school-level education, and more than one half (55.2%) were currently enrolled in either a college or vocational training program. More than 80% of these young adults were employed either full or part time. At age 21, nearly three fifths (58.4%) still lived with their parents or families of origin, and only 2.9% were married. At the time of the interview, 21 of these young adults had biological children. Although 73% of the sample identified their own employment as their main source of income, 17.9% relied primarily on financial support from their families.

Measures

A *DSM–III–R* lifetime diagnosis of major depression was determined from a structured clinical interview administered to the youths at ages 18 and 21, and young adult stressors were determined from self-reports at age 21. The history of professional mental health services received was based on both self and parent retrospective reports during the age 21 interview in 1993–1994.

Major Depression. The Diagnostic Interview Schedule (DIS–III–R; Robins, Helzer, Cottler, & Goldring, 1989), administered to subjects at ages 18 and 21 by trained interviewers with prior clinical or research experience, provided a lifetime diagnosis of major depression according to *DSM–III–R* criteria, as well as information about severity, age of onset, recency of the disorder, and number of lifetime episodes. For the present analyses, young adults were considered to have a lifetime diagnosis if they met lifetime criteria based on either the age 18 or age 21 DIS–III–R. For some additional analyses, those with a lifetime diagnosis of major depression were further classified as having either active depression or remitted depression. An active (1-year) diagnosis (Robins et al., 1991) based on DIS–III–R required the young adult to meet lifetime criteria for a full diagnosis of major depression, and to have experienced one or more episodes of depression within the year prior to the interview. For young adults who met lifetime criteria for major depression, but had not experienced any episodes during the past year, the disorder was classified as remitted.

Young Adult Stressors. Stressors in young adulthood that might be linked to major depression were drawn largely from prior research examining this developmental period. These stressors reflect both social and occupational challenges as well as the current economic and societal milieu confronting this contemporary cohort reaching adulthood in the mid-1990s. Each of the 10 domains of young adult stressors included several items taken from the age-21 assessments and were scored dichotomously:

1. Marital and family status assessed the presence of a spouse or biological children; and

2. SES factors encompassed being currently unemployed, receiving welfare, experiencing difficulty financially supporting self, and not seeking medical treatment due to costs.

3. Living arrangements constituting young adult stressors were living alone, having left the parental household, and being "not at all satisfied" with where and with whom they lived.

4. Education factors that might be stressors included current enrollment in school and being "not at all satisfied" with educational level; and

5. Career factors encompassed not having long-range career plans, believing outside factors interfered with career progress, and being "not at all satisfied" with career progress.

6. Recent health problems identified by subjects as interfering most or all of the time in the past 3 years and rating health as only "fair" or "poor" were additional young adult stressors.

7. Stressors in intimate personal relationships included not being involved with a significant other in past 3 years, an important relationship ending, and being "not at all satisfied" with friendships.

8. Poor relationships with parents, were determined by a response of "poor" or "very poor" to separate questions about the quality of young adult's relationship with their mother and with their father.

9. The perceived need for increased social support in each of five areas (assistance, material aid, advice, positive feedback, and personal confi-

dantes) was evaluated with items from the Arizona Social Support Interview Schedule (Barrera, 1980) by a response of "quite a bit" to questions about the amount of support needed in each of these areas during the past 6 months.

10. Serious negative life events occurring between ages 18 and 21 that constituted potential stressors included death of parent or someone close, the hospitalization of someone close for physical or mental problems, a suicide attempt by someone close, pregnancy of the young adult or partner, and violence targeted to the subjects themselves, including having been robbed or mugged, physical assault, and rape or sexual assault.

Mental Health Services. In the 1993–1994 interviews, both subjects and their mothers provided information about professional mental health services received by subjects, defined as contacts with psychiatrists, psychologists, social workers, other counselors or therapists, or physicians for emotional, mental, personal, family, or substance abuse problems. The recency of these services was also ascertained.

RESULTS

Prevalence of Major Depression

By 21 years of age, 54 (14.4%) of the sample met all *DSM–III–R* criteria for a lifetime diagnosis of major depression (Table 7.1). For more than 70% of these young adults, the first onset of depression occurred before age 18 and for more than 20% depression occurred before age 15. Of those with a lifetime diagnosis of depression, 40 experienced two or more episodes by age 21; nearly 20% reported six or more lifetime episodes of depression.

There were no statistically significant gender differences in prevalence, age of onset, or number of lifetime episodes. Females were significantly more likely to have experienced more severe episodes of depression (Table 7.1). Nearly three fourths (72.8%) of depressed females, compared to only one third (33.3%) of depressed males were classified by the DIS–III–R as moderately or severely depressed (based on the number of symptom groups reported).

Among the 54 young adults who met lifetime criteria for major depression, 39% had an active (1-year) diagnosis at age 21. The remainder were considered to be in remission. Young adults with depression in the last year did not differ from those with remitted depression on demographic factors or on most measures of psychosocial functioning in young adulthood. Whether depression was active or remitted was not related to gender, employment, or educational status. In addition, young adults with remitted

TABLE 7.1
Prevalence and Features of Major Depression by Gender

	Total Sample (n = 375)		Males (n = 188)		Females (n = 187)		
	n	%	n	%	n	%	χ^2
Lifetime diagnosis of major depression[a]	54	14.4	21	11.2	33	17.6	3.91
Severity of depression[b]							
Mild	23	42.6	14	66.7	9	27.2	8.23*
Moderate	16	29.6	4	19.0	12	36.4	
Severe	15	27.8	3	14.3	12	36.4	
Age of onset[b]							
By age 14	11	20.4	3	14.3	8	24.2	1.49
Ages 15–17	27	50.0	10	47.6	17	51.5	
Ages 18–21	16	29.6	8	38.1	8	24.3	
Number of lifetime episodes[b]							
1 only	14	25.9	5	23.8	9	27.3	0.30
2–5	31	57.4	13	61.9	18	54.5	
6–9	3	5.6	1	4.8	2	6.1	
10 or more	6	11.1	2	9.5	4	12.1	

[a]Percentages based on all young adults studied. [b]Percentages based on those with lifetime diagnosis of major depression.
*p < .05 for gender difference.

depression functioned just as poorly as those with active depression in several areas of young adult functioning, including having poor self-esteem and self-mastery, greater interpersonal problems, and an increased risk of suicide attempts (Reinherz, Giaconia, Carmola, Wasserman, & Silverman, 1997).

Early Versus Later Onset. We also examined whether those young adults with onset of major depression before age 18 ($n = 38$) differed in behaviors and measures of functioning from those whose depression newly emerged between ages 18 and 21 ($n = 16$). There were no significant differences between those with earlier and later onset for gender ($\chi^2 = 1.18$), employment ($\chi^2 = 0.28$), or educational status ($\chi^2 = 0.13$), or on measures of young adult functioning, including self-esteem ($t = 0.68$), interpersonal problems ($t = 0.24$), suicide attempts ($\chi^2 = 1.24$), or other active *DSM–III–R* disorders ($\chi^2 = 0.01$). Therefore in some subsequent analyses we combined these two onset groups, examining stressors associated with any lifetime depression.

Current Young Adult Stressors and Major Depression

Analyses of stressors associated with a lifetime diagnosis of major depression by age 21 were conducted separately for males and females, in light of our previous findings that risks for major depression and other psychopathol-

ogy differ by gender (Giaconia et al., 1994; Reinherz et al., 1993). A series
of univariate chi-square tests compared the proportions of young adults
with and without a lifetime diagnosis of major depression who reported
each young adult stressor; odds ratios estimated the relative odds for lifetime depression associated with each stressor; the text describes comparative rate ratios.

Young Adult Stressors and Major Depression for Males

Career difficulties, financial stress, poor relationships with parents, perceived lack of social support, life events causing physical harm to the young
adults themselves, and serious psychopathology of someone close were
among the stressors related to major depression for the young men (Table
7.2). Depressed young males, although as likely as their nondepressed
peers to have formulated long-range career plans (76.2% vs. 79.6%), and
to be satisfied with their current education level (71.4% vs. 85.9%), were
eight times more likely to report being dissatisfied with their career progress
(12.5% vs. 1.5%). Economic factors were also related to depression for
males. Although depressed and nondepressed young males were equally
likely to be currently employed (76.2% vs. 84.3%), depressed males were
twice as likely to indicate that they had difficulty supporting themselves.
Although the tendency for depressed males to report having serious health
problems in the past 3 years was not significant, depressed males (47.6%)
were nearly four times more likely than nondepressed males (13.2%) to
report a lack of access to health care due to the costs.
    Troubled adult interpersonal relationships and need for greater social
support also characterized these depressed young men. Although depressed and nondepressed young men were all likely to have been involved
in an intimate relationship in the past 3 years (100% vs. 92.2%), more
than three fifths (61.9%) of depressed males compared to only one third
(34%) of nondepressed males reported that an important intimate relationship had ended during this time period. Young men's dissatisfaction
with their current relationships with their parents was also substantially
related to major depression. Depressed young men were four times more
likely to report poor relationships with both their mothers and fathers,
with more than one third (35%) of the depressed males compared to only
8% of their nondepressed peers characterizing the quality of their relationship with their father as "poor" or "very poor." Finally, depressed males
also expressed greater need for social support; in particular they were
almost three times more likely than nondepressed males to report that
they needed "quite a bit" of positive feedback and many opportunities to
discuss personal information with family and friends (confidantes) in the
past 6 months.

TABLE 7.2
Young Adult Stressors Related to Major Depression in Males

Young Adult Risk Factor	Major Depression (n = 21)		No Depression (n = 167)		χ^2	OR (95% CI)
	%	SE	%	SE		
Marital/family status						
Married	0.0	0.0	1.2	0.8	0.25	—
Have 1 or more children	0.0	0.0	3.6	1.4	0.78	—
Economic factors						
Currently unemployed	23.8	9.5	15.7	2.8	0.89	1.68 (0.6–5.0)
Receiving welfare	0.0	0.0	1.8	1.0	0.38	—
Difficulty supporting self	33.3	10.5	15.8	2.8	3.94*	2.67 (1.0–7.3)
Medical costs prevented help	47.6	11.2	13.2	2.6	15.67***	5.99 (2.3–15.8)
Living arrangements						
Left parental household	47.6	11.2	35.3	3.7	1.21	1.66 (0.7–4.1)
Live alone	9.5	6.6	7.4	2.1	0.12	1.32 (0.3–6.3)
Dissatisfied living arrangements	19.0	8.8	6.6	1.9	3.90*	3.32 (1.0–11.6)
Education factors						
Currently in school/training	52.4	11.2	54.5	3.9	0.03	0.92 (0.4–2.3)
Dissatisfied educational level	28.6	10.1	14.1	2.7	2.93	2.43 (0.9–6.9)
Career factors						
No long-range career plans	23.8	9.5	20.4	3.1	0.14	1.22 (0.4–3.6)
Outside factors interfered	62.5	12.5	42.4	4.3	2.33	2.26 (0.8–6.6)
Dissatisfied career progress	12.5	8.5	1.5	1.1	6.55*	9.29 (1.2–71.1)
Health problems						
Fair/poor health past year	19.0	8.8	8.4	2.2	2.41	2.55 (0.8–8.6)
Health problem past 3 years	38.1	10.9	24.0	3.3	1.96	1.95 (0.8–5.1)
Personal relationships						
No signif. other past 3 years	0.0	0.0	7.8	2.1	1.76	—
Important relationship ended	61.9	10.9	33.5	3.7	6.46**	3.22 (1.3–8.2)
Dissatisfied relationships	4.8	4.8	0.6	0.6	3.05	8.25 (0.5–137.1)
Poor relationships with parents						
Mother	15.0	8.2	2.4	1.2	7.88**	7.19 (1.5–38.8)
Father	35.0	10.9	8.0	2.1	13.24***	6.17 (2.1–18.2)
Need extensive social support						
Assistance	19.0	8.8	7.8	2.1	2.88	2.79 (0.8–9.5)
Material Aid	14.3	7.8	5.5	1.8	2.38	2.87 (0.7–11.6)
Advice	33.3	10.5	17.3	3.0	3.10	2.39 (0.9–6.5)
Positive Feedback	33.3	10.5	14.5	2.7	4.80*	2.96 (1.1–8.1)
Personal Confidante	26.3	10.4	10.6	2.4	3.94*	3.03 (1.0–9.4)
Life events ages 18–21						
Death of parent	4.8	4.8	4.8	1.7	0.00	0.99 (0.1–8.4)
Death other close person	57.1	11.1	37.1	3.7	3.13	2.26 (0.9–5.7)
Close person hospitalized for:						
physical injury/illness	23.8	9.5	43.7	3.8	3.04	0.40 (0.1–1.1)
mental breakdown	14.3	7.8	1.8	1.0	9.42**	9.11 (1.7–48.5)
Close person attempted suicide	19.0	8.8	9.0	2.2	2.08	2.38 (0.7–8.0)
Robbed or mugged	19.0	8.8	3.6	1.4	8.85**	6.31 (1.6–24.6)
Physically assaulted	38.1	10.9	10.2	2.3	12.61***	5.43 (2.0–15.0)
Raped-sexually assaulted	0.0	0.0	0.0	0.0	—	—
Partner became pregnant	14.3	7.8	12.0	2.5	0.09	1.23 (0.3–4.5)

*$p < .05$. **$p < .01$. ***$p < .001$.

In the 3-year period between ages 18 and 21, depressed young men also experienced several serious negative life events. Depressed young men were nine times more likely than their nondepressed counterparts to report that someone close to them was hospitalized for a nervous breakdown or mental problem. Depressed males were also more than four times more likely to have been the target of physical violence themselves; 38% of depressed young men compared to 10% of nondepressed males were physically assaulted between ages 18 and 21, and 19% of depressed males reported being robbed or mugged during this 3-year period.

Young Adult Stressors and Major Depression for Females

Career factors, health problems, unsatisfactory social support, and serious negative life events between ages 18 and 21 were among the stressors related to major depression for females (Table 7.3). Although depressed females and nondepressed females were equally likely to have formulated long-range career goals, depressed females were six times more likely to indicate serious dissatisfaction with their progress toward their career goals. Furthermore, these depressed young women were more likely than their nondepressed counterparts to indicate that outside factors had interfered with their career progress. The outside factors cited by these young adults included financial difficulties, personal and family problems, and perceived lack of opportunities.

Recent health problems also posed a risk for depression in young adulthood for females. More than one half (54%) of depressed young women compared to one third (34%) of nondepressed young women identified one or more health problems that bothered them or interfered with daily activities most or all of the time. The most frequently cited health problems included headaches, back problems, and allergies. Furthermore, depressed females were significantly more likely to have rated their health in the past year as only fair or poor.

Almost all women in both groups were at least fairly satisfied with their relationships with their mothers. However, women with a history of depression were about twice as likely to report some dissatisfaction with their relationships with fathers, and many more women in both groups were dissatisfied with their relationships with fathers than they were with their mothers. Depressed and nondepressed young women were surprisingly similar in their overall satisfaction regarding relationships with their romantic partners. However, depressed females were significantly more likely to indicate greater need for almost all types of social support in the past 6 months, including assistance, advice, positive feedback, and personal confidantes.

Except for the (rare) death of a parent, all negative life events were reported much more frequently by women with a history of major depres-

TABLE 7.3
Young Adult Stressors Related to Major Depression in Males

Young Adult Risk Factor	Major Depression (n = 33)		No Depression (n = 154)		χ^2	OR (95% CI)	
	%	SE	%	SE			
Marital/family status							
Married	6.1	4.2	4.5	1.7	0.14	1.35	(0.3–6.8)
Have 1 or more children	12.1	5.8	9.7	2.4	0.17	1.28	(0.4–4.1)
Economic factors							
Currently unemployed	12.1	5.8	14.6	2.9	0.13	0.81	(0.3–2.5)
Receiving welfare	15.2	6.3	9.1	2.3	1.09	1.79	(0.6–5.4)
Difficulty supporting self	39.4	8.6	32.7	3.8	0.55	1.34	(0.6–2.9)
Medical costs prevented help	21.2	7.2	18.2	3.1	0.16	1.21	(0.5–3.1)
Living arrangements							
Left parental household	48.5	8.8	35.1	3.9	2.09	1.74	(0.8–3.7)
Live alone	6.1	4.2	3.9	1.6	0.31	1.59	(0.3–8.3)
Dissatisfied living arrangements	12.1	5.8	9.1	2.3	0.29	1.38	(0.4–4.5)
Education factors							
Currently in school/training	42.4	8.7	59.1	4.0	3.07	0.51	(0.2–1.1)
Dissatisfied educational level	15.2	6.3	11.1	2.5	0.42	1.43	(0.5–4.2)
Career factors							
No long-range career plans	15.2	6.3	19.5	3.2	0.33	0.74	(0.3–2.1)
Outside factors interfered	58.6	9.3	37.9	4.4	4.15*	2.32	(1.0–5.3)
Dissatisfied career progress	24.1	8.1	4.0	1.8	13.14***	7.57	(2.2–26.0)
Health problems							
Fair/poor health past year	27.3	7.9	13.7	2.8	3.69*	2.36	(1.0–5.8)
Health problem past 3 years	54.5	8.8	33.1	3.8	5.36*	2.42	(1.1–5.2)
Personal relationships							
No signif. other past 3 years	6.1	4.2	7.8	2.2	0.12	1.31	(0.3–6.2)
Important relationship ended	33.3	8.3	27.9	3.6	0.39	1.29	(0.6–2.9)
Dissatisfied relationships	0.0	0.0	1.3	0.9	0.43	—	
Poor relationships with parents							
Mother	3.1	3.1	6.5	2.0	0.56	0.50	(0.1–3.7)
Father	27.3	7.9	13.7	2.8	3.69*	2.36	(1.0–5.8)
Need extensive social support							
Assistance	33.3	8.3	16.9	3.0	4.63*	2.46	(1.1–5.7)
Material Aid	15.2	6.3	5.9	1.9	3.30	2.84	(0.9–9.1)
Advice	69.7	8.1	27.5	3.6	21.31***	6.08	(2.7–13.8)
Positive Feedback	39.4	8.6	19.0	3.2	6.49**	2.78	(1.2–6.2)
Personal Confidante	48.5	8.8	22.7	3.4	9.09**	3.20	(1.5–7.0)
Life events ages 18–21							
Death of parent	3.0	3.0	4.5	1.7	0.15	0.66	(0.1–5.5)
Death other close person	66.7	8.3	48.1	4.0	3.77*	2.16	(1.0–4.8)
Close person hospitalized for:							
physical injury/illness	63.6	8.5	39.6	4.0	6.37*	2.69	(1.2–5.8)
mental breakdown	21.2	7.2	5.2	1.8	9.45**	4.91	(1.6–14.7)
Close person attempted suicide	30.3	8.1	11.7	2.6	7.40**	3.29	(1.3–8.0)
Robbed or mugged	6.1	4.2	2.6	1.3	1.05	2.42	(0.4–13.8)
Physically assaulted	12.1	5.8	5.2	1.8	2.17	2.52	(0.7–8.9)
Raped-sexually assaulted	9.1	5.1	1.3	0.9	6.34*	7.60	(1.2–47.5)
Partner became pregnant	27.3	7.9	20.1	3.2	0.36	1.49	(0.6–3.5)

*$p < .05$. **$p < .01$. ***$p < .001$.

sion than by those without such a history. Life events between ages 18 and 21 reflecting serious harm to the young women themselves or serious problems of those close to them were experienced significantly more frequently by depressed young women than by their nondepressed counterparts. Although numbers are small, a most striking 3 of 33 depressed females compared to 1 in 75 of nondepressed females reported having been raped or sexually assaulted between the ages of 18 and 21. Depressed females were four times as likely to report that someone close was hospitalized for a nervous breakdown or mental problem. Similarly, nearly one third of depressed women reported a suicide attempt on the part of someone close to them during this 3-year period.

Number of Young Adult Stressors and Status of Depression at Age 21

In addition to identifying the specific young adult stressors related to lifetime depression, we also examined how the number of these stressors increased the likelihood of depression (Table 7.4). For each gender, the number of stressors identified as significantly related to lifetime depression were compared for these groups: (a) those with an active (1-year) diagnosis of depression; (b) those whose depression was in remission, that is, they met lifetime criteria for depression but had not experienced any depressive episodes in the year prior to the interview; and (c) those young adults who never met criteria for a lifetime diagnosis of depression.

Controlling for depression status, in all instances, females reported more stressors than males. Not surprisingly, for both genders, young adults with active depression reported significantly more stressors than did their peers with no lifetime depression. Young adults whose depression was in remission also reported experiencing significantly more current stressors than young adults with no depression, suggesting the continued vulnerability of young adults with remitted depression.

Mental Health Services Received

There were distinctive patterns of mental health services use by males and females (Table 7.5). For males, those with any lifetime diagnosis of depression (active or remitted) were not significantly more likely than their peers with no depression to have received any professional mental health services either in the past year or in the past 3 years. In contrast, females with active depression and those with remitted depression were both significantly more likely than their nondepressed counterparts to have secured some type of professional counseling in the past year or in the past 3 years.

TABLE 7.4
Number of Young Adult Stressors[a] Reported
and Status of Major Depression at Age 21

Number of Stressors	Active Depression %	Remitted Depression %	No Lifetime Depression %	χ^2	Group Diff.[b]
MALES					
1+ Stressors	100.0	83.3	66.5	5.71	None
2+ Stressors	100.0	75.0	34.7	21.47***	A,R > N
3+ Stressors	88.9	50.0	15.6	35.05***	A,R > N
4+ Stressors	77.8	33.3	3.0	71.48***	A,R > N
5+ Stressors	44.4	16.7	1.2	44.04***	A,R > N
6+ Stressors	22.2	16.7	0.0	33.26***	A,R > N
	$\bar{X}^a = 4.33$	$\bar{X} = 2.83$	$\bar{X} = 1.20$	$F = 34.81***$	A,R > N; A > R
FEMALES					
1+ Stressors	100.0	100.0	90.9	3.24	None
2+ Stressors	100.0	100.0	74.7	10.56**	A,R > N
3+ Stressors	91.7	76.2	47.4	13.67***	A,R > N
4+ Stressors	83.3	71.4	32.5	21.65***	A,R > N
5+ Stressors	75.0	66.7	20.8	31.57***	A,R > N
6+ Stressors	66.7	57.1	10.4	44.53***	A,R > N
7+ Stressors	50.0	23.8	5.2	29.31***	A,R > N
	$\bar{X} = 6.08$	$\bar{X} = 5.38$	$\bar{X} = 2.69$	$F = 24.15***$	A,R > N

[a]Number of stressors reported at age 21 of those identified as significantly related to major depression for each gender. [b]Pairs of groups that differ significantly. A = Active (1-Year) Depression; R = Remitted Depression; N = No Lifetime Depression.

Also noteworthy was the significant disparity between males and females in the rates of reported receipt of services. Seven of the 12 females with active depression had some contact with the mental health system in the past year; in contrast none of the 9 males with active depression received services ($\chi^2 = 7.88$, $p < .005$).

DISCUSSION

This study of a community population of young adults turning 21 years old in the early 1990s identifies features of major depression in the early adulthood developmental period where major work and family responsibilities emerge. These newly emerging responsibilities can add additional

TABLE 7.5
Receipt of Mental Health Services

Recency of Services[a]	Active Depression	Remitted Depression	No Lifetime Depression	χ^2	Group Differences[b]
	%	%	%		
MALES					
Past 3 years	33.3	25.0	16.8	1.99	None
Past year	0.0	0.0	4.8	1.05	None
FEMALES					
Past 3 years	75.0	52.4	24.0	19.00***	A, R > N
Past year	58.3	19.0	4.5	39.43***	A, R > N; A > R

[a]Subject and parent reports of any services provided by psychiatrists, psychologists, social workers, other counselors, or therapists, or physicians for emotional, mental, personal, family, or substance abuse problems. [b]Pairs of groups that differ significantly. A = Active (1-Year) Depression; R = Remitted Depression; N = No Lifetime Depression.
    *$p < .05$. **$p < .01$. ***$p < .001$.

stressors inherent in periods of transition. In addition the environment of the 1990s has some increased and often conflicting burdens for today's young adults. Along with increased pressures for more education ("credentialism"), there is the companion trend toward fewer higher paying jobs and corporate downsizing. Also, there may be increased inability for these young adults to achieve the developmental milestone of independent autonomous living due to economic constraints. Continuing to live in the parental household may create conflicts with parents as reported by a number of the depressed young adults in our study.

Our examination of the specific contemporary stressors experienced in common by young men and women as well as those experienced differently can enlarge our understanding of experiences and perceptions that may exacerbate distress in vulnerable young adults. Similarly, the results of the study cast some additional light on the interactive, reciprocal, and bidirectional nature of stressors and depression in young adulthood.

Features of Depression in Young Adults

Prevalence. At age 21, lifetime rates of prevalence of depression in our sample (11.2% for males and 17.6% for females) were higher than those reported for the 18- to 29-year-old group in the ECA study where the rates for males was 6% and 11% for females (Weissman, Bruce, Leaf, Florio, & Holzer, 1991). The trend toward increased incidence for depression in younger age groups has been reported in several recent publications (Fombonne, 1994; Robins, Locke, & Regier, 1991).

A plausible explanation for the increase in reported prevalence in younger age groups is the enhanced recall of youthful subjects of disorders with onset in childhood and adolescence (Prusoff, Merikangas, & Weissman, 1988). Additionally, the increasing convergent evidence found in more recent studies using different methodologies points to the validity of the observed phenomenon of increment in major depression in young adults (Fombonne, 1994).

Contemporary Stressors of Young Adulthood

The stressors addressed in the current study encompassed a number of domains identified in the literature: economic and career issues, dissatisfaction with living arrangements, conflict with parents, experiencing violence and other negative life events, health problems, and difficulties in close relationships. (Cote & Allahar, 1996; Giaconia et al., 1995; Goldscheider & Goldscheider, 1993; Katon & Sullivan, 1990; Lewinsohn et al., 1995; Valentiner et al., 1994; Weissman et al., 1991) Although the analysis compare those with lifetime prevalence with others of the same gender, the profiles of depressed males and females present some commonalities and differences with regard to these stressors.

Gender Commonalities. A number of stressors noted by both young men and women who experienced depression may reflect characteristics of the environment of the 1990s. In particular, all the young adults who had experienced depression were more dissatisfied with their career progress than peers, reflecting the salience of career advancement for contemporary young adults (Cote & Allahar, 1996). The emphasis on career at a time of economic downsizing and perceived diminished opportunity can be a source of deep disappointment.

Both depressed young men and women voiced increased need for social support more than their nondepressed peers. The importance of social support in mediating stress is noted in recent models of stress impacting mental health status (Cohen, Kessler, & Gordon, 1995). Perceived social support can serve as a buffer against stress but perceived lack of and need for unavailable social support, particularly in vulnerable individuals, can constitute stressors. Both genders expressed the need for additional positive feedback and personal confidantes. This increased need for approval and social support of depressed individuals is also reflected in recent research. Lewinsohn et al. (1995) identified the personality characteristic *emotional reliance,* as a specific risk for depression reflecting the interaction of personality variables and stressors posited by a number of recent theoretical models of depression (Coyne & Whiffen, 1995).

The importance of interpersonal stressors in depression was identified in a number of studies (Lewinsohn et al., 1995; Valentiner et al., 1994). For both depressed males and females, a poor relationship with fathers was identified as a stressor illustrating the continuing importance of family relationships in the young adult period. In our prior studies the lack of family harmony was strongly associated with depressive symptoms at age 15 (Reinherz et al., 1989) and with major depression at 18 (Reinherz et al., 1993).

Finally, the depressed young adults of both genders differed from their peers in experiencing the mental hospitalization of "someone close." This finding could be interpreted as reflective of the presence of mental disorder in the family (and therefore both a genetic and family environmental factor) or of relationships with friends vulnerable to mental illness.

Gender Differences. Some of the differences in the profiles of depressed young adults of each gender met traditional expectations and several reflected emerging societal expectations of the 1990s. For males, economic and career difficulties were stressors identified in earlier research (Conger, Lorenz, Elder, Simons, & Ge, 1993). The physical assaults experienced by depressed males were also anticipated as gender based risks. However, the prominence of negative interpersonal events including ending of personal relationships and poor relationships with both parents noted by the depressed males was not expected from reviews of earlier gender differences in stressors reported by young men (Conger et al., 1993).

The prominence of interpersonal stressors noted by the young men may be understood in the context of some recent work by Hammen (1991, 1995). Although Hammen's work has primarily focused on depressed women and their children, she developed the construct of *stress generation* (Hammen, 1995). This approach takes into account the personality characteristics and behavior of depressed individuals acting on their environment with many of the ensuing interpersonal conflicts being a consequence of the depressed individual's behaviors emphasizing the bidirectionality of the phenomena.

There were also several types of stressful events noted more frequently by female participants. The sizable number of stressful negative life events noted by females as occurring to "close persons" and family members replicates the male–female differences found in a number of past studies in which females reacted more often than males to negative events happening to family and friends (Kessler & McLeod, 1984; Turner & Avison, 1989).

The finding that the average total number of stressors reported by the young women exceeded those reported by the men reflects the results found in other studies (Gadzella, 1994; Hammen, 1995). Whether the total number of stressors noted by females reflects the fact that women are exposed to more negative events or their heightened reactivity and vulnerability to stressors (Kessler & McLeod, 1984) or a combination of the two as argued by Turner, Wheaton, and Lloyd (1995) is not clear. What still needs further research, as recently noted by Cohen et al. (1995) are continued studies to trace the pathways for both genders between exposures to negative events and mental disorders.

Status of Depression: Number of Stressors and Functioning

Our findings as to the number of stressors experienced by the 21 young adults whose depression was active at age 21 and the 33 young adults whose depression was in remission compared to the never depressed young adults in the study show a clear pattern of descending order of numbers of stressors from the actively depressed to the never depressed. However, in all instances there were significantly greater numbers of stressors for those whose depression was remitted compared to the never depressed. These results, although based on a small number of subjects, were supportive of findings of the continuing vulnerability of those who experienced major depression even when symptoms were no longer present (Garber, Kriss, Koch, & Lindholm, 1988; Rohde, Lewinsohn, & Seeley, 1994; Tweed, 1993).

The lingering impact of major depression regardless of active symptomatology was also reflected in the examination of differences and similarities of those with active depression and those in remission both in self-perceptions (low self-esteem, low sense of mastery, self-reports of behavior and interpersonal problems) of those with active depression and those in remission (Reinherz et al., 1997). Also clinically trained interviewers rated both active and remitted young adults similarly on the Global Assessment of Functioning (Reinherz et al., 1997). But, most importantly, the fact that almost one fourth of the youth with remitted depression had attempted suicide should be a strong warning for mental health professionals. Although depressive symptoms may be in remission those who have experienced major depression are a vulnerable group particularly when faced with the additional stressors of major transition periods such as entry to adulthood.

Implications for Treatment and Research

The research reported in this chapter raises several issues for mental health practice and services. The first concerns the vulnerability of young adults where depressive symptoms may be in remission but who are affected by the stressors of the transition to adulthood at a time of heightened societal uncertainty (Cote & Allahar, 1996). The second issue addresses the unmet needs for affordable mental health services for young adults who may not have medical insurance.

As the onset and peak periods of new cases of major depression emerge earlier in life (Christie et al., 1988; Giaconia et al., 1994), it is important for clinicians to be alert to young adults with past histories of depression who are reporting some major negative contemporary stressors. Services provided to these young adults may be literally life-saving due to the close link between depression and suicide.

Although mental health services were not accessed in the year prior to the last data collection wave at age 21 by one third of the actively depressed females, none of the actively depressed males had sought service in that year. When questioned as to their reasons for not seeking help, the depressed young men cited the high costs of medical care. For depressed young adults of both genders limited use of mental health professions has been reported at an age period in contemporary society where the prevalence of disorders is highest (Blazer et al., 1994) and psychosocial challenges are equally high (Kastenbaum, 1993). These unmet treatment needs may foreshadow later economic and social distress for these young adults and their larger community.

There are some limitations to the generalizability of this study which is based on a predominantly White sample of working and lower-middle class youth and thus, results cannot be applied necessarily to more racially and ethnically diverse populations. The size of the sample made it impractical to study differences in several subgroups of interest, for example, comparing those with severe and less severe depression by gender as to their experiences of stressors. However, the numbers of domains studied and the convergence of findings with those of others affirm the validity of the results (Lewinsohn et al., 1995).

ACKNOWLEDGMENTS

This research was supported by NIMH Grant MH41569.

REFERENCES

American Psychiatric Association. (1994). *Diagnostic and statistical manual of mental disorders.* Washington, DC: Author.

Barrera, M., Jr. (1980). A method for the assessment of social support networks in community survey research. *Connections, 3,* 8–13.

Bland, R. C., Stebelsky, G., Orn, H., & Newman, S. C. (1988). Psychiatric disorders and unemployment in Edmonton. *Acta Psychiatrica Scandinavica, 77*(Suppl. 338), 72–80.

Blazer, D. G., Kessler, R. C., McGonagle, K. A., & Swartz, M. S. (1994). The prevalence and distribution of major depression in a National Community Sample: The National Comorbidity Survey. *American Journal of Psychiatry, 151,* 979–986.

Brown, G. W., Bifulco, A., & Harris, T. O. (1987). Life events, vulnerability and the onset of depression: Some refinements. *British Journal of Psychiatry, 150,* 30–42.

Burke, K. C., Burke, J. D., Rae, D. S., & Regier, D. A. (1991). Comparing age at onset of major depression and other psychiatric disorders by birth cohorts in five U.S. community populations. *Archives of General Psychiatry, 48,* 789–795.

Christie, K. A., Burke, J. D., Regier, D. A., Rae, D. S., Boyd, J. H., & Locke, B. Z. (1988). Epidemiologic evidence for early onset of mental disorders and higher risk of drug abuse in young adults. *American Journal of Psychiatry, 145,* 971–975.

Cohen, S., Kessler, R. C., & Gordon, L. V. (1995). *Measuring stress.* New York: Oxford University Press.

Conger, R. D., Lorenz, F. O., Elder, G. H., Simons, R. L., & Ge, X. (1993). Husband and wife differences in response to undesirable life events. *Journal of Health and Social Behavior, 34,* 71–88.

Cote, J. E., & Allahar, A. L. (1996). *Generation on hold: Coming of age in the late twentieth century.* New York: New York University Press.

Coyne, J. C., & Whiffen, V. E. (1995). Issues in personality as diathesis for depression: The case of sociotropy-dependency and autonomy-self-criticism. *Psychological Bulletin, 118,* 358–378.

Dohrenwend, B. P. (1974). Problems in defining and sampling the relevant population of stressful life events. In B. S. Dohrenwend & B. P. Dohrenwend (Eds.), *Stressful life events: Their nature and effects* (pp. 275–313). New York: Wiley.

Dohrenwend, B. P., Shrout, P. E., Link, B. G., Skodol, A. E., & Stueve, A. (1995). Life events and other possible psychosocial risk factors for episodes of schizophrenia and depression: A case control study. In C. M. Mazure (Ed.), *Does stress cause psychiatric illness?* (pp. 43–65). Washington, DC: American Psychiatric Press.

Elder, G. H., Jr., & Caspi, A. (1990). Studying lives in a changing society: Sociological and personological explorations. In A. Rabin, R. A. Zucker, S. Frank, & R. A. Emmons (Eds.), *Studying persons and lives* (pp. 201–247). New York: Springer.

Everly, G. S., Jr., & Smith, K. J. (1987). Occupational stress and its management: A review. In J. H. Humphrey (Ed.), *Human stress: Current research* (Vol. 2, pp. 235–246). New York: AMS Press.

Finlay-Jones, R., & Eckhardt, B. (1984). A social and psychiatric survey of unemployment among young people. *Australian and New Zealand Journal of Psychiatry, 18,* 135–143.

Fiske, M., & Chiriboga, D. A. (1990). *Change and continuity in adult life.* San Francisco: Jossey-Bass.

Fombonne, E. (1994). Increased rates of depression: Updates of epidemiological findings and analytical problems. *Acta Psychiatrica Scandinavica, 90,* 145–156.

Gadzella, B. M. (1994). Student-life stress inventory: Identification of and reactions to stressors. *Psychological Reports, 74,* 395–402.

Garber, J., Kriss, M. R., Koch, M., & Lindholm, L. (1988). Recurrent depression in adolescents: A follow-up study. *Journal of the American Academy of Child and Adolescent Psychiatry, 27,* 49–54.

Giaconia, R. M., Reinherz, H. Z., Silverman, A. B., Pakiz, B., Frost, A. K., & Cohen, E. (1994). Ages of onset of psychiatric disorders in a community population of older adolescents. *Journal of the American Academy of Child and Adolescent Psychiatry, 33,* 706–717.

Giaconia, R. M., Reinherz, H. Z., Silverman, A. B., Pakiz, B., Frost, A. K., & Cohen, E. (1995). Traumas and post-traumatic stress disorder in a community population of older adolescents. *Journal of the American Academy of Child and Adolescent Psychiatry, 34,* 1269–1380.

Goldscheider, F. K., & Goldscheider, C. (1993). Whose nest? A two-generational view of leaving home during the 1980's. *Journal of Marriage and the Family, 55,* 851–862.

Hammen, C. (1991). The generation of stress in the course of unipolar depression. *Journal of Abnormal Psychology, 100,* 555–561.

Hammen, C. L. (1995). Stress and the course of unipolar and bipolar disorders. In C. M. Mazure (Ed.), *Does stress cause psychiatric illness?* (pp. 87–110). Washington, DC: American Psychiatric Press.

Helzer, J. E., Burnham, A., & McEvoy, L. T. (1991). Alcohol abuse and dependence. In L. N. Robins & D. A. Regier (Eds.), *Psychiatric disorders in America* (pp. 81–115). New York: The Free Press.

Hooley, J. M., Orley, J., & Teasdale, J. D. (1986). Levels of expressed emotion and relapse in depressed patients. *British Journal of Psychiatry, 148,* 642–647.

Karno, M., & Golding, J. M. (1991). Obsessive compulsive disorder. In L. N. Robins & D. A. Regier (Eds.), *Psychiatric disorders in America* (pp. 204–219). New York: The Free Press.

Kastenbaum, R. (1993). *Encyclopedia of adult development.* Phoenix, AZ: Oryx Press.

Katon, W. C., & Sullivan, M. D. (1990). Depression and chronic medical illness. *Journal of Clinical Psychiatry, 51,* 3–11.

Kessler, R. C., & McLeod, J. D. (1984). Sex differences in vulnerability to undesirable life events. *American Sociological Review, 49,* 620–631.

Lewinsohn, P. M., Clarke, G. N., Seeley, J. R., & Rohde, P. (1994). Major depression in community adolescents: Age at onset, episode duration, and time to recurrence. *Journal of the American Academy of Child and Adolescent Psychiatry, 33,* 809–818.

Lewinsohn, P. M., Gotlib, I. H., & Seeley, J. R. (1995). Adolescent psychopathology: IV. Specificity of psychosocial risk factors for depression and substance abuse in older adolescents. *Journal of the American Academy of Child and Adolescent Psychiatry, 34,* 1221–1229.

Mirowsky, J., & Ross, C. E. (1992). Age and depression. *Journal of Health and Social Behavior, 33,* 187–205.

Monroe, S. M., & Depue, R. A. (1991). Life stress and depression. In J. Becker & A. Kleinman (Eds.), *Psychosocial aspects of depression* (pp. 101–130). Hillsdale, NJ: Lawrence Erlbaum Associates.

Paykel, E. (1984). Life stress and psychiatric disorder. In B. S. Dohrenwend & B. P. Dohrenwend (Eds.), *Stressful life events and their contexts* (pp. 138–149). New Brunswick, NJ: Rutgers University Press.

Potthoff, J. G., Holohand, C. J., & Joiner, T. E. (1995). Reassurance seeking, stress generation, and depressive symptoms: An integrative model. *Journal of Personality and Social Psychology, 68,* 664–670.

Prusoff, B. A., Merikangas, K. R., & Weissman, M. M. (1988). Lifetime prevalence and age of onset of psychiatric disorders: Recall 4 years later. *Journal of Psychiatric Research, 22,* 107–117.

Rabkin, J. G., & Struening, E. L. (1976). Life events, stress, and illness. *Science, 194,* 1013–1020.

Reinherz, H. Z., Stewart-Berghauer, G., Pakiz, B., Frost, A., Moeykens, B. A., & Holmes, W. M. (1989). The relationship of early risk and current mediators to depressive symptomatology in adolescents. *Journal of the American Academy of Child and Adolescent Psychiatry, 28,* 942–947.

Reinherz, H. Z., Giaconia, R. M., Lefkowitz, E. S., Pakiz, B., & Frost, A. K. (1993). Prevalence of psychiatric disorders in a community sample of older adolescents. *Journal of the American Academy of Child and Adolescent Psychiatry, 32,* 369–377.

Reinherz, H. Z., Giaconia, R. M., Pakiz, B., Silverman, A. B., Frost, A. K., & Lefkowitz, E. (1993). Psychosocial risks for major depression in late adolescence: A longitudinal community study. *Journal of the American Academy of Child and Adolescent Psychiatry, 32,* 1155–1163.

Reinherz, H. Z., Giaconia, R. M., Carmola, A. M., Wasserman, M. S., & Silverman, A. B. (1997). *Major depression by early adulthood: Risks and sequelae.* Manuscript submitted for publication.

Robins, L., Helzer, J., Cottler, L., & Goldring, E. (1989). *NIMH Diagnostic Interview Schedule Version III Revised.* St. Louis, MO: Washington University, Department of Psychiatry.

Robins, L., Locke, B. Z., & Regier, D. A. (1991). An overview of psychiatric disorders in America. In L. N. Robins & D. A. Regier (Eds.), *Psychiatric disorders in America* (pp. 328–366). New York: The Free Press.

Robins, L. N., Tipp, J., & Przybeck, T. (1991). Antisocial personality. In L. N. Robins & D. A. Regier (Eds.), *Psychiatric disorders in America* (pp. 258–290). New York: The Free Press.

Rohde, P., Lewinsohn, P. M., & Seeley, J. R. (1994). Are adolescents changed by an episode of major depression? *Journal of the American Academy of Child and Adolescent Psychiatry, 33*, 1289–1298.

Rutter, M., & Rutter, M. (1993). *Developing minds: Challenge and continuity across the life span.* London: Penguin Books.

Schnaiberg, A., & Goldenberg, S. (1989). From empty nest to crowded nest: The dynamics of incompletely-launched young adults. *Social Problems, 36*, 251–269.

Starr, J. M. (1986). American youth in the 1980's. *Youth and Society, 17*, 323–345.

Swindle, R. W., Cronkite, R. C., & Moos, R. H. (1989). Life stressors, social resources, coping, and the 4-year course of unipolar depression. *Journal of Abnormal Psychology, 98*, 468–477.

Turner, R. J., & Avison, W. R. (1989). Gender and depression: Assessing exposure and vulnerability to life events in a chronically stressed population. *Journal of Nervous and Mental Disease, 177*, 443–455.

Turner, R. J., Wheaton, B., & Lloyd, D. A. (1995). The epidemiology of social stress. *American Sociological Review, 60*, 104–125.

Tweed, D. L. (1993). Depression-related impairment: Estimating concurrent and lingering effects. *Psychological Medicine, 23*, 373–386.

Valentiner, D. P., Holohan, C. J., & Moos, R. H. (1994). Social support appraisals of event controllability and coping: An integrative model. *Journal of Personality and Social Psychology, 66*, 1094–1102.

Weissman, M. M., Bruce, M. L., Leaf, P. J., Florio, L. P., & Holzer, C. (1991). Affective disorders. In L. N. Robins & D. A. Regier (Eds.), *Psychiatric disorders in America* (pp. 53–80). New York: The Free Press.

Winefield, H. R., Winefield, A. H., Tiggeman, M., & Goldney, M. (1991). A longitudinal study of the psychological effects of unemployment and unsatisfactory unemployment on young adults. *Journal of Applied Psychology, 76*, 424–431.

Zales, M. R. (1985). *Stress in health and disease.* New York: Brunner/Mazel.

Chapter 8

Explaining Transgenerational Continuity in Antisocial Behavior During Early Adolescence

Howard B. Kaplan
Texas A&M University

Xiaoru Liu
San Diego State University

The phenomenon of generational continuity has long and justifiably excited the interest of behavioral scientists (Oliver, 1993). As Atkinson and Dodder (1990) observed:

> The long standing concern over generational conflict and continuity may be because it is through generational transmission that culture is continued and the world of today becomes the world of tomorrow. . . . Generational transmission . . . serves as the mechanism through which values, attitudes, and ways of life are kept alive (and) . . . as the major mechanism for social change. Each generation determines what aspects of human culture will be retained from the previous generation and what aspects of culture will be discarded or changed. (pp. 193–194)

The significance of events at any time and in any place is gauged by the nature and moment of the adaptive responses by individuals or collectivities to the events. The extent to which such adaptations endure is a function of the transmission of the responses over time from one generation to another or of the stability of the circumstances that evoke such responses. To understand the continuity of patterns of human social behavior over time is to understand the mechanisms through which adaptations are transmitted and the forces that maintain the circumstances that evoke similar response patterns over time. Conversely, to understand individual or social change is to understand the mechanisms that impede intergenerational transmission and that modify the conditions demanding personal or collective adaptations. The analyses to be reported here should be understood in this context.

Based on the view that antisocial behavior is a patterned response to life circumstances, the present chapter addresses two objectives. First, it describes the degree of intergenerational continuity in a measure of antisocial behavior for a sample of subjects first studied in early adolescence and for their biological offspring evaluated at the same developmental stage. The second objective is to begin to explain any significant intergenerational continuity. Is the relationship between antisocial behavior of the female subjects in the first generation and their daughters accounted for by common antecedent variables, such as race or socioeconomic status, or by intervening variables including childrearing patterns or levels of psychological distress?

The present study is informed by a variety of methodological, substantive, and theoretical issues raised in the salient literature. These issues refer variously to methodological problems, the mechanisms through which intergenerational continuity is achieved (mediating processes and contextual continuity), and moderators, particularly gender.

THE PRESENT STUDY

Numerous reports of generational continuity in psychosocial phenomena have appeared in the literature. Intergenerational continuity of *psychiatric disorder* is well established (Velleman, 1992). Children of psychiatric patients were significantly more likely to manifest persisting emotional behavioral difficulties than were school classroom controls (Rutter, Quinton, & Yule, 1976). Family violence appears to be transmitted across generations (Fry, 1993; Simons, Wu, Johnson, & Conger, 1995), as are drinking practices (Peterson, Hawkins, Abbott, & Catalano, 1994). Parent–offspring similarity was shown with regard to individuation and intimacy (Harvey, Curry, & Bray, 1991), parenting styles (Van IJzendoorn, 1992), interpersonal competence (Filsinger & Lamke, 1983), marital instability (Pope & Mueller, 1976), sexual behavior (Newcomer & Udry, 1984), and sex role attitudes (Smith & Self, 1980).

Methodological Considerations

Studies of intergenerational similarity vary along two major dimensions. The first dimension concerns who provides the data pertaining to each of the two or more generations under consideration. Youths, adolescents, or adult subjects may provide data about themselves and about their parents or grandparents, or adult subjects may provide information about themselves and about their children. Alternatively, data may be provided by representatives of the respective successive generations, with parents providing data about their own behavior and offspring providing data about their own behavior.

Another methodological variation concerns the comparability of the developmental stages of the generations. For example, adults may provide information about themselves as adults and about their preadolescent children; adolescent subjects may provide information about themselves during adolescence and about their parents' attitudes and behaviors.

Studies in which the same subject provides data about both generations or where the data are provided about the different generations at different developmental stages are methodologically problematic. In the former case, validity may be compromised by common source variance, whereby associations between measures of the two generations are artificially inflated. As Simons et al. (1995) observed:

> [I]t may be that aggressive individuals tend to see others, including their parents, as displaying high rates of aggressive behavior (Straus et al., 1980), thereby producing an artifactual relationship between descriptions of their own behavior and of that of their parents. (p. 160)

Although studies based on adolescents' perceptions of their parents reveal intergenerational continuity regarding values dealing with educational goals, career, and major life concerns, the relatively few studies based on independent reports from parents and their adolescents observe relatively little intergenerational congruence (Gecas & Seff, 1990).

A different kind of problem with collecting data on the two generations from a common source is that the relationship may be artifactually reduced if we are dealing with socially undesirable data, if, for example, a parent is motivated not to appear responsible for problems in offspring. In addition, but related somewhat to issues of method variance, validity of cross-generational data is threatened by the provision of data about both generations by a representative of only one of the generations due to retrospective distortion. As Oliver (1993) observed with reference to intergenerational transmission of child abuse:

> Omission, confusion, irrationality, distortion, and most bizarre of all, idealization in accounts of cruel, rejecting or neglectful grandparents (G1) by parents (G2) with rearing difficulties and/or ill-treated children (G3) are universal findings. (p.1320)

Studies of intergenerational changes were criticized for examining the generations at different stages in the life course (e.g., Clebone & Taylor,

1992). Van IJzendoorn (1992) cited a study by Hanson and Mullis (1986) that evaluated parenting and childrearing attitudes of female college students and their parents. It is at least possible that the birth of an offspring may alter a woman's attitudes about children and childrearing.

Unfortunately, study designs avoiding these methodological pitfalls are quite rare (Blee & Tickamyer, 1986; Harburg, Gleiberman, DiFranceisco, Schork, & Weissfeld, 1990; Lefkowitz, Huesmann, & Eron, 1978). The present analyses employ data from a large in-community sample of adolescents who are followed into the fourth decade of life, and from the children of these subjects who are tested at the same developmental stage. Thus, data are provided by representatives of the two generations, and the two generations are tested at comparable developmental stages. In addition, other limitations (small sample sizes, clinical samples) are obviated by the use of a large general population sample.

Mediating Processes and Contextual Continuity

Intergenerational continuity refers to the presence of comparable responses and experiences across generations. However, comparability of outcome does not speak to the mechanisms through which the continuity occurs. Continuity may occur because characteristics of the first generation set in motion a chain of reactions serving as intervening processes that produce similarity between the generations. Alternatively, causes of the phenomenon may be constant or similar across generations. That is, the bio-psycho-social context of the phenomenon in the first generation may be stable over time, influencing the second generation in the same manner as it had in the first generation.

Parenting as a Mediating Process. First-generation parenting patterns have been observed to mediate the relationship between first- and second-generation deviance (Chassin et al., 1993; Conger, Patterson, & Ge, 1995; Roosa, Tien, Groppenbacher, Michaels, & Dumka, 1993). The influence of parental drinking on drinking by the adolescent appears to be mediated by family management practices and parental prohibitions against the child's involvement in alcohol use by other family members (Peterson et al., 1994). First-generation deviance is generally associated with poor parenting. The parents of substance abusers tend to display poor parenting skills (Kandel, 1990) and excessively punitive discipline (Smyth, Miller, Janicki, & Mudar, 1995; Tarter, Blackson, Martin, Loeber, & Moss, 1993). The mechanisms through which first-generation deviance leads to inadequate parenting are quite varied. For example, deviant adolescents often avoid spending time at home and so give parents little opportunity to carry out conventional parenting.

Poor parenting styles, in turn, influence second-generation antisocial outcomes (Barnes & Farrell, 1992; Baumrind, 1991; Chassin, Rogosch, & Barrera, 1991; Roosa et al., 1993; Sampson & Laub, 1993; Sansbury & Wahler, 1992; Simons, Johnson, & Conger, 1994; Tarter et al., 1993). Simons and his associates (1995) indicated that aggression toward family members may be a particular expression of a general antisocial syndrome that has its roots in inadequate parenting. Internalizing disorders were shown to be increased by inadequate parenting as well (Straus & Kantor, 1994).

A range of parenting patterns have been implicated in second-generation antisocial outcomes. Parenting practices that increase the probability of a range of deviant outcomes include inadequate supervision, ineffective disciplinary practices, and rejecting, distrusting, and abusive parental responses toward the child (Barber, Olsen, & Shagle, 1994; Kumpfer, 1995; Loeber & Stouthamer-Loeber, 1986). Children reared in homes in which the parents are punitive may tend to become egocentric. Both unbridled expressiveness and egocentricity increase the likelihood of antisocial behavior (McCord, 1988). Ineffective parenting patterns impede internalization of the conventional normative prescriptions and proscriptions (Brook, Brook, Gordon, Whiteman, & Cohen, 1990) that would contravene the development of antisocial behavior through the exercise of self-control (Giever, 1995). Being raised by generally aggressive parents increases the probability that aggressive behavior will be regarded as normative.

First-Generation Dysfunction as a Mechanism. The second category of salient mediating processes relate to variables that reflect or are associated with first-generation adult psychological distress. Intergenerational continuity in antisocial behavior appears to be partially mediated by first-generation adult psychological dysfunction that is secondary to earlier antisocial behavior. Psychological dysfunction is reflected in or associated with family disharmony, family violence, or the disruption of family routines, which arise in response to first-generation antisocial dispositions and anticipate second-generation antisocial outcomes (Halikas & Rimmer, 1974; Rutter, 1971; Velleman, 1992). Studies of offspring of problem drinkers and substance abusers implicate parental and family disharmony, dysfunction, and disruption in the intergenerational transmission of alcoholism and substance abuse (Bennett, Wolen, & Reiss, 1988; Keane & Roche, 1974; Velleman & Orford, 1990; Wallace, 1990). The parent's psychological dysfunction also affects second-generation outcomes primarily via its effect on the parent–child relationship. Thus, parental depression is associated with unresponsive, inattentive, and hostile attitudes and behaviors directed toward offspring (Almeida & Galambos, 1991; Belsky, 1984; Conger, McCarty, Yang, Lahey, & Kroop, 1984; Gest, Neemann, Hubbard, Masten, & Tellegen, 1993; Longfellow, Zelkowitz, & Saunders, 1982; Miller, Cowan, Cowan, Hetherington, & Clingempeel, 1993; Weissman & Paykel, 1974).

An alternative interpretation of the relationship between adult psychological dysfunction and the child's conduct disorder reflects what has been called the disruption paradigm (Loeber & Stouthamer-Loeber, 1986).

> Neglect and conflict may arise when unusual events disrupt normal family behavior patterns. Chronic conflict between spouses and breakup of the marriage may directly or indirectly affect the children's behavior. Family members affected by these stresses may be irritable and prone to aggressive outbursts. . . . Children may respond in kind or may learn to avoid the irritable parent. This pattern reduces the likelihood that the parents will teach positive social skills to their children or that they will deal with the child's problem behaviors effectively. Once, however, the stress in the parents' lives is reduced or resolved, the parents' behavior toward their children and the children's conduct problems may revert to the pre-stress level. (p. 40)

Informed by this literature, we hypothesize that parenting patterns and psychological dysfunction of first-generation adults may mediate intergenerational continuity in adolescent antisocial behavior. Although the literature supports the hypotheses that each construct would mediate the relationship between first- and second-generation adolescent antisocial behavior, it does not speak directly to the question of whether the two constructs exercise independent effects or one phenomenon exercises its influence via the other. Our analyses address this question.

Contextual Continuity. Generational similarity may also be attributed to shared genetic characteristics and to shared physical and social circumstances (Van IJzendoorn, 1992):

> Living in the same neighborhood, and even in the same family house may constitute factors stimulating intergenerational continuity. This is an example of cumulative continuity in which an individual's environment reinforces a certain interactional style, thereby sustaining the behavior pattern across the life course, and maybe even across generations (Caspi, Bem, & Elder, 1989). Therefore, the strength of intergenerational transmission of parenting will be inflated if genetic transmission of parenting determinants and contextual stability influencing the continuity of parenting attitudes and behaviors are not taken into account. (pp. 77–78)

Common experiences may be reflected in positions in the social structure such as being Black or of low socioeconomic status (SES). Insofar as these variables are proxies for the experiences of paucity of social resources or of societal rejection, continuity of such experiences across generations may lead to common adaptations such as substance abuse. Regarding being Black, Rutter and Madge (1976) observe for England a continuity of disadvantage that also characterizes the United States. SES also powerfully influences environmental circumstances across generations. Thus, Simons and his associates (1991) observed, with regard to the role of social class influences in accounting for intergenerational transmission of harsh parenting, that:

> (These) linkages ... may merely represent the tendency of adult children to replicate the lower social-class status of their parents with its accompanying stressors and life-style, a life-style that may promote irritability and increase the likelihood of harsh parenting (Burgess & Youngblade, 1988). ... (Alternatively) growing up in a lower-class family may influence people's approach to childrearing or their childrearing values regardless of the socioeconomic level that they are able to achieve. (pp. 159–160)

In the current study, we model indicators of race/ethnicity and SES as reflections of contextual continuity. We anticipate these variables will only modestly attenuate the causal effects of first-generation adolescent antisocial behavior on second-generation adolescent antisocial behavior via the intervening constructs of first-generation adult childrearing patterns and psychological dysfunction.

Moderating Processes

Although the literature suggests a number of variables that moderate the strength of intergenerational continuity (e.g., warmth of the parent–child relationship, normative definition, identification with parents and parental power), the current study is based only on the apparent moderating effect of gender. The extent to which the gender and gender congruence of the intergenerational pairs moderate the degree of continuity and its mediators have been documented in the literature. For instance, parental substance use is more strongly predictive of substance use in adolescent daughters than in adolescent sons (Clayton, 1991; Thompson & Wilsnack, 1984). Smoking by the mother is more closely related than smoking by the father to offspring smoking (Kandel & Wu, 1995). Parenting, parental relationship and violence, and parental characteristics often appear to have different effects on sons and daughters (Doumas, Margolin, & John, 1994; Harburg, Davis, & Caplan, 1982; Harvey, Curry, & Bray, 1991; O'Keefe, 1994; Rothbaum & Weisz, 1994; Spaccarelli, Sandler, & Roosa, 1994; Steinberg, Elmen, & Mounts, 1989).

In view of these moderating influences, and in further anticipation that measurement models may vary according to gender, we estimated the models separately by gender. We examined mother–daughter pairs because of the putatively greater influence of the mother than the father, and the presumably greater intensity of the mother–daughter relationship (Kandel,

1990; Rossi & Rossi, 1990; Starrels, 1994). Daughters in early adolescence are at a cognitive developmental stage when they can perceive similarity to a person with whom they have an important relationship and to idealize and identify with such persons. Mothers may be such significant role models who influence their daughters' self-esteem through their role relationship, their nearness, as well as their common gender and sex role. They are also psychologically close (Curtis, 1991).

A number of commentators suggest reasons why intergenerational transmission from mothers to daughters may be greater than in other relationships (Boyd, 1989). A daughter's identification with the mother continues throughout life, whereas the young boy's identification with the mother is broken and switched to the father (Chodorow, 1978). Women experience less social pressure to differentiate from their mothers than do men for differentiation from their fathers (Flax, 1981). Women's identity tends to be based on different values than are men's identities, especially values of affiliation and mutual relationships, which may arise from the woman's identification with a caregiving mother (Gilligan, 1982; Miller, 1986; Noddings, 1984).

METHOD

In this study of intergenerational continuity, one generation (G1) was followed from adolescence through their fourth decade of life until their offspring (G2) were the same age that G1 had been when initially studied (i.e., during early adolescence).

The G1 subjects were drawn from a study of seventh graders tested up to five times between early adolescence and their late 30s. The initial subject pool consisted of all of the seventh graders in a random one half of the junior-senior high schools in the Houston Independent School District (18 of 36 schools). Of the approximately 9,300 seventh graders in those schools, 7,618 (82%) provided usable responses. Self-administered questionnaires were distributed in common meeting areas such as auditoriums or lunchrooms in the spring of the school year. Similar instruments were given in the eighth and ninth grades. In the 1980s when they were in their 20s, 6,059 (80%) members of this panel were reinterviewed; this group is now being reinterviewed in their middle to late 30s. As part of the interview schedule, the recent wave of first-generation subjects provided detailed information on their biological, step, adopted and foster children. Those children who were ages 12 to 14 were interviewed in the household where they then resided.

The subjects for this study consist of 216 G1 female subjects who responded to questionnaires in the seventh grade and were interviewed when they were ages 35 to 39, and who have one or more biological daughters between the ages of 12 to 14. If there was more than one eligible daughter, the daughter who was closest in age to the mother when the mother was first interviewed was selected for the analysis of intergenerational continuity.

Latent Constructs and Their Indicators

Models estimated relationships among three sets of constructs: G1 and G2 antisocial behavior, indicators of contextual continuity, and intervening variables hypothesized to mediate the relationship between G1 and G2 antisocial behavior.

Antisocial Behavior. Antisocial behavior for both G1 and G2 adolescent female subjects is conceptualized as the disposition to violate shared normative expectations in membership groups. Like other research teams (e.g., Simons et al., 1995), we defined such antisocial disposition as involving "actions that are deemed risky, inappropriate, short-sighted, or insensitive by the majority of people in the society" (p. 152). Adolescent antisocial behavior is reflected in three self-reported scales reflecting official sanctions (three items), dishonesty (three items), and aggression (five items). *Official sanctions* includes suspension or expulsion from school; receiving police, sheriff, or juvenile officer attention; and being brought to the school office for punishment. *Dishonesty* includes cheating on exams, dishonesty, and telling lies often. *Aggression* includes getting angry and breaking things; starting a fist fight; often being angry, annoyed, or upset; involvement in gang fights; and beating up an innocent person.

Contextual Continuity. Two variables that were taken to reflect contextual continuity included Black or Mexican-American race/ethnicity (contrasted with White Anglo) and the educational attainment of G1's mother (G2's grandmother) reflecting family SES in three categories: didn't graduate from high school, graduated from high school, graduated from college. If the woman did not know her mother's education, the father's education was used.

Race/ethnicity and SES are conceptualized as relatively stable life circumstances that may account in part for continuity between first- and second-generation antisocial behavior. Thus, continuity may be attenuated by controlling on indices of race, ethnicity, and SES, suggesting that the successive generations respond in similar fashion to these life circumstances that can be thought of as common causes. In the absence of attenuation, it can be assumed either that the relevant circumstances associated with race and ethnicity are not invariant across time or that these circumstances are not related to antisocial behavior in one or both generations.

Mediating Constructs. Two constructs were hypothesized to mediate the putative causal relationship between G1 and G2 antisocial behavior—effective parenting practices by G1 reported during the most recent wave of data collection when they were between 35 and 39 years of age, and psychological distress of G1 reported at the same time.

Regarding effective parenting practices, consistent with the literature, early antisocial behavior was expected to be inversely related to the development of effective parenting patterns by G1, and effective parenting patterns was expected to be inversely related to the development of antisocial behavior in G2 subjects. *Effective parenting* was reflected in measures of surveillance, closeness, praise, and support. *Surveillance* was measured with seven items covering not allowing children to leave the house without telling you, knowing where they are and who they are with, knowing the children's best friends, knowing the parents of the children's best friends, talking to the children's teachers, responding when children have done something wrong or something that you do not like, and not joking about children's transgressions. *Closeness* was measured with four items including discussing things that happen at school with children, children discuss personal problems with mother, openly showing affection to children, and children show affection to mother. *Praise* was measured by six reactions to good child behavior, including praise, kissing or hugging, letting them have something special to eat, buying them something special, letting them have extra privileges, and not ignoring. *Support* was measured by denials of the following responses to child wrongdoing: making fun of them, acting cold or unfriendly, expressing anger or speaking sharply.

Psychological Distress. Consistent with current literature, psychological distress experienced by the parents is expected to be an outcome of the early development of antisocial behavior, and is expected to be positively related to the development of antisocial behavior in offspring. *Psychological distress* was measured by vulnerability, anxiety, and depression scales. *Vulnerability* was measured by eight items including being sickly, fear of going to pieces, feeling low and worthless in reaction to criticism, slow recovery from failure, confusion under pressure, feeings of losing control over self, being deeply disturbed when laughed at or blamed, and feeling close to having a nervous breakdown. *Anxiety* items included frequent unexplained shortness of breath; bad dreams; often angry, annoyed, or upset; often loses track of thoughts; attention problems; biting fingernails; pains or pressures in the head; trouble sitting still; trouble concentrating; and nervousness. *Depression* items included wishing to be as happy as others, not in good spirits, feeling downcast and dejected, not getting a lot of fun out of life, and not a happy person.

Analysis

The LISREL 8 computer program (Jöreskog & Sörbom, 1993a, 1993b) was employed to estimate model parameters. The relationships between latent constructs and observed indicators are represented in terms of factor loadings. The direct and indirect structural relationships among the latent constructs are represented as regression coefficients. Models were estimated in three stages for G1–G2 female pairs. First, we estimated the relationship between the latent construct antisocial behavior for G1 adolescent females and the same construct for G2 biologically related adolescent females measured at the same developmental stage almost 25 years later. A significant and more or less appreciable relationship between the two constructs indicated that a degree of intergenerational continuity existed between G1 adolescents and their daughters.

The second analyses estimated models in which race, ethnicity, and G1 mother's (G2 maternal grandmother's) education were specified as common antecedents of G1 and G2 antisocial behavior. The models in the third stage of the analysis added mediating constructs that might account for the remaining association between G1 and G2 antisocial behavior. The two intervening constructs used in the present analyses were G1 childrearing patterns and psychological distress, initially estimated separately, and then together. Because of the possibilities that these effects may differ by birth order we conducted analyses of the hypothesized structural models with G2 birth order specified as a common antecedent of both the mediating mechanisms and G2 antisocial behavior, and as a consequence of G1 antisocial behavior and contextual variables. The inclusion of birth order in the models produced similar results to those reported here and are, therefore, not presented separately. However, these analyses are available to interested readers upon request.

We hypothesized that significant intergenerational continuity would be observed between G1 and G2 adolescent antisocial behavior and that this continuity would be attenuated when race, ethnicity, and SES were added to the model. Finally, we hypothesized that the intergenerational continuity would be mediated by a transmission process in which antisocial behavior in G1 influences parenting patterns and the experience of psychological distress by G1 subjects later in their life course, and parenting patterns and the experience of psychological distress influences antisocial behavior in G2 adolescents.

RESULTS

A correlation matrix with means and standard deviations of all the variables included in the analyses of the hypothesized structural models are presented in Table 8.1.

Intergenerational Continuity in Antisocial Behavior

The initial model estimated the relationship between the self-reported antisocial behavior of G1 and G2 adolescent females. Before estimating the model, we determined whether the interrelationships between the observed variables and the antisocial behavior construct for the G1 and G2 females manifested similar or different patterns. We anticipated that differences are likely with regard to the strength of the interrelationships between the empirical measures and the antisocial behavior construct across the two generations. Such differences are in part expected because of the differential modes of data collection for the two generations. We also anticipated, however, that despite these differences, the observed measures should generally reflect the antisocial behavior construct well for both generations and that the patterns of the interrelationships should remain similar. To test these hypotheses, we estimated the model first by constraining to be equal both the factor loadings and the error variances of the corresponding observed variables of the G1 and G2 antisocial behavior constructs. This was followed by the estimation of the model in which the previously constrained factor loadings and the error variances were freed. A significant reduction in chi-square values between the constrained and the unconstrained models signified differences in the measurement of the G1 and G2 antisocial behavior construct. The nature of the actual differences can be ascertained by examining the differences in the magnitudes of the factor loadings (and error variances) in the unconstrained model. We present the results of the unconstrained model only in Fig. 8.1.

The constrained model generated χ^2 (14, $N = 216$) = 30.34. In contrast, the unconstrained model (see Fig. 8.1) had χ^2 (8, $N = 216$) = 9.31. Thus the difference between the models yielded χ^2 (6, $N = 216$) = 21.03, $p < .01$. These results indicate that the interrelationships between the empirical measures and the antisocial behavior construct are different for the two generations. As expected, the loadings of the measurement variables on the constructs for both generations are significant and substantial but the loadings of the measures on the antisocial behavior construct for G2 subjects are larger. This greater magnitude of loadings reflects the stronger intercorrelations among the observed measures of the latent construct (see Table 8.1 for correlations). The correlation coefficients are .22, .26, .26, respectively, among G1 measures of antisocial behavior and .38, .39, .43

TABLE 8.1
Correlations, Means, and Standard Deviations of the Variables Included in the Structural Models (N = 216)

Variables	(01)	(02)	(03)	(04)	(05)	(06)	(07)	(08)	(09)	(10)	(11)	(12)	(13)	(14)	(15)	(16)
01 SANC-1	1.00															
02 DISH-1	.22	1.00														
03 AGGR-1	.26	.26	1.00													
04 SANC-2	.22	.19	.26	1.00												
05 DISH-2	.16	.15	.19	.38	1.00											
06 AGGR-2	.04	.10	.13	.39	.43	1.00										
07 SURV	-.12	-.11	-.03	-.20	-.10	-.05	1.00									
08 CLOS	-.23	-.03	-.08	-.20	-.16	-.17	.40	1.00								
09 PRAI	-.10	-.03	-.15	-.08	-.06	.00	.30	.24	1.00							
10 SUPP	-.07	-.17	-.09	-.22	-.22	-.23	.34	.25	.18	1.00						
11 VULN	.18	.10	.18	.33	.11	.22	-.30	-.21	-.12	.36	1.00					
12 ANXI	.30	.15	.27	.40	.20	.24	-.27	-.30	-.13	-.28	.65	1.00				
13 DEPR	.19	.12	.09	.38	.18	.25	-.33	-.20	-.17	-.26	.68	.60	1.00			
14 BLAC	.09	.08	.08	.21	.05	.16	-.03	-.08	.12	.08	-.13	.01	.00	1.00		
15 MEXI	.04	.09	-.08	.00	.11	-.04	.02	.10	-.08	-.09	.04	-.03	.08	-.28	1.00	
16 MEDU	-.14	.03	-.03	-.06	-.07	.01	.06	.11	.05	.04	-.09	-.07	-.10	.03	-.28	1.00
MEAN	.32	.58	1.10	.48	.48	.72	19.21	11.02	15.60	7.33	1.68	1.91	.92	.31	.15	1.75
SD	.68	.78	.88	.80	.71	.78	1.73	1.26	1.83	1.00	1.90	2.31	1.17	.46	.36	.76

Note. SANC = official sanctions; DISH = dishonesty; AGGR = aggression; SURV = surveillance; CLOS = closeness; PRAI = praise; SUPP = supportive; VULN = vulnerability; ANXI = anxiety; DEPR = depression; BLAC = black; MEXI = Mexican Americans; MEDU = first-generation mother's or second-generation maternal grandmother's education.

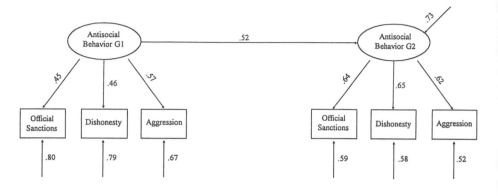

Chi-square = 9.31; d.f. = 8 (p = .32)
GFI = .99
AGFI = .96

FIG. 8.1.   Standardized regression coefficients exhibiting intergenerational
continuity of antisocial behavior (N = 216).

among the corresponding G2 measures. The greater magnitudes of the
correlation coefficients among G2 measures and consequently the stronger
factor loadings for G2 antisocial behavior construct indicate more consistency of the (mis)behavioral reports of G2 subjects. We suspect that this
consistency of the data may be partly due to the in-person interviews for
G2. It is also possible that the meanings of the indicators may vary somewhat
across generations.

Because these results indicate significant differences in the strength of
G1 and G2 measurement of antisocial behavior, we estimated the structural
models throughout the study without equality constraints on factor loadings
or the error variances of the antisocial behavior construct. The hypothesized association between antisocial behavior of G1 early adolescents and
the antisocial behavior of G2 early adolescents is reflected in the standardized coefficient of .52, indicating a noteworthy degree of intergenerational continuity in antisocial behavior. The antisocial behavior of adolescent females and of the daughters they are to give birth to later, measured
at the same developmental stage, appear to be related. However, this relationship may be accounted for by either continuity in circumstances or
by genetic and social transmission processes.

Continuity of Environmental Circumstances

In the second stage analysis, we estimate the influence of continuity of
external circumstances on the observed intergenerational continuity in
antisocial behavior by adding race, ethnicity, and SES to the models. If

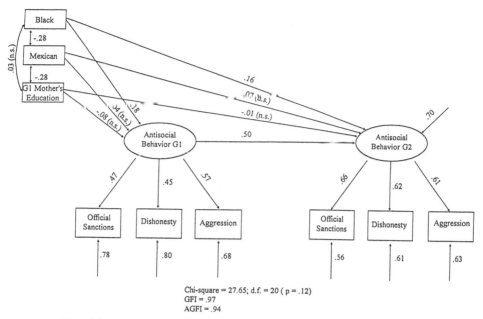

FIG. 8.2. Standardized regression coefficients exhibiting intergenerational continuity of antisocial behavior controlling race/ethinicity and SES ($N = 216$).

the circumstances of being Black, Mexican-American, or having come from a background of low education led to similar influences on antisocial behavior in the two generations, we would expect that the effect of anti-social behavior in the first generation on antisocial behavior in the second generation would be attenuated by their inclusion in the model.

The model including race, ethnicity, and SES is shown in Fig. 8.2.

The data fit the model well ($\chi^2 = 27.65$, 20df, $p = .12$). Again, the goodness-of-fit indices near 1.0. Neither Mexican-American status nor G1 mother's education had common and significant associations with G1 or G2 antisocial behavior. The status of being Black, however, was significantly associated with both G1 and G2 antisocial behavior. The strength of the association, however, was such that it did not attenuate the relationship between G1 and G2 antisocial behavior. In the absence of theoretically informed specification of alternative common antecedents indicating con-tinuing influences on antisocial behavior in successive generations, the intergenerational continuity may be explained in terms of a causal effect of G1 antisocial behavior on G2 antisocial behavior.

Mediating Constructs

On the assumption that the relationship between antisocial behavior in the first generation and antisocial behavior in the second generation is causal in nature, we offered two models that specified intervening variables.

The causal relationship between G1 and G2 antisocial behavior was hypothesized to be mediated by childrearing patterns and psychological distress experienced by G1 mothers. We summarize the results of the analyses in which first child-rearing, then psychological distress, and then both constructs are included in the model.

Childrearing as a Mediating Construct. The model with G1 childrearing as a mediating construct is shown in Fig. 8.3. The measurement variables had significant and appreciable loadings on the latent childrearing variable. Surveillance and Closeness were more strongly associated with the construct than were Praise and Support. The overall fit of the model is good χ^2 = 73.75 (53 df, N = 216, p =.03), goodness-of-fit index = .95, and adjusted goodness-of-fit index = .91.

The intergenerational relationship in antisocial behavior was attenuated by including the childrearing construct in the model. The intergenerational effect was somewhat reduced from .50 in the previous model to .41. As hypothesized, antisocial behavior in G1 subjects was inversely related to the development of effective childrearing patterns later in the life cycle. First-generation childrearing patterns in turn, were inversely related to G2 antisocial behavior. Inadequate childrearing patterns were one apparent

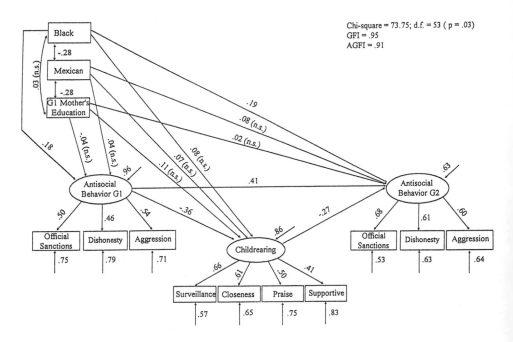

FIG. 8.3. Standardized regression coefficients exhibiting childrearing as mediating intergenerational continuity of antisocial behavior (N = 216).

outcome of an earlier rule-breaking proclivity, and influenced later contranormative dispositions in G2.

Psychological Distress as a Mediating Variable. The second construct hypothesized to mediate the intergenerational continuity in antisocial behavior is psychological distress. The estimated model including psychological distress as an intervening variable is shown in Fig. 8.4. The three measures reflecting psychological distress had significant and appreciable loadings on the construct. Indeed, the relationships from the construct to the three measures were stronger than in the case of any of the other constructs. The hypothesized intervening influence of psychological distress appears to be present. The intergenerational continuity of antisocial behavior was attenuated when psychological distress was included in the model. The effect of G1 antisocial behavior on G2 antisocial behavior was reduced from .50 in the model reported in Fig. 8.2 to .33 in this model, suggesting a stronger mediating influence than childrearing patterns. G1 adolescent antisocial behavior was related to their experience of psychological distress in the later half of the fourth decade of life. Psychological distress in turn appears to have had adverse effects on G2 adolescent antisocial behavior.

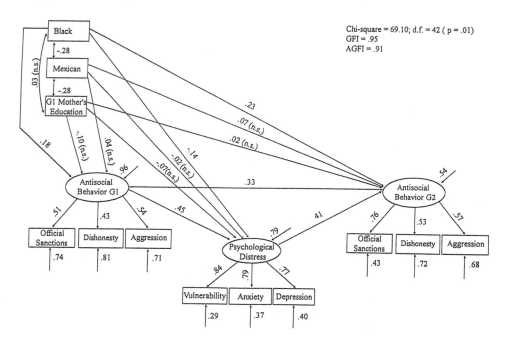

FIG. 8.4. Standardized regression coefficients exhibiting psychological distress as mediating intergenerational continuity of antisocial behavior (N = 216).

This model was a good fit to the data $\chi^2 = 69.10$ (42 *df*, $N = 216$, $p = .01$), a goodness-of-fit index of .95, and an adjusted goodness-of-fit index of .91.

Both Intervening Variables Included. The mediating influence of child-rearing and psychological distress considered separately raises the question of whether each exercise a unique mediating influence when both are considered in the same model. The estimation of this model is summarized in Fig. 8.5. The fit of the model is acceptable with $\chi^2 = 131.43$ (86 *df*, $N = 216$, $p < .001$), a goodness-of-fit index of .93, and an adjusted goodness-of-fit index of .89. The inclusion of both mediating variables did not attenuate the intergenerational effect of antisocial behavior appreciably beyond that which was observed when only psychological distress was specified as a mediating variable. The intergenerational effect was reduced only from .33 in Fig. 8.4 to .32 in the present model. However, with psychological distress in the model, child-rearing patterns no longer exercised an independent effect on G2 antisocial behavior. G1 antisocial behavior continued to be significantly and inversely related to childrearing effectiveness, but childrearing effectiveness of G1 adults had no direct effect upon G2 antisocial behavior. Either of two interpretations would account for these pat-

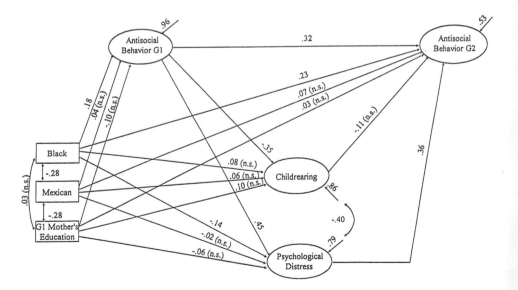

Chi-square = 131.43; d.f. = 86 (p = .00)
GFI = .93
AGFI = .89

FIG. 8.5. Standardized regression coefficients exhibiting childrearing and psychological distress as mediating intergenerational continuity of antisocial behavior ($N = 216$).

terns. Either G1 psychological distress is a common antecedent of childrearing patterns and G2 antisocial behavior, or childrearing patterns have an indirect effect upon G2 antisocial behavior via its influence upon G1 psychological distress. In the former case, maternal childrearing patterns, contrary to conventional wisdom, would not directly influence antisocial behavior of their children. Under such conditions, the belief that childrearing influences the genesis of antisocial behavior would be a spurious inference from the existence of a common antecedent (adult psychological distress) of both maternal childrearing patterns and offspring antisocial behavior. This interpretation would suggest a causal sequence that is inconsistent with the current model. Childrearing patterns had no independent direct effect on G2 antisocial behavior when G1 adult psychological distress was included in the model.

DISCUSSION

Methodological Implications

Our study is characterized by the use of a panel design, multigeneration measurements of successive biologically related panels at a comparable developmental stage, specification of mediating variables and contextual continuity, and consideration of the potential moderating influence on intergenerational continuity (and on intervening causal linkages) of a range of variables including the genders of G1 and G2 subjects. Many of these features approximate those that are thought to be ideal for the study of intergenerational transmission of, for example, parenting (Van IJzendoorn, 1992). These methodological features, and the further consideration of the potential modulating influences of gender, were associated with the demonstration of a stronger degree of intergenerational continuity than that observed in other longitudinal studies including various psychosocial characteristics such as parenting (Van IJzendoorn, 1992). However, whether these differences are due to the methodological features, the substantive phenomena under consideration, the focus on only female–female dyads, or other considerations, remains to be determined.

Substantive Implications

A number of findings were compatible with our expectations. First, a substantial effect of G1 adolescent female antisocial behavior on G2 adolescent female antisocial behavior was observed. Second, this effect was attenuated marginally by the few indices of contextual continuity that were considered. Third, the relationship between G1 and G2 antisocial behavior was accounted for in part by hypothesized intervening causal linkages. These findings are in many ways the most interesting because they suggest further intervening mediating processes. G1 parenting practices and psychological dysfunction each mediated in part the relationship between G1 and G2 adolescent female's antisocial behavior when considered separately. However, when the model included both, only G1 psychological dysfunction had a direct effect on G2 antisocial behavior. This suggests that any effect that parenting had on the transmission of antisocial behavior between the generations was attributable to mother's psychological dysfunction or to a correlate of the mother's psychological dysfunction that has not yet been modeled. Because our measures of G1 psychological dysfunction were taken at the same time as the measures of G1 parenting and G2 antisocial behavior, it is possible that the more commonly anticipated ordering of these variables is incorrect. A model whereby G1 female antisocial dispositions lead to ineffective parenting skills which contribute to G1 emotional distress is also consistent with the data. Mothers who are unable to control the behavior of their daughters and who are the object of the daughter's hostile responses to an inadequate parenting style may develop psychological dysfunction. The mother's psychological distress may preclude the transmission of adequate coping styles, a sense of self-efficacy, and self-acceptance to the daughter who then adapts to her circumstance with an antisocial coping style.

Several findings in the literature are consistent with these speculations. Conger, Ge, Elder, Lorenz, and Simons (1994) report that adolescent externalizing and internalizing symptoms are the outcome of parent hostility secondary to parent–adolescent conflict, marital conflict, parent depressed mood, and economic pressure. These dynamics are compatible with Rossi's (1980) suggestion (cited by La Sorsa & Fodor, 1990) that low morale and family strain occur when the parent undergoes "mid-life crisis" stress and is therefore unable to cope with the adolescent child and contributes to the adolescent's experience of stress. The intense distress experienced by the parent precludes the transmission of adequate coping resources to the adolescent child, and, in effect, invites the child to adopt antisocial responses in more or less effective attempts to reduce his or her own experience of psychological distress. Our findings that parental psychological distress accounted for the influence of parenting is consistent also with observations by Gest and associates (1993) that the experience of negative life events (presumably associated with subjective distress) involving the parents of the subjects was associated with increase in conduct problems. Effective parenting was associated with fewer parent-related negative events during offspring adolescence. Effective parenting did not compensate for the negative effects of the adversity and it did not moderate the effects of adversity. These results are also interpretable (along with our own) as indicating that effective parenting occurs when there are few subjectively distressing experiences. Parental psychological dysfunction may reflect both prior inability to cope with children in particular and inability to cope more generally. If so, parental psychological dysfunction may lead to transmission of inadequate coping patterns to the next generation and, offspring adoption of deviant adaptations to deal with life stress. Holloway and Machida (1991) reported that the use of coping strategies involving distancing, escape/avoidance, and seeking social support was associated with symptoms of distress. However, the use of active behavioral and cognitive coping strategies was associated with feelings of control in childrearing situations and was associated with authoritative parenting.

Limitations

These results should be regarded as preliminary for a number of reasons. First, the G1 and G2 data collected during the initial wave for each generation were gathered by different procedures. For G1, the data were gathered by self-administered questionnaires in common locations in the school setting, whereas data for G2 subjects were gathered at their place of residence by personal interview. These differences in data collection procedures may have attenuated the intergenerational continuity in antisocial behavior and affected the validity and reliability of the empirical measures reflecting the antisocial behavior constructs.

Second, the present analyses are based on a sample that disproportionately represents adolescents born to the younger mothers from the G1 cohort. Only the daughters born when mothers were still very young had reached the ages of 12 to 14 years. Most G2 daughters were still younger than that. In addition to any influences that might be associated with minority group status, SES, or other correlates of childrearing at earlier ages, it is known that age of the mother at the time of giving birth moderates the putative relationships between life experiences and adverse outcomes. Brooks-Gunn and Furstenberg (1986) and Furstenberg, Brooks-Gunn, and Morgan (1987) reported that the offspring of teenage parents manifested more symptoms of maladjustment than did children who were born to older mothers. Lefkowitz and associates (1978) cited findings that sons born to mothers older than 35 years of age at parturition were significantly more aggressive than sons of mothers who were younger (between the ages 18 and 35 years) at parturition. This difference could reflect insufficiency of the intrauterine environment or childrearing practices, as well as other correlates of age at parturition. Furthermore, early and continuous father-presence had a positive impact on cognitive and behavioral adjustment primarily for children born to older mothers. The lack of a significant effect of the father's presence on the adjustment of children born to teenage mothers may reflect the fewer skills and resources that the father in a teenage relationship is able to bring to the family and the greater resources that the husband or father who is older may bring to the family (Crockett et al., 1993). Thus, the findings reported must be replicated as new members of the cohort become eligible for interview at later dates as the result of the mothers having been older at the time of birth. Third, findings regarding the relationship between parental characteristics in the fourth decade of life and the characteristics of their adolescent children do not necessarily reflect unidirectional causal relations. Characteristics of the child may influence parents in addition to influence of parents on children. The concurrent measurement of psychological dysfunction in the parent and antisocial behavior in the child does not permit easy separation of the causal relationships:

> Parental rejection may drive children to rebel. However, it is also difficult to love children who make one's life miserable. Thus, parental rejection can be both cause and consequence of children's behavior. (Loeber & Stout-hamer-Loeber, 1986, p. 54)

Although we have interpreted the relationship between maternal distress and the adolescent's antisocial behavior as a one-way causal relationship, adolescent behavior may feed back into the mother's experience of distress. These "antisocial" responses are implicated in the adolescent's developmental task of separating from the mother. La Sorsa and Fodor (1990) observed that:

> the adolescent daughter's devaluation and distancing, which can often be hostile, may result in a loss of self-esteem for the mother. Mothers may perceive this normal aspect of adolescence as an indication of maternal inadequacy, particularly during this vulnerable period of midlife when they are also evaluating themselves. In addition, the mother experiences a deep sense of loss and rejection in the pulling-away process. (p. 601)

Teasing out the nature of the reciprocal relationship remains for future analyses and subsequent follow-up of the G2 subjects.

Fourth, the information regarding parental characteristics was gathered when the children were between 12 and 14 years of age. This measurement point is perhaps not the best for determining the causal impact of parental characteristics because children's antisocial behavior may have been formed in earlier years of their developmental span and parenting in those years may exert a greater or perhaps more unidirectional influence on children's antisocial behavior. Fifth, our measures of parent childrearing practices were derived entirely from parents' self-report rather than including children's reports of parental practices. Offspring reports of parenting practices may be more related to children's distress and hence their antisocial behavior outcomes. However, such a relationship might have been artificially inflated (or deflated) if children's reports of parenting practices and their own antisocial behavior are both consequences of common underlying personality traits. Future research should seek solutions for these problems. Sixth, the selection of only one of several eligible G2 children for investigating, although having the merit of avoiding variance inflation due to the sharing of a common household, may underestimate the influence of multichildren families on intergenerational continuity. A true estimate of the effect of G1 on G2 requires estimation of this effect for all G2 children who reach the developmental stage of interest. Future analyses may find ways of making appropriate corrections for design effects in structural equation methodology and should include all eligible G2 subjects. Seventh, we limited our analyses to psychosocial factors that may explain the intergenerational continuity of antisocial behavior. It is quite likely, however, that the intergenerational continuity of antisocial behavior is in part genetically determined. Thus, genetically transmitted IQ (Lefkowitz et. al., 1978) and biologically based disorders (Oliver, 1993) are implicated in intergenerational transmission of child abuse and related phenomena. Future analyses will consider variables impinging on the possibility of genetic transmission as well as the range of theoretically informed contexual and psychosocial mediating variables that might contribute to the continuity of antisocial behavior.

Finally, we have yet to examine secular trends over the generations that might account for the presence or absence of intergenerational continuity. Intergenerational trends in deviant behavior, societal responses to deviant behavior, and related phenomena may attenuate or exacerbate intergenerational continuity in antisocial behavior. Exposure to such secular trends may differentially moderate the nature and explanation of intergenerational continuity. In the absence of a cohort-sequential design, it is not possible to evaluate the degree to which findings relating to intergenerational continuity (or their absence) are due to patterns of sociocultural change. During periods of social stability, intergenerational transmission becomes a major mechanism for maintaining the stability of attitudes. The mass media and contemporary peers will tend to reinforce intergenerationally transmitted attitudes and behaviors. In times of rapid social change, however, the inevitable intergenerational influences will be attenuated by the transmission of the nature and acceptability of novel ideas in the mass media and by heterogeneous peers who model such novel ideas and behaviors. The interpretation of our findings must take such circumstances into account.

Future Research Agenda

Substantive Issues. Even the most complex model estimated failed to completely decompose the observed intergenerational continuity in antisocial behavior. It still remains to specify what other common antecedents or intervening processes (both in terms of biogenetic and psychosocial factors) explain the intergenerational relationship in antisocial behavior between adolescent females who will become mothers of adolescent females and the G2 adolescent females themselves at the same developmental stage. With regard to *common antecedents*, intergenerational continuity in one form of deviant behavior may reflect a common circumstance to which the members of the respective generations adapt in like fashion, as with substance abuse. A variety of common circumstances may be summarized, for example, in the general experience of psychological dysfunction. Continuity in psychological dysfunction across the generations (whether due to common experiences or not) may lead to common deviant adaptations. Regarding intervening processes, understanding intergenerational transmission requires the ever more precise specification of mediating mechanisms. As Velleman (1992) observes:

> in seeking to account for the intergenerational transmission of alcohol problems, researchers have suggested an explanation couched in terms of marital and family problems. Yet explaining the transmission of problems by simply citing such factors as violence, parental conflict, parental loss, and parental inconsistency is in itself no explanation, for the same question can be re-asked about these factors: why should these factors lead to a greater incidence of problems. (p. 382)

Furthermore, before we approximate a fuller explanatory model accounting for intergenerational continuity in antisocial behavior and the mechanisms that account for such continuity, we must initiate further investigation of potential moderators, such as gender. Future work will examine fully the intergenerational continuities in other parent–offspring gender combinations. Both on empirical and theoretical grounds we may expect that the degree of intergenerational continuity and the factors that account for such continuity will vary according to the genders of the intergenerational pairs. If we find that gender moderates the processes accounting for intergenerational continuity, we must further seek out the more proximal moderators of causal linkages.

Methodological Issues. It is always possible that measures used for one generation are no longer valid indicators of the latent constructs for a later generation. This is a special case of the situation that exists even in studies in which data are collected at a single point in time. That is, it is possible that subgroups of the population reflect psychosocial phenomena in different ways than other subgroups. Males, for example, may reflect alienation from conventional society with different behaviors than females. Certain behaviors that are considered deviant for females are considered acceptable for males. Hence, these indicators may not be appropriate measures of alienation for males, while they remain valid indicators of alienation for females. Similarly, subcultural variation in ethnic groups may preclude one ethnic group from expressing self-derogation with what are face-valid indicators of self-derogation for other groups. One ethnic group may by normative consent be precluded from admitting to self-derogatory feelings, whereas another group may be permitted to express such feelings when self-derogation is truly present. Or, one ethnic group may be required as a matter of good form to depreciate their personal qualities. In such groups the expression of self-deprecatory feelings would not be valid indicators of self-derogation.

Measurement variables may not reflect the same underlying meanings across time and in different gender, ethnic, racial, or SES groups. Even where measurement items cohere, the internally reliable scale may reflect different constructs. Therefore, all analyses will examine the internal reliability and construct validity of measures for groups differentiated in terms of gender, race/ethnicity, and SES at different times. Where measurement models vary over time and across SES, the decision will have to be made as to whether the functionally equivalent but metrically dissonant measurement models reflect the same underlying theoretical construct. If they do, the models will be estimated for different groups using functionally equivalent but metrically different indicators. This issue has been all but ignored in the discipline. It is necessary to begin thinking of how one deals with the problem of temporal and sociocultural differences in reflections of underlying constructs.

The present analyses were designed to further the goal of a full understanding of the processes underlying intergenerational continuity and discontinuity.

ACKNOWLEDGMENTS

This work was supported by research grants (R01 DA 02497 and R01 DA 10016) and by a Research Scientist Award (K05 DA00136) to Kaplan from the National Institute on Drug Abuse.

REFERENCES

Almeida, D. M., & Galambos, N. L. (1991). Examining father involvement and the quality of father–adolescent relations. *Journal of Research on Adolescence, 1*(2), 155–172.

Atkinson, L. P., & Dodder, R. A. (1990). Differences over time and generation in sexual attitudes. *International Review of Modern Sociology, 20*, 193–210.

Barber, B. K., Olsen, J. E., & Shagle, S. C. (1994). Associations between parental psychological and behavioral control and youth internalized and externalized behaviors. *Child Development, 65*, 1120–1136.

Barnes, G. M., & Farrell, M. P. (1992). Parental support and control as predictors of adolescent drinking, delinquency, and related problem behaviors. *Journal of Marriage and the Family, 54*, 763–776.

Baumrind, D. (1991). The influence of parenting style on adolescent competence and substance use. *Journal of Early Adolescence, 11*, 56–95.

Belsky, J. (1984). Determinants of parenting: A process model. *Child Development, 55*, 83–96.

Bennett, L., Wolin, S., & Reiss, D. (1988). Deliberate family process: A strategy for protecting children of alcoholics. *British Journal of Addiction, 83*, 821–829.

Blee, K. M., & Tickamyer, A. R. (1986). Black–White differences in mother-to-daughter transmission of sex-role attitudes. *Sociological Quarterly, 28*(2), 205–222.

Boyd, C. J. (1989). Mothers and daughters: A discussion of theory and research. *Journal of Marriage and the Family, 51*, 291–301.

Brook, J. S., Brook, D. W., Gordon, A. S., Whiteman, M., & Cohen, P. (1990). The psychosocial etiology of adolescent drug use: A family interactional approach. *Genetic, Social, and General Psychology Monographs, 116*(2).

Brooks-Gunn, J., & Furstenberg, F. F., Jr. (1986). The children of adolescent mothers: Physical, academic and psychological outcomes. *Developmental Review, 6*, 224–251.

Burgess, R. L., & Youngblade, L. M. (1988). Social incompetence and the intergenerational transmission of abusive parental practices. In G. T. Hotaling, D. Finkelhor, J. Kirkpatrick, & M. A. Straus (Eds.), *Family abuse and its consequence: New directions in research* (pp. 38–60). Newbury Park, CA: Sage.

Caspi, A., Bem, S., & Elder, G. H. (1989). Continuities and consequences of interactional styles across the life course. *Journal of Personality, 57*, 375–406.

Chassin, L., Pillow, D. R., Curran, P. J., Molina, B. S. G., & Barrera, J. M. (1993). Relation of parental alcoholism to early adolescent substance use: A test of three mediating mechanisms. *Journal of Abnormal Psychology, 102*, 3–19.

Chassin, L., Rogosch, F., & Barrera, J. M. (1991). Substance use and symptomatology among adolescent children of alcoholics. *Journal of Abnormal Psychology, 100*, 449–463.

Chodorow, N. (1978). *The reproduction of mothering.* Berkeley: University of California Press.

Clayton, S. (1991). Gender-differences in psychosocial determinants of adolescent smoking. *Journal of School Health, 61*(3), 115–120.

Clebone, B. L., & Taylor, C. M. (1992). Family and social attitudes across four generations of women of maternal lineage. *Psychological Reports, 70*, 268–270.

Conger, R. D., Ge, X., Elder, G. H., Jr., Lorenz, F. O., & Simons, R. L. (1994). Economic stress, coercive family process, and developmental problems of adolescents. *Child Development, 65*, 541–561.

Conger, R. D., McCarty, J. A., Yang, R. K., Lahey, B., & Kroop, J. P. (1984). Perception of child, child-rearing values, and emotional distress as mediating links between environmental stressors and observed maternal behavior. *Child Development, 55*, 2234–2247.

Conger, R. D., Patterson, G. R., & Ge, X. J. (1995). It takes 2 to replicate—A mediational model for the impact of parents' stress on adolescent adjustment. *Child Development, 66*(1), 80–97.

Crockett, L. J., Eggebeen, D. J., & Hawkins, A. J. (1993). Father's presence and young children's behavioral and cognitive adjustment. *Journal of Family Issues, 14*(3), 355–377.

Curtis, A. (1991). Perceived similarity of mothers and their early adolescent daughters and relationship to behavior. *Journal of Youth and Adolescence, 20*(3), 381–397.

Doumas, D., Margolin, G., & John, R. S. (1994). The intergenerational transmission of aggression across three generations. *Journal of Family Violence, 9*(2), 157–175.

Filsinger, E. E., & Lamke, L. K. (1983). The lineage transmission of interpersonal competence. *Journal of Marriage and the Family, 45,* 75–80.

Flax, J. (1981). The conflict between nurturance and autonomy in mother–daughter relationships and within feminism In E. Howell & M. Dayes (Eds.), *Women and mental health* (pp. 51–68). New York: Basic Books.

Fry, D. P. (1993). The intergenerational transmission of disciplinary practices and approaches to conflict. *Human Organization, 52*(2), 176–185.

Furstenberg, F. F., Jr., Brooks Gunn, J., & Morgan, S. P. (1987). *Adolescent mothers in later life.* Cambridge, MA: Cambridge University Press.

Gecas, V., & Seff, M. A. (1990). Families and adolescents: A review of the 1980's. *Journal of Marriage and the Family, 52,* 941–958.

Gest, S. D., Neemann, J., Hubbard, J. J., Masten, A. S., & Tellegen, A. (1993). Parenting quality, adversity, and conduct problems in adolescence: Testing process-oriented models of resilience. *Development and Psychopathology, 5,* 663–682.

Giever, D. (1995, November). *An empirical assessment of the core elements of Gottfredson and Hirschi's general theory of crime.* Paper presented at the 47th Annual Meeting of the American Society of Criminology, Boston.

Gilligan, C. (1982). *In a different voice.* Cambridge, MA: Harvard University Press.

Halikas, J., & Rimmer, J. (1974). Predictors of multiple drug use. *Archives of General Psychiatry, 31,* 414–418.

Hanson, R. A., & Mullis, R. L. (1986). Intergenerational transfer of normative parental attitudes. *Psychological Reports, 59,* 711–714.

Harburg, E., Davis, D. R., & Caplan, R. (1982). Parent and offspring alcohol use: Initiative and aversive transmission. *Journal of Studies on Alcohol, 43,* 497–516.

Harburg, E., Gleiberman, L., DiFranceisco, W., Schork, A., & Weissfeld, L. (1990). Familial transmission of alcohol use: III. Impact of imitation/non-imitation of parent alcohol use (1960) on the sensible/problem drinking of their offspring (1977). *British Journal of Addiction, 85,* 1141–1155.

Harvey, D. M., Curry, C. J., & Bray, J. H. (1991). Individuation and intimacy in intergenerational relationships and health: Patterns across two generations. *Journal of Family Psychology, 5*(2), 204–236.

Holloway, S., & Machida, S. (1991). *Child-rearing effectiveness of divorced mothers: Relationship to coping strategies and social support.* New York: Haworth Press.

Jöreskog, K. G., & Sörbom, D. (1993a). *LISREL 8: Structural equation modeling with the SIMPLIS command language.* Hillsdale, NJ: Lawrence Erlbaum Associates.

Jöreskog, K. G., & Sörbom, D. (1993b). *New features in LISREL 8.* Chicago: Scientific Software.

Kandel, D. B. (1990). Parenting styles, drug use, and children's adjustment in families of young adults. *Journal of Marriage and the Family, 52,* 183–196.

Kandel, D. B., & Wu, P. (1995). The contribution of mothers and fathers to the intergenerational transmission of cigarette smoking in adolescence. *Journal of Research Adolescence, 5,* 225–252.

Keane, A., & Roche, D. (1974). Developmental disorders in the children of male alcoholics. In *Proceedings of the 20th International Institute on the Prevention and Treatment of Alcoholism,* Manchester.

Kumpfer, K. L. (1995, November). *Impact of maternal characteristics and parenting processes on children of drug abusers.* Paper presented at the 47th annual meeting of the American Society of Criminology, Boston.

La Sorsa, V. A., & Fodor, I. G. (1990). Adolescent daughter/midlife mother dyad. *Psychology of Women Quarterly, 14,* 593–606.

Lefkowitz, M. M., Huesmann, L. R., & Eron, L. D. (1978). Parental punishment: A longitudinal analysis of effects. *Archives of General Psychiatry, 35,* 186–191.

Loeber, R., & Stouthamer-Loeber, M. (1986). Family factors as correlates and predictors of juvenile conduct problems and delinquency. In M. Tonry & N. Morris (Eds.), *Crime and justice: An annual review of research* (pp. 29–149). Chicago: University of Chicago Press.

Longfellow, C., Zelkowitz, P., & Saunders, E. (1982). The quality of mother–child relationships. In D. Belle (Ed.), *Lives in stress: Women and depression* (pp. 163–179). Beverly Hills, CA: Sage.

McCord, J. (1988). Parental behavior in the cycle of aggression. *Psychiatry, 51,* 14–23.

Miller, J. B. (1986). *Toward a new psychology of women* (2nd ed.). Boston: Beacon Press.

Miller, N. B., Cowan, P. A., Cowan, C. P., Hetherington, E. M., & Clingempeel, W. G. (1993). Externalizing in preschoolers and early adolescents: A cross-study replication of a family model. *Developmental Psychology, 29,* 3–18.

Newcomer, S. F., & Udry, J. R. (1984). Mothers' influence on the sexual behavior of their teenage children. *Journal of Marriage and the Family, 46,* 477–485.

Noddings, N. (1984). *Caring: A feminine approach to ethics and moral education.* Berkeley: University of California Press.

O'Keefe, M. (1994). Linking marital violence, mother–child/father–child aggression, and child behavior problems. *Journal of Family Violence, 9*(2), 63–78.

Oliver, J. E. (1993). Intergenerational transmission of child abuse: Rates, research, and clinical implications. *American Journal of Psychiatry, 150*(9), 1315–1324.

Peterson, P. L., Hawkins, J. D., Abbott, R. D., & Catalano, R. F. (1994). Disentangling the effects of parental drinking, family management, and parental alcohol norms on current drinking by Black and White adolescents. *Journal of Research on Adolescence, 4*(2), 203–227.

Pope, H., & Mueller, C. W. (1976). The intergenerational transmission of marital instability: Comparisons by race and sex. *Journal of Social Issues, 32,* 39–66.

Roosa, M. W., Tien, J., Groppenbacher, N., Michaels, M., & Dumka, L. (1993). Mothers' parenting behavior and child mental health in families with a problem drinking parent. *Journal of Marriage and the Family, 55,* 107–118.

Rossi, A. (1980). Aging and parenthood in the middle years. In P. B. Baltes & O. G. Brim (Eds.), *Life-span development and behavior* (Vol. 3, pp. 138–205). New York: Academic Press.

Rossi, A. S., & Rossi, P. H. (1990). *Of human bonding: Parent–child relations across the life course.* New York: Aldine DeGruyter.

Rothbaum, F., & Weisz, J. R. (1994). Parental caregiving and child externalizing behavior in nonclinical samples: A meta-analysis. *Psychological Bulletin, 116*(1), 55–74.

Rutter, M. (1971). Parent–child separation: Psychological effects on the children. *Journal of Child Psychology and Psychiatry, 12,* 233–260.

Rutter, M., & Madge, N. (1976). *Cycles of disadvantage: A review of research.* London: Heinemann.

Rutter, M., Quinton, D., & Yule, B. (1976). *Family pathology and disorder in the children.* Chichester, England: Wiley.

Sampson, R. J., & Laub, J. H. (1993). *Crime in the making: Pathways and turning points through life.* Cambridge, MA: Harvard University Press.

Sansbury, L. E., & Wahler, R. G. (1992). Pathways to maladaptive parenting with mothers and their conduct disordered children. *Behavior Modification, 16*(4), 574–592.

Simons, R. L., Johnson, C., & Conger, R. D. (1994). Harsh corporal punishment versus quality of parental involvement as an explanation of adolescent maladjustment. *Journal of Marriage and the Family, 56,* 591–607.

Simons, R. L., Wu, C., Johnson, C., & Conger, R. D. (1995). A test of various perspectives on the intergenerational transmission of domestic violence. *Criminology, 33*(1), 141–171.

Smith, M. D., & Self, G. (1980). The congruence between mothers' and daughters' sex-role attitudes: A research note. *Journal of Marriage and the Family, 42,* 105–109.

Smyth, N. J., Miller, B. A., Janicki, P. I., & Mudar, P. (1995, November). *Mothers' protectiveness and child abuse: The impact of her history of childhood sexual abuse and alcohol diagnosis.* Paper presented at the 47th annual meeting of the American Society of Criminology, Boston.

Spaccarelli, S., Sandler, I. N., & Roosa, M. (1994). History of spouse violence against mother: Correlated risks and unique effects in child mental health. *Journal of Family Violence, 9*(1), 79–98.

Starrels, M. E. (1994). Gender differences in parent–child relations. *Journal of Family Issues, 15*(1), 148–165.

Steinberg, L., Elmen, J. D., & Mounts, N. (1989). Authoritative parenting, pspychosocial maturity, and academic success among adolescents. *Child Development, 60,* 1424–1436.

Straus, M. A., Gelles, R. J., & Steinmetz, S. K. (1980). *Behind closed doors: Violence in the American family.* Garden City, NY: Anchor Books.

Straus, M., & Kantor, G. K. (1994). Corporal punishment of adolescents by parents: A risk factor in the epidemiology of depression, suicide, alcohol abuse, child abuse, and wife beating. *Adolescence, 29*(115), 543–561.

Tarter, R. E., Blackson, T., Martin, C., & Loeber, R., Moss, H. B. (1993). Characteristics and correlates of child discipline practices in substance abuse and normal families. *American Journal on Addictions, 2*(1), 18–25.

Thompson, K. M., & Wilsnack, R. W. (1984). Drinking and drinking problems among female adolescents: Patterns and influences. In S. C. Wilsnack & L. J. Beckman (Eds.), *Alcohol problems in women* (pp. 37–65). New York: Guilford.

Van IJzendoorn, M. H. (1992). Intergenerational transmission of parenting: A review of studies in nonclinical populations. *Developmental Review, 12,* 76–99.

Velleman, R. (1992). Intergenerational effects—A review of environmentally oriented studies concerning the relationship between parental alcohol problems and family disharmony in the genesis of alcohol and other problems: II. The intergenerational effects of family disharmony. *International Journal of the Addictions, 27*(4), 367–389.

Velleman, R., & Orford, J. (1990). Adult offspring of parents with drinking problems: Recollection of parent's drinking and its immediate effects. *British Journal of Clinical Psychology, 29,* 297–317.

Wallace, B. (1990). Crack cocaine smokers as adult children of alcoholics: The dysfunctional family link. *Journal of Substance Abuse Treatment, 7*(2), 89–100.

Weissman, M. M., & Paykel, E. S. (1974). *The depressed woman.* Chicago: University of Chicago Press.

Chapter 9

Maternal Disciplinary Practices and Offspring Temperament Across Two Generations

Stephanie Kasen
Columbia University College of Physicians & Surgeons
New York State Psychiatric Institute

Patricia Cohen
Columbia University College of Physicians & Surgeons
New York State Psychiatric Institute

Cheryl Slomkowski
Columbia University

Judith S. Brook
Mount Sinai School of Medicine

This chapter examines relationships between maternal discipline and offspring temperament across two generations of families, G1 and G2. Both samples are derived from families with a child between 1 and 10 years old randomly selected from two upstate New York counties in 1975 (Kogan, Smith, & Jenkins, 1977). Since then, children from these families were followed up in three subsequent waves of data collection (Cohen et al., 1993). A related study was undertaken toward the end of the 1980s in order to examine reciprocal models of parenting and offspring temperament among those children from the original 1975 cohort who had become parents.

For the current study, we include the 199 children who were 1 or 2 years old in the 1975 survey (G1). They are compared to the 123 2-year-old offspring of the 1975 cohort of children who were examined, on the average, some 18 years later (G2). We limit the G1 sample to children who were less than 3 years old in 1975 in order to enhance comparability with children in the G2 sample. Because the older G1 children were more likely to become parents first, only one of the G1 children examined here is a parent of a G2 offspring also included in this investigation. However, these analyses of generational effects do compare two geographically related samples followed prospectively, and interviewed with parallel protocols.

Conceptualization of the reciprocal nature of parent–child interactions has been advanced by a number of theorists and researchers, and supported empirically as well (e.g., Bates, 1980; Bell, 1968; Belsky, 1984; Brazelton, Koslowski, & Main, 1974; Chess & Thomas, 1984; Crockenberg, 1981, 1987; Sameroff, 1975; Thomas, Chess, Birch, Hertzig, & Korn, 1963). It is widely accepted that not only the parent but also the child is an active agent, each of whom influences the behaviors and expectations of the other, and particularly with regard to socialization (Bell & Chapman, 1986; Buss, 1981; Goldsmith & Campos, 1982; Lee & Bates, 1985; Lerner, 1978, 1979; Lerner & Spanier, 1978). For example, Lee and Bates reported that difficult temperament in early infancy predicted subsequent maternal use of power assertive control strategies, whereas Buss (1981) found that children who were overactive and difficult to control at 3 and 4 years of age induced higher levels of punitive and hostile parenting when they were 5 years old than did their nonoveractive, more easily controlled peers. Children who are better adjusted and more responsive to socializing attempts, on the other hand, are reported to inspire more positive caretaking efforts (e.g., Bugental, Caporael, & Shennum, 1980; Cantor & Gelfand, 1977; Kandel & Wu, 1995). Parents may actively modify socializing strategies contingent on the child's response to earlier methods employed, thus making discipline and control efforts a product of as well as a predictor of offspring temperament.

There is overwhelming empirical support that earlier problematic adjustment and poor parenting both are predictive of subsequent delinquent and antisocial behaviors in adolescence and adulthood (e.g., Cohen & Brook, 1987, 1995; Farrington, 1990, 1991; Loeber & Dishion, 1983; Loeber & Stouthamer-Loeber, 1986; McCord, 1979; Patterson, DeBaryshe, & Ramsey, 1989; Robins, 1966). Further, exposure to physically punitive parenting in childhood has also been implicated in adult depression and suicidal ideation (Straus, 1995). Given these powerful long-term effects of early adjustment and parenting on later functioning, as well as their dynamic interactive nature, parental discipline and control, particularly when coercive and punitive in nature, may contribute to a more robust trajectory of problematic adjustment across childhood and adolescence. Thus, it is important to study societal trends in the parenting disciplinary practices that shape enduring behavioral patterns in very young children.

The primary purpose here is to examine generational changes in maternal use of punitive coercive strategies (i.e., aversive discipline) and reasoning–distracting strategies (i.e., cognitive discipline) to control children, offspring temperament, and relationships between them in G1 and G2 mothers who have children under 3 years old. The age-stratified G1 sample of children and their mothers was obtained through rigorous random sampling procedures (implemented for the original 1975 cohort), and is representative of families who had children under 3 years old and lived in the northeastern section of the United States in 1975 (Kogan et al., 1977). In contrast, G2 mothers, although offspring in the original 1975 cohort, were selected for being a parent of a 2-year-old child within a specific time frame. As G2 parents were followed since childhood, at each point of data collection we were informed about impending pregnancies and births. Thus, the study design enhanced the likelihood of recruiting younger mothers of firstborn children for the G2 sample.

As G2 mother–offspring dyads are a selected subsample (albeit derived from a randomly obtained sample), it is important to reconcile any confounding qualities in G2 that may account for differences in outcomes attributed to generational effects. Variations in maternal characteristics, including age (Furstenberg, 1976; García Coll, Hoffman, & Oh, 1987; Roosa, Fitzgerald, & Carlson, 1982; Schilmoeller & Baranowski, 1985), maternal intelligence or education or both (Crockenberg, 1988; Elardo, Bradley, & Caldwell, 1975; Hannan & Luster, 1991), maternal employment (Belsky, 1988; Crockenberg, 1988; Crockenberg & Litman, 1991; Weinraub, Jaeger, & Hoffman, 1988), family SES (Sameroff & Chandler, 1975; Tulkin, 1977), and presence of a supportive spouse or partner (Crockenberg, 1986; Emery & Tuer, 1993; Quinton & Rutter, 1985), all have been reported to shape or alter the quality of childrearing practices. Moreover, some reports indicate that maternal characteristics such as personality, social class, and education influence maternal perceptions of infant temperament (e.g., Bates, Freeland, & Lounsbury, 1979; Matheny, Wilson, & Thoben, 1987; Sameroff, Seifer, & Elias, 1982; Vaughn, Taraldson, Crichton, & Egeland, 1981). Thus, given the nonrandom nature of the G2 sample, generational differences in maternal age at birth of offspring, as well as educational, marital, work, and welfare status are tested, and, where relevant, controlled. In addition, generational differences in offspring age, sex, and birth order are tested and controlled in all analyses. The following questions are addressed:

1. Do the G1 and G2 samples differ on offspring characteristics (age, sex, birth order) or temperament, or on maternal characteristics (age at birth of offspring, and educational, marital, work, and welfare status)?

2. What proportions of G1 and G2 mothers use the aversive and cognitive disciplinary strategies measured here to control offspring under 3 years old, and does usage differ between generations after adjusting

for offspring characteristics and temperament and maternal characteristics?

3. Are offspring or maternal characteristics related to offspring temperament or maternal discipline?

4. Does the relationship between maternal characteristics and offspring temperament or maternal discipline differ across the two generations?

5. Is there a relationship between offspring temperament and maternal discipline net of offspring and maternal characteristics, and does the relationship differ across the two generations?

METHOD

Sample Description

The G1 sample was comprised of 199 mother–offspring pairs. Offspring age range was 12 to 35 months ($M = 24.2$ months), and about one half were female and firstborn. The G2 sample was comprised of 123 mother–offspring pairs. Offspring age range was 24 to 32 months ($M = 24.7$ months), and almost two thirds were female and firstborn. Descriptive characteristics of mothers and offspring in the G1 and G2 study samples are given in Table 9.1.

Procedure

In 1975 and during the 1990 to 1994 time period, respectively, G1 and G2 mothers responded to parallel interviews approximately 1-hour long covering family characteristics, parenting practices, and offspring temperament and behavior. Interviews were administered by trained lay interviewers (see Lewis, Gorsky, Cohen, & Hartmark, 1985, for a description of interviewer selection and training, and explanation to study participants).

Measures

Although the G2 study also included standardized observations of mother–child interactions, developmental scales, and other measures, only the protocol segment that was the same for the two generations is used in this study.

Individual items describing specific methods of discipline were examined. G1 and G2 mothers indicated which of a series of aversive and cognitive strategies they had used to discipline or control their children in the past month. The seven aversive strategies were reflective of a coercive

TABLE 9.1
Descriptive Characteristics of G1 and G2 Samples

	G1	*G2*
Mothers		
Year interviewed	1975	1990–1994
Number	199	123
Mean age at birth	24.3 years	22.1 years
Age range at birth	16–43.3 years	15.8–32.1 years
Offspring		
Number	199	123
Percent female	47.2	63.4
Mean age	24.2 months	24.7 months
Age range	12–35 months	24–32 months
Percent firstborn	52.3	64.2
Mean birth order	1.8	1.4

punishment method of behavioral control, and included scolding, spanking or slapping, screaming, threatening to punish (whether or not followed through), removal of privileges, confinement to room, and verbal withdrawal of love or security (i.e., saying "I don't love you" or "I will send you away"). The six cognitive strategies included removing a controversial object, distracting with another activity, demonstrating the correct behavior, explaining why the behavior is not acceptable, rewarding for compliance, and using other children as a standard of reference for correct behavior (i.e., saying "other children don't do that"). Empirical evidence of the predictive validity of these disciplinary practices has been reported by others: Maternal use of physical punishment, threats, and restriction, and the verbal expression of anger and criticism have been related to increased defiance in toddlers and preschool-aged children (e.g., Crockenberg, 1986; Kuczynski, 1984; Kuczynski, Kochanska, Radke-Yarrow, & Girnius-Brown, 1987; Power & Chapieski, 1986), whereas maternal use of reasoning and guidance to socialize toddlers has been linked to increased compliance or less defiance or both (Crockenberg & Litman, 1990; Kuczynski, 1984; Lytton, 1980). Interviewers read the list of strategies asking whether each of these disciplinary practices had been used to correct the child's behavior in the month prior to the interview; a *yes* response was coded 1, a *no* response was coded 0. In addition, three scaled measures of discipline were employed. The seven aversive strategies were added together to create the Aversive Discipline scale ($r_{xx} = .50$), and the six cognitive strategies were added together to create the Cognitive Discipline scale ($r_{xx} = .33$). A high individual score on either of these two scales reflected the use of more aversive or cognitive strategies; a high group (G1 or G2) mean reflected the combined effects of use of more aversive or cognitive strategies by more mothers. The third discipline scale was a one-item measure of level of strictness reflecting the degree of control and structure provided, "How strict are you with your child about following rules?," on a 4-point scale (*very strict, strict, easy, very easy*). These scales were found to demonstrate predictive validity and consistency over time (Cohen & Brook, 1987, 1995).

The two offspring temperament scales used here, Anger and Fearfulness, were derived from factor analysis of 97 items (Cohen & Brook, 1987), and reflect a range of infant–toddler behaviors that capture the temperament constructs originally defined by Thomas, Chess, and Birch (1968). The six-item Anger scale ($r_{xx} = .58$) measures whether or not the child usually cries or complains loudly, screams, kicks, throws things, or rolls on the floor when angry (on a 2-point scale: *no, yes*), and how often the child gets angry on an average day (on a 5-point scale: *never* to *constantly*). High scores on the Anger scale indicate an undercontrolled child who responds with high intensity. The four-item Fearfulness scale ($r_{xx} = .67$) measures how often the child is afraid, shy with familiar people, and timid or fearful about doing things (on a 4-point scale: *never* to *often*), and the usual first reaction of the child to strangers (on a 3-point scale: *very friendly* to *unfriendly*). High scores on Fearfulness indicate a withdrawn child with poor adaptability in social situations. The temperament scales have predicted adolescent externalizing and internalizing disorders in the larger sample of G1 children from which this sample is taken (Bezirganian & Cohen, 1992; Kasen, Cohen, Brook, & Hartmark, 1996).

Zero-order correlations among the three discipline scales and two temperament scales are given in Table 9.2. Although statistically significant, relationships between the Anger scale and the Fearful, Aversive, Cognitive, and Strictness scales, and between the Aversive and Strictness scales are very modest, with coefficients ranging from $-.11$ to $.17$.

All G1 and G2 measures, including offspring age, sex, and birth order, and maternal characteristics, including age at birth of offspring, years of education completed, marital status (married vs. single), work status (working full time out of the home vs. not working or working part time), and welfare status (supported whole or in part by welfare vs. no welfare sup-

TABLE 9.2
Zero-Order Correlations Between Temperament and Discipline Scales

	Fearfulness	Aversive	Cognitive	Strictness
Anger	.14	.13	.14	−.11
Fearfulness		−.08	.03	−.06
Aversive			.05	.17
Cognitive				.05

Note. Coefficients ≥ .11 significant at the $p < .05$.

port), were derived from the G1 and G2 mother interviews conducted in, respectively, 1975 and 1990–1994.

Overview of Analytic Methods

To examine generational differences in offspring age, sex, birth order, and temperament, and maternal age at birth of offspring and educational, marital, work, and welfare status, we employed the chi-square coefficient at the categorical level and analyses of variance (ANOVA) at the scale level. We used logistic regression to examine whether use of specific aversive and cognitive strategies differed between G1 and G2 mothers net of other influences. Logistic regression is the procedure of choice for examining effects of continuous or categorical risk variables on a binary outcome, and is interpreted in terms of the odds of being in one of the two categories (of outcome) versus the other (Fleiss, Williams, & Dubro, 1986). Each strategy was regressed against generation membership (coded 0 and 1 for, respectively, G1 and G2) after adjusting for offspring characteristics and temperament and maternal characteristics; thus an odds ratio of more than 1.00 reflected more use of a particular strategy by G2 mothers (compared to G1 mothers), whereas an odds ratio of less than 1.00 reflected less use of a particular strategy by G2 mothers (compared to G1 mothers). Multivariate regression analyses also were used to examine relationships among offspring temperament, maternal discipline (at the scale level), offspring and maternal characteristics, and generation membership; potential generational differences in temperament–discipline relationships were examined. Temperament and discipline scales were standardized for regression analyses so that unit changes in the dependent variables would be comparable across all predictors.

RESULTS

Do the G1 and G2 Samples Differ on Offspring or Maternal Characteristics?

Significant differences between G1 and G2 offspring and between G1 and G2 mothers were observed (see Table 9.3). There were about 15% more girls (for unknown reasons) and about 12% more firstborns (for expected reasons) among G2 offspring than among G1 offspring, and, net of the effects of age, sex, birth order and fearfulness, G2 offspring were reported to be significantly more angry than G1 offspring by about one quarter of a unit ($SD = 0.26$). As anticipated, G2 mothers were younger at the time of offspring birth than were G1 mothers, with a mean difference of over

TABLE 9.3
Mean Differences Between G1 and G2 Offspring
Temperament and Offspring and Mother Characteristics

	G1 N = 199	G2 N = 123	t^a	Chi-Square
Offspring temperament[b]				
Anger	−0.10	0.16	2.39[d]	
Fearfulness	−0.08	0.13	1.19	
Offspring characteristics[c]				
Mean age (in months)	24.2	24.7	0.80	
Percent female	47.2	63.4		8.00[d]
Percent firstborn	52.3	64.2		4.44[d]
Mother characteristics[c]				
Mean age at birth (in years)	24.3	22.1	−4.43[d]	
Mean years education	12.7	12.5	−0.97	
Percent single	12.6	14.6		0.28
Percent work full time	15.6	33.3		13.80[d]
Percent on welfare	9.6	24.4		12.98[d]

[a]two-tail t test. [b]standardized mean group scores adjusted for age, sex, birth order, and other temperament scale. [c]bivariate group comparisons. [d]$p < .05$.

2 years. In addition, twice as many G2 mothers worked full time and more than twice as many received welfare benefits than did G1 mothers.

What Proportions of G1 and G2 Mothers Use the Aversive and Cognitive Disciplinary Strategies Measured Here to Control Offspring Under 3 Years Old, and Do They Differ After Adjusting for Offspring Characteristics and Temperament and Maternal Characteristics?

Table 9.4 gives the proportion of G1 and G2 mothers employing the 13 methods of discipline in the month preceding the interviews. Scolding and spanking or slapping were the two most common aversive disciplinary practices reported, and were utilized by a majority of mothers in each generation. Screaming and threatening were employed by at least one half of the mothers in each generation group. However, withdrawal of love or security was rare to nonexistent in either group. Cognitive disciplinary practices used by a clear majority in both generations of mothers included removal of the controversial object, distracting with another activity, demonstrating what should be done, and explaining why it should not be done. Referring to other children's behavior as normative was the least used cognitive strategy in the two generations, and suggestive of mothers' awareness of age-related cognitive limitations in their children.

TABLE 9.4
Disciplinary Practices of Two Generations
of Mothers of Children Under 3 Years Old

Disciplinary Practices	G1 (N = 199) % used	G2 (N = 123) % used	OR[a]	CI
Aversive strategies				
Scolded	92.5	82.1	0.18	(0.07, 0.46)
Spanked or slapped	87.4	71.5	0.21	(0.10, 0.44)
Screamed at	60.8	49.6	0.60	(0.36, 1.01)
Threatened to punish	52.8	66.7	1.39	(0.80, 2.39)
Took a privilege away	16.1	34.4	3.21	(1.69, 6.12)
Confined to room	19.6	25.2	1.64	(0.89, 3.02)
Told "I don't love you" or "I will send you away"	1.5	0.0		—
Cognitive strategies				
Removal of controversial object	88.9	91.8	1.34	(0.57, 3.17)
Distracted with another activity	88.4	86.2	0.85	(0.39, 1.85)
Demonstrated what should be done	86.9	95.9	1.25	(0.36, 4.35)
Explained why it shouldn't be done	71.9	95.9	6.94	(2.46, 19.56)
Offered a reward for compliance	45.7	83.7	5.38	(2.95, 9.82)
Told "other children don't do that"	21.6	31.7	1.08	(0.48, 2.42)

[a]Odds ratios (OR) and 95% confidence intervals (CI) adjusted for offspring age, sex, birth order, and temperament, and maternal age at birth and educational, marital, work, and welfare status.

The odds of using each aversive and cognitive strategy for G2 mothers versus G1 mothers (net of offspring age, sex, birth order, and temperament, and maternal age at birth and educational, marital, work, and welfare status) also are given in Table 9.4. Regarding the use of aversive strategies, G2 mothers were at significantly decreased odds of scolding and spanking or slapping, at marginally decreased odds of screaming, but at significantly increased odds of taking privileges away compared to G1 mothers. Regarding the use of cognitive strategies, G2 mothers were at significantly increased odds of explaining why something should not be done and offering a reward for compliance compared to G1 mothers.

Generational differences in discipline at the scale level net of all other offspring and maternal variables were tested (not tabled). These analyses supported significantly less overall use of aversive discipline in G2 mothers than in G1 mothers (mean group scores: $SD = 0.29$ vs. $SD = 0.18$; unit change in aversive discipline given G2 membership, $B -0.11$, $p < .001$), and significantly more overall use of cognitive discipline in G2 mothers than in G1 mothers (mean group scores: $SD = 0.46$ vs. $SD = -0.28$, unit change in cognitive discipline given G2 membership, $B = 0.16$, $p < .001$). No generational difference between G1 and G2 in strictness was observed (mean group scores: $SD = -0.004$ vs. $SD = 0.003$ for G1 and G2, respectively).

Are Offspring or Maternal Characteristics Related to Offspring Temperament or Maternal Discipline?

Partial regression coefficients of relationships between characteristics of offspring and mothers with temperament and discipline in the combined G1 and G2 sample are given in Table 9.5. Net of all other background characteristics, offspring age, sex, and birth order predicted maternal discipline: Mothers of older offspring used more of both kinds of discipline; mothers of later born offspring used less cognitive discipline, were less strict, and tended to use less aversive discipline as well; and, mothers of male offspring tended to be more strict. Older offspring were reported to be somewhat more fearful; however, none of the effects of offspring characteristics on temperament reached conventional levels of statistical significance. There were also independent effects of maternal characteristics on discipline and temperament. Mothers who worked full time used less aversive disciplinary strategies but more cognitive ones, single mothers tended to use more aversive discipline, and mothers receiving welfare benefits tended to be somewhat more strict. In addition, mothers on welfare reported higher levels of angry temperament in offspring, and to a lesser extent, higher levels of fearfulness.

TABLE 9.5
Effects of Background Characteristics on Offspring Temperament
and Maternal Discipline in a Combined G1 and G2 Sample
(322 mother–offspring pairs)

	Anger	Fearfulness	Aversive	Cognitive	Strictness
Offspring characteristics					
Age	.01	.02[a]	.03[b]	.06[b]	−.00
Male gender	.11	−.15	.11	−.01	.21[a]
Birth order	.08	−.09	−.11[a]	−.15[b]	−.15[b]
Mother characteristics					
Age at birth of offspring	−.01	.02	−.00	−.01	.03
Education	.00	.05	−.03	−.02	.05
Single mother	.00	.07	.29[a]	−.14	−.21
G1					−0.54[b]
G2					0.24
Full-time worker	.17	−.01	−.35[b]	.32[b]	−.07
G1			−.49[b]		
G2			.05		
Welfare-supported	.49[b]	.34[a]	−.26	.03	.30[a]
G1				−.56[b]	
G2				.04	

Note. Temperament and discipline scales are standardized. Tabled coefficients are partial regression coefficients in simultaneous equations. Within-generation coefficients tabled only when characteristic X generation interaction was significant at the .05 level.
[a]$p < .10$. [b]$p < .05$.

Does the Relationship Between Maternal Characteristics
and Offspring Temperament or Maternal Discipline Differ
Across the Two Generations?

Generational differences in relationships between maternal characteristics and offspring temperament were not observed; however, there was some evidence of generational differences in relationships between maternal characteristics and maternal discipline. We tabled partial regression coefficients describing within-generation relationships where generational differences reached conventional levels of significance (see Table 9.5): G1 mothers who worked full time used less aversive discipline than G1 mothers who didn't work or worked only part time, whereas no comparable difference was observed between working and nonworking–part-time working G2 mothers; single G1 mothers were less strict than married G1 mothers, whereas no comparable difference was observed between single and married G2 mothers; and, G1 mothers on welfare used less cognitive discipline than G1 mothers not on welfare, whereas no comparable difference was observed between welfare-supported and nonwelfare G2 mothers.

Is There a Relationship Between Offspring Temperament
and Maternal Discipline Net of Offspring and Maternal
Characteristics, and Does the Relationship Differ
Across the Two Generations?

Reports of offspring temperament and maternal discipline used here were obtained at the same time. Thus, in order to avoid an arbitrary choice regarding directionality, we examined each measure of offspring temperament and maternal discipline as a dependent variable net of, respectively, the other temperament scale or discipline scales. These analyses were adjusted for generation and all offspring and maternal background characteristics as well. Partial regression coefficients for the discipline → temperament and temperament → discipline perspectives are given in, respectively, Tables 9.6 and 9.7.

From the discipline → temperament perspective, offspring responded with increasingly angry temperament with mothers who used more aversive discipline, with mothers who were less strict, and, marginally, with mothers who used more cognitive discipline. Maternal discipline did not influence fearfulness in offspring.

From the temperament → discipline perspective, mothers responded to increasing angry temperament in offspring with more use of aversive discipline, and, marginally, more use of cognitive discipline and less strictness. Degree of fearfulness in offspring, on the other hand, did not influence maternal discipline.

To determine whether there were any significant differences between the two generations of mothers in temperament–discipline relationships,

TABLE 9.6
Effects of Maternal Discipline on Offspring Temperament in G1 and G2[a]

Maternal Discipline Scales	Offspring Temperament Scales			
	Anger		Fearfulness	
	B	(SE)	B	(SE)
Aversive	.20[c]	(.06)	−.03	(.06)
Cognitive	.12[b]	(.06)	−.03	(.07)
Strictness	−.16[c]	(.06)	−.09	(.06)

[a]Coefficients are partial regression coefficients in simultaneous equations. Effects are net of offspring age, sex, birth order, and other discipline scales; maternal age at birth and educational, marital, work, and welfare status; and generation. [b]$p < .10$. [c]$p < .01$.

TABLE 9.7
Adjusted Effects of Offspring Temperament
on Maternal Discipline in G1 and G2[a]

Offspring Temperament Scales	Maternal Discipline Scales					
	Aversive		Cognitive		Strictness	
	B	(SE)	B	(SE)	B	(SE)
Anger	.16[c]	(.05)	.10[b]	(.05)	−.10[b]	(.06)
Fearfulness	−.06	(.05)	−.04	(.05)	−.08	(.06)

[a]Partial regression coefficients in simultaneous equations. Effects are net of offspring age, sex, and birth order; maternal age at birth and educational, marital, work, and welfare status; the other temperament scale; and generation. [b]$p < .10$. [c]$p < .01$.

interaction effects (generation X temperament effects and generation X discipline effects on, respectively, discipline and temperament) were tested in regression analyses; however none reached conventional levels of significance. Furthermore, inspection of within-generation coefficients revealed a particularly close similarity in G1 and G2 relationships between angry temperament and disciplinary practices.

IMPLICATIONS AND EXTENSIONS

Differences in Background Characteristics and Temperament

Most of the generational differences in offspring and maternal background characteristics found here may be explained to a large degree by differing methods of sample selection (more firstborn offspring and younger maternal age at birth in G2) or historical change (more mothers working full time in G2), or both (more mothers supported by welfare in G2). The higher levels of angry temperament in offspring reported by G2 mothers compared to G1 mothers were net of these and other background characteristics. However, maternal characteristics measured here were primarily demographic, and did not include those of a psychological nature that have been linked to perceptions of infant temperament and behavior (e.g., depression and adjustment, Cox, Owen, Lewis, & Henderson, 1989; social dominance and emotional stability, Matheny et al., 1987; and negative and positive affectivity, Mangelsdorf, Gunnar, Kestenbaum, Lang, & Andreas, 1990). It may be that generational differences in maternal psychological adjustment account for this difference, particularly given the variation in sample selection methods and demographic characteristics. We have no viable rationale for the predominance of female offspring in G2. Further, any speculation we could offer would hardly be plausible given the constraints of the data used here. Thus, we call it an inexplicable phenomenon (for now), and return to it at some later point in time.

Differences in Maternal Disciplinary Practices

Maternal use of aversive discipline decreased, but maternal use of cognitive discipline increased from the first generation to the second, net of generational variations in offspring age range, female to male ratio, proportion of firstborns, and degree of anger and fearfulness, and maternal background characteristics, including age at birth of offspring and educational, marital, work, and welfare status. The simultaneity of these disciplinary changes across the two generations of mothers is suggestive of a complementary exchange of disciplinary strategies, and may be an indicator that aversive methods of socializing children under 3 years old are becoming less normative in our society. A trend for less parental use of punitive disciplinary practices was supported by others (Simons, Whitbeck, Conger, & Chyi-In, 1991). However, whether this will continue into the next generation may depend on how effective parents are in socializing offspring with other, more positive methods of behavioral control.

It is also very important to note that, despite the significant reduction in the use of aversive disciplinary strategies across generations, scolding and spanking or slapping still were used by about three quarters of the mothers in the second generation to control offspring under 3 years old. This level of usage is comparable to the rates of spanking and scolding toddlers reported by the National Family Violence Survey in 1975 and 1985 (as cited by Straus, 1994). Furthermore, experiencing corporal punishment as a child is predictive of employing corporal disciplinary measures with one's own children (Elder, Liker, & Cross, 1984; Herrenkohl, Herrenkohl, & Toedter, 1983; Simons et al., 1991). Given the very high prevalence of maternal use of aversive discipline in the original 1975 epidemiological sample, then we expect that G2 mothers were exposed to aversive discipline from their mothers (who were also part of the 1975 cohort of mothers) before they were 3 years old. This may explain, in part, the high rates of scolding and spanking or slapping reported here by G2 mothers despite the significant historical decrease. Generational change in a desirable direction (i.e., less aversive discipline) but with continued high rates of aversive practices in effect is comparable to the historical struggle to ban corporal punishment in our nation's schools, begun in 1974. Despite a significant increase in the number of states that have banned corporal punishment over two decades (27 as of 1994), almost one half still have not done so, with the delay in progress attributed to a general acceptance of high levels of punitiveness in our society (Hyman, 1995).

Influence of Offspring and Maternal Characteristics on Temperament and Discipline

Offspring characteristics influenced maternal discipline in expected directions. Mothers used more of both types of discipline with older offspring, but less with later born, and mothers of male offspring were more strict. These findings held across both generations of mothers. Mothers may need to exert more control as offspring age out of infancy due to developmental changes such as increases in mobility, alert states, and in general, more autonomous behavior. Furthermore, as offspring age mothers are reported to ascribe more intentionality to negative behavior (Dix, Ruble, & Zambarano, 1989), thus they may perceive the need for increased disciplinary efforts. That later born children are disciplined less is most likely attributable to a number of factors related to having an older child, among them less maternal time and energy and increasing maternal tolerance for social trangressions with each successive child. More strictness with male offspring is most likely due to a combination of the higher activity level reported in male infants as well as to gender stereotypes still in force, particularly those related to a need for increased control.

Mothers who worked full time used less aversive and more cognitive discipline. Less negative control of young children by their working mothers was supported by others (e.g., Crockenberg & Litman, 1991), and was attributed in part to greater motivation to make the reduced mother–child interaction time more positive, and to increased financial resources for the purchase of time-saving conveniences that reduce the burden of household demands and the ensuing stress. However, the use of less aversive discipline among mothers who worked full time occurred only in G1 mothers. In contrast, work status did not influence the use of aversive discipline among G2 mothers. This suggests that maternal employment may no longer relate to parenting as it did in the 1970s. Since then, employment among mothers of children under 3 years of age has become more normative (Hofferth & Phillips, 1987). According to recent U.S. Department of Labor statistics, due to an increasing number of mothers in the workforce, fewer than one half of infants and toddlers are cared for by their parents (Clarke Stewart, 1993). Consequently, more infants and toddlers in the 1990s are in alternative child-care arrangements. Variations in child-care experiences affect child behavior (Belsky & Braungart, 1991; Crockenberg & Litman, 1991; Scarr & Eisenberg, 1993), which in turn influences maternal discipline. Thus, a negative child-care situation may very well have an indirect but adverse effect on parenting. It also may be that the effects of maternal employment on parenting are contingent on other unmeasured prevailing factors. For example, parenting competence among working women is reported to be contingent on satisfaction with the parenting and work roles (Crockenberg & Litman, 1991; Hock & DeMeis, 1990) and spousal approval and support (Spitze, 1988). That the proportion of mothers of very young children who work full time has increased significantly is reflected in these data. Thus, it is also important to keep in mind that, as working full time was less normative in first-generation mothers, those who did so also may have differed with regard to selective individual characteristics relevant to parenting not examined here.

Single mothers tended to use more aversive discipline to control offspring. In the current study, 56% of G1 single mothers and 83% of G2 single mothers never married, a status that has been linked to a host of concomitant stressors, particularly economic disadvantage and lack of a caring partner with whom to share parenting responsibilities (Crittenden, 1985; Weinraub & Wolf, 1983); these in turn have a negative influence on mothers' personal resources and, consequently, parenting competence (Vondra & Belsky, 1993). It is possible, too, that single mothers are attempting to compensate for lack of paternal discipline by increasing the use of negative controls.

Although G1 and G2 mothers did not differ with regard to the influence of being single on the relative use of aversive discipline, inspection of within-generation group means revealed a distinctive picture for each generation: Standardized mean aversive scores for married mothers versus single mothers were, respectively, $SD = 0.15$ versus $SD = 0.39$ in G1 and $SD = -0.33$ vs. $SD = -0.06$ in G2. Thus, single mothers in the G2 sample, although meting out more aversive discipline than their married counterparts (as did single mothers in the G1 sample), were part of the overall generational decrease in the use of aversive discipline noted for all G2 mothers.

Effects of being single on maternal discipline also may be a function of other factors such as social attitudes and stigmatization, which could change over time. For example, we also found that single G1 mothers were less strict than married G1 mothers, whereas marriage status did not influence strictness in G2 mothers. Strictness as measured here (i.e., how strict about following rules) is a component of Baumrind's (1973) conceptualization of the authoritative parent, and has related negatively to poor child outcome in our studies (Cohen & Brook, 1987). This interpretation of strictness is supported by our current finding of lower angry temperament in offspring of families with higher strictness. Thus, we view this generational change as desirable. Although single motherhood may be related to a number of stressors, current norms regarding marital status and motherhood are more flexible than those in effect two decades ago, with social support systems being much more in evidence. (Note the social phenomenon in 1992 of the popular television character Murphy Brown, a single pregnant woman whose impending motherhood generated a political debate in the media over alternatives of acceptable family structure.) Consequently, single mothers may have more resources to alleviate potential stressors, enabling them to provide a more consistent and structured approach to socializing their offspring. It also is possible that increased availability of legal abortion over the past two decades has given pregnant women without support systems more of a choice about carrying the pregnancy to term than past generations have had; thus, sample characteristics of unmarried mothers from different generations may vary due to selection bias brought about by historical changes.

Welfare-supported mothers reported significantly more angry temperament, and to a lesser extent, more fearfulness in offspring and more strictness than mothers not supported by welfare. Because of a marginal generational difference in the relationship between welfare status and angry temperament (i.e., $p = .07$), we examined within-generation mean scores: The difference between welfare status groups was significant in G2 ($SD = 0.65$ vs. $SD = 0.01$; unit change in angry temperament given welfare support after adjusting for offspring and maternal characteristics, $B = 0.62$, $p < .05$) but not in G1 ($SD = 0.02$ vs. $SD = -0.11$ in G1); unit change in angry temperament given welfare support after adjusting for offspring and maternal characteristics, $B = 0.10$ (ns). Furthermore, examination of within-generation fearful temperament and strictness mean scores for welfare status groups revealed a similar picture: The links between welfare support with more offspring fearfulness and with more strictness were reflective of G2 mothers, not G1 mothers. On the other hand, welfare support was related to significantly less maternal use of cognitive discipline in the first generation, but not in the second.

Some of these findings have been supported by other research (e.g., a link between economic disadvantage and maternal reports of increased problematic offspring temperament: Sameroff, Seifer, & Elias, 1982); however, others have not (e.g., the link between economic disadvantage and an increase in rules and structure). The generational differences in welfare status effects found here suggest that these inconsistencies may be contingent on historical changes involving social attitudes and policy toward welfare support Welfare was just beginning to be viewed as an entitlement in the 1970s, a view that was probably predominant by the 1990s; consequently, criteria for benefits have become less stringent. (Note that welfare mothers were more normative in the G2 sample than in the G1 sample, a finding most likely due to social changes as well as to sample selection factors). Thus, easier access to welfare benefits may have allowed more women without financial resources or family support systems to have and care for their child, suggesting that characteristics of welfare-supported mothers may have changed over time. For example, lack of a family support system to alleviate stressors among economically disadvantaged mothers of young children might work to negatively influence perceptions of offspring temperament, whereas if closely involved or living with a family support system others might share the parenting role, thus altering maternal disciplinary practices. It is also possible that welfare status is not an altogether suitable proxy variable for economic disadvantage, and that such status implies other factors not considered here that would explain findings that may appear counterintuitive.

Relationships Between Offspring Temperament and Maternal Discipline

Angry temperament was associated with increased maternal use of aversive discipline in both generations, and supports other reports of a link between punitive parenting and anger, defiance, and noncompliance in children under 3 years old (e.g., Crockenberg, 1987; Crockenberg & Litman, 1990; Lee & Bates, 1985). Angry temperament was also associated with increased maternal use of cognitive discipline across generations. As we view cognitive discipline in a positive light, this finding would at first appear to be counterintuitive. However, Crockenberg and Litman (1990) reported a link between defiant behavior in 2-year-olds and maternal control by guidance and reasoning, and attributed it to lack of a clear directive to discontinue the inappropriate behavior. Clear directives (such as those implied by rules) may be a necessary ingredient to more cognitive-oriented discipline, which by itself may be too permissive by leaving open the option of refusal. It also is possible that some mothers overdiscipline their offspring with cognitive as well as aversive strategies, thus evoking increasing anger, or, that mothers increase their use of cognitive as well as aversive discipline in order to control escalating anger in offspring. Others have reported that mothers of offspring with difficult temperament were more engaged with their children than were mothers of offspring without difficult temperament (Klein, 1984; Pettit & Bates, 1984). Furthermore, there is evidence that parents often combine reasoning strategies with power assertive control strategies to socialize children (Grusec & Kuczynski, 1980; Holden, 1983), and that this reduces the effectiveness of the former (Lytton, 1980).

This prompted us to examine the relationship between angry temperament and the overall use of discipline (aversive and cognitive scores combined). Angry temperament was regressed against the total discipline score and, given the higher rates of offspring anger reported by second generation mothers, adjusted for generation membership. Independent effects of total discipline ($B = 0.17$ SD, $p < .01$) and generation membership ($B = 0.23$, $p < .05$) on angry temperament were observed. (The interaction effect between generation membership and total disciplne on angry temperament was tested, but was not significant.) Thus, the amount of discipline used may be as important a factor as type or pattern of strategies used in determining the links between parenting and offspring temperament. (Note also that second generation mothers used a greater variety of disciplinary methods than did first generation mothers (mean group scores: $SD = 0.12$ vs. $SD = -0.07$, two-tailed $t = 1.68$, $p < .10$), which may explain in part the higher levels of anger reported for second-generation offspring.) However, the link between difficult temperament and parenting also may be moderated by other influences not measured here (e.g., parental beliefs about reinforcing difficult temperament and degree of social support) (Crockenberg, 1981; Crockenberg & McCluskey, 1986), influences that may vary across the two generations of mothers studied here.

High levels of strictness, in contrast to high levels of aversive and cognitive discipline, appeared to be a remedy for both increasing anger and increasing fearfulness. This finding supports in part the link between providing a firm structure of rules and guidelines and positive outcome in children (Baumrind, 1973). Given the modest relationship between strictness and aversive discipline, this finding takes on added import. Providing a set of clear guidelines, when not coupled with punitive discipline, may be an effective means of socializing children.

Limitations

Certain limitations in the current data should be addressed. First, measures of maternal disciplinary strategies and offspring temperament were obtained contemporaneously; thus, causality cannot be determined. However, causality, which was not the focus of the current analyses, was most likely bidirectional given the substantial empirical support for the more dynamic, transactional models of mother–offspring interactions. Second, mothers provided reports of both disciplinary strategies and offspring temperament; thus there were no independent measures of either. However we have found the disciplinary strategies to be related to combined mother–child reports of later conduct disorder (Cohen & Brook, 1987, 1995). Finally, maternal characteristics measured here were primarily of a sociodemographic nature. Sociodemographic influences on parenting may be mediated by the effects of psychological or social relationship factors (Belsky, 1984; Belsky & Vondra, 1985). For example, among high-risk mothers of infants, psychological integration differentiated between those who were punitive and those who provided adequate or excellent care (Brunnquell, Crichton, & Egeland, 1981), and, among adolescent, economically disadvantaged mothers of 2-year-olds, social support differentiated between those who were punitive and those who were nurturant and responsive (Crockenberg, 1987; García Coll, Hoffman, & Oh, 1987). Psychological characteristics are reported to be linked to parenting practices in low-risk middle-class mothers as well (e.g., Benn, 1986; Cox et al., 1989).

CONCLUSIONS

In summary, we did find evidence of change in mother–offspring pairs across the two generations, namely, a significant increase and decrease in, respectively, cognitive discipline and aversive discipline. However, despite the significant decrease in the latter, high rates of punitive discipline still prevail, most notably scolding and spanking or slapping. In addition, there is indication that although disciplinary tactics may have changed in a desirable direction, the overall amount of discipline used bears examination as well. We have also attributed generational differences in disciplinary practices to historical changes involving the marital, work, and welfare status of mothers of young children. Although these interpretations may be considered somewhat speculative and certainly in need of replication, we hope they inspire others to examine the social forces at work and the consequences for the individual. We also found strong evidence of stability across generations, primarily in the positive links between angry temperament and more punitive control and less strictness, and, to a lesser extent, more cognitive control. Given the significant decrease in aversive discipline across generations, it will be very important that mothers have a repertoire of more effective strategies with which to substitute, ones that are compatible with a reasonable degree of compliance in offspring. These findings suggest that having rules and guidelines even for very young children may be an effective way in which to reduce angry or fearful behavior or both.

ACKNOWLEDGMENTS

The research described was supported by grants from the National Institute of Mental Health and by the W. T. Grant Foundation.

REFERENCES

Bates, J. E. (1980). The concept of difficult temperament. *Merrill-Palmer Quarterly, 26,* 299–319.

Bates, J. E., Freeland, C. A., & Lounsbury, M. L. (1979). Measurement of infant difficultness. *Child Development, 50,* 794–803.

Baumrind, D. (1973). The development of instrumental competence through socialization. In A. D. Pick (Ed.), *Minnesota symposium on child psychology* (Vol. 7, pp. 3–46). Minneapolis: University of Minnesota Press.

Bell, R. Q. (1968). A reinterpretation of the direction of effects in studies of socialization. *Psychological Review, 75,* 81–95.

Bell, R. Q., & Chapman, M. (1986). Child effects in studies using experimental or brief longitudinal approaches to socialization. *Developmental Psychology, 22,* 595–603.

Belsky, J. (1984). The determinants of parenting: A process model. *Child Development, 55,* 83–96.

Belsky, J. (1988). The "effects" of infant day care reconsidered. *Early Childhood Research Quarterly, 3,* 235–272.

Belsky, J., & Braungart, J. M. (1991). Are insecure-avoidant infants with extensive day-care experience less stressed by and more independent in the Strange Situation. *Child Development, 62,* 567–571.

Belsky, J., & Vondra, J. (1985). Characteristics, consequences, and determinants of parenting. In L. L'Abate (Ed.), *Handbook of family psychology and therapy* (pp. 523–536). Homewood, IL: The Dorsey Press.

Benn, R. K. (1986). Factors promoting secure attachments relationships between employed mothers and their sons. *Child Development, 57,* 1224–1231.

Bezirganian, S., & Cohen, P. (1992). Sex differences in the interaction between temperament and parenting. *Journal of the American Academy of Child and Adolescent Psychiatry, 31,* 790–801.

Brazelton, T. B., Koslowski, B., & Main, M. (1974). The origins of reciprocity in mother–infant interaction. In M. Lewis & L. A. Rosenblum (Eds.), *The effect of the infant on its caregiver* (pp. 49–76). New York: Wiley.

Brunnquell, D., Crichton, L., & Egeland, B. (1981). Maternal personality and attitude in disturbances of child rearing. *American Journal of Orthopsychiatry, 51,* 680–691.

Bugental, D. B., Caporael, L., & Shennum, W. A. (1980). Experimentally-produced child controllability: Effects on the potency of adult communication patterns. *Child Development, 51,* 520–528.

Buss, D. M. (1981). Predicting parent–child interactions from children's activity level. *Developmental Psychology, 17,* 59–65.

Cantor, N. L., & Gelfand, D. M. (1977). Effects of responsiveness and sex of children on adults' behavior. *Child Development, 48,* 232–238.

Chess, S., & Thomas, A. (1984). *The origins and evolution of behavior disorders: From infancy to early adult life.* New York: Brunner/Mazel.

Clarke-Stewart, A. (1993). *Day-care.* Cambridge, MA: Harvard University Press.

Cohen, P., & Brook, J. S. (1987). Family factors related to the persistence of psychopathology in childhood and adolescence. *Psychiatry, 50,* 332–345.

Cohen, P., & Brook, J. S. (1995). The reciprocal influence of punishment and child behavior disorder. In J. McCord (Ed.), *Coercion and punishment in long-term perspectives* (pp. 154–164). Cambridge, England: Cambridge University Press.

Cohen, P., Cohen, J., Kasen, S., Velez, C. N., Hartmark, C., Johnson, J., Rojas, M., Brook, J., & Struening, E. L. (1993). An epidemiological study of disorders in late childhood and adolescence - I. Age- and gender-specific prevalence. *Journal of Child Psychology and Psychiatry, 34,* 851–867.

Cox, M. J., Owen, M. T., Lewis, J. M., & Henderson, V. K. (1989). Marriage, adult adjustment, and early parenting. *Child Development, 60,* 1015–1024.

Crittenden, P. (1985). Social networks, quality of child rearing, and child development. *Child Development, 56,* 1299–1313.

Crockenberg, S. (1981). Infant irritability, mother responsiveness, and social support influences on the security of infant–mother attachment. *Child Development, 52,* 857–865.

Crockenberg, S. (1986). Are temperamental differences in babies associated with predictable differences in caregiving? In J. V. Lerner & R. M. Lerner (Eds.), *Temperament and child development: New directions for child development* (pp. 53–73). San Francisco: Jossey-Bass.

Crockenberg, S. (1987). Predictors and correlates of anger toward and punitive control of toddlers by adolescent mothers. *Child Development, 58,* 964–975.

Crockenberg, S. (1988). Stress and role satisfaction experienced by employed and nonemployed mothers with young children. *Lifestyles: Family and Economic Issues, 9,* 97–110.

Crockenberg, S., & Litman, C. (1990). Autonomy as competence in 2-year-olds: Maternal correlates of child defiance, compliance, and self-assertion. *Developmental Psychology, 26,* 961–971.

Crockenberg, S., & Litman, C. (1991). Effects of maternal employment on maternal and two-year-old child behavior. *Child Development, 62,* 930–953.

Crockenberg, S., & McClusky, K. (1986). Change in maternal behavior during the baby's first year of life. *Child Development, 57,* 746–753.

Dix, T., Ruble, D. N., & Zambarano, R. J. (1989). Mothers' implicit theories of discipline: Child effects, parent effects, and the attribution process. *Child Development, 60,* 1373–1391.

Elardo, R., Bradley, R., & Caldwell, B. M. (1975). The relation of infants' home environments to mental test performance from six to thirty-six months: A longitudinal analysis. *Child Development, 46,* 71–76.

Elder, G., Liker, J., & Cross, C. (1984). Parent–child behavior in the great depression: Life course and intergenerational influences. *Life-Span Development and Behavior, 6,* 109–158.

Emery, R. E., & Tuer, M. (1993). Parenting and the marital relationship. In T. Luster & L. Okagaki (Eds.), *Parenting: An ecological perspective* (pp. 121–148). Hillsdale, NJ: Lawrence Erlbaum Associates.

Farrington, D. P. (1990). Implications of criminal career research for the prevention of offending. *Journal of Adolescence, 13,* 93–113.

Farrington, D. P. (1991). Antisocial personality from childhood to adulthood. *The Psychologist: Bulletin of the British Psychological Society, 4,* 389–394.

Fleiss, J. L., Williams, J. B., & Dubro, A. F. (1986). The logistic regression analysis of psychiatric data. *Journal of Psychiatric Research, 20,* 145–209.

Furstenberg, F. (1976). The social consequences of teenage parenthood. *Family Planning Perspectives, 81,* 48–164.

García Coll, C. T., Hoffman, J., & Oh, W. (1987). The social ecology and early parenting of caucasian adolescent mothers. *Child Development, 58,* 955–963.

Goldsmith, H. H., & Campos, J. J. (1982). Toward a theory of infant temperament. In R. M. Emde & R. Harmon (Eds.), *Attachment and affiliative systems: Neurobiological and psychobiological aspects* (pp. 161–193). New York: Plenum Press.

Grusec, J. E., & Kuczynski, L. (1980). Direction of effect in socialization: A comparison of the parent's versus the child's behavior as determinants of disciplinary techniques. *Developmental Psychology, 16,* 1–9.

Hannan, K., & Luster, T. (1991). Influence of parent, child, and contextual factors on the quality of the home environment. *Infant Mental Health Journal, 12,* 17–30.

Herrenkohl, E. C., Herrenkohl, R. C., & Toedter, L. J. (1983). Perspectives on the intergenerational transmission of abuse. In D. Finkelhor, R. J. Gelles, G. T. Hotaling, & M. A. Straus (Eds.), *The dark side of families: Current family violence research* (pp. 305–316). Beverly Hills, CA: Sage.

Hock, E., & DeMeis, D. K. (1990). Depression in mothers of infants: The role of maternal employment. *Developmental Psychology, 26,* 285–291.

Hofferth, S., & Phillips, D. A. (1987). Child care in the United States, 1970 to 1995. *Journal of Marriage and the Family, 49,* 559–571.

Holden, G. W. (1983). Avoiding conflict: Mothers as tacticians in the supermarket. *Child Development, 54,* 233–240.

Hyman, I. (1995). Corporal punishment, psychological maltreatment, violence, and punitiveness in America: Research, advocacy, and public policy. *Applied and Preventive Psychology, 4,* 113–130.

Kandel, D. B., & Wu, P. (1995). Disentangling mother-child effects in the development of antisocial behavior. In J. McCord (Ed.), *Coercion and punishment in long-term perspectives* (pp. 106–123). Cambridge, England: Cambridge University Press.

Kasen, S., Cohen, P., Brook, J. S., & Hartmark, C. (1996). A multiple-risk interaction model: Effects of temperament and divorce on psychiatric disorders in children. *Journal of Abnormal Child Psychology, 24,* 121–150.

Klein, P. (1984). The relation of Israeli mothers toward infants in relation to infants' perceived temperament. *Child Development, 55,* 1212–1218.

Kogan, L., Smith, J., & Jenkins, S. (1977). Ecological validity of indicator data as predictors of survey findings. *Journal of Social Service Research, 1,* 117–132.

Kuczynski, L. (1984). Socialization goals and mother–child interaction: Strategies for short-term and long-term compliance. *Developmental Psychology, 20,* 1061–1073.

Kuczynski, L., Kochanska, G., Radke-Yarrow, M., & Girnius-Brown, O. (1987). A developmental interpretation of young children's noncompliance. *Developmental Psychology, 23,* 799–806.

Lee, C., & Bates, J. (1985). Mother-child interaction at age two years and perceived difficult temperament. *Child Development, 56,* 1314–1325.

Lerner, R. M. (1978). Nature, nurture, and dynamic interactionism. *Human Development, 21,* 1–20.

Lerner, R. M. (1979). A dynamic interactional concept of individual and social relationship development. In R. Burgess & T. Huston (Eds.), *Social exchange in developing relationships* (pp. 271–305). New York: Academic Press.

Lerner, R. M., & Spanier, G. B. (1978). A dynamic and interactional view of child and family development. In R. M. Lerner & G. B. Spanier (Eds.), *Child influences on marital and family interaction: A life-span perspective* (pp. 1–22). New York: Academic Press.

Lewis, S. A., Gorsky, A., Cohen, P., & Hartmark, C. (1985). The reactions of youth to diagnostic interviews. *Journal of the American Academy of Child and Adolescent Psychiatry, 24,* 750–755.

Lytton, H. (1980). *Parent-child interaction.* New York: Plenum Press.

Loeber, R., & Dishion, T. J. (1983). Early predictors of male delinquency: A review. *Psychological Bulletin, 94,* 68–99.

Loeber, R., & Stouthamer-Loeber, M. (1986). Family factors as correlates and predictors of juvenile conduct problems and delinquency. In M. Tonry & N. Morris (Eds.), *Crime and justice: An annual review of research* (pp. 29–149). Chicago: University of Chicago Press.

Mangelsdorf, S., Gunnar, M., Kestenbaum, R., Lang, S., & Andreas, D. (1990). Infant proneness-to-distress temperament, maternal personality, and mother-infant attachment: Associations and goodness of fit. *Child Development, 61,* 820–831.

Matheny, A. P., Jr., Wilson, R. S., & Thoben, A. S. (1987). HOME and mother: Relations with infant temperament. *Developmental Psychology, 23,* 323–331.

McCord, J. (1979). Some child-rearing antecedents of criminal behavior in adult men. *Journal of Personality and Social Psychology, 9,* 1477–1486.

Patterson, G. R., DeBaryshe, B. D., & Ramsey, E. (1989). A developmental perspective on antisocial behavior. *American Psychologist, 44,* 329–335.

Pettit, G., & Bates, J. (1984). Continuity of individual differences in the mother-infant relationship from 6 to 13 months. *Child Development, 55,* 729–739.

Power, T. G., & Chapieski, M. L. (1986). Childrearing and impulse control in toddlers: A naturalistic investigation. *Developmental Psychology, 22,* 271–275.

Quinton D., & Rutter, M. (1985). Parenting behavior of mothers raised "in care." In R. Nichol (Ed.), *Longitudinal studies in child psychology and psychiatry* (pp. 157–201). Chichester, England: Wiley.

Robins, L. (1966). *Deviant children grown up.* Baltimore. Williams & Wilkins.

Roosa, M. W., Fitzgerald, H. E., & Carlson, N. A. (1982). A comparison of teenage and older mothers: A systems analysis. *Journal of Marriage and the Family, 47,* 367–377.

Sameroff, A. L. (1975). Transactional models in early social relations. *Human Development, 18,* 65–79.

Sameroff, A. L., & Chandler, M. J. (1975). Reproductive risk and the continuum of caretaking casualty. In F. D. Horowitz (Ed.), *Review of child development research* (Vol. 4, pp. 187–244). Chicago: University of Chicago Press.

Sameroff, A. L., Seifer, R., & Elias, P. K. (1982). Sociocultural variability in infant temperament ratings. *Child Development, 53,* 164–173.

Scarr, S., & Eisenberg, M. (1993). Child care research: Issues, perspectives, and results. *Annual Review of Psychology, 44,* 613–644.

Schilmoeller, G. L., & Baranowski, M. D. (1985). Childrearing of firstborns by adolescent and older mothers. *Adolescence, 20,* 805–822.

Simons, R. L., Whitbeck, L. B., Conger, R. D., & Chyi-In, W. (1991). Intergenerational transmission of harsh parenting. *Developmental Psychology, 27,* 159–171.

Spitze, G. (1988). Women's employment and family relations: A review. *Journal of Marriage and the Family, 50,* 595–618.

Straus, M. A. (1994). *Beating the devil out of them: Corporal punishment in American families.* New York: Lexington Books.

Straus, M. (1995). Corporal punishment of children and adult depression and suicidal ideation. In J. McCord (Ed.), *Coercion and punishment in long-term perspectives* (pp. 59–77). Cambridge, England: Cambridge University Press.

Thomas, A., Chess, S., & Birch, H. (1968). *Temperament and behavioral disorders in childhood.* New York: New York University Press.

Thomas, A., Chess, S., Birch, H. G, Hertzig, M. E., & Korn, S. (1963). *Behavioral individuality in early childhood.* New York: New York University Press.

Tulkin, S. R. (1977). Social class differences in maternal and infant behavior. In P. H. Leiderman, S. R. Tulkin, & A. Rosenfield (Eds.), *Culture and infancy* (pp. 495–538). New York: Academic Press.

Vaughn, B., Taraldson, B. J., Crichton, L., & Egeland, B. (1981). The assessment of infant temperament. *Infant Behavior and Development, 4,* 1–17.

Vondra, J., & Belsky, J. (1993). Developmental origins of parenting: Personality and relationship factors. In T. Luster & L. Okagaki (Eds.), *Parenting: An ecological perspective* (pp. 1–33). Hillsdale, NJ: Lawrence Erlbaum Associates.

Weinraub, M., Jaeger, E., & Hoffman, L. W. (1988). Predicting infant outcomes in families with employed and nonemployed mothers. *Early Childhood Research Quarterly, 3,* 361–378.

Weinraub, M., & Wolf, B. (1983). Effects of stress and social supports on mother–child interactions in single- and two-parent families. *Child Development, 54,* 1297–1311.

Chapter 10

I Felt the Earth Move: A Prospective Study of the 1994 Northridge Earthquake

Jodie B. Ullman
California State University, San Bernadino

Michael B. Newcomb
University of Southern California

On January 17, 1994, at 4:30 a.m., residents of Los Angeles were awakened by a 6.6 magnitude earthquake centered in Northridge, a suburb of Los Angeles. The earthquake was felt throughout Southern California and aftershocks continued to shake the Los Angeles area for months afterward. In the week immediately following the quake there were more than 245 aftershocks of magnitude 3 or higher, 26 were greater than 4, and 2 were larger than a 5 magnitude on the Richter scale. The initial earthquake and the subsequent aftershocks created widespread damage. Freeways and buildings collapsed, gas and water lines exploded, and trains derailed. Many people were without gas, electricity, and water for several days. Surprisingly, fewer than 50 people were killed; however, many people were injured and hundreds were left homeless.

The goal of this chapter is to examine the relationship between location and psychological distress, substance use, and general control beliefs before and after a natural disaster using a pre–post quasi-experimental design. Within the 6 months immediately prior to the earthquake we had finished data collection for an ongoing longitudinal project. Many of respondents in this longitudinal project were still located in the Los Angeles area; therefore, the earthquake provided us with a natural pretest–posttest quasi-experiment.

PAST RESEARCH

People who survive a disaster often experience some degree of psychological distress (Cardena & Spiegel, 1993; Goenjian et al., 1994; Kaniasty & Norris, 1993; Manuel & Anderson, 1993; see North, Smith, McCool, & Lightcap, 1989, for an exception). Unfortunately, most of the studies that have tested the link between a disaster and psychological distress have had neither prospective predisaster data available for the survivors nor control groups of unaffected individuals. Without this baseline information, it is difficult to ascertain whether the disaster was responsible for the heightened psychological distress or whether something idiosyncratic to the sample might have yielded the same results regardless of the disaster.

Three studies have prospectively examined a direct link between a disaster and psychological distress. Kaniasty and Norris (1993) found prospective evidence of increased depression following a severe flood in a population of elderly adults. Grady et al. (1991) also prospectively examined a direct link between psychological distress after a disaster (both a hurricane and an earthquake) and found evidence of greater depression following a disaster in a sample of older adults. Unfortunately, the combined disaster sample was not equivalent to the general sample. The disaster sample was in the later stages of rheumatoid arthritis and experienced more flare-ups of arthritis than the general sample; therefore, it is not clear whether the greater depression was due to the disaster or the later disease progression. Both of these studies used samples of elderly adults. It is unclear if younger adults respond similarly to disasters. Among younger adults, is there a direct relationship between a disaster and Psychological Distress?

In a pre–post study with control group, Robins, Lishbach, Smith, Cottler, and Solomon (1986) found little evidence that experiencing a disaster (flood, dioxin contamination). In contrast to Kaniasty and Norris (1993) and Grady et al. (1991), the Robins et al. sample ranged in age from less than 25 to over 65. Prior to the disasters, the exposed and control groups were similar in terms of pre-existing Psychological Distress. They hypothesized that one reason for the lack of association might be the mild nature of these disasters. They also hypothesized that the pre–post design with control group allowed for more precise assessment of the relationship between Psychological Distress following a disaster. A second reason for the lack of association between the disasters and Psychological Distress might be related to the measurement time frame. It is unclear how long after experiencing these disasters the survivors were reinterviewed. It may be that a disaster does increase Psychological Distress but only for a brief period of time.

Given these conflicting results, it seems relevant to further examine the direct link between experiencing a disaster and Psychological Distress.

Other factors such as amount of damage, proximity, gender, and social support may serve moderating or mediating roles in the relationship between disasters and Psychological Distress.

Proximity

Proximity to a disaster may be associated with greater Psychological Distress. Smith, North, McCool, and Shea (1990) examined symptoms of posttraumatic stress disorder (PTSD), major depression, generalized anxiety, and alcohol–drug abuse approximately 4 to 6 weeks after a plane crashed into a hotel. Survivors were categorized into three groups: those on site at the time of the crash; those who were supposed to be at the hotel, but for some reason were not there at the time of the crash; and those not scheduled to work. The group that was in the hotel when the plane crashed reported twice as much anxiety as the groups that were off-site when the crash occurred. Depression was the most common problem in all of the groups regardless of location. It may be that proximity to a disaster is predictive of only some aspects of Psychological Distress.

Smith et al. (1990) found no differences in prevalence of alcohol abuse in the on- and off-site individuals after a plane crash. However, some survivors, regardless of location, did meet the criteria for alcohol abuse following the crash. Those who met the criteria for alcohol abuse also met the criteria for at least one other psychiatric diagnosis.

In an improvement over the studies that employed posttest only designs, Smith et al. (1990) also obtained retrospective information on participants' histories of psychiatric disorders. Of the 50% of the participants who met criteria for psychiatric diagnoses after the disaster, 72% were individuals with a predisaster history of a psychiatric disorder. Previous psychopathology was a strong predictor of posttrauma psychopathology; however, symptoms of PTSD arose in individuals without predisaster histories of the disorder. They concluded that individuals with psychiatric histories may be particularly susceptible to psychiatric disorders following a disaster.

This raises several questions. Are individuals with nonclinical levels of Psychological Distress prior to a disaster also more susceptible to distress following a disaster? PTSD symptoms arose in survivors without histories of PTSD. What are the antecedents for PTSD? Does Psychological Distress prior to the disaster make individuals susceptible for PTSD as well as general Psychological Distress?

Goenjian et al. (1994) also found a relationship between location and Psychological Distress. Survivors who were closer to the epicenter of an earthquake had more symptoms of Psychological Distress than did those participants who were farther away. Unfortunately, neither the Goenjian et al. (1994) nor the Smith et al. (1990) study was prospective. Therefore, were the study participants who were closer to the disaster sites more susceptible to Psychological Distress for reasons independent of the disaster? For example, if a community in close proximity to a disaster is already chronically stressed, would greater stress in that community, relative to other communities, be expected regardless of a disaster? Conversely, if a disaster is centered in a community with good resources and community support, perhaps less stress would be evident regardless of the disaster. North et al. (1989) cited strong community support as a possible explanation for their null findings. The study reported in this chapter is prospective and does include characteristics of the communities and therefore can examine the relationship between location and Psychological Distress with less ambiguity than previous research.

Generally, people who live close to the center of a disaster also experience the most physical damage. Which is the more important predictor of Psychological Distress: absolute damage or sheer proximity? Following the Sierra Madre earthquake, Freddy, Saladin, Kilpatrick, Resnick, and Saunders (1994) found the earthquake-related resource loss was associated with Psychological Distress.

Gender

Smith et al. (1990) found no gender differences in Psychological Distress. However, Freddy et al. (1994) found that women experienced greater Psychological Distress than men 4 to 7 months following an earthquake. Manuel and Anderson (1993) and Solomon et al. (1987) found that men and women respond differently to disasters. Manuel and Anderson examined duration of stress and found that women reported more stress than men; however, these relationships changed over time. Women were higher in intrusive thoughts, but not avoidant thoughts at 2 weeks after the earthquake; however, by 1 to 2 weeks following the quake, women were higher on both intrusive and avoidant thoughts. Differences in general Psychological Distress disappeared by the second measurement.

In a prospective study, Solomon, Smith, Robins, and Fischbach (1987) reinterviewed individuals in the midwest after a flood and discovery of unsafe levels of dioxin. Males who were personally or indirectly exposed to the disaster used more alcohol and were more depressed than were their female counterparts. They concluded that major catastrophes have a greater effect on men than on women.

Social Support

Social Support, specifically nonkin support, mediates the relationship between a disaster and Psychological Distress. More nonkin support led to less Psychological Distress (Kaniasty & Norris, 1993). Although helping may be beneficial for the person being helped, it may also be burdensome to the Social Support giver. Solomon et al. (1987) also found that survivors of the flood who were most heavily relied on by network members were also more likely to somatize (women) or abuse alcohol (men) than those with moderate network demands. Additionally, excellent spousal support helped men but hindered women.

These studies primarily examined help and support burden. Neither study examined the degree to which strong emotional support from family and friends may buffer the negative psychological effects of a disaster. It may be that the perception of strong emotional support may lessen the impact of a disaster on psychological distress and symptoms of PTSD (Newcomb, 1990).

Perceived Control

To our knowledge, none of the disaster studies examined the relationship between sense of control and Psychological Distress or substance use following a disaster. Solomon et al. (1987) suggested that perceived control may mediate the relationship between disaster and social involvement.

Nor have studies established a relationship between proximity to a disaster and sense of control. Do individuals who are very near a disaster experience a greater loss of control than individuals who are more distant? Taylor (1983) asserted that an important aspect of recovering from a trauma is gaining a sense of control over it. Therefore, although disasters are characterized by a loss of control, perhaps the degree to which the loss of control is experienced is associated with an increase in psychological distress. To this end, Solomon et al. (1987) suggested further research that examines the extent to which a sense of loss of control explains negative effects of disasters.

THE CURRENT STUDY

The current study uses a pre–post design to examine the effect of an earthquake on Psychological Distress, sense of control, and substance use. Pre-earthquake measures of distress, sense of control, substance use, and social support are employed as well as specific characteristics of the earthquake (i.e., perceived force, damage).

Proximity

The Northridge earthquake was felt over a wide area; however, not all of the area sustained damage. Due to soil conditions, specifically liquefaction, some areas farther from the epicenter felt more shaking and sustained more damage than did areas closer to the epicenter. The relationship between proximity to the epicenter of the earthquake and perceived control and psychological distress before and after the disaster are examined. We hypothesize that individuals closer to the epicenter or who sustained greater damage regardless of proximity to the epicenter will (a) perceive greater loss of control; (b) report greater depression, anxiety, or panic; and (c) report more substance use. Increased predisaster alcohol and drug use may be predictors of postdisaster Psychological Distress. Although Psychological Distress has been widely examined in the disaster literature, few studies have explored alcohol and drug use, or marijuana and cigarette use following a disaster.

Pre-existing stress within a community may also exacerbate Psychological Distress and loss of control following an earthquake, even if the community is further from the epicenter. The south central area of Los Angeles is a primarily African American community. This area had suffered widespread damage in the civil unrest following the Rodney King beating trial the prior year. Because this community was still recovering from this human-made disaster, the residents of this area may have been chronically stressed at the time of the earthquake. This might explain their experiencing higher levels of Psychological Distress and loss of control than did residents in areas near the epicenter of the earthquake.

Antecedents of PTSD

Prior studies have not examined the precursors of symptoms of PTSD following a disaster. An exploratory analysis is performed to develop a parsimonious prediction model for two facets of PTSD (avoidant and intrusive thoughts). The independent variables of interest are: predisaster levels of Psychological Distress, social support, damage, perceived force, proximity to epicenter, gender, and sense of control.

This first hypothesized model is presented in Fig. 10.1. In all figures, circles represent latent variables and rectangles represent measured variables. A line connecting variables represents a hypothesized direct effect. Lack of a line connecting variables indicates no hypothesized direct effect. For clarity within the text, latent variables are referred to with initial capital letters.

High levels of Psychological Distress pre-earthquake may predispose individuals to have more avoidant and intrusive thoughts. This path reflects a control for emotional distress prior to the earthquake. After controlling for distress pre-earthquake, it may still be difficult for survivors to achieve a sense of "normalcy" if they live in communities that have experienced extensive damage. Survivors who live in these areas are constantly faced with reminders of the earthquake and may experience more avoidant and intrusive thoughts. Therefore, amount of damage should increase both avoidant and intrusive thoughts.

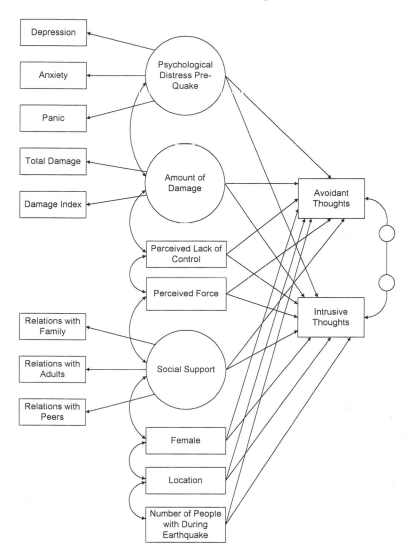

FIG. 10.1. Hypothesized model for prediction of posttraumatic stress disorder (PTSD).

Individuals who have an external locus of control or a low general sense of control may be more sensitive to their surroundings. After a disaster, such individuals may take longer to focus on normal day-to-day activities than do other individuals. Therefore, a low sense of control pre-earthquake may lead to more avoidant and intrusive thoughts after the earthquake.

Survivors who perceived a lot of shaking (strong perceived force) may tend to relive the earthquake more, for example, by experiencing intrusive thoughts; alternatively, they may avoid thinking about the earthquake. Additionally, having felt the initial earthquake strongly, they may have been more sensitive to aftershocks. Thus, stronger perceived force should lead to more PTSD symptoms.

Strong emotional Social Support pre-earthquake may reduce the number of avoidant and intrusive thoughts in survivors postearthquake. Whether or not family and friends are able to actually help with cleaning up or with contacting disaster agencies, they can serve as someone to talk to, and sharing the experience may result in fewer avoidant and intrusive thoughts. Schachter and Singer (1962) found that in stressful situations people preferred to wait with others rather than alone. It may also be that if survivors experienced the earthquake with others, they may experience fewer avoidant and intrusive thoughts than survivors who were alone. This hypothesis may not apply if the people they experienced the earthquake with were their direct responsibility, for example, their children. Although presence of others may reduce the impact of a stressful event, presence of children may increase stress because of a need to care for and protect them. Finally, women may experience more avoidant and intrusive thoughts than men.

Mediational Models

The relationships among preexisting Psychological Distress, substance use, and sense of control, closeness to the earthquake, and damage to the area are examined with a multivariate mediational model. Psychological outcomes following an earthquake are complex and multidimensional. To begin to understand the dynamics of Psychological Distress following an earthquake, multivariate models need to be developed that take the complex nature of a disaster into account. Many factors contribute to how survivors of a disaster respond.

Past research has generally been limited to univariate examination of specific constructs hypothesized to be related to a facet of distress following a disaster. These univariate models are helpful but limited. This study examines Psychological Distress (including alcohol use and PTSD) within a model that includes pre-earthquake measures of distress and sense of control. The relationship among Psychological Distress, location, damage, perceived force and gender are also examined and controlled.

It is hypothesized that a sense of loss of control postearthquake will mediate the relationship between the sense of control pre-earthquake and Psychological Distress and alcohol consumption postearthquake. This second hypothesized model is presented in Fig. 10.2. Perceived force and amount of damage will mediate the relationship between location and Psychological Distress and PTSD. Strong Social Support pre-earthquake will predict less Psychological Distress and PTSD postearthquake. Women will experience more Psychological Distress and PTSD postearthquake than will men.

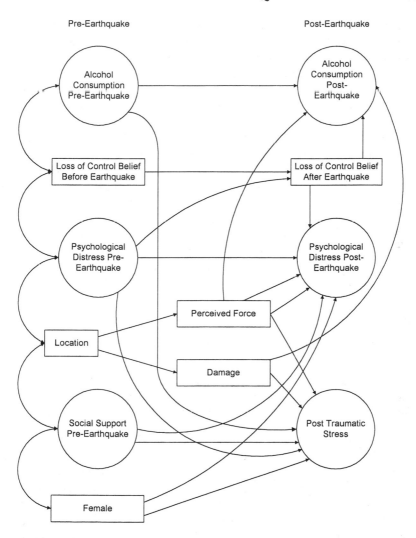

Pre-Earthquake   Post-Earthquake

FIG. 10.2. Hypothesized pre–post model of psychological functioning after the earthquake.

METHOD

Participants and Procedures

Participants in this project were from an ongoing longitudinal study (Newcomb, 1997; Newcomb & Bentler, 1986; Newcomb, Huba, & Bentler, 1986). The focus of this project is on adolescent and adult development with a particular emphasis on substance use. Those individuals who currently reside in Los Angeles, Ventura, or northern Orange County had completed a survey as part of the ongoing longitudinal study within the 6 months prior to the earthquake. Two months following the earthquake, the respondents who lived in either Los Angeles, Ventura, or northern Orange County were sent a brief questionnaire. Some questions were specific to the earthquake, whereas others were repeated assessments of critical factors (i.e., Psychological Distress and substance use). Sixty-eight percent agreed ($N = 225$; 170 women and 55 men). Every respondent in the hardest hit area returned a survey. The respondents who did not return the survey all lived in outlying regions. The average age of the participants was 30. This was a well-educated sample; most (83%) report having at least 1 year of college. Education in this sample ranges from junior high through doctorate. Sixty-eight percent had full-time jobs (average income $30,000–$40,000), 60% were married, and 43% had children. More details about this sample were published elsewhere (Newcomb, 1992, 1994, 1997; Newcomb & Bentler, 1988; Newcomb, Huba, & Bentler, 1986; Newcomb & Rickards, 1995).

Measures

Location. The proximity variable was created by plotting each participant's zip code on a map of Los Angeles, Ventura, and northern Orange Counties. Four major groupings of participants were created based on distance from epicenter, preliminary estimates of damage in the area, and liquefaction estimates of the soil to assess the degree of shaking experienced.

The first group was comprised of respondents who lived closest to the epicenter, in the areas with the most shaking and most damage. This area was comprised of San Fernando Valley (e.g., Canoga Park, Northridge, Pasadena), the west side of Los Angeles (e.g., Santa Monica), and Ventura County (e.g., Moorpark, Simi Valley). The second group was comprised of respondents who lived in an area that also experienced some damage and shaking but less than the group closest to the epicenter. This group all resided in areas badly affected by the civil unrest over the trial of the policemen involved in the Rodney King beating the prior year in which buildings were destroyed and vandalized (e.g., Compton, south central Los Angeles). This community had still not fully recovered from the prior year's unrest and was still suffering in its aftermath. The final two groups of respondents were comprised of communities that experienced less shaking and damage than either of the two first groups. One group consisted of outlying areas in the South Bay (e.g., El Segundo, Long Beach, and the Pomona area). The other outlying area consisted of north Orange County and the Whittier area.

Damage and Force. A damage index was created by summing the responses to questions about how many types of damage occurred to the respondent's house or apartment and how many types of damage occurred to the respondent's personal property. The damage index had a range 0 to 9. The perceived force variable was a single Likert scale item that asked how strong the earthquake felt, ranging from 0 (*I didn't feel it at all*) to 7 (*I never have felt anything stronger*).

Social Support. Social Support was assessed with three scales comprised of four items per scale. These scales focused on perceived emotional support from family, adults, and peers (Newcomb & Bentler, 1986). These items probe social embeddedness and satisfaction with the support given. A second social support measure asked the number of people a respondent was with during the earthquake (excluding children). Although presence of others may reduce the impact of a stressful event, presence of children may increase stress because of a need to care for and protect them. The number of people a respondent was with was summed to create this scale.

Perceived Control. The perceived control scale consisted of four items that are rated on a 7-point Likert scale. These items assess general control beliefs such as "My life is in my hands and I am in control of it" (Newcomb & Harlow, 1986).

Psychological Distress. Psychological Distress was assessed with three scales: depression, panic, and anxiety. The depression scale is a three-item scale from a short version of the Hopkins Symptom Checklist (SCL; Newcomb, Bentler, & Fahy, 1987). Prior to the earthquake, respondents had been asked how often in the past year they had experienced symptoms such as "feeling sad or crying without a good reason." They chose one of five points on a Likert scale. This question was modified for the postearthquake questionnaire by changing "post year" to "since the earthquake."

The panic and anxiety scales are also from a short version of the Hopkins SCL (Newcomb et al., 1987). A sample item for the panic scale is "feeling afraid or scared without good reason." The anxiety items ask how often respondents have felt nervous, fidgety, or tense.

PTSD Symptoms. PTSD symptoms were assessed with the Impact of Event scale that is comprised of two subscales: avoidant thoughts and intrusive thoughts (Koopman, Classen, Spiegel, in press; Cardena & Spiegel, 1993). Respondents were asked to rate on a 5-point scale how frequently each item had been true for them during the past week. The avoidant scale contains items such as "I tried not to think about the earthquake." The intrusive scale contains items such as "I had dreams about the earthquake."

Drug Use. Measures of frequency of use of alcohol (beer, wine, and liquor), cigarettes, marijuana, and minor tranquilizers (Librium, Valium, Equanil, Miltown) were employed in this study. Additionally, the quantity of alcohol and cigarettes used was assessed. Frequency of use alcohol, cigarettes, marijuana, and minor tranquilizers pre-earthquake was assessed by asking how many times in the last 6 months a respondent had used a particular substance. In the postearthquake questionnaire respondents were asked how many times since the earthquake they had used a particular substance. On both the pre- and postearthquake surveys, quantity of alcohol and cigarette use was assessed by asking when a respondent drank or smoked, how much of the substance was consumed.

RESULTS

Mean Comparisons

The hypothesized interactions between respondents' location at the time of the earthquake and pre–postearthquake measures of Psychological Distress, substance use, and control beliefs were assessed thorough a series of six MANOVAs. Each MANOVA employed the same two independent variables: location with four levels (individuals living near epicenter, in chronically stressed community, more distant from epicenter in communities with less damage and motion, more distant from epicenter in communities with more motion and less damage), and time with two levels (before and after the earthquake).

The dependent variable means and standard deviations for each analysis are presented in Table 10.1. The plausibility of the assumptions of normality, linearity, and homogeneity of variance–covariance matrices were examined. Box's M test for homogeneity of variance–covariance matrices test was significant ($p < .001$) in the substance frequency and quantity, and perceived control MANOVAs. This test is quite conservative; however, because sample sizes were also quite discrepant, Pillai's criterion was employed as the test statistic for all of the MANOVA analyses (Tabachnick & Fidell, 1996). The variables employed in the separate MANOVAs are correlated; therefore a more appropriate analysis strategy may have been to use all the variables in a single MANOVA; however, due to the prohibitive number of subjects necessary per cell, separate MANOVA analyses were performed. Therefore, due to potential overlapping variance, caution should be used in interpreting these results independently.

TABLE 10.1

Means and Standard Deviations of Variables Used in MANOVA Analyses ($N = 214$)

Variables	Before Earthquake				After Earthquake			
	Location 1[a]	Location 2	Location 3	Location 4	Location 1	Location 2	Location 3	Location 4
	($N = 17$)	($N = 19$)	($N = 87$)	($N = 91$)	($N = 17$)	($N = 19$)	($N = 87$)	($N = 91$)
Control								
My life is in my hands and I am in control of it.	5.88	5.33	5.49	5.40	4.71	4.22	4.94	5.30
	(1.17)	(1.71)	(1.50)	(1.49)	(1.83)	(2.16)	(1.65)	(1.75)
I feel I am not in control of my life.	1.94	2.33	2.34	2.43	2.47	3.11	2.69	2.19
	(1.43)	(1.78)	(1.66)	(1.64)	(1.59)	(1.97)	(1.74)	(1.45)
I feel that whether or not I am successful is just a matter of luck and chance rather than my own doing.	2.18	2.33	2.23	2.25	2.18	1.94	2.24	2.00
	(1.23)	(1.61)	(1.57)	(1.50)	(1.33)	(1.43)	(1.44)	(1.38)
I feel that things just happen to me.	2.65	2.78	2.56	2.63	2.59	1.89	2.65	2.38
	(1.50)	(1.93)	(1.61)	(1.72)	(1.70)	(1.53)	(1.52)	(1.46)
Depression								
Feeling sad or crying without a good reason	1.88	1.95	2.13	2.14	2.35	2.05	2.29	2.25
	(.70)	(.85)	(.93)	(.94)	(.61)	(.91)	(.76)	(.88)
Feelings are easily hurt	2.35	2.63	2.47	2.53	2.41	2.53	2.47	2.45
	(.93)	(.68)	(.86)	(.91)	(.79)	(1.07)	(.97)	(.87)
Crying easily or a lot	2.00	2.00	2.03	2.13	2.12	1.95	1.95	2.11
	(.79)	(.94)	(.87)	(.97)	(.78)	(.91)	(.89)	(1.01)
Panic								
Feeling afraid or scared without good reason	1.71	1.63	1.87	1.86	2.12	1.53	2.05	1.92
	(.59)	(.76)	(.94)	(.96)	(.86)	(.61)	(.86)	(.87)
Avoiding certain places, people, or things because they frighten me	1.88	1.95	1.99	1.88	2.12	1.84	1.77	1.88
	(.78)	(.62)	(.96)	(.87)	(1.11)	(1.42)	(1.10)	(1.08)

(*Continued*)

TABLE 10.1
(Continued)

Variables	Before Earthquake				After Earthquake			
	Location 1[a]	Location 2	Location 3	Location 4	Location 1	Location 2	Location 3	Location 4
	(N = 17)	(N = 19)	(N = 87)	(N = 91)	(N = 17)	(N = 19)	(N = 87)	(N = 91)
Feeling afraid in open places or on the street	1.59	1.89	1.44	1.55	1.29	1.53	1.40	1.53
	(.79)	(.74)	(.68)	(.83)	(.47)	(.96)	(.81)	(.75)
Anxiety								
Feeling nervous, fidgety, or tense	2.29	2.05	2.26	2.25	2.47	2.05	2.37	2.36
	(.98)	(.85)	(.88)	(.90)	(.80)	(.97)	(.95)	(.83)
Feeling keyed up or overexcited	2.77	2.42	2.39	2.47	2.76	2.21	2.44	2.43
	(.97)	(.84)	(.94)	(.84)	(.90)	(.98)	(.94)	(.83)
Being so restless I can't sit still	2.06	1.58	1.91	2.10	2.29	1.63	2.00	2.22
	(.97)	(.69)	(.83)	(.81)	(.85)	(.83)	(.91)	(.82)
Substance quantity								
How much did you drink on a usual day?	2.23	2.16	2.87	2.57	1.47	.90	1.79	1.16
	(1.20)	(2.45)	(2.18)	(2.07)	(1.07)	(1.52)	(2.02)	(1.27)
How much did you smoke on a usual day?	1.18	1.63	1.64	1.79	1.29	1.79	1.65	1.68
	(.53)	(1.06)	(1.39)	(1.50)	(.69)	(1.18)	(1.35)	(1.34)
Substance frequency								
How often did you use alcohol?	2.73	1.93	2.62	2.29	2.23	1.59	2.10	1.68
	(.97)	(1.13)	(1.38)	(1.18)	(1.18)	(.97)	(1.25)	(.92)
How often did you use cigarettes?	1.31	2.56	2.10	2.30	2.12	2.33	2.22	2.33
	(1.01)	(2.45)	(2.21)	(2.37)	(2.28)	(2.09)	(2.34)	(2.35)
How often did you use marijuana?	1.00	1.22	1.63	1.57	1.00	1.11	1.45	1.60
	(.01)	(.73)	(1.44)	(1.50)	(.01)	(.47)	(1.24)	(1.46)
How often did you use minor tranquilizers?	1.25	1.06	1.13	1.16	1.25	1.00	1.10	1.10
	(1.00)	(.24)	(.45)	(.78)	(.68)	(.01)	(.46)	(.48)

[a]Location refers to area: 1 = community near epicenter, 2 = chronically stressed community, 3 = outlying Area 1, 4 = outlying Area 2.

Perceived Control. Four control items (see Table 10.1) were employed as dependent variables (DVs) in the first MANOVA. Using Pillais criterion there was a significant main effect for time for sense of control beliefs, $F_{4,203} = 7.63$, $p < .05$, $\eta^2 = .13$. Participants reported less perceived control after the earthquake. Univariate and stepdown F ratios were examined Stepdown F-ratios control for potential overlapping variance among DVs. The DVs are prioritized and each successive DV is tested with the higher priority DVs as covariates. In the univariate analyses the responses to both "My life is in my hands and I am in control of it" and "I feel things just happen to me" significantly differed. Participants felt less control after the earthquake. The results of the univariate and stepdown tests are presented in Table 10.2. The main effect of location was not significant.

TABLE 10.2
Univariate and Stepdown F-Ratios, Degrees of Freedom, and
Effect Size (η^2) for Significant Multivariate MANOVA Analyses

MANOVA	Dependent Variables	Univariate F	Stepdown F	η^2
Depression				
Time	Feeling sad or crying without a good reason.	6.76* (1,211)	6.76* (1,211)	.03
	Feelings are easily hurt.	.16 (1,211)	1.30 (1,210)	
	Crying easily or a lot.	.01 (1,211)	.92 (1,209)	
Panic				
Time	Feeling afraid or scared without good reason.	2.36 (1,210)	2.36 (1,210)	
	Avoiding certain places, people, or things because they frighten me.	.04 (1,210)	.43 (1,209)	
	Feeling afraid in open places or on the street.	4.74* (1,210)	5.44* (1,205)	.02
Location	Feeling afraid or scared without good reason.	1.55 (3,210)	1.55 (3,210)	
	Avoiding certain places, people, or things because they frighten me.	.14 (3,210)	.54 (3,209)	
	Feeling afraid in open places or on the street.	1.36 (3,210)	3.74* (3,208)	.05
Perceived control				
Time	My life is in my hands and I am in control of it.	23.53* (1,206)	23.53* (1,206)	.10
	I feel I am in control of my life.	3.84 (1,206)	.04 (1,205)	
	I feel that whether or not I am successful is just a matter of luck and chance rather than my own doing.	1.16 (1,206)	2.03 (1,204)	

(Continued)

TABLE 10.2
(Continued)

MANOVA	Dependent Variables	Univariate F	Stepdown F	η^2
	I feel that things just happen to me.	4.33*	4.47*	.02
		(1,206)	(1,203)	
Time × location	My life is in my hands and I am in control of it.	3.55*	3.55*	.05
		(3,206)	(3,206)	
	I feel I am in control of my life.	2.28	.88	
		(3,206)	(3,205)	
	I feel that whether or not I am successful is just a matter of luck and chance rather than my own doing.	.60	.52	
		(3,206)	(3,204)	
	I feel that things just happen to me.	2.59	2.24	
		(3,206)	(3,203)	
Frequency of substance use				
Time	Alcohol	36.62*	36.62*	.15
		(1,205)	(1,205)	
	Cigarettes	3.30	3.77	
		(1,205)	(1,204)	
	Marijuana	.76	.15	
		(1,205)	(1,203)	
	Minor tranquilizers	.26	.18	
		(1,205)	(1,202)	
Quantity of substance use				
Time	Alcohol	47.79*	47.79*	.19
		(1,209)	(1,209)	
	Cigarettes	.91	.51	
		(1,209)	(1,208)	

*$p < .05$.

Using Pillais criterion there was a significant location-by-time interaction, $F_{12,615} = 1.80$, $p < .05$, $\eta^2 = .10$. Univariate and stepdown F-ratios were again examined. In both methods only the item, "My life is in my hands and I am in control of it" was significant. Figure 10.3 presents the interaction of location and time and the main effect for time. The area nearest the epicenter and the chronically stressed community both experienced a larger decrease in sense of control than did either of the outlying areas.

Psychological Distress. Three MANOVAs examined mean differences in anxiety, panic, and depression. Levels of anxiety did not significantly differ from pre-earthquake levels by location or as a combined function of time and location.

There was a small significant main effect for panic items as a function of time, $F_{3,208} = 2.76$, $p < .05$, $\eta^2 = .04$. However, on examination of the univariate and stepdown F-ratios, only the mean differences for the panic

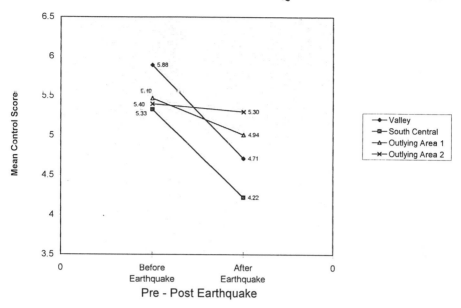

FIG. 10.3.   Plot of interaction of time and location and main effect of time on perceived control scores.

indicator, "Feeling afraid in open places or on the street" was significant (*M* before earthquake = 1.54, *SD* = .77, *M* after earthquake = 1.46, *SD* = .78). There was also a small effect of panic items as a function of location, $F_{9,630} = 1.90$, $p < .05$, $\eta^2 = .08$. Examination of the univariate and stepdown F-ratios revealed only a significant effect in the stepdown analysis for the panic indicator, "Feeling afraid in open places or on the street." Contrary to our hypotheses, endorsement of this item decreased over time. However, this may not indicate a reduction in panic following the earthquake but rather pragmatism. After the earthquake many people felt safer outside of their homes and in open places where nothing could fall on them! Prior to the earthquake respondents who lived in south central Los Angeles reported the highest levels of "feeling afraid in open places or on the street." After the earthquake the residents of south central Los Angeles also reported the highest levels of feeling afraid outside, however, the level was lower than prior to the earthquake. Before the earthquake south central Los Angeles was the most dangerous community (of those measured) to be out-of-doors. After the earthquake crime throughout Los Angeles dropped; therefore, it was relatively safer outside even in south central Los Angeles after the earthquake.

Using Pillais criterion, evidence of a small effect for time was detected for depression items, $F_{3,209} = 2.99$, $p < .05$, $\eta^2 = .04$. When univariate and stepdown F-ratios were examined, only "Feeling sad or crying without a good reason" was significant in both the univariate and stepdown analyses. Respondents reported slightly more depression on this item after the earthquake than they reported before (before earthquake $M = 1.88$, $SD = .91$, after earthquake $M = 2.53$, $SD = .79$). Neither the main effect of location nor the interaction of location and time were significant.

Substance Use. Two MANOVAs were performed to examine substance use. One analysis examined frequency of alcohol, cigarette, marijuana, and minor tranquilizer use as a function of location and time and the other examined quantity of alcohol and cigarettes used as a function of location and time.

For the quantity measures, there was a significant main effect of time, $F_{2,208} = 24.10$, $p < .05$, $\eta^2 = .19$. In both the univariate and the stepdown F-ratios only the mean difference in alcohol quantity was significant (before earthquake alcohol quantity $M = 2.63$, $SD = 2.10$; after earthquake alcohol quantity $M = 1.42$, $SD = 1.64$). Regardless of location, respondents drank less after the earthquake. Neither the main effect of location nor the interaction of location and time were significant.

Similar results were found when substance use frequency measures were examined. Again, a significant multivariate effect of time was detected, $F_{4,202} = 10.22$, $p < .05$, $\eta^2 = .17$. Both the univariate and stepdown F analyses revealed significant mean differences for frequency of alcohol use. As with the quantity measures, respondents reported drinking less frequently after the earthquake (before earthquake alcohol frequency $M = 2.43$, $SD = 1.26$; after earthquake alcohol frequency $M = 1.89$, $SD = 1.11$).

The finding that respondents drank less frequently after the earthquake was contrary to our predictions. Perhaps only the very heavy drinkers drank less? Perhaps only the social drinkers drank less (i.e., becoming nondrinkers). A second analysis was performed to explore this finding. We performed McNemar's test of symmetry on the quantity of alcohol used at one time (see Table 10.3). Alcohol quantity was clearly less after the earth-

TABLE 10.3
McNemar's Test of Symmetry for Alcohol
Quantity Before and After Earthquake

Alcohol Quantity After Quake	Alcohol Quantity Before Quake				
	Nondrinker	< 1 Drink	1 Drink	2 Drinks	3 or More Drinks
Nondrinker	45	4	20	16	10
< 1 Drink	3	4	9	10	6
1 Drink	3	2	9	17	9
2 Drinks	0	0	4	15	10
3 or More Drinks	0	0	0	6	20

quake (i.e., the table was asymmetric), χ^2 (10, $N = 225$) = 77.21, $p < .01$. The diagonal represents responses that did not change from before or after the quake. The upper and lower diagonals are not symmetric and indicate that all levels of drinking before the quake declined after the quake.

Structural Equation Models

Structural equation modeling (SEM) techniques (Newcomb, 1990; 1994) were employed to examine: the predictors of PTSD and relationships among Psychological Distress, substance use, control beliefs, and location and damage. SEM techniques were employed because they allow simultaneous examination of multiple systems of equations. Concepts such as Psychological Distress and Social Support are higher order constructs and as such an analysis that allows examination of constructs directly is advantageous. Through the use of latent variables, the relationship between constructs that are free of measurement error can be examined and multiple regression of factors can be performed (Newcomb, 1990).

The assumptions underlying SEM were evaluated for each model. Due to nonnormality of several of the variables employed in the models, all models were estimated with maximum likelihood estimation with an adjustment made to the chi-square and standard errors for the extent of the nonnormality (Bentler & Dijkstra, 1985; Satorra & Bentler, 1988). The means, standard deviations, and z scores for skewness and kurtosis for the variables used in the SEM analyses are presented in Table 10.4. All chi-squares reported are Satorra-Bentler scaled chi-squares. The fit of models is evaluated with the model chi-square, the comparative fit index (CFI), the ratio of chi-square to degrees of freedom (ratios less than 2:1 are considered evidence of good fitting models), and the Akaike Information Criteria (AIC; Akaike, 1987). The CFI has a range of 0 to 1, with higher numbers indicating better fitting models (Bentler, 1988). The AIC is a measure that assesses parsimony that can be employed when SEM models are not nested. This is a relational index. When models are compared, lower values indicate greater parsimony (Ullman, 1996).

Predicting Symptoms of PTSD. Three latent variables and six measured variables were hypothesized to predict two components of PTSD: avoidant and intrusive thoughts. The means and standard deviations for the measured variables are presented in Table 10.4. The hypothesized model is presented in Fig. 10.1. *Psychological Distress* is a latent construct that is indicated by three summed scales: depression, anxiety, and panic. *Amount of Damage* is a latent construct predicted by two indicators: amount of damage to house–apartment and property, and number of different types

TABLE 10.4
Means, Standard Deviations, Skewness, and Kurtosis of
Measured Variables Employed SEM Analyses ($N = 225$)

Variables	Mean	Standard Deviation	Z Score for Skewness	Z Score for Kurtosis
Pre-earthquake measures				
Distress				
Depression	2.21	.74	2.74	−.91
Anxiety	2.22	.72	2.44	−.38
Panic	1.89	.76	4.16*	.45
Alcohol consumption				
Frequency	2.45	1.26	4.27*	−.90
Quantity	2.64	2.06	3.80	.28
Perceived lack of control	2.44	1.13	5.66*	2.91
Social support				
Relationship with family	15.85	3.55	−6.39*	2.64
Relationship with adults	16.86	2.14	−3.73*	.28
Relationship with peers	16.51	2.87	−6.01*	2.39
Postearthquake measures				
Number of people with				
during earthquake	1.37	1.41	16.96*	32.12*
Perceived lack of control	2.51	1.13	4.16*	.02
Perceived force	5.23	1.50	−6.76*	4.88*
Amount of damage				
How much damage to				
house and property	3.05	1.90	12.15*	10.35*
Number of different				
kinds of damage	.79	1.37	10.51*	6.47*
Distress				
Depression	2.25	.75	1.69	−1.76
Anxiety	2.31	.77	1.82	−.07
Panic	1.92	.82	2.43	−.52
PTSD				
Avoidant thought	11.95	4.17	3.61*	−1.63
Intrusive thought	11.80	4.52	5.74*	1.11
Alcohol consumption				
Frequency	1.92	1.12	7.78*	2.42
Quantity	1.45	1.65	6.41*	1.96
Near epicenter	.07	.26	19.54*	25.16*

*$p < .01$.

of damage. *Social Support* prequake is a latent construct reflected by three summed scales that assess relations with family, adults, and peers. *Perceived lack of control* is a measured variable that is the sum of the four control items. *Perceived force* is a single item that asks how strongly the earthquake was felt. *Female* is coded 1 for man, 2 for woman. *Location* is a dichotomous variable representing near epicenter or not. Finally, we used the number of people, excluding children, that a respondent was with during the quake.

There was substantial support for the hypothesized model, $\chi^2(62, N = 225) = 67.43$, $p = .30$, CFI $= 1.00$, AIC $= -56.57$, Consistent AIC $= -330.37$. However, one goal of the analysis was the development of a parsimonious model; therefore with the aid of the Wald test, nonsignificant paths that did not significantly degrade the model were dropped (Bentler & Chou, 1990). To make the model still more parsimonious, variables that were not significantly related to either avoidant or intrusive thoughts were dropped (gender, location, and number of people with during earthquake). The final model presented in Fig. 10.4 also fit the data well, $\chi^2(45,$

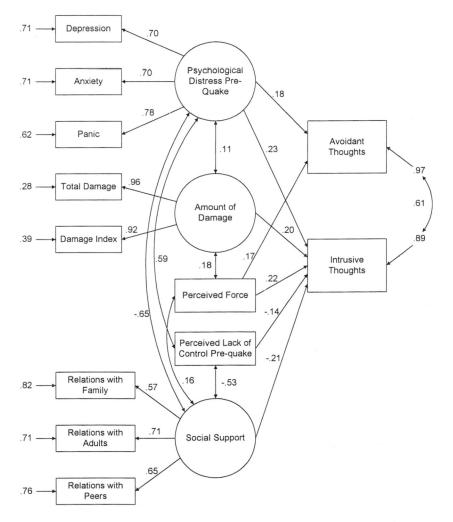

FIG. 10.4. Final model for prediction of PTSD. All paths are significant ($p < .05$). Path coefficients are presented in standardized form.

$N = 225) = 46.88$, $p = .39$, CFI $= 1.00$, AIC $= -40.22$, CAIC $= -330.37$. Because variables were completely removed from the final model, the hypothesized and final models are not nested. Therefore a chi-square difference test between models is inappropriate. Instead the models can be compared with the AIC and the CAIC. Both of these indicators of parsimony offer evidence that the final model is a more parsimonious model than the hypothesized model.

The final model accounts for more of the variance in intrusive thoughts than in avoidant thoughts (R^2 intrusive thoughts $= .21$; R^2 for avoidant thoughts $= .06$). The correlation between the residuals associated with avoidant and intrusive thoughts was .61. Avoidant and intrusive thoughts could be considered indicators of an underlying construct representing PTSD (posttraumatic stress syndrome) and analyzed as such. However, one goal of the analysis was to explore differences in the predictors of each scale.

Greater Psychological Distress and perceived force led to more avoidant thoughts after the earthquake. Greater Psychological Distress and perceived force also led to more intrusive thoughts. Additionally, the greater the Amount of Damage the more intrusive thoughts. Less Social Support predicted more intrusive thoughts. Finally greater perceived lack of control led to more intrusive thoughts.

Mediational Model. The process by which pre–post measures of Psychological Distress, substance use, and sense of control were related was examined in a second SEM model. This SEM model specifically tested the relationship among pre–post measures of Psychological Distress, PTSD, Alcohol Consumption, location, damage, perceived earthquake force, perceived control, and gender. Psychological Distress, Alcohol Consumption, Social Support, and Posttraumatic Stress were all latent constructs. Psychological Distress was indicated by three measured variables: depression; anxiety; and panic. Alcohol Consumption was indicated by both frequency and quantity of alcohol use. Social Support was indicated by three measured variables that assess relations with adults, peers, and family. The PTSD construct was reflected by two scales: avoidant thoughts and intrusive thoughts. The means and standard deviations for the measured variables in this model are presented in Table 10.4. The hypothesized model is presented in Fig. 10.2.

Alcohol Consumption after the earthquake was hypothesized to be predicted by perceived force, loss of sense of control, and prequake levels of Alcohol Consumption. Loss of control after the earthquake was predicted by prior sense of control and Psychological Distress prequake. Psychological Distress postquake was predicted by loss of control, perceived force, social support prequake, gender, and Psychological Distress prequake. Posttraumatic Stress was predicted by perceived force, amount of damage, Psychological Distress prequake, Alcohol Consumption prequake, Social Support, and gender.

Loss of sense of control postearthquake was hypothesized to mediate the relationship between Psychological Distress prequake and both Alcohol Consumption and Psychological Distress postearthquake. Both perceived force and amount of damage were hypothesized to mediate the relationship between location and Psychological Distress as well as Posttraumatic Stress after the earthquake.

There was substantial support for the hypothesized model, $\chi^2(159, N = 225) = 249.07, p < .05$, CFI = .94. To aid in parsimony the nonsignificant paths were dropped from the model and the model was re-estimated. This final model (see Fig. 10.5) also fit the data well, $\chi^2(182, N = 225) = 263.58, p < .05$, CFI = .94. This more parsimonious model did not significantly differ from the hypothesized model, $\chi^2_{\text{difference}}(23, N = 225) = 14.51, p > .05)$.

The final model is given in Fig. 10.5. Prequake levels of Alcohol Consumption accounted for 77% of the variance in postearthquake Alcohol Consumption. Prequake loss of control beliefs and Psychological Distress accounted for 39% of the variance in postearthquake loss of control beliefs. Psychological Distress prequake accounted for 27% of the variance in postearthquake Psychological Distress. Location, perceived force, damage, gender, and prequake levels of Alcohol Consumption, and Psychological Distress accounted for 24% of the variance in Posttraumatic Stress.

Higher levels of Alcohol Consumption postearthquake were associated with higher prequake levels of Alcohol Consumption. Loss of control beliefs after the earthquake was associated with loss of control after the earthquake and greater Psychological Distress prequake. Greater Psychological Distress after the earthquake was predicted by greater Psychological Distress prequake. Greater symptoms of PTSD were predicted by higher levels of Alcohol Consumption prequake, greater levels of Psychological Distress prequake, greater perceived force, and more damage. Women also reported more symptoms of PTSD.

The relationship between PTSD and location was mediated by both perceived force and damage. Living in the most affected areas led to a greater perception of force and more damage, which in turn, led to more symptoms of PTSD (unstandardized indirect effect of location on PTSD = .21, standard error = .07).

DISCUSSION

Experiencing the Northridge earthquake affected survivors in complex ways. Pre-existing Psychological Distress, control beliefs, and substance use were related to components of Psychological Distress after the earthquake.

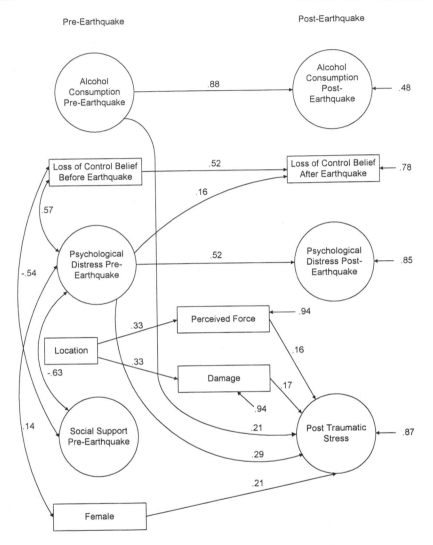

FIG. 10.5. Final model for full pre–post model of psychological functioning. All paths are significant ($p < .05$). Path coefficients are presented in standardized form.

Characteristics of a community before the earthquake were also related to survivors' perceptions after the earthquake. In addition to community characteristics, location, perceived force, and damage were associated with facets of Psychological Distress following the earthquake. The pre–post design of this study combined with multivariate statistical techniques allowed us to tease apart some of the complex relationships associated with psychological functioning after this disaster.

Characteristics of a community where a disaster occurs relate to psychological outcomes following an earthquake. Although none of the areas differed on perceived control prior to the earthquake, survivors who lived in the hardest hit areas experienced a greater loss of control than participants in outlying areas. South central Los Angeles is a community that was less severely effected by the earthquake. However, this area was also recovering from civil unrest that occurred during the year prior to the earthquake. During the unrest, buildings were destroyed and vandalism was widespread throughout the community. This area is also plagued by high crime and gang activity. Although south central Los Angeles was not as badly damaged as the area closest to the epicenter, the participants' perceived control dropped as much as the participants in the harder hit area. It may be that the pre-existing stress in the community predisposed these individuals to experience a greater loss of control than other areas that were equally affected by the earthquake. The other two outlying areas experienced virtually no change in perceived control from before to after the earthquake.

Location was not related to changes in most measures of Psychological Distress (depression, anxiety, or panic) nor substance use. Regardless of location, participants felt more depressed following the earthquake. This finding is in accord with Smith et al. (1990), but contrary to Goenjian et al. (1994), who found that respondents closer to the epicenter had greater Psychological Distress than those farther away. Perhaps the difference in results can be explained by the differences in the design of the two studies. Goenjian et al. (1994) used only retrospective assessments, whereas our study used prospective data. The ability to assess a baseline for Psychological Distress may have contributed to our findings of no differences among locations. A second reason may also account for the lack of differences among locations. The Northridge earthquake was widely covered by the media. Radio, TV, and newspapers were saturated with earthquake news. This widespread coverage may have washed out differences between locations in terms of Psychological Distress.

After the earthquake our respondents reported less panic regardless of location. Examination of the panic items revealed that participants felt less afraid in open places and on the street. Indeed this does not reflect a reduction in panic as much as reality. Following the quake many people felt safer outside than they did inside. Again the media coverage may have increased this belief. Much coverage was given to the tent cities where both newly homeless survivors and frightened survivors of the earthquake were living. Media coverage of a disaster may play an important role in psychological functioning in the aftermath of a disaster.

Interestingly, PTSD was associated with location. Perceived force and damage mediated the relationship between location (a dichotomized variable, near epicenter or not) and PTSD. It may be that only particular facets of psychological distress are associated with location. Survivors who felt the earthquake very strongly and had a lot of damage experienced more PTSD (avoidant and intrusive thoughts). Watching the media coverage of the earthquake may engender feelings of depression about losses of others, but perhaps does not relate to avoidant and intrusive thoughts. It may be that symptoms of PTSD are only related to strong firsthand experience (i.e., remembering the sensation of the earthquake and living in an area surrounded by damage).

When location was placed within the context of a pre–post model of psychological outcomes following an earthquake, location was only associated with PTSD, not loss of control or Psychological Distress postquake. Additional methodological reasons may account for this finding. In the structural equation models, location was dichotomized into the area hardest hit versus all other areas. This dichotomization resulted in a loss of power (Cohen, 1977). The purpose of this dichotomization was to examine the mediators (force and damage) of the relationship between location and Psychological Distress and PTSD. Therefore, dichotomizing the variable as hardest hit area or not was warranted. In this dichotomization the distinction between areas that were less severely affected was lost. Due to pre-existing conditions, South Central Los Angeles may have experienced the earthquake quite differently than other outlying areas. Therefore, combining groups with seemingly different pre-existing characteristics may have served to cloud the analysis.

Contrary to our hypotheses, alcohol use (frequency and quantity) declined after the earthquake. Regardless of how much participants drank before the earthquake, they drank less after the earthquake. Two post hoc explanations may account for this counterintuitive finding. This finding may relate to earthquake preparedness. Participants may have felt that if they drank they would be less able to respond to a major aftershock or to another earthquake, therefore they drank less. It may also be that respondents were socializing less and therefore drinking less.

An intriguing path emerged in the pre–post model of psychological outcomes. After controlling for prequake levels of Psychological Distress and alcohol consumption, prequake alcohol consumption was positively associated with symptoms of PTSD postearthquake but not with Psychological Distress after the earthquake. Greater alcohol consumption prequake led to more symptoms of PTSD postearthquake. The Opponent-Process model (Solomon, 1980) may help explain this finding. Light drinkers experience positive affect with few drinks. As drinking becomes heavier, the tolerance for alcohol increases. More alcohol is necessary for the same level of positive affect. However, as drinking increases in both frequency and quantity, more negative affectivity also emerges. Therefore, the person drinks more and more in an attempt to experience positive affectivity but actually the reverse happens and more negative affectivity occurs. Therefore, heavy drinking may lead to higher sensitivity to the specific stress related to the earthquake. Greater alcohol consumption led only to more PTSD symptoms not more general distress. This may have occurred because the PTSD scales are specific to the earthquake and therefore may be more sensitive to earthquake stress.

Social Support was not directly related to Psychological Distress postearthquake or to PTSD. However, social support was highly correlated with Psychological Distress prequake ($r = -.63$). Respondents who reported high levels of emotional Social Support reported little Psychological Distress prequake. Psychological Distress prequake was strongly associated with postearthquake Psychological Distress and PTSD. Therefore, when Psychological Distress and emotional Social Support are considered together within the same model, only Psychological Distress emerged as a predictor of PTSD and Psychological Distress postearthquake. This high correlation may also indicate that there is an underlying mediational process relating Social Support and Psychological Distress. The relationship between Social Support and Psychological Distress postearthquake may be mediated by Psychological Distress prequake. Future research should examine this hypothesis with data from more than one time point predisaster.

The Social Support indicators employed in this study are basically broad measures of emotional support. If specific measures of support directly related to coping with an earthquake had been employed (i.e., "I have friends who will help me clean up earthquake debris"), perhaps these measures would have related more strongly to Psychological Distress postearthquake and PTSD.

Few gender differences were found in this study. Prior research found that men and women respond differently to disasters. This prior research argues for gender as a moderating variable. Evidence from the full pre–post model of Psychological Distress does indicate that men and women did not differ on general Psychological Distress, but only on PTSD symptoms. This may indicate a greater sensitivity to the specific distress related to the earthquake. Women reported more symptoms of PTSD than men after controlling for prior Psychological Distress levels. This finding may provide support for gender as a moderating variable. If prequake levels of Psychological Distress is viewed as a proxy for PTSD symptoms prequake, then the PTSD symptoms on which the women were higher than the men were essentially the change in distress symptoms after controlling for prequake distress levels. Therefore it could be inferred that women's levels of distress changed more than did men's level of distress. Unfortunately, our sample is dominated by women and sample size constraints would not allow a complete examination of moderating effects. Further research should continue to examine gender as a moderator of Psychological Distress. Additionally, research should continue to examine the process by which gender is a moderator of distress following a disaster.

Prior perceived control was not related to postearthquake Psychological Distress, alcohol consumption, or PTSD. The control measures were highly correlated with Psychological Distress ($r = .57$). The greater the loss of perceived control, the higher the level of Psychological Distress. As was seen with Social Support and Psychological Distress, when loss of control and Psychological Distress are included in the same model, only prequake levels of distress predict postearthquake levels of Psychological Distress and PTSD. This correlation indicates that future research should test mediational hypothesis that Psychological Distress predisaster mediates the relationship between control beliefs and postdisaster Psychological Distress.

Outcomes associated with psychological functioning after an earthquake are complex. The pre-existing psychological states of the survivors are critically important in determining how well survivors cope in the aftermath of a disaster. The characteristics of a community are also important in determining psychological functioning after a disaster. Proximity to a disaster may be important for particular specific facets of distress, such as symptoms of PTSD, but not for others that are more general (i.e., depression or anxiety). Preexisting characteristics of the community may also be important for psychological outcomes. If communities are stressed prior to a disaster, then more negative outcomes may occur. Further research should include multilevel analyses that can explicitly incorporate specific community level variables into analyses.

ACKNOWLEDGMENTS

This research was supported by grant DA01070 from the National Institute on Drug Abuse. The production assistance of Wendy Sallin is gratefully acknowledged.

REFERENCES

Akaike, H. (1987). Factor analysis and AIC. *Psychometrika, 52*, 317–332.
Bentler, P. M. (1988). Comparative fit indexes in structural models. *Psychological Bulletin, 107*, 238–246.
Bentler, P. M., & Chou, C.-P. (1990). Model modification in covariance structure modeling: A comparison among likelihood ratio, Lagrange multiplier, and Wald tests. *Multivariate Behavioral Research, 25*, 115–136.
Bentler, P. M., & Dijkstra, T. (1985). Efficient estimation via linearization in structural models. In. P. R. Krishnaiah (Ed.), *Multivariate analysis* (Vol. 6, pp. 9–42). Amsterdam: North-Holland.

Cardena, E., & Spiegel, D. (1993). Dissociative reactions to the San Francisco Bay area earthquake of 1989. *American Journal of Psychiatry, 150,* 474–478.

Cohen, J. (1977). *Statistical power analysis for the behavioral sciences* (rev. ed.). New York: Academic Press.

Freddy, J. R., Saladin, M. E., Kilpatrick, D. G., Resnick, H. S., & Saunders, B. E. (1994). Understanding acute psychological distress following natural disaster. *Journal of Traumatic Stress, 7,* 257–273.

Goenjian, A., Najarian, L. M., Pynoos, R. S., Steinberg, A. M., Manoukian, G., Tavosian, A., & Fairbanks, L. A. (1994). Posttraumatic stress disorder in elderly and younger adults after the 1988 earthquake in Armenia. *American Journal of Psychiatry, 151,* 895–901.

Grady, K. E., Reisine, S. T., Fifield, J., Lee, N. R., McVay, J., & Kelsey, M. E. (1991). The impact of Hurricane Hugo and the San Francisco earthquake on a sample of people with rheumatoid arthritis. *Arthritis Care and Research, 4,* 106–110.

Kaniasty, K., & Norris, F. H. (1993). A test of the social support deterioration model in the context of natural disaster. *Journal of Personality and Social Psychology, 64,* 395–408.

Koopman, C., Classen, C., & Spiegel, D. (in press). Predictors of post-traumatic stress symptoms among Oakland/Berkeley Firestorm survivors. *American Journal of Psychiatry.*

Manuel, S. J., & Anderson, K. M. (1993). Stress and coping: The Loma Prieta earthquake. *Current Psychology, 12,* 130–141.

Newcomb, M. D. (1990). What structural modeling techniques can tell us about social support. In I. G. Sarason, B. R. Sarason, & G. R. Pierce (Eds.), *Social support: An interactional view* (pp. 26–63). New York: Wiley.

Newcomb, M. D. (1992). Understanding the multidimensional nature of drug use and abuse: The role of consumption, risk factors, and protective factors. In M. D. Glantz & R. Pickens (Eds.), *Vulnerability to drug abuse* (pp. 255–298). Washington, DC: American Psychological Association.

Newcomb, M. D. (1994). Drug use and intimate relationships among women and men: Separating specific from general effects in prospective data using structural equations models. *Journal of Consulting and Clinical Psychology, 62,* 463–476.

Newcomb, M. D. (1997). Psychosocial predictors and consequences of drug use: A developmental perspective within a prospective study. *Journal of Addictive Diseases, 16,* 51–89.

Newcomb, M. D., Bentler, P. M., & Fahy, B. (1987). Cocaine use and psychopathology: Associations among young adults. *International Journal of the Addictions, 22,* 1167–1188.

Newcomb, M. D., & Bentler, P. M. (1986). Loneliness and social support: A confirmatory hierarchical analysis. *Personality and Social Psychology Bulletin, 12,* 520–535.

Newcomb, M. D., & Harlow, L. L. (1986). Life events and substance use among adolescents: Mediating effects of perceived loss of control and meaninglessness in life. *Journal Personality and Social Psychology, 51,* 565–577.

Newcomb, M. D., Huba, G. J., & Bentler, P. M. (1986). Desirability of various life change events among adolescents: Effects of exposure, sex, age, and ethnicity. *Journal of Research in Personality, 20,* 207–227.

Newcomb, M. D., & Rickards, M. A. (1995). Parent drug use and intimate relations: Associations among community samples of young adult women and men. *Journal of Counseling Psychology, 42,* 141–154.

North, C. S., Smith, E. M., McCool, R. E., & Lightcap, P. E. (1989). Acute postdisaster coping and adjustment. *Journal of Traumatic Stress, 2,* 353–360.

Robins, L. N., Lishbach, R., Smith, E. M., Cottler, L. B., & Solomon, S. D. (1986). The impact of disaster on previously assessed mental health. In J. H. Shore (Ed.), *Disaster stress studies: New methods and findings* (pp. 21–48). Washington, DC: American Psychiatric Association.

Satorra, A., & Bentler, P. M. (1988). Scaling corrections for chi-square statistics in covariance structure analysis. *Proceedings of the American Statistical Association,* 308–313.

Schachter, S., & Singer, J. E. (1962). Cognitive, social and physiological determinants of emotional state. *Psychological Review, 69,* 379–399.

Smith, E. M., North, C. S., McCool, R. E., & Shea, J. M. (1990). Acute postdisaster psychiatric disorders: Identification of persons at risk. *American Journal of Psychiatry, 147,* 202–206.

Solomon, R. L. (1980). Opponent-process theory of acquired motivation: The cost of pleasure and benefits of pain. *American Psychologist, 35,* 691–712.

Solomon, S. D., Smith, E. M., Robins, L. N., & Fischbach, R. L. (1987). Social involvement as a mediator of disaster-induced stress. *Journal of Applied Social Psychology, 17,* 1092–1112.

Tabachnick, B. G., & Fidell, L. S. (1996). *Using multivariate statistics* (3rd ed.). New York: HarperCollins.

Taylor, S. E. (1983). Adjustment to threatening events: A theory of cognitive adaptation. *American Psychologist, 38,* 1161–1173.

Ullman, J. B. (1996). Structural equations modeling. In B. G. Tabachnick & L. S. Fidell (Eds.), *Using multivariate statistics* (3rd ed., pp. 709–812). New York: Harper Collins.

Part II

COMPARISON OF NATIONAL
AND GEOGRAPHICAL COHORTS

Antisocial Personality Disorder: Comparisons of Prevalence, Symptoms, and Correlates in Four Countries

Mark Zoccolillo
McGill University

Rumi Price
Washington University

Ted Hyun Chul Ji
Washington University

Hai-Gwo Hwu
National Taiwan University

Antisocial personality disorder (ASP) is a disabling psychiatric disorder defined by pervasive and persistent antisocial behavior that begins in childhood and persists in adulthood, often to middle age (American Psychiatric Association [APA], 1994; Robins, 1966, 1978; Zoccolillo, Pickles, Quinton, & Rutter, 1992). It carries an increased risk of early mortality and substance dependence (Robins, 1966; Robins, Tipp, & Pryzbeck, 1991). The disorder is familial, with evidence for both genetic and environmental factors (APA, 1994; Crowe, 1974; Lyons et al., 1995).

Although the specific criteria for the disorder vary from *DSM–III* (APA, 1980) to *DSM–III–R* (APA, 1987) to *DSM–IV* (APA, 1994), the defining characteristic—pervasive antisocial behavior in both childhood and in adulthood—does not. This requirement of both persistent and pervasive antisocial behaviors (which is well validated by longitudinal studies) defines the syndrome. The findings that these symptoms are all highly intercorrelated and form a coherent syndrome support the validity of ASP as a psychiatric disorder, and not just an assemblage of deviant behaviors (Robins, 1966, 1978; Robins et al., 1991; Robins & Price, 1991; Zoccolillo et al., 1992).

The National Institute of Mental Health Epidemiologic Catchment Area (NIMH-ECA) study of psychiatric disorders in the adult population in the

United States (using *DSM–III* criteria) was the first general population survey of ASP (Robins et al., 1991). Some key findings from that study were: (a) the expected associations between child and adult antisocial behavior found in previous studies in special populations were confirmed; (b) the rates of ASP differed between men (4.5%) and women (0.8%); (c) there were variations in prevalence among age cohorts (prevalence decreased with increasing age); (d) there were no prevalence differences across three ethnic groups (White, Black, Hispanic); (e) there were differences in prevalence by study site in the youngest cohort only; (f) the mean age of onset was between ages 8 and 9; (g) substance use disorders occurred commonly in those with ASP.

A fortuitous consequence of the development of the NIMH Diagnostic Interview Schedule (DIS; Robins, Helzer, Croughan, & Ratliff, 1981) and the adoption of the *DSM–III* classification worldwide was that several countries conducted their own equivalent of the NIMH-ECA study (Eaton & Kessler, 1985), using translated forms of the DIS, and retained the same scoring algorithms and *DSM–III* criteria. Prior to this development, there were no general populations surveys of ASP in other countries. Although data on special populations showed that ASP existed in countries other than the United States (Zoccolillo et al., 1992), it had not been possible to compare the prevalence rates across countries.

Why compare rates in different countries? Because it is difficult to do controlled experimental studies of risk factors for psychopathology, it is important to examine populations that may differ naturally in potential risk factors. Examining rates across countries has the advantage of revealing risk factors that may be diffuse within a country. An excellent example of this is diet, which varies more across countries than within countries. Cross-national and immigration studies of diet and heart disease were critical pieces of evidence in discovering the etiology of arteriosclerotic heart disease (Benfante, 1992). Certain risk factors for ASP may vary little within a country but widely across countries. There may also be novel risk or protective factors present in one country but not another.

The comparison of rates is only a first and exploratory step. If there are large differences, then further studies need to be carried out to determine the cause(s) of the differences. It is likely that a series of studies, using different methods and samples, would be needed to clarify cross-national differences. The necessary first step is determining whether there are differences in prevalence rates.

A key assumption in comparing prevalence rates is that the disorder measured is the same in different countries. For diseases with objective laboratory measures (e.g., HIV infection), it is possible to be certain that the disorder measured is the same, even though its natural history or manifestations may differ by country. For psychiatric disorders, the issue is much more problematic, because there are no universal laboratory measures. Several papers recently discussed some of the difficulties of cross-cultural and cross-national psychiatry and the pitfalls of assuming that the same criteria measure the same disorder in different countries (Kleinman 1987; Leff, 1990; Littlewood, 1990).

The purpose of this chapter is to present comparative data on the general population rates and correlates of ASP, as measured using the DIS and *DSM–III* criteria, in four countries: Taiwan, New Zealand, Canada, and the United States. We address whether ASP measures the same construct in the four countries by comparing the following across countries: whether those with ASP had the same pattern of adult symptoms; whether those with ASP had the same pattern of child antisocial symptoms; whether the age of onset of ASP is the same; whether ASP is associated with substance use disorders.

We address whether those with the full syndrome of ASP look the same in different countries. However, a key element in the construct of ASP is that pervasive adult antisocial behavior is preceded by child antisocial behavior (APA, 1994; Robins, 1966, 1978). We tested this construct by comparing the proportion of those with and without the adult criterion of ASP (four or more adult antisocial behaviors) who had a history of the *DSM–III* child criterion for ASP (three or more antisocial criteria occurring before age 15) across countries.

METHODS

Overview

Four existing general population epidemiologic surveys were examined for cross-national differences and similarities of antisocial personality: the St. Louis ECA Survey in the United States (Robins et al., 1991); the Edmonton Survey of Psychiatric Disorders in Canada (Swanson, Bland, & Newman, 1994; Orn, Newman, & Bland, 1988); the Christchurch Psychiatry Epidemiology Study in New Zealand (Wells, Bushnell, Hornblow, Joyce, & Oakley-Brown, 1989); and the Taiwan Psychiatric Epidemiologic Project (TEPE, 1981–1986; Hwu, Yeh, & Chang, 1989). A larger project on the international epidemiology of psychopathology and substance abuse, for which these datasets were acquired, was described in Price, Wada, and Murray (1995).

Comparable measures are also available from the Epidemiological Study of Mental Disorders in South Korea (Lee, Kovak, & Rhee, 1987; Lee, 1992), which we plan to analyze in the near future. Three other ECA-like datasets were considered but could be not be used for our investigation of antisocial personality and substance use. The dataset from Puerto Rico, which was used in a cross-national comparison of alcohol use disorders (Helzer et al., 1990), was excluded because antisocial personality and drug use were not assessed. The dataset from Shanghai, China, could not be used because childhood conduct symptoms were not included in their version of the DIS due to the researchers' doubt about ensuring cultural appropriateness of these symptoms in China without extensive modifications (Wang et al., 1992). The dataset from Hong Kong (Chen et al., 1993) used a two-phase design, making prevalence comparisons across sites more difficult to interpret.

All surveys were conducted in the early to mid-1980s. Target populations ranged from 181,000 to 1.6 million, with sample sizes ranging from approximately 1,500 to 11,000. The three surveys outside the United States are comparable to the NIMH-ECA study (Eaton & Kessler, 1985) with respect to ascertainment and assessment methods (see Table 11.1).

Site Descriptions.   The four survey sites are located in three broad regions around the Pacific: two sites from North America, one from Oceania, and one from Southeast Asia.

United States (St. Louis, Missouri).   St. Louis is the largest city in Missouri, located on the Mississippi River just south of its confluence with the Missouri River. St. Louis forms the core of a metropolitan area that ranks

TABLE 11.1
Unweighted Demographic Characteristics of Samples

Country Locale	U.S. St. Louis	New Zealand Christchurch	Canada Edmonton	Taiwan
Target population	277,000	181,000	394,950	1,570,590
Year data collected	1981	1986	1983	1982
Number of respondents	3,004	1,498	3,258	11,004
Completion rate (%)	79	70	72	70
Age (%) 18–24	16	20	18	23
25–44	41	55	49	45
45–64	24	24	22	25
65+	19	0	11	7
Sex (%) Male	40	48	41	34
Race (%) White	58	96	—	0
Black	39	—	—	0
Other	3	4	—	100

Note. — Not included in the sample or data not collected; Other race in New Zealand includes 2% Maori and 2% others; and in Taiwan includes 83% native Taiwanese, 14% mainland Chinese and 2% aborigines. Sources: Helzer et al. (1990), Helzer and Canino (1992), Compton et al. (1991).

17th in population in the United States. The city proper lost more than one half of its population in the last 40 years, as surrounding suburbs grew. Nevertheless, St. Louis City continues to be the 14th most densely populated city in the country. Presently, about one half the city's population is African American, compared to 17% in the metropolitan area as a whole. The city maintains relatively high unemployment rates (around 10%), despite recent improvements in the economy of the region.

Canada (Edmonton, Alberta). Reflecting the extreme northern location of much of its area, Canada is the second largest country by area in the world, has a population of just over 28 million, and a population density one tenth that of the United States. Edmonton, capital of the western Province of Alberta, is the fifth largest city and the northernmost population center in Canada. Canada's population as a whole is overwhelmingly of European descent (40% British, 27% French, 20% other European), with 1.5% being Native American or Eskimo. Alberta's population likewise is almost exclusively White, although without a sizeable French representation. Canadians as a whole enjoy a high standard of living, with a 99% literacy rate. The historical importance of agriculture to the economy of Edmonton and the rest of Alberta was challenged after World War II, and especially in the 1970s, by the rapid development of gas and oil deposits. The population increased rapidly at this time.

New Zealand (Christchurch). New Zealand comprises an island chain about 1,400 miles southeast of Australia. Its two main islands combined are about the size of Colorado. The 3.4 million New Zealanders are nearly 90% European (mostly British) and about 9% Polynesian (mostly Maori). The population is 85% urban. Christchurch is located on the northeast coast of the South Island and, with a population of about 300,000, is the country's second largest city. The proportion of non-European citizens in the population is smaller in Christchurch than in the nation as a whole. Two thirds of New Zealand's labor force are in services and government. New Zealand is a leading livestock and timber producer with a high standard of living and a 99% literacy rate. A former British colony, organized European settlement did not begin until after 1840. A progressive political tradition, with state ownership or control of many industries, extends back to the 1800s.

Taiwan. A densely populated island the size of Connecticut and New Hampshire combined, Taiwan lies 100 miles east of China. Its population of about 20.3 million is highly urbanized (75%), with native Taiwanese (largely descendants of Chinese immigrants from the 17th century) accounting for 84% of the population. Chinese Nationalist immigrants and families, arriving in 1949, now account for about 14% of the population. A very small proportion of the population is non-Chinese Taiwanese, with ancestry predating Chinese influxes. The island was ruled by Japan between 1895 and 1945. Despite increasing industrialization, 16% of the labor force remains in agriculture. Literacy is at 90%. Although Taiwan currently has one of the world's strongest economies, political isolation as a result of its severance from mainland China characterizes Taiwan's current situation (Hwu et al., 1989; TEPE, 1981–1986).

Sampling Methods

The methods for selecting catchment areas and sampling varied according to the specific sites' scientific inquiry; however, they all used sampling methods commonly used for survey research for general populations.

United States (St. Louis, Missouri). Three federally defined community mental health catchment areas were selected within the inner city of St. Louis, an inner suburb, and a three-county small town and rural area on the outskirts of the metropolitan area. A five-stage stratified cluster probability design was used. Census enumeration districts were selected for each of the three areas. Districts with large African American populations were oversampled (Robins et al., 1991).

Canada (Edmonton, Alberta). The city of Edmonton proper was selected for the sample, excluding suburban and neighboring rural areas. A two-stage design was used, with households systematically sampled from a list of residential addresses and one household member then chosen through a respondent selection grid. Hospitals and nursing homes were excluded; a separate institutional sample taken at a later date is not contained within the present dataset (Orn et al., 1988).

New Zealand (Christchurch). The sampling area was Christchurch's central city, neighboring suburban boroughs, and semirural areas along the margin of the city. A three-stage sampling design was used. Long-term institutional care facilities were excluded but employee quarters and other group living situations were included. In two out of every three dwellings a usual resident between the ages of 18 and 64 was eligible. For every third household, only a woman aged 18 to 44 years was eligible, to oversample cases of eating disorders and depression (Wells et al., 1989).

Taiwan. The entire metropolitan area of Taipei, two townships, and six rural counties comprised the sampling frame. One of the selected townships, Su-Lin, is close to Taipei, and had experienced rapid population growth at the time of the sampling. The other, Tsau-Tung, is farther from Taipei and had more gradual growth. Of the counties selected, two were in the north, two in the central region, and two in the south of Taiwan. They were chosen to provide the three rural village-types present in Taiwan; farming, fishing, and both combined A multistaged, stratified cluster probability design was used. Respondents were selected from rosters including name, age, sex, marital status, education, occupation, place of birth, and current addresses for all adults.

Sample Description

The sample characteristics are shown in Table 11.1 including the target population size, year of data collection, the sample size, completion rate, and unweighted distributions of age, sex, and race. The interview response rate ranged from 70% to 79%. Respondents were all 18 years of age or older. With proper weights applied, women are about 50% of the samples. In all societies, distributions of the samples' demographic characteristics are representative of the compositions of the target populations, including racial or ethnic minorities. Unweighted distributions show that Blacks composed 39% of the St. Louis sample due to the site's oversampling scheme. Race information was not collected in the Edmonton site, but is predominantly White with a small number of Native Americans, Blacks, and Asians. In New Zealand, 96% were White and 2% were Maori. The population of Taiwan is almost all Asian of Chinese descent: 83% were native Taiwanese (descendants of early Chinese settlers), 14% mainland Chinese, and 2% Aborigines.

Data Analysis

The data analyses were performed at the Washington University School of Medicine in St. Louis. The centralized reanalysis became possible over time through collaborations in which entire datasets were transferred from the Taiwan and Christchurch teams (Compton et al., 1991; Helzer & Canino, 1992; Wells, Robins, Bushnell, Jarosz, & Oakley-Browne, 1994). The Edmonton dataset was also transferred during the planning phase for the international epidemiology project (Price et al., 1995).

The algorithms used to derive psychiatric diagnoses based on *DSM–III* (APA, 1980) were written in the Statistical Analysis System (SAS) by the investigators of the original St. Louis ECA (NIMH, 1984). The same algorithms were applied to survey data obtained at each site so that the prevalence estimates of psychiatric disorders and syndromes are also comparable across international sites. The Canada site did not score a series of supplemental questions on antisocial behavior that were used in the other sites. These questions asked about age of first sexual relations, promiscuity, infidelity, prostitution and pimping, other illegal activities, and repeatedly incurring bad debt. Previous analyses from the St. Louis ECA site found that omitting these questions resulted in lower rates of ASP. Although we could have omitted the supplemental questions from the analyses to make all the sites comparable, we chose to keep the supplemental questions because the comparison of greatest interest was Taiwan to other sites, and we wanted comparisons on the broadest number of symptoms. This probably results in an underestimation of ASP in Canada.

For the current study, we made several adjustments to maximize the comparability of the samples. The age range of respondents was restricted to 18 to 64 years old across four sites. The institutional sample of the St. Louis site was removed. These adjustments reduced the sample sizes for each site, broken down by sex (Male:female) to: United States 985:1,441; New Zealand 504:994; Taiwan 5,247:4,914; Canada 1,208:1,692. We also modified missing data codes assigned separately at each site to make them consistent across the four sites. For each analysis, sample sizes vary somewhat because of missing or invalid responses. A notable difference across sites was that 17% to 21% of the female and 8% to 9% of male respondents in Taiwan had missing data for the conduct disorder symptoms that required misbehavior in school, including starting fights (which asks about fights in school), compared to missing values of 2% or less in other sites. The missing values were accounted for by subjects who either never attended school or left school before completing sixth grade. Because of these sample size adjustments, prevalence estimates of ASP and substance abuse and their symptoms are different from those in previously published reports (Swanson et al., 1994).

Weighting Strategy. When stratification, clustering and weighting are involved in the sampling design, variance estimates for the means and rates are biased. Three methods were considered for reducing the bias: balanced repeated replication (BRR), Jackknife replication (JR), and the delta method (Taylor series approximation). Earlier published reports of the NIMH-ECA study frequently used the Taylor series using the SE-SUDAAN program (Shah, 1981). For the current work, we applied the weighting strategy previously used for the NIMH-ECA study to the St. Louis dataset (Leaf, Myers, & McEvoy, 1991; Robins & Price 1991). In this scheme, the St. Louis sample was weighted to the 1980 population of the catchment areas of the St. Louis ECA, correcting for intentional oversampling of Blacks, and for household size and nonresponse. The increased sampling error was then corrected by downweighting the sample size to the size that would have provided the standard deviations had there been simple random sampling, correcting for design effects and clustering (Leaf et al.,

1991). This strategy was found to produce results similar to BRR, JR, and the delta methods (Robins & Price, 1991).

A similar downweighting scheme developed by the investigators of New Zealand was used for this site. For the Canada dataset, only the design and poststratification weights were used in our analyses because an over-sampling scheme was not involved in the original study. A multistage clustering sampling was used in Taiwan; however, we treated the Taiwan dataset as if it were collected randomly and no weights were applied. Given the geographical coverage of the Taiwan sampling and its sample size, we considered the sampling bias to be negligible. Previous analyses performed by the original study investigators found little differences in demographic distributions or prevalence rates by study sites (Hwu et al., 1989).

Terminology. Each site is referred to by its country (United States, Canada, New Zealand, Taiwan) for ease in differentiating the four sites in presenting data. It is, of course, recognized that the samples are not national samples. *Prevalence* refers to unweighted prevalence and *weighted prevalence* refers to prevalences weighted back to be representative of that site's population as described earlier.

Statistical Inference. This study is largely descriptive and the sample sizes are so large that it is expected that differences that are not meaningful would still be statistically significant. For these reasons, the only comparisons on which tests of statistical significance were done were for the prevalence rates of ASP, the associations between ASP and substance abuse, and for the association between the adult and child criteria for ASP.

RESULTS

Table 11.2 shows the 12 child antisocial symptoms, of which 3 must occur before age 15, to fulfill the child criterion for a diagnosis of ASP and the 9 adult antisocial behaviors, 4 of which must occur after age 18 to meet the adult criterion for ASP.

Table 11.3 shows the number with ASP along with the prevalence (unweighted and weighted) rates separately for each gender and site. Except as noted, the diagnosis of ASP is by the full *DSM–III* criteria, including the exclusion criteria (does not also meet criteria for schizophrenia or mania) and the criterion that at least one of the adult criterion symptoms had occurred between the ages 18 and 25. This latter was a modification of *DSM–III* criterion D, (which requires a pattern of continuous antisocial behavior with no intervening period of at least 5 years without antisocial behavior) created for the NIMH-DIS in order to ascertain lifetime prevalence of ASP in subjects who had recovered by the time of interview. There

TABLE 11.2

DSM–III Diagnostic Criteria for Antisocial Personality Disorder

Conduct Symptoms (Three or More Must Occur Before Age 15)

Truancy, at least 5 days per year in 2 years
Expelled or suspended from school
Arrested or sent to juvenile court
Told a lot of *lies*
Ran away from home overnight more than once
Any *sexual relations*
Used drugs or *drunk* more than once
Stole more than once
Vandalism
Poor grades and teachers thought could do better
Frequently *in trouble* with teacher–principal *at school*
Got into trouble for *starting fights*

Adult Antisocial Behaviors (Four or More Must Occur After Turning 18)

Work problems: three or more different jobs; quit three or more different jobs; often late or
    absent to work; lengthy unemployment
Negligent parenting: left young children home alone; neighbor fed or kept child overnight;
    professional said child not cared for; ran out of money for food more than once
Illegal activities: arrested more than once or convicted of a felony; prostitution or pimping;
    made money by buying–selling stolen property, selling drugs, or running numbers
Marital–relationship problems: Two or more divorces or separations; walked out on spouse
    for at least several weeks; promiscuity (10 or more sexual partners in a year)
Violence: Hit or threw things at partner more than once; spanked a child hard enough to
    bruise; more than one physical fight (other than spouse)
Debts: Was sued for a bad debt or had things repossessed for failure to pay three or more
    times
Vagrancy: Traveled around for a month or more without plans (not on vacation); no regu-
    lar place to live for at least a month
Lying: Used alias or assumed name; lied often
Traffic offenses: Four tickets for moving violations; accident or arrest for drunk driving

was a marked difference between Taiwan and the other three sites. The
statistical significance of the difference in the prevalence between Taiwan
and the other three sites is presented by examining the odds ratio (and
its 95% confidence limit) of ASP in each of the other three sites compared
to Taiwan. The unweighted prevalence data were used, because it is still
not clear if downweighting schemes can be applied to associations (Shrout,
1994). Confidence limits were not calculated for females, because only
one female in Taiwan had ASP, but the differences between Taiwan and
the other three sites are large. As can be seen, the odds of ASP were 14
to 39 times greater in the other countries.

The weighted prevalence of specific criterion symptoms in childhood
and adulthood by sex and country were examined next to see if differences

TABLE 11.3
Antisocial Personality Disorder by Sex and Site

	Number With ASP	Prevalence	Weighted Prevalence
Males			
U.S. (970)	109	11.2%	9.9%
New Zealand (504)	22	4.4%	4.3%
Canada (1,206)	86	7.1%	6.9%
Taiwan (5,216)	17	0.3%	
Females			
USA (1,432)	33	2.3%	1.6%
New Zealand (994)	22	2.2%	1.9%
Canada (1,092)	12	0.7%	0.7%
Taiwan (4,899)	1	0.0%	

Odds Ratios and 95% Confidence Limits for ASP in Males Compared to Taiwan

Comparison	Odds Ratio	Confidence Limit
U.S.–Taiwan	38.7	23.1–64.9
New Zealand–Taiwan	13.9	7.36–26.5
Canada–Taiwan	23.5	13.9–39.6

among countries occur at the level of individual symptoms. Table 11.4 shows the prevalence rates for the individual child antisocial symptoms separately by sex and country, along with the proportion meeting the child criterion for ASP, and Table 11.5 provides the same information on adult symptoms. The striking finding is the much lower prevalence rate of all the child and adult antisocial symptoms (except negligence with children) in Taiwan relative to the other three countries.

Because the symptom of child neglect was the only one more common in Taiwan, it was examined more closely. In the United States, Canada, and New Zealand samples, negligence of children was highly predictive of definite or probable ASP (38% to 61% of those reporting negligence were so diagnosed), but this was not the case for Taiwan, where only 3% were so diagnosed. The criterion for child neglect is met if a positive answer is given to any of the following: (a) left children under 6 home alone while out shopping or doing something else; (b) neighbor fed a child because respondent did not get around to shopping for food or cooking or neighbor kept a child overnight because no one was taking care of the child at home; (c) nurse, social worker, or teacher said child was not being cared for; (d) ran out of money more than once for food for family because food money had been spent on the respondent or on going out. At all four sites the difference between Taiwan and the other three sites was

TABLE 11.4
Prevalence of Childhood Conduct Symptoms
(Weighted Prevalences in Percent) by Sex

	U.S.	New Zealand	Canada	Taiwan
Males				
Truancy	10.6	9.1	22.5	3.2
Expelled, suspended	11.0	3.5	8.4	0.3
Arrested	6.4	3.0	4.5	0.2
Ran away	2.5	3.6	2.9	0.3
Lies	15.3	11.8	13.3	5.1
Sexual relations	23.1	8.7	n/a	0.8
Drug use or drunk	9.1	8.0	16.5	2.0
Stole	30.7	34.1	28.7	6.7
Vandalism	8.0	8.6	7.8	2.2
Poor grades	7.4	6.7	5.8	4.2
Trouble at school	17.7	19.6	20.1	3.6
Starting fights	16.6	19.0	17.5	9.7
Three or more of the above	24.7	18.5	20.4	3.2
Females				
Truancy	5.0	6.0	10.5	0.5
Expelled, suspended	5.5	2.3	2.3	<0.1
Arrested	1.1	0.7	0.5	0.0
Ran away	1.8	2.9	2.9	0.1
Lies	10.1	10.2	9.9	2.4
Sexual relations	7.3	5.6	n/a	0.8
Drug use or drunk	2.6	2.7	7.3	0.4
Stole	12.9	17.8	14.5	2.4
Vandalism	1.0	1.6	1.4	0.8
Poor grades	3.7	2.2	2.4	2.3
Trouble at school	6.5	10.9	4.1	1.0
Starting fights	7.1	4.9	4.5	1.8
Three or more of the above	7.3	8.3	8.4	0.6

largely due to the first question: 4% versus 0.6% to 1.3% in the other three sites (unweighted prevalences in those who had ever parented a child). For the other three questions, the responses in Taiwan were 0.1%, 0.4%, and 0.8%, respectively, and for the other three sites were: New Zealand (0.4%, 0.1%, 0.5%); Canada (0.6%, 0.3%, 0.8%); and the United States (0.1%, 0.4%, and 0.8%). Leaving a young child home alone does not appear to associated with other antisocial behavior in Taiwan, and raises the question of its legitimacy as part of the criterion of negligent parenting for Taiwan.

The next analyses examined the question of whether subjects who were diagnosed with ASP in different countries have the same pattern of child and adult antisocial behavior, substance abuse, and age of onset. The

TABLE 11.5
Prevalence of Adult Antisocial Behaviors
(Weighted Prevalences in Percent) by Sex

	U.S.	New Zealand	Canada	Taiwan
Males				
Work problems	45.5	36.8	48.4	16.3
Negligent parenting	1.1	0.4	0.9	3.0
Illegal activities	15.9	8.2	13.5	2.3
Marital–relationship problems	27.3	16.3	14.6	6.5
Violence	28.9	27.0	24.6	16.1
Debts	0.5	0.7	n/a	0.2
Vagrancy	8.4	6.4	10.5	1.5
Lying	6.2	7.1	5.5	3.4
Traffic offenses	36.8	25.3	45.6	5,8
Four or more of the above	15.0	15.7	13.1	1.3
Females				
Work problems	37.6	26.1	27.2	11.5
Negligent parenting	0.8	2.1	0.9	4.8
Illegal activities	3.7	1.9	1.3	0.3
Marital–relationship problems	24.5	18.3	15.5	2.2
Violence	20.2	16.9	10.8	9.6
Debts	0.3	0.2	n/a	0.1
Vagrancy	4.4	5.6	3.6	0.6
Lying	5.2	5.0	2.2	2.6
Traffic offenses	6.1	2.1	7.5	0.2
Four or more of the above	4.5	3.8	2.3	0.2

prevalence of individual child and adult antisocial criteria in those with probable or definite ASP is presented by sex and country in Tables 11.6 and 11.7. Probable ASP is defined the same as definite ASP except only three adult antisocial criteria and two child antisocial criteria are required. Subjects with probable ASP were included because of the low number (17) of males with definite ASP in Taiwan; because the goal of this section was to examine similarities and differences in those with pervasive and persistent antisocial behavior expanding the definition to probable ASP appeared reasonable.

As can be seen in Table 11.6, if traffic offenses are excluded, for men in all four countries job troubles, marital problems, and violence were the top three symptoms, occurring with remarkably similar frequencies in all four countries. Traffic offenses, arrests–criminality, and vagrancy were notably less common in the Taiwanese men with ASP than in the men from the other three countries. There were no meaningful differences among the symptom patterns of the men from the United States, Canada, and New Zealand. Among the three Western sites, the pattern is the same among women. The number of Taiwanese women meeting the probable or definite ASP criteria was only four; it was not meaningful to compare their symptom patterns to other sites.

Early substance use and early sexual activity occur infrequently in ASP in Taiwan. School expulsion or suspension is also rare and much lower than in the United States, but the other school symptoms (truancy, trouble at school, and poor grades) approached levels seen in the United States sample. Fighting was the most frequent symptom in the Taiwan sample. Juvenile arrests, however, were less common in Taiwan. Vandalism, along with all the school symptoms except suspension–expulsions, were similar across all four sites.

Table 11.7 also shows the conduct disorder symptoms among the women with definite or probable ASP. Because there were only four such cases in Taiwan, no strong conclusions are possible.

The prevalence of *DSM-III* alcohol abuse or dependence and drug abuse or dependence in those with definite ASP compared to those without ASP

TABLE 11.6
Adult Symptoms of ASP Among Those
With Definite or Probable ASP by Sex

	U.S.	New Zealand	Canada	Taiwan
Males	(194)	(52)	(182)	(67)
Of those with ASP percent with:				
Work problems	83	77	87	69
Negligent parenting	2	4	5	12
Illegal activities	64	50	54	33
Marital–relationship problems	73	54	48	63
Violence	71	75	71	89
Debts	4	8	n/a	3
Vagrancy	28	37	36	19
Lying	22	37	26	36
Traffic offenses	72	63	86	36
Females	(98)	(40)	(43)	(4)
Of those with ASP percent with:				
Work problems	87.8	85	88	75
Negligent parenting	11	15	21	0
Illegal activities	34	30	23	33
Marital–relationship problems	87	78	72	50
Violence	64	68	77	50
Debts	4	3	n/a	0
Vagrancy	35	40	30	25
Lying	36	53	33	75
Traffic offenses	24	25	37	25

TABLE 11.7
Conduct Symptoms in Those With Definite or Probable ASP by Sex

	U.S.	New Zealand	Canada	Taiwan
Males	(194)	(52)	(182)	(67)
Truancy	38	35	61	38
Expelled, suspended	37	13	30	2
Arrested	21	17	22	4
Ran away	13	21	14	6
Lies	42	35	38	39
Sexual relations	61	35	n/a	3
Drug use or drunk	36	28	46	7
Stole	64	69	68	41
Vandalism	26	29	23	31
Poor grades	19	15	17	23
Trouble at school	47	58	62	48
Starting fights	44	44	50	66
Females	(98)	(40)	(43)	(4)
Truancy	34.7	33	45	50
Expelled, suspended	35	21	17	25
Arrested	13	12	7	0
Ran away	21	20	26	50
Lies	52	55	40	50
Sexual relations	47	40	n/a	0
Drug use or drunk years	18.8	23	40	0
Stole	51	65	67	75
Vandalism	7	8	14	25
Poor grades	17.7	3	19	0
Trouble at school	41	74	31	50
Starting fights	36	30	35	50

by country was determined and the statistical significance of the association examined through the use of the odds ratio. Table 11.8 shows the association between substance use disorders in those with and without definite ASP in the four sites for men and the three sites (excluding Taiwan, where there was only one case of ASP) for women. In all sites, there were high rates of alcoholism associated with ASP. There were also high rates for drug abuse or dependence except for Taiwan. Although drug abuse–dependence was over 30 times more common in those with ASP in Taiwan than in those without, 94% of those with ASP did not have a drug use disorder.

The mean age of occurrence of the first *DSM–III* child criterion for ASP, in those with definite ASP, is presented in Table 11.9. The United States, New Zealand, and Canadian samples were all within 6 months of one another, between ages 7 and 8. The sample in Taiwan had a mean onset almost 2 years later but still in middle childhood. For the women,

TABLE 11.8
Substance Abuse or Dependence in Those
With and Without Definite ASP by Sex

Antisocial Personality Disorder (yes or no)	Percent With Alcohol Abuse or Dependence	Percent With Drug Abuse or Dependence
Males		
U.S.		
No (859, 860)[a]	26	7
Yes (109)	75	36
Odds ratio	8.7 (5.5–13.7)[b]	7.8 (4.9–12.6)[b]
New Zealand		
No (482, 477)	30	5
Yes (22)	82	50
Odds ratio	10.7 (3.5–32.1)[b]	19.7 (7.8–50.3)[b]
Canada		
No (1,120, 1,117)	28	9
Yes (86)	87	48
Odds ratio	17.8 (9.3–34.0)[b]	9.4 (5.9–15)[b]
Taiwan		
No (4,954, 5,079)	14	0.2
Yes (17)	76	6
Odds ratio	20.4 (6.7–62.9)[b]	31.7 (3.8–262)[b]
Females		
U.S.		
No (1,395, 1,396)[a]	6	5
Yes (32, 33)	47	39
Odds ratio	13.4 (6.5–27.8)[b]	12.7 (6.1–26.6)[b]
New Zealand		
No (972, 967)	6	4
Yes (22)	50	50
Odds ratio	15.2 (6.3–36.5)[b]	25.9 (10.5–63.6)[b]
Canada		
No (1,680, 1,678)	7	3
Yes (12)	75	33
Odds ratio	38.0 (10.1–142)[b]	15 (4.4–51.5)[b]

[a]Number of subjects with complete alcoholism data, number of subjects with complete drug data. [b]95% confidence intervals.

the mean age was somewhat older than the men but there were no striking differences among the three sites other than Taiwan.

The last section examines the association between pervasive adult antisocial behavior (meeting the adult criterion for ASP of four or more adult antisocial behavior symptoms) and pervasive child antisocial behavior (meeting the child criterion for ASP of three or more antisocial behavior symptoms before age 15) in the four sites (Table 11.10). The odds ratio

TABLE 11.9
Age of First ASP Symptom, in Those With Definite ASP, by Sex

Site	Age First ASP Symptoms (SD) (min–max)
Males	
U.S. (109)	7.8 (2.2, 2–12)
Canada (86)	7.6 (2.2, 4–14)
New Zealand (22)	7.4 (2.4, 3–13)
Taiwan (17)	9.5 (3.2, 1–14)
Females	
U.S. (33)	8.4 (2.9, 1–14)
Canada (12)	9.2 (3.4, 5–14)
New Zealand (22)	9.2 (2.7, 5–14)
Taiwan (1)	6

and 95% confidence limits were examined to determine if any associations were statistically significant. For all four sites, men and women with four or more adult antisocial behaviors were much more likely to have had three or more child antisocial symptoms.

DISCUSSION

This study confirms that the syndrome of ASP disorder exists in different countries. Of those who have ASP, the broad pattern of adult and child symptoms, early age of onset, and co-morbidity with substance abuse–dependence is similar across all four countries, suggesting it is the same disorder in all four countries. The criteria used in *DSM–III*, derived from studies of samples in the United States, appear relevant in other countries, including one non-Western country (Taiwan). The association between pervasive adult antisocial behavior and child pervasive antisocial disorder also seems to hold in all four countries, even though there appear to be quantitative differences in continuity.

Although the disorder assessed by the criteria appears the same, the prevalence rates vary somewhat across the three Western countries. It is the similarities that are more striking than the differences among the United States, New Zealand, and Canada. The most striking difference is between the prevalence rates in males in the United States and New Zealand. This difference, however, needs to be put into context relative to differences across the five ECA sites in the United States. The lifetime prevalence rate for ASP was highest in St. Louis of all the five ECA sites, and double the rate of Durham, North Carolina, the site with the lowest rate (3.38% vs. 1.63%, weighted prevalences, both sexes combined; Robins et al., 1991). Some of

TABLE 11.10
Rate of Meeting Childhood Criteria in Those Who
Did and Did Not Meet Adult ASP Criteria, by Sex

	% With Three or More Conduct Symptoms
Males	
U.S.	
No (786)	17
Yes (178)	66
Odds ratio	9.2 (6.4–13.1)[a]
New Zealand	
No (464)	15
Yes (40)	55
Odds ratio	7.0 (3.6–13.7)[a]
Canada	
No (1,034)	15
Yes (171)	55
Odds ratio	6.9 (4.9–9.8)[a]
Taiwan	
No (4,774)	3
Yes (61)	30
Odds ratio	14.1 (7.9–25)[a]
Females	
U.S.	
No (1,332)	8
Yes (94)	38
Odds ratio	7.1 (4.5–11.3)[a]
New Zealand	
No (949)	8
Yes (42)	57
Odds ratio	16.0 (8.3–30.8)[a]
Canada	
No (1,643)	5
Yes (45)	29
Odds ratio	8.0 (4.1–15.9)[a]
Taiwan	
No (4,011)	0.6
Yes (9)	11
Odds ratio	19.9 (2.4–165.3)[a]

[a]95% confidence intervals.

this difference may be attributable to questions that were omitted in the Durham protocol. Controlling for sex and education, the spread between the rates in St. Louis and Durham becomes even larger: 5.4% of those between the ages of 18 and 44 who did not graduate high school met criteria for ASP compared to 10.9% in St. Louis. Whether the difference between New Zealand and the United States is explainable by factors peculiar to the

United States or just to the St. Louis ECA site is not known. Although all three countries share a common heritage derived from Great Britain, the similarity in rates of ASP cannot be solely related to this heritage because a significant proportion of the St. Louis sample was Black and rates of ASP and substance use disorders in Blacks and Whites do not differ (Robins et al., 1991).

The absence of major differences is most useful in eliminating potential risk factors from consideration and in estimating potential social policy effects. For example, Canada has more extensive social welfare programs than the United States and legal penalties for drug possession and selling are less harsh. These different policies seem to have little effect on prevalence of both substance use disorders and ASP, assuming the prevalence rates found in these studies are stable across time. Geographical contiguity seems to have little effect, since the rates of substance use disorders and ASP in New Zealand, geographically distant from Canada and the United States, are no different than in the United States and Canada, which share an unguarded and very long border.

The prevalence rate of ASP is strikingly lower in Taiwan compared to the other three countries. One possibility to be considered is whether rates of *DSM–III* defined ASP in Taiwan are falsely lower. This could occur because: (a) there was a relatively high proportion of subjects who did not attend school in Taiwan past the sixth grade (and who were not asked questions regarding school misbehavior and thus had missing data for 5 of the 12 conduct symptoms); (b) the DIS does not adequately assess psychiatric disorders in Taiwan; (c) the sampling technique missed a large proportion of those with ASP.

The subjects with missing data for school-related conduct symptoms cannot account for the differences because almost all of these same subjects had valid data for the adult antisocial symptoms. Only 0.5% of the females and 1.5% of the males with missing child antisocial symptoms had four or more adult symptoms, rates similar to the overall rates of four or more adult antisocial symptoms in the whole Taiwan sample (Tables 11.8 and 11.9).

In support of the possiblity that the DIS may not adequately assess psychiatric disorders in Taiwan is the study by Compton et al. (1991) comparing the prevalence rates of 14 psychiatric diagnoses from the same Taiwan ECA dataset analyzed in this study to all ECA sites in the United States. Prevalence rates for all disorders were markedly lower in Taiwan and for 10 of the disorders the differences were statistically significant; for the other 4 disorders all had very low prevalence rates in both sites. This globally lower rate of disorders raises the possibility of a problem specific to the version of the DIS used in Taiwan, the Chinese Modified Diagnostic Interview Schedule (DIS–CM).

The authors of the DIS–CM described the development, reliability, and validity of the DIS–CM (Hwu, Yeh, & Chang, 1986; Hwu, Yeh, Chang, & Yeh, 1986). They noted that questions were modified for cultural reasons and to increase reliability. A validity study was carried out comparing diagnoses obtained by the DIS–CM and Taiwanese psychiatrists using a semi-structured interview in both a clinical and a community sample (Hwu, Yeh, & Chang, 1986). No examination on the validity of ASP was done, but kappas for three diagnoses (schizophrenia, manic episode, depressive episode) in the clinical sample ranged from .54 to .96. In the community sample, kappas for seven diagnoses ranged from .45 to .7, except for phobic disorder (.18). When physician and DIS–CM assessments were compared, the authors concluded that the DIS–CM was more powerful in discriminating mentally healthy and unhealthy groups than the physician interview and that the DIS–CM had reasonable diagnostic power.

The same authors also examined the validity of lifetime estimates of ASP (Hwu, Yeh, Chang, & Yeh, 1986). To examine the validity of a lifetime estimate of ASP, they compared the expected number of cases by age cohort and the deviation of estimation of lifetime prevalence by analyzing age of onset against current age groups. They concluded that ASP was underestimated. However, the same finding occurs in the New Zealand, Canada, and U.S. samples, where there is a decline in the lifetime prevalence of ASP with age (Robins, Tipp, & Przybeck, 1991; Swanson et al. 1994; Wells et al., 1989).

The validity of alcoholism was also reported on (Hwu, Yeh, Yeh, & Chang, 1988). Because alcoholism often co-occurs with ASP, and because some of the criterion behaviors for a diagnosis of alcoholism include antisocial behaviors, evidence for underreporting of alcoholism would suggest underreporting of ASP also. In the community validity sample described, there were 18 cases of *DSM–III* alcohol abuse–dependence; 17 were diagnosed by the DIS–CM and 8 by the clinician interview, suggesting the DIS misses very few cases. In a further examination of the validity of the cases identified by the DIS, the authors first noted other studies indicating generally low rates of alcoholism in the Chinese and that their epidemiologic study found considerably higher rates than previous studies. They also noted the extremely low prevalence of isolated alcohol problem behaviors and heavy drinking in those without a DIS diagnosis of alcoholism. They also noted the lower rates of treatment for alcoholism in Taiwan (Yeh & Hwu, 1992). Finally, in discussing the considerable discrepancy between rates of alcoholism in Korea and Taiwan, the authors noted both biologic differences in response to alcohol use (the flushing response) and cultural differences which support the differences in prevalence between the two countries (Helzer et al., 1990).

Overall, it seems unlikely that the large differences in prevalence rates for ASP between Taiwan and the other three sites are solely due to underreporting of antisocial behavior, for two reasons. First, although the rates of all disorders are lower in Taiwan, the ratio of the prevalence of ASP to other disorders is much lower in Taiwan relative to the ratios in the U.S. sample. Using the data provided in the paper by Compton et al. (1991) for major depression, generalized anxiety disorders, and alcoholism the ratios of prevalence of ASP–prevalence of the other disorder are respectively .49, .29, and .19, whereas for Taiwan they are .15, .023, and .025. Second, alcoholism appears to be reported truthfully in Taiwan, even though its symptoms are not socially desirable and are those most closely related to ASP. It is unlikely that a general tendency in Taiwan to underreport psychiatric symptoms could account for the much lower ratios of ASP relative to other disorders yet at the same time result in a relatively truthful reporting of alcoholism.

Is it possible that, relative to the other three countries, more of those with ASP in Taiwan were missed by the survey? This could occur, for example, if those with ASP in Taiwan were more likely to be in institutions (because residents in institutions were not interviewed) or less likely to be in the household sampling frames (for example, if they were more likely to emigrate from the country). Only detailed analyses undertaken in collaboration with colleagues in Taiwan can test these possiblities but the difference between Taiwan and the other sites is so much larger that they seem unlikely explanations for the large differences. Furthermore, the differences for women between Taiwan and the other countries (which are even greater than those for men) would be much more difficult to explain by institutionalization (because few women with ASP end up in institutions) or emigration, because men are more likely to emigrate than women. Urban–rural differences across the four countries can also be dismissed as explanations. The prevalence rates for ASP in Taiwan also showed the expected higher urban rates for ASP found in other studies, but even the highest rate in males in metropolitan Taipei (0.24%) was much lower than those of the other countries (Hwu et al., 1989).

Another possible source of error is that the criteria for ASP do not appropriately ascertain the underlying construct in Taiwan because they are culturally biased or measure society's response to the behavior. For example, if criminal behavior in Taiwan is less likely to result in formal court sentencing or if criminal activity takes a different form than that ascertained by the DIS questions, true criminality will be underrated relative to the other sites. Similar reasoning could be applied to other criteria. However, behaviors that are directly assessed and do not assess society's response (such as lying and stealing) are also lower, suggesting that cultural biases could not fully explain the lower rates.

Could ASP be less severe in Taiwan but with a similar prevalence? Rates of probable and definite ASP combined in Taiwan are still much lower

(.08% of females and 1.3% of males) than rates of definite ASP in the other three countries, thus this is an unlikely explanation.

Why, then, are the rates of ASP so much lower in Taiwan? We have no good answer but in the next section discuss some potential research strategies to pursue why the rates may be lower in Taiwan. Nonetheless, two potential explanations can be dismissed.

First, the low rates of alcoholism and drug use disorders in Taiwan relative to the other countries may explain some of the differences in ASP rates, but cannot explain them all. For example, the higher rates of drug abuse may lead to drug dealing or a felony drug conviction, thus "pushing" a proportion of moderately antisocial subjects in the three Western countries over the threshold to ASP; in a society where drug abuse is less prevalent (such as Taiwan) the same subjects might not meet the criteria for ASP. However, studies of the natural history of drug abuse and the co-morbidity of substance abuse and antisocial personality disorder have shown consistently that the child behavior symptoms of antisocial personality disorder precede the onset of drug use and abuse and are themselves risk factors for drug abuse (Robins & McEvoy, 1990; Young et al., 1995). Because the prevalence of the child symptoms of ASP are also much lower in Taiwan, the lower rates of substance use disorders cannot be the only explanation of the differences in the rates of ASP. It is also possible that the higher rates of substance use disorders in the United States, Canada, and New Zealand are in part caused by the higher rates of those with conduct disorder and ASP. Overall, the lower rates of substance use disorders do not seem to be a major explanation of the differences, even though it is possible that they may explain some of the differences.

Second, Chinese nationalists who emigrated to Taiwan in 1949 constitute only 14% of the sample and of the population. The low rate of ASP cannot be explained by differential migration occurring at that time.

Future Directions for Research in Taiwan

The first step is to make certain that the low rates in Taiwan are real and not due to underreporting of the *DSM–III* criteria, underascertainment of subjects, or because the ASP syndrome in Taiwan has symptoms not fully captured by *DSM–III* criteria. Comparisons of other indices of ASP such as crime statistics, delinquency statistics, and substance use treatment rates would be useful in addressing the first two issues. Investigations of the adult outcome of children considered in Taiwan to have antisocial behavior problems and of the child histories of adult criminals need to be done to see if they have the same pattern of behaviors found in similar studies in the United States and elsewhere.

Assuming the differences are real, the next step is to use what is currently known about the risk factors for ASP to see how well they may explain the lower rates in Taiwan. The most consistent risk factor for ASP and its child precursor of conduct disorder is a biologic parent with the same disorder (Cadoret, Yates, Troughton, Woodworth, & Stewart, 1995; Cohen & Brook, 1987; Lahey et al., 1995; Robins, 1966, 1978). Adoption and twin studies suggest both genetic and environmental components, which suggest several strategies (Cadoret et al., 1995; Kendler, 1995; Lyons et al., 1995).

It is possible that the lower rate of ASP may be explained in part by genetic differences between Taiwan Chinese and other ethnic groups. For alcoholism, the lower rate of alcoholism in Taiwan compared to Korea is paralleled by higher rates of a fast flushing response which is believed to be due to an inability to metabolize acetaldehyde, a metabolic product of alcohol (Park et al., 1984). Within Taiwan, the majority Chinese Han have much higher rates of a deficiency of the enzyme (ALDH–I) that metabolizes acetaldehyde than aboriginal groups, which also parallels the rates of alcohol dependence in the different groups (Chen, Hwu, Yeh, Morimoto, & Otsuki, 1991; Thomasson et al., 1994). However, the finding of rates of ASP in Hong Kong Chinese that are closer to the Western sites and Korea but rates of alcohol abuse and dependence that are similar to those in Taiwan suggests that differences in a genetic susceptibility to alcoholism may not be related to differences in rates of ASP. Although it would be desirable to be able to carry out similar research on ASP, there are no known genetic defects or markers for ASP. The most consistent data are on the relationship between aggression and altered rates of metabolism of serotonin, including low cerebral spinal fluid (CSF) metabolites of serotonin (5–hydroxyindoleacetic acid) and low monoamine oxidase (MAO) activity (Brunner, Nelen, Breakefield, Ropers, & van Oost, 1993; Kruesi et al., 1990). Because not all those with ASP are aggressive, and many of those who are aggressive do not meet criteria for ASP (Robins et al., 1991), it is not clear whether these results are generalizable to ASP. One study found that patients with borderline personality disorder (BPD) had lower MAO activity than nonpsychiatric controls, and those with BPD and ASP had even lower rates (Yehuda, Southwick, Edell, & Giller, 1989). At present, the general lack of data on biochemical and genetic markers for ASP makes comparisons between Taiwan and other countries difficult, but a potential candidate for study would be MAO activity and the genes that code for this activity (Brunner et al., 1993).

Other strategies can also be used to determine if the differences in the rates of ASP between Taiwan and other countries are due to genetic differences. One tactic is to see if rates of ASP are similarly low in Taiwanese who live in the United States, New Zealand, or Canada. If the rate rises to that seen in the host country, then this would suggest a nongenetic explanation. A persistently lower rate, however, would not necessarily suggest a genetic explanation because it may reflect cultural transmission as well as genetic transmission. Another strategy is to determine if ASP in Taiwan has a larger genetic component than in countries with higher prevalence rates, using twin studies. If ASP were more "genetic" in Taiwan than in other countries this would suggest that the difference in the prevalence rates of ASP between Taiwan and the other countries must be due to an excess of "environmental" cases in the other countries. If the genetic components are equal then this would suggest that the genetic cases are responsible for the excess cases in the countries with the higher prevalence.

A comparison of environmental risk factors across countries is complicated because most putative environmental risk factors also occur much more commonly in families where one or more of the biologic parents also had ASP (Patterson, Reid, & Dishion, 1992; Robins, 1966; Rutter & Quinton, 1984). Few studies of these risk factors attempted to control for having an antisocial biologic parent (Patterson et al., 1992; Robins, 1966, 1978). For example, neither divorce nor having a teenage mother are risk factors for conduct disorder, once their association with parental ASP is controlled (even though both risk factors are much more common in the families of children with conduct disorder; Christ et al., 1990; Lahey et al., 1988). In a recent adoption study, family risk factors in the adoptive environment contributed to juvenile antisocial behavior only when there was a biologic parent who had ASP (Cadoret et al., 1995). The adoptive home environment did make an independent contribution to the development of adult antisocial behavior. The consequence of the confounding with a diagnosis of ASP is that, with the possible exception noted below, it is difficult to come up with clear unequivocal environmental risk factors for ASP for comparison across countries. Any investigation of environmental risk factors would have to take steps to control for possible genetic confounders.

One risk factor, ineffective parenting practices (including inadequate monitoring and supervision), was shown to be a predictor of continuation of child antisocial behavior (including continuation to ASP), independent of its association with parental ASP (Patterson et al., 1992; Robins, 1966). Furthermore, parental stresses (such as substance abuse and absence of one parent) lead to ineffective parenting practices (Patterson et al., 1992). These findings suggest one strategy, which is to determine first if the rate of progression from conduct disorder to ASP differs in Taiwan, and whether parenting practices explain this difference. Such a study would have to be careful to make sure the samples are matched as closely as possible on the level of severity of conduct disorder and that any differences in parental ASP are controlled for. If sustained, then a next natural question would be whether parents in Taiwan are more effective parents because of the overall lower rates of substance abuse and marital breakup in Taiwan. It is also possible that there are stronger extrafamilial social control mechanisms (e.g., school and neighbors) in Taiwan than in the other sites that also have the effects of preventing the progression of antisocial behaviors. Studies on the community response to children with similar levels of antisocial behavior in the different countries may shed light on the differences in rates of antisocial behavior. A comparison between Hong Kong and Taiwan may be particularly instructive as to risk factors unrelated to parental substance use disorders, because the rates of substance use disorders are similar in the two countries but the rates of ASP are considerably higher in Hong Kong.

Although this model might explain lower rates of progression from conduct disorder to ASP in Taiwan, it would not explain why the rates of child and adolescent antisocial behavior problems are also so much lower to begin with. Longitudinal studies suggest that at least some children who become persistently antisocial already differ in their behaviors from their peers by age 3 (Richman, Stevenson, & Graham, 1982; White, Moffitt, Earls, Robins, & Silva, 1990). Cross-national studies would have to study children very early in life to capture the period before the onset of behavioral problems. Because aggression and disruptive behavior are relatively common, but over 90% of children will not grow up to have ASP, cross-national studies will have to be careful when making inferences about ASP from cross-national differences for aggressive or disruptive behavior. Potential areas of study include cross-national differences in maternal sensitivity to the infant and parental response to normative disruptive behavior (e.g. the terrible twos). One model to consider is that there may be no qualitative differences between Taiwan and the other three countries in parenting but that the lower rate of substance abuse and disrupted marital relationships in Taiwan results in proportionately fewer families with highly deviant parenting styles and fewer children with antisocial behavior.

Finally, it would be important to determine if the low rates of ASP are peculiar to Taiwan or are found elsewhere. Published rates of ASP in Korea (Lee et al., 1987) were much closer to those in the three Western sites (2.1% in Seoul) and the rate of alcoholism was the highest of all countries studied (Helzer et al., 1990). However, a preliminary analysis of the actual datafile from Korea revealed that the rate of ASP in the paper by Lee et al. (1987) included subjects with "possible ASP" (Maeng-Je Cho, personal communication) and that the rates of definite ASP (using the criteria specified in this chapter) may be much closer to those of Taiwan than the other three countries. The Korean dataset is currently being analyzed by our research group. The lifetime prevalence of ASP in Hong Kong (Chen et al., 1993) was similarly closer to those in the Western sites (2.78%), but the rates of alcohol and drug abuse or dependence were similar to those of Taiwan. Although no ECA type study has been done in Japan, rates of substance abuse and antisocial behavior appear to be low there (Price et al., 1995). In an epidemiologic study using the DIS of psychiatric disorders in Shanghai (China; Wang et al., 1992), rates of antisocial personality disorder were not determined but the rate of alcoholism was low. Findings of low rates in several countries would suggest that the low rates in Taiwan are not due to an unreplicable historical accident and could serve as "natural experiments" to test possible risk or protective factors found in Taiwan.

Differences and similarities in the rates of ASP and substance use disorders across nations are evidence of "experiments of nature." Interpreting and extending the results of these experiments, although not always straightforward, may prove useful in understanding the causes of ASP and substance use disorders and lead to new intervention strategies.

ACKNOWLEDGMENTS

We would like to acknowledge the site investigators:

United States: Lee N. Robins; John Helzer, Department of Psychiatry, Washington University School of Medicine.

New Zealand: Christchurch Psychiatric Epidemiology Study Team: Elisabeth Wells, Ph.D.; Peter Joyce, M.B., Ch.B, FRANZCP; Marck Oakley-Browne, M.B., Ch.B., FRANZCP; John Bushnell, M.A., Dip. Clin. Psych.; Andrew Hornblow, Ph.D., Dip. Clin. Psych. Christchurch School of Medicine, University of Otago.

Canada: Edmonton Survey of Psychiatric Disorders: Roger C. Bland, M.B.; Stephen C. Newman, M.D.; Helene Orn, B.Ed., Department of Psychiatry, University of Alberta, Alberta.

Taiwan: Taiwan Psychiatric Epidemiologic Study (TEPE): Eng-KungYeh, M.D., Hai-Gwo Hwu, M.D., Department of Psychiatry, National Taiwan University.

REFERENCES

American Psychiatric Association. (1980). *Diagnostic and statistical manual of mental disorders* (3rd ed.). Washington, DC: Author.

American Psychiatric Association. (1987). *Diagnostic and statistical manual of mental disorders* (rev. 3rd ed.). Washington, DC: Author.

American Psychiatric Association. (1994). *Diagnostic and statistical manual of mental disorders* (4th ed.). Washington, DC: Author.

Benfante, R. (1992). Studies of cardiovascular disease and cause-specific mortality trends in Japanese-American men living in Hawaii and risk factor comparisons with other Japanese populations in the Pacific Regions: A review. *Human Biology, 64,* 791–805.

Brunner, H. G., Nelen, M., Breakefield, X. O., Ropers, H. H., & van Oost, B. A. (1993). Abnormal behavior associated with a point mutation in the structural gene for monoamine oxidase A. *Science, 262,* 578–580.

Cadoret, R. J., Yates, W. R., Troughton, E., Woodworth, G., & Stewart, M. (1995). Genetic-environmental interaction in the genesis of aggressivity and conduct disorders. *Archives of General Psychiatry, 52,* 916–924.

Chen, C. C., Hwu, H. G., Yeh, E. K., Morimoto, K., & Otsuki, S. (1991). Aldehyde dehydrogenase deficiency, flush patterns and prevalence of alcoholism: An interethnic comparison. *Acta Medica Okayam, 45,* 409–416.

Chen, C. N., Wong, J., Lee, N., Chan-Ho, M. W., Lau, J. T., & Fung, M. (1993). The Shatin community mental health survey in Hong Kong. *Archives of General Psychiatry, 50,* 125–133.

Christ, M. A. G., Lahey, B. B., Frick, P. J., Russo, M. F., McBurnett, K., Loeber, R., Stouthamer-Loeber, M., & Green, S. (1990). Serious conduct problems in the children of adolescent mothers: Disentangling confounded correlations. *Journal of Consulting and Clinical Psychology, 58,* 840–844.

Cohen, P., & Brook, J. (1987). Family factors related to the persistence of psychopathology in childhood and adolescence. *Psychiatry, 50,* 332–345.

Compton, W. M., Helzer, J. E., Hwu, H. G., Yeh, E. K., McEvoy, L., Tipp, J. E., & Spitznagel, E. L. (1991). New methods in cross-cultural psychiatry: Psychiatric illness in Taiwan and the United States. *American Journal of Psychiatry, 148,* 1697–1704.

Crowe, R. C. (1974). An adoption study of antisocial personality disorder. *Archives of General Psychiatry, 31,* 785–791.

Eaton, W. W., & Kessler, L. G. (Eds.). (1985). *Epidemiologic field methods in psychiatry: The NIMH Epidemiologic Catchment Area Program.* Orlando, FL: Academic Press.

Helzer, J. E., & Canino, G. J. (Eds.). (1992). *Alcoholism in North America, Europe, and Asia.* New York: Oxford.

Helzer, J. E., Canino G. J., Yeh, E. K., Bland, R. C., Lee, C. K., Hwu, H. G., & Newman, S. (1990). Alcoholism—North America and Asia: A comparison of population surveys with the Diagnostic Interview Schedule. *Archives of General Psychiatry, 47,* 313–319.

Hwu, H. G., Yeh, E. K., & Chang, L. Y. (1986). Chinese diagnostic interview schedule I. Agreement with psychiatrist's diagnosis. *Acta Psychiatrica Scandinavica, 73,* 225–233.

Hwu, H. G., Yeh, E. K., & Chang, L. Y. (1989). Prevalence of psychiatric disorder in Taiwan defined by the Chinese Diagnostic Interview Schedule. *Acta Psychiatrica Scandinavica, 79,* 136–147.

Hwu, H. G., Yeh, E. K., Chang, L. Y., & Yeh, Y. L. (1986). Chinese diagnostic interview schedule II. A validity study on estimation of lifetime prevalences. *Acta Psychiatrica Scandinavica, 73,* 348–357.

Hwu, H. G., Yeh, E. K., Yeh, Y. L., & Chang, L. Y. (1988). Alcoholism by Chinese diagnostic interview schedule: A prevalence and validity study. *Acta Psychiatrica Scandinavica, 77,* 7–13.

Kendler, K. S. (1995). Genetic epidemiology in psychiatry. *Archives of General Psychiatry, 52,* 895–899.

Kleinman, A. (1987). Anthropology and psychiatry. *British Journal of Psychiatry, 151,* 447–454.

Kruesi, M. J. P., Rapoport, J. L., Hamburger, S., Hibbs, E., Potter, W. Z., Lenane, M., & Brown, G. L. (1990). Cerebrospinal fluid monoamine metabolites, aggression, and impulsivity in disruptive behavior disorders of children and adolescents. *Archives of General Psychiatry, 47,* 419–426.

Lahey, B. B., Hartdargen, S. E., Frick, P. J., McBurnett, K., Connor, R., & Hynd, G. W. (1988). Conduct disorder: parsing the confounded relation to parental divorce and antisocial personality. *Journal of Abnormal Psychology, 97,* 334–337.

Lahey, B. B., Loeber R., Hart E. L., Frick, P. J., Applegate, B., Zhang, Q., Green, S. M., & Russo, M. F. (1995). Four-year longitudinal study of conduct disorder in boys: Patterns and predictors of persistence. *Journal of Abnormal Psychology, 104,* 83–93.

Leaf, P. J., Myers, J. K., & McEvoy, L. T. (1991). Procedures used in the Epidemiologic Catchment Area Study. In L. N. Robins & D. A. Regier (Eds.), *Psychiatric disorders in America* (pp. 11–32). New York, NY: The Free Press.

Lee, C. K. (1992). Alcoholism in Korea. In J. E. Helzer & G. J. Canino (Eds.), *Alcoholism in North America, Europe, and Asia* (pp. 247–263). New York, NY: Oxford University Press.

Lee, C. K., Kovak, Y. S., & Rhee, H. (1987). The national epidemiologic study of mental disorders in Korea. *Journal of Korean Medical Science, 2,* 19–34.

Leff, J. (1990). The 'new cross-cultural psychiatry'. *British Journal of Psychiatry, 156,* 305–307.

Littlewood, R. (1990). From categories to contexts: A decade of the "new cross-cultural psychiatry." *British Journal of Psychiatry, 156,* 308–327.

Lyons, M. J., True, W. R., Eisen, S. A., Goldberg, J., Meyer, J. M., Faraone, S. V., Eaves, L. J., & Tsuang, M. T. (1995). Differential heritability of adult and juvenile antisocial traits. *Archives of General Psychiatry, 52,* 906–915.

National Institute of Mental Health. (1984). *NIMH DSM-III scoring algorithm.* Rockville, MD: National Institute of Mental Health.

Orn, H., Newman, S. C., & Bland, R. C. (1988). Design and field methods of the Edmonton survey of psychiatric disorders. *Acta Psychiatrica Scandinavica,* 77(Suppl. 338), 17–23.

Park, Jy., Huang, Hy., Nogoshi, C. T., Yuen, S., Johnson, R. C., Ching, C. A., & Bowman, K. S. (1984). The flushing response to alcohol use among Koreans and Taiwanese. *Journal of Studies on Alcohol, 45,* 481–485.

Patterson, G. R., Reid, J. B., & Dishion, T. J. (1992). *Antisocial boys.* Eugene, OR: Castalia.

Price, R. K., Wada, K., & Murray, K. S. (1995). Protective factors for drug abuse: A prospectus for a Japanese - U.S. epidemiologic study. In R. K. Price, B. M. Shea, & H. N. Mookherjee (Eds.), *Social psychiatry across cultures: Studies from North America, Europe, Asia and Africa* (pp. 169–172). New York: Plenum.

Richman, N., Stevenson, J., & Graham, P. J. (1982). *Pre-school to school: A behavioural study.* London: Academic Press.

Robins, L. N. (1966). *Deviant children grown up.* Baltimore: Williams & Wilkins.

Robins, L. N. (1978). Sturdy childhood predictors of adult antisocial behaviour: Replications from longitudinal studies. *Psychological Medicine, 8,* 611–622.

Robins, L. N., Helzer, J. E., Croughan, J., & Ratliff, K. S. (1981). The NIMH Diagnostic Interview Schedule: Its history, characteristics, and validity. *Archives of General Psychiatry, 38,* 381–389.

Robins, L. N., & McEvoy, L. (1990). Conduct problems as predictors of substance abuse. In L. N. Robins & M. Rutter (Eds.), *Straight and devious pathways from childhood to adulthood* (pp. 182–204). Cambridge, England: Cambridge University Press.

Robins, L. N., & Price, R. K. (1991). Adult disorders predicted by childhood conduct problems: Results from the Epidemiologic Catchment Area Program. *Psychiatry, 54,* 116–132.

Robins, L. N., Tipp, J., & Pryzbeck, T. (1991). Antisocial personality disorder. In L. N. Robins & D. A. Regier (Eds.), *Psychiatric disorders in America* (pp. 258–290). New York: The Free Press.

Rutter, M., & Quinton, D. (1984). Parental psychiatric disorder: Effects on children. *Psychological Medicine, 14,* 853–880.

Shah, B. V. (1981). SESUDAAN: *Standard errors. Program for computing standardized rates from sample survey data* (RTI/5250100-015). Research Triangle Park, NC: Research Triangle Institute.

Shrout, P. E. (1994). The NIMH Epidemiologic Catchment Area Program: Broken promises and dashed hopes? *International Journal of Methods in Psychiatric Research, 4,* 113–122.

Swanson, M. C. J., Bland, R. C., & Newman, S. C. (1994). Antisocial personality disorders. *Acta Psychiatrica Scandinavica Supplementum, 376,* 63–70.

TEPE. *Taiwan Psychiatric Epidemiological Study Project.* (1981–1986). China: Department of Health, Executive Yuan, Republic of China.

Thomasson, H. R., Crabb, D. W., Edenberg, H. J., Li, T. K., Hwu, H. G., Chen, C. C., Yeh, E. K., & Yin, S. J. (1994). Low frequency of the ADH2*2 allele among Atayal natives of Taiwan with alcohol use disorders. *Alcoholism, Clinical & Experimental Research, 18*, 640–643.

Wang, C.-H., Liu, W. T., Zhang, M.-Y., Yu, E. S. H., Xia, Z.-Y., Fernandes, M., Lung, C.-T., Xu, C.-L., & Qu, G.-Y. (1992). Alcohol use, abuse, and dependency in Shanghai. In J. H. Helzer & G. L. Canino (Eds.), *Alcoholism in North America, Europe, and Asia* (pp. 264–286) New York: Oxford University Press.

Wells, E. J., Bushnell, J. A., Hornblow, A. R., Joyce, P. R., & Oakley-Browne, M. A. (1989). Christchurch psychiatric epidemiology study: Part 1. Methodology and lifetime prevalence for specific psychiatric disorders. *Australian New Zealand Journal of Psychiatry 23*, 315–326.

Wells, E. J., Robins, L. N., Bushnell, J. A., Jarosz, D., & Oakley-Browne, M. A. (1994). Perceived barriers to care in St. Louis (USA) and Christchurch (NZ): Reasons for not seeking professional help for psychological distress. *Social Psychiatry and Psychiatric Epidemiology, 29*, 155–164.

White, J., Moffitt, T. E., Earls, F., Robins, L. N., & Silva, P. A. (1990). How early can we tell?: Predictors of childhood conduct disorder and adolescent delinquency. *Criminology, 28*, 507–533.

Yeh, E.-K, & Hwu, H.-G. (1992). Alcoholism in Taiwan Chinese communities. In J. H. Helzer & G. L. Canino (Eds.), *Alcoholism in North America, Europe, and Asia* (pp. 215–248). New York: Oxford University Press.

Yehuda, R., Southwick, S. M., Edell, W. S., & Giller, E. L., Jr. (1989). Low platelet monoamine oxidase activity in borderline8 personality disorder. *Psychiatry Research, 30*, 265–273.

Young, S. E., Mikulich, S. K., Goodwin, M. B., Hardy, J., Martin, C. L., Zoccolillo, M., & Crowley, T. J. (1995). Treated delinquent boys' substance use: Onset, pattern, relationship to conduct and mood disorders. *Drug & Alcohol Dependency 37*, 149–162.

Zoccolillo, M., Pickles, A., Quinton, D., & Rutter, M. (1992). The outcome of childhood conduct disorder: Implication for defining adult personality disorder and conduct disorder. *Psychological Medicine, 22*, 971–986.

Chapter 12

Same Place, Different Children:
White and American Indian Children
in the Appalachian Mountains

E. Jane Costello
Elizabeth M. Z. Farmer
Adrian Angold
Duke University

American Indian children living mainly on a reservation, and White children living in the surrounding countryside, can inhabit one geographic world but two different social worlds. Of the two communities described in this chapter, one (American Indian) enjoys a wide range of support services provided by the tribe and the federal government, such as subsidized housing and health care. There is a strong tradition of family togetherness and pride in tribal identity. On the other hand, employment opportunities are scarce and seasonal and as a result, family incomes are low. The predominantly White community that lives in the surrounding area is proud of its Appalachian heritage, and is resentful of being viewed as "mountain folk" by outsiders. It has a higher mean income than that of the American Indians, with fewer families living in dire poverty, but lacks the safety net of support services provided through the Indian Health Service and the Bureau of Indian Affairs. In the study described here, we were interested in effects of the interplay between community resources and family strengths and weaknesses on the development of children, in particular, their vulnerability to psychiatric disorders.

There is little reliable information about the development of psychiatric disorders in American Indian youth. This ignorance extends to the prevalence of psychopathology, its developmental course, and its causes and correlates. In their review of the data on American Indian adolescent mental health for the Congressional Office of Technology Assessment, Manson and Bergeisen (Office of Technical Assessment, 1990) concluded that:

No comparable (to the Epidemiologic Catchment Area) (Robins & Regier, 1991) epidemiologic studies have been undertaken with Indian adolescents nor have Indians ever been included to a meaningful degree in any national survey. Indeed, it is not surprising, then, that a recent draft report by the IHS (Indian Health Service) Office of Mental Health Programs—based on a survey of providers, planners, and investigators—listed a large-scale psychiatric epidemiologic study of children and adolescents as among the highest priorities for future Indian mental health research.

After reviewing the limited data available at the time, Manson and Bergeisen concluded that ". . . Indian adolescents have more serious mental health problems than the United States all races population with respect to developmental disabilities . . . ; depression; suicide; anxiety; alcohol and substance abuse; self-esteem and alienation; running away; and school dropout" (Office of Technical Assessment, 1990). Although figures of those reporting having ever used alcohol are similar for American Indian and White youth (Office of Technical Assessment, 1990), the former were described as particularly vulnerable to poly-drug use, (Oetting, Swaim, Edwards, & Beauvais, 1989) and liable to begin abusing various substances earlier in life (Oetting & Goldstein, 1979). However, Jensen (1977) pointed to marked differences among tribes in rates of both alcohol abuse and conduct problems. Similarly, Beiser and Manson (1987) noted that studies of self-esteem—a concept with links to depression and suicidal behavior—find very diverse rates of low self-esteem among American Indian communities (Beiser & Manson, 1987). The present study provides information for one tribe only, but uses standardized methods applicable to other racial and ethnic groups. The study is taking place in the context of a representative-sample survey of an 11-county area in the southeastern United States, in which an American Indian reservation is located. Comparable data are thus available on a sample of White children of the same age as the American Indian children, living in the same geographical area and using many of the same community services.

METHODS

Sampling Design

The study is an accelerated cohort design (Schaie, 1965), in which children of ages 9, 11, and 13 were recruited and are interviewed annually. Overlapping cohorts permit us to test for cohort effects. At the end of the study's 4 years of data collection, information will be available on the age range 9 through 16. Here, we report on findings from the first wave.

Sampling Frame: The Eastern Band of Cherokee Indians

The Qualla Boundary, the federal reservation of the Eastern Band of Cherokee Indians, extends into two counties in North Carolina, and covers some 55,000 acres. Most American Indians in the southern Appalachians are members of the Cherokee tribe. The Cherokee share with the rest of the population of the region the problem of making a living in an area rich in timber and natural beauty, but in little else. Employment is hard to find and frequently seasonal. The birth rate is high, and the average age about 10 years younger than that of the U.S. population in general. Incomes are low (in 1990, 50.4% of households had an annual income below $15,000), and unemployment is high (14.4% compared with 9% among all American Indians in 1990). On the other hand, educational levels are higher than those found in other American Indian groups; for example, only 4.3% of the North Carolina Cherokee left school before Grade 9, compared with 14% of American Indians as a whole (U.S. Census Bureau, 1990).

Definition of American Indian Ethnicity

Children were defined as American Indian for the purposes of this study if they met the criterion of being an enrolled member of a recognized tribe or band, or the first- or second-generation descendent of an enrolled member. There were 431 children at ages 9, 11, and 13 during the year of sample recruitment (November 1992–October 1993) who were identified in this way; 380 living on the Qualla Boundary, and the rest in the surrounding counties. All but 25 were Cherokee. The majority attend schools on the reservation, but at the time of the first assessment, 19.2% were in public schools in the surrounding community.

Comparison With the White Sample

The American Indian study is taking place in the context of a community study of psychopathology and service use in 11 contiguous counties in the southern Appalachians. Data are available on a sample of more than 1,000 children of the same age as the American Indian children (9, 11, and 13 at intake), selected to be representative of the general population of the area. Most are White; a small subgroup (82 children, 8.1% of the total) is African American. Because the African American sample is so small, it is not included in these analyses; a note on the findings from this group is included in the appendix. Full details of the sampling procedures and results of the baseline assessment for the main sample can be found in other publications (Burns et al., 1995; Costello, Angold, Burns, Erkanli, et al., 1996; Costello, Angold, Burns, Stangl, et al., 1996). Interview measures and procedures were identical for all subjects.

Interviewing Measures

The following areas are included in the analyses reported here: (a) diagnosable psychiatric disorders, symptoms, and functional impairment; (b) mental health service use; (c) family risk factors, including mental illness, family deviant behavior, poverty, and family adversity. The measures used for each area are reviewed briefly here; further details, including psychometric properties, may be obtained from other study publications (Angold & Costello, 1995; Angold, Prendergast, et al., 1995; Ascher, Farmer, Burns, & Angold, 1996; Farmer, Angold, Burns, & Costello, 1994).

Diagnoses, Symptoms, and Functional Impairment

The *Child and Adolescent Psychiatric Assessment* (CAPA; Angold & Costello, 1995; Angold, Prendergast, et al., 1995) is an interview that elicits information about symptoms that contribute to a wide range of diagnoses according to the *ICD–10, DSM–III–R* and *DSM–IV* taxonomies. It also contains ratings of interviewers' observations of the child's behavior and affect during the interview. The CAPA is an *interviewer-based* rather than a *respondent-based* interview (Angold, Prendergast, et al., 1995). That is, the onus throughout is on the interviewer to use the questions and probes provided in the interview schedule to ensure that subjects understand the question being asked, provide clear information on behavior or feelings relevant to the symptom, and have the symptom at a clinical level of severity. The CAPA is thus more adaptable to the ways in which different ethnic groups think about mental illness than is a respondent-based interview that asks the identical questions of every child, regardless of age, developmental level, or culture. The CAPA has good retest reliability in use with White and African American children (Angold & Costello, 1995), but its test–retest reliability in American Indian populations has not been established. James E. Sanders, director of Bureau of Indian Affairs Social Services on the Qualla Boundary, served as consultant to the study on the appropriateness and cultural competence of the interview.

Service Use, Access and Barriers to Care

The *Child and Adolescent Services Assessment* (CASA; Burns, Angold, Magruder-Habib, Costello, & Patrick, 1992) is an interview designed to elicit information about recent (past 3 months) and lifetime use of a wide range of services for mental health problems. It assesses the use of specialty mental health providers, pediatricians, and other medical care providers; school counselors; probation officers; Department of Social Services staff; self-help groups; spiritual advisors; family; and friends. A comparison of

CASA parent reports of mental health service use with the records of local mental health agencies (Ascher et al., 1996) showed complete agreement for inpatient services, 91% agreement for outpatient services, and 79% agreement overall. Farmer et al. (1994) reported excellent test–retest reliability for outpatient service use.

Family Risk Factors

Part of the CAPA consists of a series of assessments of family characteristics that previous studies have linked with child psychopathology. The measures come from various parts of the interview but are analyzed in this chapter under four headings: family mental illness, family deviance, poverty, and family adversity.

Family Mental Illness. The interviewed parent completes a self-report depression questionnaire, the *Mood and Feelings Questionnaire* (*MFQ*; Angold, Costello, et al., 1995; Messer et al., 1995). Parents are judged to be depressed if they reported five or more symptoms; a rough approximation to the *DSM–III–R* criterion for major depressive episode (American Psychiatric Association, 1987). The interviewed parent also provides a brief history of psychiatric treatment and hospitalization, for the child's biological and, if appropriate, nonbiological parents. A family is defined as having a history of mental illness if there are three or more individuals or episodes of mental illness reported (e.g., the mother [respondent] is currently depressed, and reports a previous psychiatric hospitalization, and father received medication for panic attacks).

Family Deviance. The same informant also provides information about parental drug and alcohol problems and treatment, criminal convictions and violent behavior. Family deviance is counted as present if there are two or more problems reported.

Poverty and Family Adversity. The parent is asked about annual household income; sources of income, including welfare payments; unemployment of one or more parental figures; number of parental figures who did not complete high school; and number of children in the household (four or more are counted as a risk factor). Poverty is defined as a family income below the federal guideline for a family of that size. Family adversity is counted as present if two or more of the following indicators—welfare, unemployment, low parental education, or large family—are reported.

Interviewers and Interviewer Training

Interviewers are residents of the area in which the study is taking place; three are American Indians, of whom two are Cherokee. All have at least bachelor's level degrees. They receive 1 month of training and constant quality control, maintained by postinterview reviews of each schedule by experienced interviewer supervisors.

Procedures for the First Wave

Children were interviewed within 1 month of the birthday on which they became 9, 11, or 13. Families recruited for the interview stage of the study were visited by two interviewers, either at home or in a location convenient for them. Before the interviews began, parent and child signed informed consent forms. They were then interviewed in separate rooms. Each parent and child was paid $10 after the interview was completed.

Data Collection, Reduction and Analysis. Of the 431 Cherokee children whose names were provided, 375 were recruited into the study, and 59 refused (86.3% compliance). Severe weather blocked access to parts of the reservation on two occasions during the interviewing period, so that 52 scheduled Wave 1 interviews (12%) could not be completed during the "window" for those subjects. Wave 1 interviews were thus completed on 323 children (75%). Table 12.1 shows the distribution by age, sex, and residence. Analysis of available information on families who refused or could not be interviewed for Wave 1 showed no significant differences from the rest in age, sex, or age-by-sex distribution, family income, reported need for mental health care, recent use of mental health services, or score

TABLE 12.1
Demographic Characteristics of the American Indian and White samples

	American Indian (N = 323) %	White (N = 933)[a] %
Age:		
9	33.5	36.1
11	36.3	34.5
13	30.1	29.4
Sex:		
Female	46.8	49.9
Male	53.2	50.1
Residence:		
Urban	8.0	30.8
Rural	92.0	69.2

[a]For explanation of stratification, please see text.

on a brief child behavior problems scale obtained from the mother when the family was first contacted.

RESULTS

Child Psychiatric Disorders

Table 12.4 shows the 3-month prevalence of the major types of *DSM–III–R* psychiatric disorder in the American Indian and White children (American Psychiatric Association, 1987). The American Indian children had a slightly lower overall prevalence of psychiatric disorder than did the White sample: American Indian (AI) = 16.7%, White (W) = 19.2%, Odds Ratio (OR) = 0.9, 95% Confidence Interval (CI) = 0.6 – 1.2, p = .382), accounted for largely by the difference in rates of tic disorders in 9-year-old boys (AI = 0.0%, W = 10.6%, OR = 0.8, 95% CI = 0.8 – 0.9, p = .010).

On the other hand, although substance abuse or dependence was rare in both groups, as expected in this age range, it was significantly more common in the American Indians (AI = 1.2%, W = 0.1%, OR 11.7, 95% CI 2.1 – 65.2, p = .005). Use of tobacco, alcohol, or illegal drugs during the past 3 months was reported by 9% of American Indian children and 3.8% of White children (OR = 2.6, 95% CI = 1.6 – 4.3, p < .001). Alcohol

TABLE 12.2
Risk and Protective Factors in American Indian and White Families

Risk and Protective Variables[a]	American Indian %	White %	Test Statistic (p) %
1. Poverty: Household income below the federal poverty line	**62.5**	25.5	17.3 (p < .0001)
2a. Parental history of drug/alcohol problems	**42.2**	21.3	10.8 (p < .0001)
2b. Parental history of arrest	**60.6**	30.9	13.4 (p < .0001)
2c. Parental violence to spouse or children	**20.4**	12.6	4.9 (p < .0001)
2. Family deviance	**42.5**	18.4	13.3 (p < .0001)
3a. Parental history of psychiatric treatment	20.9	**29.6**	−3.9 (p < .0001)
3b. Current maternal depression	7.2	7.2	0.6 (p = .5781)
3. Parental mental illness	16.9	**23.0**	−3.0 (p = .0024)
4a. Household partly or wholly dependent on welfare	**36.3**	17.2	11.0 (p < .0001)
4b. One or both parental figures unemployed	**23.8**	11.6	8.3 (p < .0001)
4c. Four or more children in household	**23.4**	10.1	8.9 (p < .0001)
4d. One or both parental figures did not graduate from high school	**60.6**	33.5	11.9 (p < .0001)
4. Family adversity	**44.4**	18.2	14.8 (p < .0001)

[a]Figures in bold indicate that the rate in this group is significantly higher than in the other group.

was the most commonly reported substance used. Analysis by age group showed almost no reported use at ages 9 and 11; but at age 13, 6.2% of the American Indian children reported using alcohol recently, compared with 3.0% of the White sample (OR = 2.1, 95% CI = 0.7 − 6.1, p = .167). Comorbidity of substance use and psychiatric disorder was also more common among American Indian youth (AI = 2.5%, W = 0.9%, OR = 2.9, 95% CI = 1.1 − 7.4, p = .026).

Family Risk Factors

The prevalence of these factors is shown in Table 12.2, and the correlations among them in Table 12.3. Although poverty and family adversity were highly correlated (AI = .48, W = .53), they were kept separate because of our interest in whether poverty showed a different pattern of relationships with child psychopathology from that of the problems that often, but not inevitably, accompany it.

Risk for Child Psychiatric Disorder. Table 12.5 shows the percentage of children with each type of family risk factor who had a psychiatric disorder, by ethnic group. Looking first at the within-race comparisons, American Indian children were significantly more likely to report psychiatric disorder if they had a family history of mental illness, but none of the other risk factors increased their risk. White children, like the Cherokees, were at increased risk if they had a family psychiatric history, but they were also at risk in the presence of family deviance, family adversity, and poverty. The American Indian children showed the same pattern of relationship to risk in relation to both emotional and behavioral problems—an association with family mental illness but with nothing else. The White children were more likely to have an emotional disorder in the face of any type of family risk factor, but the association with behavioral disorders was significant only for poverty and family adversity.

TABLE 12.3
Correlations Among Risk Factors for Child
Psychiatric Disorder in Two Communities

	Income	Family Adversity	Family Deviance	Family Mental Illness
Income		−.48 (p < .0001)	−.25 (p < .0001)	−.08 (p = .1469)
Family adversity	−.53 (p < .0001)		.30 (p < .0001)	.16 (p = .0039)
Family deviance	−.25 (p < .0001)	.39 (p < .0001)		.26 (p < .0001)
Family mental illness	−.23 (p < .0001)	.18 (p < .0001)	.31 (p < .0001)	

Note. Upper triangle = American Indians; Lower triangle = Whites.

TABLE 12.4

3-Month Prevalence Rates of *DSM–III–R* Disorders, by Sex and Ethnic Group

| | American Indian | | | | | | White | | | | | |
| | Girls (N = 151) | | Boys (N = 172) | | Both (N = 323) | | Girls | | Boys | | Both | |
Diagnosis	%	SE	%	SE	%	SE	%	SE	%	SE	%	SE
Any anxiety disorder	6.0	1.9	4.7	1.6	5.3	1.2	6.7	1.6	4.6	1.2	5.6	1.0
Any depressive disorder	0.7	0.7	0	—	0.3	0.3	1.4	0.7	1.6	0.7	1.5	0.5
Conduct or oppositional disorder	4.6	1.7	8.1	2.1	6.5	1.4	2.8	0.8	7.8	1.4	5.3	0.8
ADHD	0.7	0.7	1.7	1.0	1.2	0.6	1.0	0.23	2.9	0.8	1.9	0.4
Substance abuse or dependence[a]	2.0	1.1	0.6	0.6	1.2	0.6	0.1	0.1	0.1	0.1	0.1	0.1
One or more disorders	11.9	3.0	14.5	3.0	13.3	2.1	10.6	1.9	13.7	1.9	12.2	1.3

[a]More common in Cherokee than White sample (OR = 11.9%, CI = 2.1 – 65.5).

TABLE 12.5
Percent of Children With Psychiatric Disorder, by Ethnic Group and Family Risk

	Family Mental Illness	Family Deviance	Family Adversity	Poverty
Core psychiatric disorder				
American Indian	29.6***[a]	15.4[a]	16.7[a]	15.2[a]
White	21.3***[a]	20.2***[a]	18.6*[a]	23.1***[a]
Odds ratio (95% CI)[b]	1.5 (0.8–3.0)[b]	0.7 (0.4–1.3)[b]	0.9 (0.4–1.7)[b]	0.6 (0.4–1.0)*[b]
One or more emotional disorders				
American Indian	14.8***[a]	6.6[a]	6.5[a]	6.8[a]
White	14.0***[a]	12.5*[a]	12.7*[a]	13.9***[a]
Odds ratio (95% CI)[b]	1.0 (0.4–2.4)[b]	0.5 (0.2–1.1)[b]	0.5 (0.2–1.2)[b]	0.5 (0.2–0.9)*[b]
One or more behavioral disorders				
American Indian	14.8*[a]	8.1[a]	11.1[a]	9.5[a]
White	9.5[a]	9.5[a]	11.6*[a]	11.6***[a]
Odds ratio (95% CI)[b]	1.7 (0.7–4.1)[b]	0.8 (0.4–1.9)[b]	1.0 (0.4–2.2)[b]	0.9 (0.5–1.5)[b]

[a]Within-race comparison with youth without the risk factor. [b]Between-race comparison of rates of psychiatric disorder in youth with the risk factor.
*$p < .05$. **$p < .01$. ***$p < .001$.

Table 12.5 also shows the results of tests of between-group differences in rates of disorder in those children exposed to a family risk factor. Poverty was the only risk factor on which the two ethnic groups differed significantly. More White than Cherokee children living in poverty had a psychiatric disorder, in particular an emotional disorder. Thus, the bivariate analyses show a picture of equal vulnerability to family psychiatric history, but less vulnerability to extreme poverty, family deviance, and family adversity in the American Indian children. Table 12.6 shows the results of weighted logistic regression analyses of all risk factors together. Family mental illness was strongly associated with childhood disorder in both ethnic groups. It increased the likelihood of both behavioral disorders (attention deficit hyperactivity disorder, conduct disorder, oppositional defiant disorder, substance abuse and dependence) and emotional disorders (anxiety and depression). Family adversity had relatively little effect on rates of disorder in either group, over and above its association with other risk factors. The two groups differed markedly in the relationship between poverty and child psychopathology. Among the Cherokee, there was no link between any disorder and poverty. Among the White children, there was a strong association between poverty and both behavioral and emotional disorders. Family deviance showed a similar pattern, to a lesser degree, with a marginally significant association with child psychiatric disorder in White families, but none in the Cherokee.

Thus, results of the multivariable analysis reinforce those of the bivariate analyses, showing that the impact of adversity and deviance on child psychiatric disorder in the White families was largely the result of their asso-

TABLE 12.6
Model of Risk for Child Psychiatric Disorder,
in American Indian and White Families

	Parameter Estimate	Standard Error	χ^2	p	Odds Ratio	95% Confidence Limits
American Indian: Likelihood ratio 13.3, df 11, p = .276						
Intercept	1.4	0.21	42.4	<.0001		
Poverty	0.4	0.22	<0.1	.8688	1.0	0.4–2.3
Family mental illness	0.6	0.20	8.0	.0047	3.4	1.6–7.1
Family adversity	0.2	0.22	0.6	.4227	1.5	0.7–3.3
Family deviance	<0.1	0.19	<0.1	.9643	0.9	0.5–1.9
White: Likelihood ratio 5.9, df 11, p = .879						
Intercept	1.5	0.12	134.3	<.0001		
Poverty	0.5	0.12	13.6	.0002	2.5	1.5–4.0
Family mental illness	0.4	0.11	10.0	.0016	2.1	1.3–3.2
Family adversity	0.1	0.13	0.3	.5059	1.2	0.7–2.0
Family deviance	0.2	0.12	3.6	.0575	1.5	0.9–4.0

ciation with poverty. To assess the robustness of the associations, we used a bootstrapping approach, splitting the samples into two halves, randomly selected, and repeating the analysis. Over 100 replications, the model remained essentially unchanged for each ethnic group.

POSSIBLE REASONS FOR THE DIFFERENT IMPACT OF POVERTY

Geography and Culture

Most of the Cherokee children lived and went to school on the reservation, but 62 (19% of the interviewed sample) lived ($n = 28$) and/or went to school ($n = 59$) in the surrounding 11-county area. They remained eligible for health benefits as members of the tribe. We examined whether this group differed from those who lived and went to school on the reservation in the prevalence of child psychiatric disorder, exposure to family risk, effect of risk on psychopathology, or use of services. The off-reservation group showed no differences from the others on any of these analyses. Nor was the possibility that urban-dwelling children were at higher family risk than rural children supported in either ethnic group, controlling for family risk.

Use of Mental Health Services

It seemed possible that the Cherokee children were protected from the direct impact of poverty on pathology because, under the Indian Health Service, they had access to mental health care without cost barriers. Rates of service use overall were slightly, but not significantly, lower for American Indian than for White children. The rate of professional mental health care was low relative to the rate of disorder. Only one child in seven with a current disorder had used professional mental health services in the past 3 months (compared with one in eight in the White sample). In general, therefore, the data did not support the idea that use of mental health services was sufficiently high to moderate the effect of poverty.

The low rate of use was surprising given the lower cost barriers for tribal members. We compared rates of specialty mental health care for children with psychiatric disorders as a function of the insurance status of White families. The comparison was made for rural children only, as there were very few urban American Indian families, and rates of mental health care were higher for urban youth (Burns et al., 1995). Rates of service use were lower for American Indian than for White youth with public insurance. Furthermore, even among children with free access to mental health care and a current psychiatric disorder, only about one child in seven had seen a mental health care professional in the past 3 months, compared with one in four White youth with a disorder and public insurance. Logistic regression, controlling for poverty, family mental illness, family deviance, and family adversity showed similar results.

Relative Deprivation

The idea that where everyone is poor, no one perceives poverty as a disadvantage, is one that the Cherokee themselves certainly espouse (Joyce Dugan, chief of the Eastern Band of the Cherokee, personal communication, January 1996). The corollary is that poverty would be a risk factor only in those who are in the poorest group within their own community, irrespective of their absolute income or of their standing relative to neighboring communities. We tested this by identifying the one third of each sample with the lowest income within that ethnic group, and comparing rates of disorder by "low" and "high" income so defined. For each type of diagnosis, two thirds of the White children with a psychiatric disorder were in the "low" income third of the sample. In the Cherokee sample, three fifths of the children with a diagnosis were in the "low" income third (nonsignificant difference). This suggests that poverty, interpreted in terms of relative deprivation, had an effect on the American Indians as well as the White children, though perhaps somewhat attenuated by other protective factors.

Social Selection

Social selection theories of the distribution of mental illness (Dohrenwend et al., 1992) suggest that, in societies where upward mobility is possible, there develops over time a correlation between social status and psychiatric disorder; that is, those at risk for mental illness are also the most likely to experience poverty and social adversity. As Table 12.3 shows, income was negatively associated with family mental illness ($r = -.23$, $p < .0001$) in the White sample, but not in the Cherokee. The same result held if both variables were treated as categorical rather than continuous, with federally defined poverty as the criterion (phi = .20, $p < .001$ vs. phi = $-.014$, ns). This is consistent with Dohrenwend et al.'s theory, elegantly demonstrated in their study of North African immigrants to Israel (Dohrenwend et al., 1992) that in societies where upward mobility is checked, for example by racial discrimination, the downward drift of the mentally ill does not occur to the same extent.

Effect of Multiple Risk Factors

Several research groups (e.g., Rutter & Sandberg, 1992; Sameroff & Seifer, 1995) have published data showing that most children can cope with one or two disadvantages or disasters, but that with the accumulation of disadvantage beyond that point, rates of disorder increase exponentially. To examine this in the present study, a scale of family risk factors was created that included having one or more parents who did not complete high school, were unemployed, had been arrested, had received psychiatric treatment, or had had a substance abuse problem; living in a single-parent household, a violent household; or a household with four or more children. Rates of disorder rose linearly from 2% in youth with no risk factors to 21.6% in those with four or more. Neither race, poverty, nor their interaction was significantly associated with prevalence of disorder at any risk level. Thus the data from these two samples do not support a "threshold" for an effect of adversity on pathology. Because poverty did not increase the likelihood of psychiatric disorder at any risk level, this suggests that poverty has little impact on its own, but operates as a risk factor by increasing the likelihood of other factors.

DISCUSSION

The data from the first wave of this study show that up to the age of 13 the mental health problems of one group of American Indian children had much in common with those of other children living in the same part of southern Appalachia. Furthermore, the 3-month prevalence rates of *DSM–III–R* psychiatric disorder found in both samples was very much what would be expected given rates found in other epidemiological studies in the United States and elsewhere (see Costello, 1989). The only diagnosis that occurred more frequently in Cherokee than in White children was substance abuse, although all forms of substance use also began to appear earlier in the Cherokee. This is consistent with Oetting and Beauvais' observation that American Indian children are liable to begin abusing substances earlier in life (Oetting et al., 1989). Later waves of the study will show whether the experience of these Cherokee children replicates the rapid increase in substance use across adolescence reported by Yates (1987) and others in other tribes and using different methods.

The lack of difference between the two ethnic groups in the prevalence of childhood disorder is in contrast to studies showing that emotional and behavioral problems occur more frequently in children from poor, urban families (Offord et al., 1987; Rutter, Cox, Tupling, Berger, & Yule, 1975). Little is known about rates of mental illness in poor, rural youth (Donnermeyer & Park, 1995; Hagen, 1987; Kelleher, Rickert, Hardin, Pope, & Farmer, 1992; Metzner, Harburg, & Lamphiear, 1982; Napier, Carter, & Pratt, 1981). Urban poverty is often found together with low educational levels, unemployment, welfare dependency, and a high risk of criminal activity and substance abuse: the syndrome described by Wilson (1987) as characteristic of the urban underclass. This study addresses the question of whether these phenomena co-occur in the same way in poor rural communities, and what the impact is on children's mental health. The data presented here (Table 12.3) show that, in both White and American Indian communities, poverty is highly correlated with parental unemployment, lack of education, and income from welfare (family adversity), and to a lesser but still considerable extent with parental crime, violence, and substance abuse (family deviance). However, controlling for family mental illness, family adversity and deviance did not increase the risk of child psychopathology significantly, whereas the association with poverty was a significant risk factor only for the White community, not for the American Indians. Thus, the underclass phenomenon described by Wilson may not inevitably be a risk factor for children; its effect, at least for the 9- to 13-year-olds studied here, could be mitigated by other aspects of family or community life; perhaps in this case by a feeling of sharing a common economic fate. As Dugan said to us when we discussed the findings with her: "Yes, but we didn't feel poor, because we all were." One of the longitudinal aims of the study is to see whether the patterns of risk and protection observed in the first wave of data continue to operate as the children grow older.

The study showed that, within a shared geographical environment, the two groups of children lived in family environments that were alike in some ways, but different in others. The burden of family mental illness was high in both communities, but somewhat higher in the White community. Many families had a history of drug and alcohol problems, criminal convictions, and intrafamilial violence; however, the risk was twice as high for the Cherokee youth. Poverty was much more likely among the Cherokee, as were the concomitants of poverty: welfare dependency, unemployment, low educational level, and large family size. Ignoring poverty for the moment, the Cherokee children were under a much higher burden of family risk than the White youth: Two thirds of them had one or more of the family risk factors compared with one third of the White children, three quarters compared with one half if poverty is included. The correlational pattern among these types of family risk was, however, similar for the two communities, with one exception: All risk factors were highly correlated in the White families, but poverty and family mental illness showed a low correlation in the Cherokee families (Table 12.3). This pattern of family risk is consistent with the thesis that social selection was operating in the White community, but not among the American Indians, perhaps because of external discriminatory pressures that kept the whole community living in poverty, with little capacity to undergo the sort of "sorting and sifting" processes observed to be associated with downward mobility for the mentally ill. The present study is, to our knowledge, the first to present evidence of transgenerational transmission of this phenomenon.

The various explanations for the findings tested in the previous section of this chapter do not show a clear victory for one model over the others. Our best understanding of the picture presented here is as follows: (a) the more problems that a child's family has to cope with, the more likely the child is to suffer from a psychiatric disorder; (b) family mental illness is the single most dangerous of the range of economic, cultural, and economic risks examined; (c) poverty is an added risk in the presence of high levels of other types of risk, for children coming from a community where poverty is the exception, but not when poverty is the norm; (d) there is little evidence that the simple absence of a cost barrier to mental health services throughout life is protective, given the low rates of utilization observed even where services were effectively free.

As time goes on, we will be able to test whether the pattern described here stands up to the challenge of replication in later waves of data collection, and whether it persists as the children grow older (the overlapping cohorts design permits us to examine both developmental and historical effects). Even in this cross-sectional analysis, the value of a cross-cultural comparison is immense, forcing us to examine some beliefs that would have gone unchallenged if we had only been studying a single population, and to look harder for answers. Just as life course developmental studies have shown how time, or history, can shape children's psychosocial development (Conger, Ge, Elder, Lorenz, & Simons, 1994; Elder, 1996), studies like this one show how place, or community expecations and values, can mediate the impact of stress on psychopathology.

Looking first at the impact of an increasing burden of risk, there was a steadily increasing rate of disorder as the number of risk factors increased, irrespective of ethnic group or income. Starting at 2% prevalence for children with no risk factors, there was a steady 4% to 6% increase with each additional factor (2%, 6.6%, 11%, 16%, 21.6% in four or more risk factors). The fact that poverty, ethnic group, and their interaction did not affect this steady increase argues that poverty operates as a risk factor by way of its effect on the likelihood of other types of risk. It appears from Table 12.3 that poverty is correlated with family deviance and adversity, and with family mental illness in the White community. This cross-sectional analysis does not permit us to test for the direction of causality, but it certainly makes sense that lack of money in itself would not function as a risk factor. The ethnic differences observed in the impact of poverty on child psychopathology can be understood by asking what poverty serves as a marker for in the two communities. In the White community, poverty signals inability to climb the ladder to higher family income, a ladder whose rungs include a good education and steady employment. For those at the bottom of the ladder, the community offers few resources, especially for children's mental health problems, unless poverty is so extreme as to open the door to Medicaid. Among the American Indians, by contrast, poverty is a marker for being like everyone else. Employment is so chancy that, except for the very able, there is little incentive to use education as an escape route. On the other hand, federal and tribal resources are available to alleviate the worst effects of poverty. It is particularly interesting that the services directly targeted on child mental health—the specialty mental health services provided on and off the reservation—are little used even by families with disturbed children. It seems unlikely that they can have much to do with the apparent resilience of these children. As the study continues, we shall be looking at whether this apparent resilience lasts as children grow to adulthood and move away from the shelter of family and school.

ACKNOWLEDGMENTS

This project was supported by grant MH48085 from the National Institute of Mental Health. Additional support was provided through Faculty Scholar awards from the William T. Grant Foundation to Costello and Angold, and a Center grant from the Leon Lowenstein Foundation to Angold.

The field work for this study was supervised by Teresa Sweeney, and Ralph Folsom of Research Triangle Institute consulted on the sampling design. We acknowledge with gratitude the help of superintendents of schools in the 11-county area of the study; James E. Sanders, director of B.I.A. Social Services on the Qualla Boundary; and Joyce Dugan, principal chief of the Eastern Band of the Cherokee and the director of education there. The cooperation of the entire community of western North Carolina is warmly appreciated.

APPENDIX:
Psychiatric Disorder, Family Risk Factors, and Social Adversity in the African American Sample

There were 82 African American children in the main community sample of 1,015 interviewed at Wave 1. Most live in the one city encompassed by the study area. We are reluctant to generalize on the basis of so small a number of African American children, and so have not included them in the analyses presented in the chapter. Readers may, however, be interested to know how these 82 children compared with the Cherokee and White children in rates of psychiatric disorder and their relationship to family risk and social adversity.

The 3-month prevalence of one or more *DSM–III–R* disorders was high in African American children (34.3%, SE 8.0%), but this was due almost entirely to the very high rate of functional enuresis (17.9%, SE 7.2%) and other minor problems. The rate of core psychiatric disorder was similar to that of White children (11.5%, SE 4.0%).

Poverty was experienced by 44.6% of African American children, family adversity by 36.0%, family deviance by 12.3%, and family mental illness by 15.3%. Thus, they fell between the White and American Indian children in exposure to poverty and adversity, but reported less family deviance and mental illness than either of the other groups. In weighted least squares logistic regression, none of the risk factors was significantly associated with child mental illness.

REFERENCES

American Psychiatric Association. (1987). *Diagnostic and statistical manual of mental disorders (DSM-III-R)* (rev. 3rd ed.). Washington, DC: Author.

Angold, A., & Costello, E. J. (1995). A test-retest reliability study of child-reported psychiatric symptoms and diagnoses using the Child and Adolescent Psychiatric Assessment (CAPA-C). *Psychological Medicine, 25,* 755–762.

Angold, A., Costello, E. J., Messer, S. C., Pickles, A., Winder, F., & Silver, D. (1995). The development of a short questionnaire for use in epidemiological studies of depression in children and adolescents. *International Journal of Methods in Psychiatric Research, 5,* 237–249.

Angold, A., Prendergast, M., Cox, A., Harrington, R., Simonoff, E., & Rutter, M. (1995). The Child and Adolescent Psychiatric Assessment (CAPA). *Psychological Medicine, 25,* 739–753.

Ascher, B. H., Farmer, E. M. Z., Burns, B. J., & Angold, A. (1996). The Child and Adolescent Services Assessment (CASA): Description and psychometrics. *Journal of Emotional and Behavioral Disorders, 4*(1), 12–20.

Beiser, M., & Manson, S. M. (1987). Prevention of emotional and behavioral disorders in North American Native children. *Journal of Preventive Psychiatry, 3*(3), 225–240.

Burns, B. J., Angold, A., Magruder-Habib, K., Costello, E. J., & Patrick, M. K. S. (1992). *The Child and Adolescent Services Assessment (CASA): Version 3.0.* Durham, NC: Duke University Medical Center.

Burns, B. J., Costello, E. J., Angold, A., Tweed, D., Stangl, D., Farmer, E. M. Z., & Erkanli, A. (1995). Children's mental health service use across service sectors. *Health Affairs, 14*(3), 147–159.

Conger, R. D., Ge, X., Elder, G. H., Lorenz, F. O., & Simons, R. L. (1994). Economic stress, coercive family process, and developmental problems of adolescents. *Child Development, 65,* 541–561.

Costello, E. J. (1989). Developments in child psychiatric epidemiology. *Journal of the American Academy of Child and Adolescent Psychiatry, 28,* 836–841.

Costello, E. J., Angold, A., Burns, B. J., Erkanli, A., Stangl, D., & Tweed, D. (1996). The Great Smoky Mountains Study of Youth: Functional impairment and severe emotional disturbance. *Archives of General Psychiatry, 53*, 1137–1143.

Costello, E. J., Angold, A., Burns, B. J., Stangl, D., Tweed, D., Erkanli, A., & Worthman, C. M. (1996). The Great Smoky Mountains Study of Youth: Goals, design, methods, and the prevalence of DSM–III–R disorders. *Archives of General Psychiatry, 53*, 1129–1136.

Dohrenwend, B. P., Levav, I., Shrout, P. E., Schwartz, S., Naveh, G., Link, B. G., Skodol, A. E., & Stueve, A. (1992). Socioeconomic status and psychiatric disorders: The causation-selection issue. *Science, 255*, 246–255.

Donnermeyer, J. F., & Park, D. S. (1995). Alcohol use among rural adolescents: Predictive and situational factors. *International Journal of the Addictions, 30*, 459–479.

Elder, G. H. (1996). Human lives in changing societies: Life course and developmental insights. In R. B. Cairns, G. H. Elder, & E. J. Costello (Eds.), *Developmental science* (pp. 31–62). New York: Cambridge University Press.

Farmer, E. M. Z., Angold, A., Burns, B. J., & Costello, E. J. (1994). Reliability of self-reported service use: Test-retest consistency of children's responses to the Child and Adolescent Services Assessment (CASA). *Journal of Child and Family Studies, 3*(3), 307–325.

Hagen, B. H. (1987). Rural adolescents and mental health: Growing up in the rural community. *Human Services in the Rural Environment, 11*(2), 23–28.

Jensen, G. F., Strauss, J. H., & Harris, V. W. (1977). Crime, delinquency, and the American Indian. *Human Organization, 36*, 252–257.

Kelleher, K. J., Rickert, V. I., Hardin, B. H., Pope, S. K., & Farmer, F. L. (1992). Rurality and gender: Effects on early adolescent alcohol use. *American Journal of Diseases of Children, 146*, 317–322.

Messer, S. C., Angold, A., Costello, E. J., Loeber, R., Van Kammen, W., & Stouthamer-Loeber, M. (1995). Development of a short questionnaire for use in epidemiological studies of depression in children and adolescents: Factor composition and structure across development. *International Journal of Methods in Psychiatric Research, 5*, 251–262.

Metzner, H. L., Harburg, E., & Lamphiear, D. E. (1982). Residential mobility and urban-rural residence within life stages related to health risk and chronic disease in Tecumseh, Michigan. *Journal of Chronic Disease, 35*, 359–374.

Napier, T. L., Carter, T. J., & Pratt, M. C. (1981). Correlates of alcohol and marijuana use among rural high school students. *Rural Sociology, 46*, 319–332.

Oetting, E. R., & Goldstein, G. S. (1979). Drug use among Native American adolescents. In G. Beschner & A. Friedman (Eds.), *Youth drug abuse.* Lexington, MA: Lexington Books.

Oetting, E. R., Swaim, R. C., Edwards, R. W., & Beauvais, F. (1989). Indian and anglo adolescent alcohol use and emotional distress: Path models. *American Journal of Alcohol Abuse, 15*(2), 153–172.

Office of Technical Assessment. (1990). *Indian Adolescent Mental Health OTA-H-446.* Washington, DC: U.S. Government Printing Office.

Offord, D. R., Boyle, M. H., Szatmari, P., Rae-Grant, N. I., Links, P. S., Cadman, D. T., Byles, J. A., Crawford, J. W., Munroe-Blum, H., Byrne, C., Thomas, H., & Woodward, C. A. (1987). Ontario child health study: II. Six-month prevalence of disorder and rates of service utilization. *Archives of General Psychiatry, 44*, 832–836.

Rutter, M., Cox, A., Tupling, C., Berger, M., & Yule, W. (1975). Attainment and adjustment in two geographical areas: I. The prevalence of psychiatric disorder. *British Journal of Psychiatry, 126*, 493–509.

Rutter, M., & Sandberg, S. (1992). Psychosocial stressors: Concepts, causes, and effects. *European Child and Adolescent Psychiatry, 1*(1), 3–13.

Sameroff, A. J., & Seifer, R. (1995). *Accumulation of enviromental risk and child mental health.* New York: Garland.

Schaie, K. W. (1965). A general model for the study of developmental problems. *Psychological Bulletin, 64*(2), 92–107.

U. S. Census Bureau. (1990). *1990 census of population and housing summary.* Washington, DC: U. S. Government Printing Office.

Wilson, W. J. (1987). *The truly disadvantaged: The inner city, the underclass, and public policy.* Chicago: University of Chicago Press.

Yates, A. (1987). Current status and future directions of research on the American Indian child. *American Journal of Psychiatry, 144*(9), 1135–1142.

Chapter 13

Transatlantic Replicability of Risk Factors in the Development of Delinquency

David P. Farrington
University of Cambridge

Rolf Loeber
Western Psychiatric Institute and Clinic
University of Pittsburgh

This chapter investigates the replicability of risk factors for delinquency across time and place. It compares the development of offending in the Cambridge Study in Delinquent Development, which is a prospective longitudinal survey of 411 London boys originally of ages 8 to 9 in 1961–1962, and in the middle sample of the Pittsburgh Youth Study, comprising 508 Pittsburgh boys originally between the ages of 10 and 11 in 1987–1988. It seeks to establish which risk factors during childhood (age 8–10) predict court appearances for delinquency in adolescence (age 10–16) in English and U.S. samples of inner-city boys in different time periods (1963–1971 in London and 1987–1994 in Pittsburgh).

Systematic comparisons of results obtained in two longitudinal surveys are rare. Some researchers compared their results with previously published data from other surveys. For example, Pulkkinen (1988) analyzed her Finland longitudinal survey of males to see how comparable their criminal career features were to the London data reported by Farrington (1983, 1986). Direct, point-by-point, collaborative comparisons are less common. However, Farrington and Wikström (1994) systematically compared criminal career features (e.g., prevalence and frequency of offending at different ages, and also ages of onset) for the London boys and for working-class Stockholm boys from Project Metropolitan, also born in 1953 (Janson, 1984; Wikström, 1987). They took various steps to increase comparability, for example by restricting the analyses to the same range of offenses in both samples. They found some similarities between the samples (e.g., in the cumulative prevalence curves) but also some dissimilarities (e.g., in the frequency of offending at different ages).

Pulkkinen and Tremblay (1992) investigated similarities between two longitudinal studies of boys, in Jyvaskyla, Finland, and Montreal, Canada. They cluster analyzed five scales derived from teacher ratings (aggression, anxiety, inattention, hyperactivity, and prosocial behavior) and found that eight similar clusters of boys were obtained in each country. The multiple-problem boys were most likely to have later delinquent outcomes. This study has some similarities with the cross-sectional comparison of U.S. and Dutch boys by Achenbach, Verhulst, Baron, and Althaus (1987). They factor analyzed Child Behavior Checklists completed by parents in each country, and concluded that seven empirically derived behavioral syndromes were replicable.

The only previous systematic comparisons of risk factors for delinquency in two prospective longitudinal surveys in different countries were carried out by Farrington, Biron, and LeBlanc (1982) and Moffitt, Caspi, Silva, and Stouthamer-Loeber (1995). Farrington et al. compared the relationship between personality factors and delinquency in London and Montreal. Moffitt et al. investigated the relationship between personality and intelligence measures and delinquency in the Dunedin (New Zealand) and Pittsburgh studies. They found that constraint (risk-taking as opposed to caution), negative emotionality (a low threshold for emotions such as anger and fear) and verbal intelligence were correlated with delinquency in both countries. The present comparison includes a much wider range of risk factors and focuses on their ability to predict later offending.

Cross-national comparisons of risk factors for delinquency are important for addressing the question of how far the causes of delinquency are similar in different times and places, and hence how far theories of delinquency can be generalized over time and place. A related issue is how far interventions needed to reduce or prevent the development of delinquency are similar in different times and places. To the extent that causes, theories, and interventions differ, this shows the importance of cultural and national contexts.

Cross-national delinquency comparisons are not easy, because of differences in legal definitions of offenses and in court processing. Cross-national comparable self-report surveys have many advantages (Junger-Tas, Terlouw, & Klein, 1994). However, England and the United States are quite similar in definitions of offenses and in court processing (Farrington, Langan, & Wilkström, 1994). There are problems in comparing different studies, because of differences in theoretical constructs studied and in the operational definition and measurement of theoretical constructs. Some variables may be harder to measure in some times and places; for example, it is difficult to measure criminal records of biological fathers in the United States in the

1990s, partly because of the problem of establishing the identity of the biological father, and partly because of problems of getting access to records and the adequacy of records for a mobile population. Nevertheless, because of investigator overlap, the London and Pittsburgh studies have many similarities in theoretical constructs and empirical variables.

THE CAMBRIDGE STUDY IN DELINQUENT DEVELOPMENT

The Cambridge Study in Delinquent Development is a prospective longitudinal survey of the development of offending and antisocial behavior in 411 London males. Table 13.1 summarizes key features of this project. At the time they were first contacted in 1961–1962, these males were all living in a working-class inner-city area of London. The sample was chosen by taking all the boys who were then 8 to 9 years of age and on the registers of six state primary schools within a 1-mile radius of a research office that had been established. Hence, the most common year of birth of these males was 1953. In nearly all cases (94%), their family breadwinner at that

TABLE 13.1
Key Features of London and Pittsburgh Studies

London	Pittsburgh
411 boys first studied at ages 8 to 9	508 boys first studied in fourth grade
97% White	44% White
Small inner-city area of London	City of Pittsburgh
Ages 8 to 9 in 1961–1962	Ages 10 to 11 in 1987–1988
All boys in six state primary schools	Random sample of public schools
Complete population	259 high risk, 249 low risk
Data from boy, mother, teacher, peers, records	Data from boy, mother, teacher, records
Individual, family, peer, school constructs	Individual, family, peer, neighborhood constructs
Initial data from all boys and 95% of mothers	Initial data from 86% of boys and mothers
Eight interviews at 3-year intervals up to age 32	Seven interviews at 6-month intervals up to age 14
94% interviewed in last wave	94% interviewed in last wave
Court records of convictions ages 10 to 16	Court records of petitions ages 10 to 16
21% convicted	28% petitioned
94% living with acting father at ages 8 to 9	59% living with acting father at ages 10 to 11
40% have three or more siblings	26% have three or more siblings
Average age of mother at boy's birth = 27.5	Average age of mother at boy's birth = 23.7
Average age of mother at first birth = 23.3	Average age of mother at first birth = 19.9
51% living in four or fewer rooms[a]	24% living in five or fewer rooms[a]
20% on welfare	43% on welfare

[a]London figures excluded bathrooms; 32% of boys had no fixed bath in their home.

time (usually the father) had a working-class occupation (skilled, semi-skilled, or unskilled manual worker). Most of the males were White (97%) and of British origin. The study was originally directed by Donald J. West, and it has been directed since 1982 by David P. Farrington, who has worked on it since 1969. It has been mainly funded by the British Home Office. The major results can be found in four books (West, 1969, 1982; West & Farrington, 1973, 1977), in more than 60 papers listed by Farrington and West (1990), and in a summary paper by Farrington (1995). These publications should be consulted for more details about the variables measured in this chapter.

A major aim in this survey was to measure as many factors as possible that were alleged to be causes or correlates of offending. The males were interviewed and tested in their schools when they were about the ages of 8, 10, and 14, by male or female psychologists. They were interviewed in a research office at about 16, 18, and 21, and in their homes at about 25 and 32, by young male social science graduates. At all ages except 21 and 25, the aim was to interview the whole sample, and it was always possible to trace and interview a high proportion: 389 out of 410 still alive at age 18 (95%) and 378 out of 403 still alive at age 32 (94%), for example. The tests in schools measured individual characteristics such as intelligence, attainment, personality, and psychomotor impulsivity, whereas information was collected in the interviews about such topics as living circumstances, employment histories, relationships with females, leisure activities such as drinking and fighting, and offending behavior.

In addition to interviews and tests with the males, interviews with their parents were carried out by female social workers who visited their homes. These took place about once a year from when the male was about 8 until when he was age 14 to 15 and was in his last year of compulsory education. The primary informant was the mother, although most fathers were also seen. The parents provided details about such matters as family income, family size, their employment histories, their childrearing practices (including attitudes, discipline, and parental disharmony), their degree of supervision of the boy, and his temporary or permanent separations from them.

The teachers completed questionnaires when the males were about 8, 10, 12, and 14 years of age. These furnished data about their troublesome and aggressive school behavior, their attention deficits, their school attainments and their truancy. Ratings were also obtained from their peers when they were in the primary schools, about such topics as their daring, dishonesty, troublesomeness, and popularity.

Searches were also carried out in the central Criminal Record Office in London to try to locate findings of guilt of the males, of their biological parents, of their full brothers and sisters, and (in recent years) of their wives and cohabitees. The minimum age of criminal responsibility in England is 10. The Criminal Record Office contains records of all relatively serious offenses committed in Great Britain or Ireland. In the case of 18 males who had emigrated outside Great Britain and Ireland by age 32, applications were made to search their criminal records in the eight countries where they had settled, and searches were actually carried out in four countries. Because most males did not emigrate until their 20s, and because the emigrants had rarely been convicted in England, it is likely that the criminal records are quite complete.

Convictions were only counted if they were for offenses normally recorded in the Criminal Record Office, thereby excluding minor crimes such as common assault, traffic infractions, and drunkenness. The most common offenses included were thefts, burglaries, and unauthorized takings of vehicles, although there were also quite a few offenses of violence, vandalism, fraud, and drug abuse. In order not to rely on official records for information about offending, self-reports of offending were obtained from the males at every age from 14 onward. In general, predictors and correlates of convictions were very similar to predictors and correlates of self-reported delinquency (Farrington, 1992).

This chapter compares explanatory variables measured at age 8 to 10 with convictions between ages 10 and 16, inclusive. Hence, this is a genuinely predictive study and the age-8 to age-10 variables could not be biased by the knowledge of who became delinquent. The recorded age of offending is the age at which an offense was committed, not the age on conviction. There can be delays of several months or even more than a year between offenses and convictions, making conviction ages different from offending ages. Offenses are defined as acts leading to convictions. Between ages 10 and 16 inclusive (the years of juvenile delinquency in England at that time), 85 males (21%) were convicted. Altogether, up to age 40 in 1994, 164 males (40%) were convicted (Farrington, Barnes, & Lambert, 1996).

The Cambridge Study in Delinquent Development has a unique combination of features:

1. Eight personal interviews with the males have been completed over a period of 24 years, from age 8 to age 32.
2. The main focus of interest is on offending.
3. The sample size of about 400 is large enough for many statistical analyses but small enough to permit detailed case histories of the boys and their families.
4. There has been a very low attrition rate, because 94% of the males still alive provided information at age 32.
5. Information has been obtained from multiple sources: the males, their parents, teachers, peers, and official records.

6. Information has been obtained about a wide variety of theoretical constructs, including intelligence, personality, parental childrearing methods, peer delinquency, school behavior, employment success, marital stability, and so on.

THE PITTSBURGH YOUTH STUDY

The Pittsburgh Youth Study is a prospective longitudinal survey of the development of offending and antisocial behavior in three samples of about 500 Pittsburgh boys ($N = 1,517$). At the time they were first contacted in 1987–1988, random samples of first, fourth, and seventh grade boys enrolled in the city of Pittsburgh public schools were selected. At that time, 72% of all children resident in the city of Pittsburgh attended public schools. The city of Pittsburgh covers the inner city population of about 370,000 in 1990 out of the Pittsburgh–Beaver Valley Metropolitan Statistical Area of about 2,243,000 (Hoffman, 1991). Many of the assessments in the Pittsburgh Youth Study were designed to be comparable to those used in two other contemporaneous longitudinal surveys conducted in Denver, Colorado (Huizinga, Esbensen, & Weiher, 1991) and Rochester, New York (Thornberry, Lizotte, Krohn, Farnworth, & Jang, 1991).

Out of about 1,000 boys in each grade selected at random for a screening assessment, about 850 boys (85%) were actually assessed. The boys completed a self-report questionnaire about antisocial behavior and delinquency (Loeber, Stouthamer-Loeber, van Kammen, & Farrington, 1989), while their primary caretakers completed an extended Child Behavior Checklist (Achenbach & Edelbrock, 1983) and their teachers completed an extended Teacher Report Form (Edelbrock & Achenbach, 1984). We refer to the primary caretaker as the mother because this was true in 94% of cases. Participants did not differ significantly from the comparable male student population in their scores on the California Achievement Test (CAT) and in their ethnic composition (African American or White).

From the screening assessment, a risk score was calculated for each boy indicating how many of 21 serious antisocial acts he had ever committed (including types of stealing, running away, firesetting, truancy, vandalism, robbery, gang fighting, attacking with a weapon, joyriding, burglary, liquor use, and marijuana use). Information from all three sources was taken into account. The risk score was used to select the sample for follow-up, consisting of approximately the 250 most antisocial boys in each grade and about 250 boys randomly selected from the remaining 600. Hence, the screening sample of about 850 per grade was reduced to a follow-up sample of about 500 per grade. The 500 boys in each grade were then assessed every 6 months for 3 years, with data collection from the boy, the mother and the teacher on each occasion. Regular data collection from the middle sample then ceased, but the oldest and youngest sample were still being followed up at yearly intervals as of 1997. Rolf Loeber is the principal investigator of the Pittsburgh Youth Study, with Magda Stouthamer-Loeber, Welmoet van Kammen, David P. Farrington, and Benjamin B. Lahey as coinvestigators. The study has mainly been funded by the U.S. Office of Juvenile Justice and Delinquency Prevention and the U.S. National Institute of Mental Health.

For the closest comparability to the London data, the present analyses are based only on the middle sample of boys, who were aged about 10 when they were first assessed. Variables measured in the screening assessment and first follow-up 6 months later are compared with petitions to the juvenile court up to 1994. The middle follow-up sample comprises 508 boys, 259 of whom were high risk and 249 of whom were randomly chosen from the remainder who were screened. Of the sample, 56% were African American, 91% were living with their natural mother, and 41% were living with their natural father at the time of the first follow-up. At this time, their median age was 10.6 years, and they were then followed up in court records for 5.8 years up to a median age of 16.4 years. The Pittsburgh boys were more variable in age than the London boys, although both were grade samples. In England, advancement from one grade to the next depends on age, not an achievement; hence, children are not "held down" in age-inappropriate grades because of low achievement.

Table 13.1 shows some differences between the London and Pittsburgh samples. As already mentioned, 97% of London boys were White, compared with 44% of Pittsburgh boys. Although 94% of London boys were living with an acting (biological or nonbiological) father, this was true of only 59% of Pittsburgh boys. The London boys had more siblings (defined as other children born to their biological mothers) on average than the Pittsburgh boys (where all related siblings, including paternal half-siblings, were included). However, Pittsburgh mothers were younger at the time of the boy's birth and at the time of the birth of their first child. London homes were smaller and hence more crowded, but twice as many of the Pittsburgh families (43%, compared with 20% in London) were dependent on welfare.

As in the London study, a major aim in the Pittsburgh Youth Study was to measure as many factors as possible that were alleged to be causes or correlates of offending. The first follow-up was much more extensive than the screening assessment. The boys completed the Self-Reported Delinquency scale of Elliott, Huizinga, and Ageton (1985), while the mothers again completed the extended Child Behavior Checklist and the teachers again completed the extended Teacher Report Form. These questionnaires yielded data on antisocial behavior and on individual factors such as hyperactivity, anxiety, and shyness. In addition, the mothers completed a demographic questionnaire yielding information about adults and children living with the boy, and the Revised Diagnostic Interview Schedule for Children (DISC–R; Costello et al., 1985) that yielded child psychiatric diagnoses such as attention deficit disorder with hyperactivity (ADHD). The boys completed the Recent Mood and Feelings Questionnaire (Costello & Angold, 1988) as a measure of depressed mood. Also, CAT results on reading, language, and mathematics were obtained from the schools.

Various questionnaires were used to assess parental discipline and supervision, parent–child communication, parental attitudes to child antisocial behavior, parental disharmony (where two parents were present), parental stress, parental anxiety and parental substance use. Socioeconomic status (SES) was assessed using the Hollingshead (1975) index, based on parental occupational prestige and educational level. Where two parents were present, the higher score was recorded. Housing quality was assessed by the interviewer, based on such features as the structural condition of the house and visible signs of peeling paint. Neighborhood quality was rated by the mother and also assessed from census data (e.g., on median family income, percentage unemployed, percentage separated or divorced).

In order to maximize the validity of all variables, information from different sources was combined as far as possible, as was information from the screening and first follow-up assessments. For example, the combined measure of delinquency seriousness based on mothers, boys, and teachers was a better predictor of court petitions than self-reported delinquency alone (Farrington, Loeber, et al., 1996). Only brief descriptions of variables are included in this chapter; more extensive descriptions can be found in previous papers (e.g., Loeber, Stouthamer-Loeber, van Kammen, & Farrington, 1989, 1991; Stouthamer-Loeber, Loeber, & Thomas, 1992; Stouthamer-Loeber et al., 1993; van Kammen et al., 1991) and in the first book on the study (Loeber, Farrington, Stouthamer-Loeber, & van Kammen, 1998). Measurement methods were better in Pittsburgh than in London, especially for family variables.

Court records were obtained from Allegheny County Juvenile Court (paper files). The city of Pittsburgh is included in and surrounded by Allegheny County, which had a population of about 1,336,000 in 1990 (Hoffman, 1991). Six boys who moved outside Allegheny County within 2 years were excluded from the analyses, as were seven boys with no consent forms or incomplete records. In order to carry out a genuinely predictive analysis, 10 boys with court records before the first follow-up assessment were excluded, leaving 485 boys in the analysis who had no official record at age 10.

Detected juvenile offenders in Allegheny County may be referred to the juvenile court by the police or other agencies (e.g., the school board). The intake officer (in the probation department) reviews all cases and almost always meets with the alleged offender, the family, and the victim. The intake officer may dismiss or withdraw cases because of doubts about whether the offender is in fact guilty, doubts about whether there is sufficient evidence to prove that the offender is guilty, or for procedural reasons such as the victim not turning up. The intake officer may divert the offender (e.g., by giving a warning or requiring informal probation) if the case is minor or the offender is young and criminally inexperienced. If the intake officer believes that there is sufficient evidence that the juvenile is guilty, and that the case is too serious for diversion, the case will be petitioned to the juvenile court. We have only counted petitioned cases. Therefore, our recorded juvenile offenders are relatively serious cases where there is convincing evidence of guilt.

Offense types were coded according to the FBI Uniform Crime Reports system. For comparability with London offenses, we included index and nonindex delinquency. Nonindex delinquency included simple assault, forgery, fraud, receiving stolen property, weapons offenses, vandalism, drug offenses, prostitution, statutory rape, disorderly conduct, threats and endangering, indecent assault and indecent exposure. Other offenses (e.g., liquor law violations, drunkenness, traffic offenses, violations of ordinances, status offenses) were excluded. The London and Pittsburgh offenses leading to juvenile court delinquency records are quite comparable. Of the 485 boys in the middle sample with no court record before the follow-up assessment, 137 (28%) were petitioned afterward. Most of these (104 out of 137) were petitioned for the index offenses of homicide, forcible rape, robbery, aggravated assault, burglary, larceny, motor vehicle theft, or arson.

The Pittsburgh Youth Study has a unique combination of features:

1. It is a multiple-cohort accelerated longitudinal design (Bell, 1954; Farrington, 1991), although only the middle cohort is studied in this chapter.
2. It contains a high-risk sample and a representative sample, thus maximizing the yield of problem boys while still permitting conclusions about the general population.
3. Information from the males, their mothers, and their teachers was obtained every 6 months on seven occasions for the middle sample, and data collection is continuing annually for the youngest and oldest samples 9 years after the start of the project.
4. The main focus of interest is on offending and on child psychiatric disorders.
5. The sample size of about 500 per cohort is relatively large.
6. The multiple-cohort design means that results obtained with one sample can be tested for replication with others.

7. There has been a very low attrition rate from the first follow-up onward; 94% of the follow-up sample of boys in the middle cohort were interviewed in the seventh assessment.
8. Information has been obtained about a wide variety of theoretical constructs, including individual, family, SES, peer, and neighborhood measures.

KEY EXPLANATORY VARIABLES

The London and Pittsburgh studies were not designed to test one particular theory but to test hypotheses derived from numerous theories. Major longitudinal surveys are so uncommon and so difficult to carry out that it is desirable to measure numerous theoretical constructs and outcome variables in them (e.g., not only delinquency but also substance use, sexual intercourse, etc.). The major theoretical constructs and hypotheses to be tested were derived from important theories such as the following:

1. Cohen (1955) and Cloward and Ohlin (1960), highlighted the importance of socioeconomic deprivation, low social class, low school attainment, the inability to achieve status goals, and the inability to delay gratification.
2. Shaw and McKay (1969) and Sutherland and Cressey (1974), emphasized the influence of criminal and socially disorganized neighborhoods, delinquent schools, delinquent friends, and criminal parents.
3. Bowlby (1951) and Hirschi (1969), focused on the importance of attachment to and separation from parents, and the strength of bonding to family and society.
4. Eysenck (1977) and Trasler (1962), concentrated on the importance of internal inhibitions against offending built up in a social learning process, of consistent parenting, and of anxiety as an inhibitor.
5. Akers (1973), Patterson (1982), and Widom (1989), focused on the importance of differential reinforcement by parents of good and bad behavior, and of direct imitation of parental aggression.
6. Robins (1966), highlighted the continuity and stability of an underlying construct such as antisocial personality.
7. Gottfredson and Hirschi (1990), Wilson and Hernstein (1985), and Moffitt (1990), emphasized the importance of self-control, impulsivity and intelligence.

Most modern delinquency theories (see, e.g., Hawkins, 1996) include several of these key theoretical ideas.

For both samples, explanatory variables were dichotomized to discriminate the approximately 25% of males who were in the highest risk group from the remainder. The 25%–75% split was chosen to match the prior expectation that about one quarter of the sample would be convicted as juveniles. Because most variables in the London study had been coded into a small number of categories (typically three or four), this dichotomizing did not usually involve a great loss of information.

There are certain advantages to dichotomized variables. They permit a "risk factor" approach, and also make it possible to use a simple sum to study the cumulative effects of several risk factors. Second, they make it easy to investigate interactions between variables, although they also carry some risk of misrepresenting the interaction between the full scaled variables. Hence, they encourage a focus on types of individuals as well as on variables, permitting the investigation of relationships within different subgroups of individuals. Information about individuals is more useful for interventions than information about variables. Dichotomization also makes it more straightforward to compare effects between necessarily dichotomous variables (e.g., broken family, family on welfare) and variables that may also be represented as a scale.

Dichotomous data permit the use of the odds ratio as a measure of strength of relationship, which is readily understood as the (multiplicative) increase in risk associated with a risk factor (Fleiss, 1981). It is a more intuitively compelling measure of predictive efficiency than the percentage of variance explained (Rosenthal & Rubin, 1982). For example, an odds ratio of 2, doubling the risk of delinquency, might correspond to a correlation of .12 or less, which translates into 1.4% of the variance explained. The percentage of variance explained gives a misleading impression of unimportance. However, because of the mathematical relationship between the logarithm of the odds ratio and the phi correlation (Agresti, 1990), conclusions about relative strengths of associations based on odds ratios and phi correlations are similar.

The use of the odds ratio encourages the study of the worst affected individuals. In delinquency research, there is often more interest in predicting extreme cases (e.g., "chronic" offenders) than the whole range of variation. Dichotomization is also a convenient means of handling problems in the distribution of variables and of nonlinear relationships among variables. Variables reflecting deviancy often have a highly skewed distribution. Some variables are nonlinearly related to delinquency, with a large increase in delinquency in the most extreme category compared with the remainder. For example, in the Pittsburgh study, the percentage of boys petitioned to the juvenile court was 40% of those with three or more siblings, compared with 24.5% of those with two siblings, 24.5% of those with one sibling, and 22.4% of those with no siblings.

There was a great deal of data reduction in London and Pittsburgh to try to produce distinct measures of a relatively small number of key theoretical constructs. The aim was to eliminate redundancy without significant loss of information, using only clearly explanatory variables as predictive factors. For example, peer delinquency was excluded, because it may merely be measuring the boy's own delinquency (because 76% of seriously delinquent acts in the middle sample in Pittsburgh were committed with others). Amdur (1989) pointed out that a common fault in much delinquency research is to include measures of the outcome variable as predictors. If two variables are measuring the same underlying construct, using one as a predictor of the other will artifactually increase the percentage of variance explained, without adding practical significance to the explanation of delinquency.

In order to avoid collinearity problems in regression analyses, we deleted variables that were highly correlated $(r > .40)$ with other, conceptually similar variables. For example, in London, low family income was retained in preference to the father's poor job record $(r = .48)$ and living on welfare $(r = .57)$, and low junior school attainment in preference to low verbal intelligence $(r = .48)$. However, both large family size (four or more siblings) and low family income were retained, despite their intercorrelation $(r = .46)$, because they were judged to be distinctly different constructs. In Pittsburgh, behavior problems of the father was retained in preference to parental substance use $(r = .54)$, age of the mother at first birth in preference to age of the mother at the birth of the boy $(r = .45)$, and broken family (not living with two biological parents) in preference to living in a single-parent, female headed household $(r = .59)$. However, African American ethnicity and bad neighborhood (according to census data) were both retained $(r = .52)$, as were African American ethnicity and living on welfare $(r = .42)$ and broken family and living on welfare $(r = .43)$, because distinctions between these effects were judged to be substantively important.

Table 13.2 shows the key explanatory variables, divided into four categories: individual, childrearing, SES, and parental. In general, dichotomization of variables in Table 13.2 left between 15% and 35% of boys in the high-risk group. However, some variables fell outside of that range (e.g., family on welfare, broken family, African American ethnicity in Pittsburgh, and few friends and boy not praised in London). The Pittsburgh data were analyzed without weighting back to the screening sample because, although weighting changed prevalence estimates, it did not change measures of association, which are the focus of this chapter.

In previous analyses of the London data, variables were excluded if information was missing for 10% or more of the sample. This rule could not be applied to the Pittsburgh data, because of the large number of absent

TABLE 13.2
Explanatory Variables, Prevalence of High Risk, and Missing Data

London (n = 411)			*Pittsburgh (n = 485)*		
Individual Characteristics	% *High*	% *Miss*	*Individual Characteristics*	% *High*	% *Miss*
Low nonverbal intelligence (B)	25	0	Low achievement (R)	25	4
Low school achievement (T)	23	6	Hyperactive (M,T)	19	0
High daring (M,P)	30	1	High attention deficit (M)	24	0
Lacks concentration or			Lacks guilt (M,T)	30	13
restless (T)	20	0	High anxiety (M,T)	30	0
High psychomotor			Shy or withdrawn (M,T)	30	0
impulsivity (B)	25	0	Few friends (B,M)	29	3
High nervousness (M)	24	7	Depressed mood (B)	23	1
Shy or withdrawn (M)	22	7	High religiosity (B)	21	27
Few friends (M)	12	5			
Unpopular (P)	32	4			
Regular church attender (M)	19	14			
Childrearing			*Childrearing*		
Poor supervision (M)	19	7	Poor supervision (B,M)	28	2
Harsh maternal discipline			Physical punishment by		
(M)	16	7	mother (B,M)	36	1
Harsh paternal discipline			Low parental reinforcement		
(M)	21	11	(B,M)	26	1
Authoritarian parental atti-			Poor family communication		
tude (M)	24	27	(B,M)	25	1
Boy not praised (M)	12	12	Boy not involved (B,M)	30	1
Boy's leisure outside home (M)	17	19	Boy not close to mother (B)	18	2
Father doesn't join in (M)	28	27	Disagree on discipline (B,M)	24	44
Parental conflict (M)	24	9	Unhappy parents (M)	31	41
Socioeconomic			*Socioeconomic*		
Low SES (M)	19	0	Low SES (M)	25	2
Low family income (M)	23	0	Family on welfare (M)	43	7
Mother at home (M)	30	5	Unemployed father (M)	22	42
Poor housing (I)	33	0	Unemployed mother (M)	27	10
Three or fewer rooms (M)	19	6	Poor housing (I)	23	5
Separated from parent (M)	22	0	Five or fewer rooms (M)	24	3
High delinquency school (R)	21	10	Broken family (M)	61	3
			Bad neighborhood (M)	24	1
			Bad neighborhood (C)	26	8

(Continued)

TABLE 13.2
(Continued)

London (n = 411)			Pittsburgh (n = 485)		
Parental	% High	% Miss	Parental	% High	% Miss
Convicted parent (R)	27	0	Father behavior problems (M)	18	8
Young mother (< 20) (M,R)	22	0	Mother antisocial attitude (M)	24	1
Nervous mother (M)	32	6	Young mother (<18) (M)	28	10
Nervous father (M)	22	10	Anxious parent (M)	27	0
Four or more siblings (M,R)	24	0	High maternal stress (M)	23	1
			Poorly educated mother (M)	27	3
			Poorly educated father (M)	23	43
			Three or more siblings (M)	26	0
			Ethnicity		
			African American (M)	56	0

Note. B = boy, M = mother, F = father, T = teacher, P = peer, R = record, I = interviewer, C = Census.

fathers. More than 40% of the sample were missing on father variables (e.g., poorly educated father, unemployed father) and on variables based on two parents (e.g., disagree on discipline, unhappy parents). This difficulty did not arise with behavior problems of the father, because this variable was based on currently absent fathers as well as currently present fathers. The notes to Table 13.2 show that the source of this variable was the mother.

PREDICTORS OF JUVENILE COURT DELINQUENCY SHARED BY THE TWO STUDIES

Table 13.3 shows odds ratios obtained with reasonably comparable predictors of juvenile court delinquency in London and Pittsburgh. A one-tailed .05 significance criterion was used because all the predictions were directional. Hyperactivity or impulsivity and poor concentration or attention deficit approximately doubled the odds of delinquency in both London and Pittsburgh, as did low junior school attainment in London (from school records) and low achievement in Pittsburgh (measured by the CAT). However, the measures of nervous boy and shy–withdrawn in London (based on mothers) and of anxious boy and shy–withdrawn in Pittsburgh (both derived from mothers and teachers) did not predict delinquency. Nor did having few or no friends (rated by mothers in London and by mothers and boys in Pittsburgh). Similarly, neither attending church regu-

TABLE 13.3
Comparable Predictors of Juvenile Court Delinquency

London		Pittsburgh	
Individual	*OR*	*Individual*	*OR*
High impulsivity	2.3*	Hyperactive	1.9*
Poor concentration	2.3*	High attention deficit	1.8*
Low achievement	2.6*	Low achievement	2.2*
High nervousness	1.0	High anxiety	0.8
Shy or withdrawn	0.8	Shy or withdrawn	1.2
Few friends	0.6	Few friends	1.2
Church attender	0.7	High religiosity	1.0
Childrearing		*Childrearing*	
Poor supervision	2.2*	Poor supervision	2.0*
Harsh discipline	3.3*	Physical punishment	1.2
Low reinforcement	1.4	Low reinforcement	1.5*
Leisure outside home	2.1*	Boy not involved	1.4
Parental conflict	2.6*	Unhappy parents	2.3*
Socioeconomic		*Socioeconomic*	
Low SES	1.5	Low SES	2.5*
Low family income	2.6*	Family on welfare	3.2*
Poor housing	1.9*	Poor housing	1.4
Small home	0.8	Small home	1.5
Separated from parent	2.4*	Broken family	3.5*
Parental		*Parental*	
Convicted parent	4.0*	Father behavior problems	1.9*
Young mother	1.6	Young mother	1.8*
Nervous mother	1.6	Anxious parent	0.9
Large family size	2.5*	Large family size	2.1*

*$p < .05$, one-tailed.

larly in London (according to mothers) nor low participation in religious services in Pittsburgh (according to boys) predicted court delinquency.

Generally, childrearing measures were based on mother reports in London and on questionnaires completed by mothers and boys in Pittsburgh. Poor parental supervision doubled the odds of delinquency in London (Odds Ratio; [OR] = 2.2) and in Pittsburgh (OR = 2.0). In Pittsburgh, the main measure of parental discipline was whether the mother used physical punishment (hitting, slapping, or spanking the boy). This did not predict delinquency. The most comparable variable in London was a combined measure of harsh or erratic discipline and cruel or neglecting attitude of the mother, and a harsh or neglecting mother. This variable was one of the strongest risks for subsequent delinquency (OR = 3.3).

In London, boys who were not praised or rewarded for being good were marginally (not significantly) more likely to become delinquents (OR = 1.4). Pittsburgh boys who received little parental reward or reinforcement for positive behavior were similarly more at risk (OR = 1.5), but this time the OR was marginally significant. In London, boys who spent most of their leisure time outside the home (according to a questionnaire completed by mothers) were about twice as likely to become delinquents (OR = 2.1). However, in Pittsburgh, boys who were not involved in family activities were not significantly more likely to become delinquents (OR = 1.4). In London, parental disharmony at age 8 (chronic disagreement or raging conflicts between the parents) more than doubled the odds of delinquency (OR = 2.6). In Pittsburgh, unhappiness between the parents at age 10 had a very similar effect (OR = 2.3).

Turning to socioeconomic factors, low SES (low occupational prestige of the family breadwinner based on the Registrar General's scale) did not significantly predict delinquency in London (OR = 1.5). This could be because the Registrar General's scale did not realistically reflect social standing. For example, dockers and printers in London at that time were relatively well paid (and had high prestige locally), but these blue-collar occupations ranked lower on the Registrar General's scale than did more poorly paid white-collar occupations such as bank clerks. In Pittsburgh, the Hollingshead (1975) index of SES was used, which reflects not only occupational prestige but also the educational level of the parents. Low SES on this index significantly predicted the boy's delinquency (OR = 2.5).

Low family income in London significantly predicted delinquency (OR = 2.6) as did the family being on welfare in Pittsburgh (OR = 3.2). Poor housing in London (dilapidated or slum conditions) predicted delinquency (OR = 1.9), but the relationship was not significant in Pittsburgh (OR = 1.4). Living in a relatively small home (three or fewer rooms in London, five or fewer rooms in Pittsburgh) did not predict delinquency in either London or Pittsburgh. In London, separation of a boy from a parent (for reasons other than death or hospitalization) increased the odds of delinquency (OR = 2.4). Similarly, in Pittsburgh, boys who were not living with both biological parents were at 3.5 times the risk of delinquency as those who did live with both biological parents.

A convicted parent (usually the father) strongly predicted delinquency in London (OR = 4.0). Similarly, in Pittsburgh, a father with a history of behavior problems was predictive, although less strongly (OR = 1.9). A mother who was relatively young at the time of her first birth (younger than 20 in London, than 18 in Pittsburgh) predicted delinquency in both studies, but relatively weakly in London. In London, nervousness of the mother was based on mother reports, evidence of psychiatric treatment (received by 21% of mothers by the boy's age 8), and a Health Questionnaire completed by mothers. This was a marginal (nonsignificant) predictor of delinquency (OR = 1.6). In Pittsburgh, boys were considered to have an anxious parent if either their mother or their father had sought help for anxiety, depression or suicidal problems, but this variable did not predict the boy's delinquency. Finally, large family size (four or more siblings in London, three or more siblings in Pittsburgh) significantly predicted delinquency in both studies.

These variables are not all closely comparable. Nevertheless, the agreement between London and Pittsburgh results is quite impressive. Based on the odds ratio, 9 of the 12 significant predictors in London were also significant in Pittsburgh, and 6 of the 9 nonsignificant predictors in London were also nonsignificant in Pittsburgh. Out of 21 comparisons, there were only two large discrepancies. First, harsh maternal discipline significantly predicted delinquency in London (OR = 3.3), but maternal physical punishment was not predictive in Pittsburgh (OR = 1.2). Second, low SES significantly predicted delinquency in Pittsburgh (OR = 2.5) but not in London (OR = 1.5).

There were four smaller discrepancies. The boy spending his leisure time outside the home predicted delinquency in London (OR = 2.1), but his low involvement in family activities was not predictive in Pittsburgh (OR = 1.4). Poor housing was more strongly related to delinquency in London (OR = 1.9) than Pittsburgh (OR = 1.4), and a convicted parent was more predictive in London (OR = 4.0) than the father's behavior problems in Pittsburgh (OR = 1.9). Finally, a broken family was more strongly predictive in Pittsburgh (OR = 3.5) than was separation from a parent in London (OR = 2.4).

OTHER PREDICTORS OF JUVENILE COURT DELINQUENCY

Quite a number of variables measured in London had no directly comparable variable measured in Pittsburgh, and vice-versa. Identifying these variables has implications for measurement. For example, if a London variable, not measured in Pittsburgh, proved to be an important predictor of delinquency, one implication is that this variable should be measured in Pittsburgh. Table 13.4 shows the extent to which these noncomparable variables predicted delinquency.

In London, high daring (adventurousness or taking many risks, rated by peers and parents) was a strong predictor of delinquency (OR = 4.2). In Pittsburgh, lack of guilt was a strong predictor (OR = 3.8). Low nonverbal IQ (90 or less on the Progressive Matrices) predicted delinquency in London (OR = 2.3). Unpopularity in London (rated by peers) was a weak but significant predictor of delinquency (OR = 1.7), while in Pittsburgh depressed mood was not a significant predictor.

TABLE 13.4
Predictors of Juvenile Court Delinquency Measured in Only One Study

London		Pittsburgh	
Individual	*OR*	*Individual*	*OR*
Low nonverbal intelligence	2.3*	Lacks guilt	3.8*
High daring	4.2*	Depressed mood	1.2
Unpopular	1.7*		
Childrearing		*Childrearing*	
Harsh paternal discipline	2.5*	Poor family communication	1.5*
Authoritarian parental attitude	2.1*	Boy not close to mother	1.2
Father doesn't join in	1.9*	Disagree on discipline	1.3
Socioeconomic		*Socioeconomic*	
Mother at home	1.4	Unemployed father	1.6
High delinquency school	2.6*	Unemployed mother	1.7*
		Bad neighborhood (M)	1.8*
		Bad neighborhood (C)	2.0*
Parental		*Parental*	
Nervous father	1.3	Mother antisocial attitude	1.2
		High maternal stress	1.2
		Low mother education	2.7*
		Low father education	2.5*
		Ethnicity	
		African American	3.4*

Note. M = Mother. C = Census. *$p < .05$, one-tailed.

In London, fathers with harsh attitude and discipline tended to have delinquent sons (OR = 2.5), as did parents who expressed authoritarian and punitive childrearing attitudes on a questionnaire (OR = 2.1) and fathers who did not join in their sons' leisure activities (OR = 1.9). In Pittsburgh, poor communication between the boy and his parents (e.g., not telling them about his problems) was a weak predictor of delinquency (OR = 1.5). However, the boy reporting that he did not feel close to his mother, and disagreement between the parents on disciplining the boy, were not significant predictors.

In London, having a mother who stayed home and did not work outside the home was not a predictor of delinquency. However, going to a high-delinquency-rate secondary school at age 11 was a significant predictor (OR = 2.6). In Pittsburgh, a poor employment record of the mother (unemployed for at least 26 weeks in the previous year) was a weak but significant predictor of delinquency (OR = 1.7), whereas a comparably poor employment record of the father had a similar OR but was not statistically significant, perhaps because of the smaller numbers (42% of fathers missing on this variable). Also, information from the mother about the father's unemployment may have been inaccurate. For the mother variable, homemakers were not coded as unemployed. Living in a bad neighhorhood in Pittsburgh, according to either mother reports (OR = 1.8) or census data (OR = 2.0), significantly predicted the boy's delinquency. Finally, in Pittsburgh, African-American boys were significantly likely to be petitioned to the juvenile court (OR = 3.4). As already mentioned, 97% of the London boys were White; 7 of the 12 African-Caribbean males in London were convicted as juveniles.

In London, ratings of the nervousness of the father were based on mother reports and evidence of psychiatric treatment (received by 11% of fathers by the boy's age 8). However, this variable did not predict the boy's delinquency. In Pittsburgh, the mother's antisocial attitude (e.g., approving the boy's fighting and truancy) and her perceived stress were not significant predictors. However, a poor education (not reaching Grade 12) of the mother (OR = 2.7) and the father (OR = 2.5) both predicted the boy's delinquency.

MULTIVARIATE ANALYSES

In order to provide some indication about the predictors of delinquency that were independently important in each study, regression analyses were carried out. Strictly speaking, logistic regression analysis should be carried out with dichotomous data. However, a problem with logistic regression is that a case that is missing on any one variable has to be deleted from the whole analysis, causing a considerable loss of data. As already mentioned, missing data was especially a problem in Pittsburgh, because there were so many absent fathers. Fortunately, with dichotomous data, ordinary least squares (OLS) regression produces very similar results to logistic regression (Cleary & Angel, 1984), and the results obtained by the two methods are mathematically related (Schlesselman, 1982). Missing data were handled in the OLS regression by pairwise deletion, using all the available data for estimation of the relationship between all possible pairs of variables.

Hierarchical regression analyses entered variable sets from proximal to distal predictors. It was expected that childrearing factors (e.g., poor supervision) would increase the prevalence of individual risks (e.g., high daring), that SES (e.g., low family income) would increase the probability of poor childrearing (e.g., poor supervision), and that parental characteristics (e.g., young mother) would increase the probability of risky SES and structural factors (e.g., low family income). There is a surprising degree of consensus among longitudinal researchers (e.g., Larzelere & Patterson, 1990; Rutter, 1981) and contextual researchers (e.g., Gottfredson, McNeil, & Gottfredson, 1991; Simcha-Fagan & Schwartz, 1986) that neighborhood and SES factors have indirect effects on delinquency via their affects on childrearing and individual factors. African American ethnicity was entered last, because it could not be caused (changed) by any other factor. Other causal orders are of course possible. For example, SES factors could influence parental factors rather than the reverse, and nonindividual factors may have direct effects on delinquency rather than indirect effects via individual ones. An empirical justification for the causal ordering is presented later, and direct and indirect effects are investigated in regression analyses.

Table 13.5 shows the results of the regression analyses. The multiple regressions may be misleadingly low because of the use of dichotomous variables, and because proxy measures of the outcome variable (e.g., peer delinquency) were excluded as predictors. The best predictors of delinquency—high daring and lack of guilt—are measuring constructs that are theoretically distinct from delinquency. These analyses indicate which

TABLE 13.5
Hierarchical Regression Analyses for Juvenile Court Delinquency

London	F change	p	Pittsburgh	F change	p
Individual (.36)			Individual (.35)		
High daring	29.66	.0001	Lacks guilt	29.41	.0001
Low achievement	10.33	.0007	Low achievement	10.66	.0006
Low intelligence	4.81	.015	Low anxiety	3.24	.04
Unpopular	2.20	.07			
Childrearing (.40)			Childrearing (.38)		
Harsh maternal discipline	6.22	.007	Unhappy parents	3.53	.03
Authoritarian parents	2.44	.06	Poor supervision	2.09	.07
Socioeconomic (.41)			Socioeconomic (.43)		
Separated from parent	3.11	.04	Family on welfare	9.01	.002
			Broken family	4.00	.02
Parental (.45)			Parental (.45)		
Convicted parent	10.30	.0008	Poorly educated mother	4.11	.02
			Poorly educated father	2.14	.07
			Ethnicity (.46)		
			African American	3.08	.04

Note. Multiple R values in parentheses; p values one-tailed.

explanatory variables are important independently of more proximal variables.

In both London and Pittsburgh, separate tests of each set of predictors showed that the individual variables were the best predictors, as measured both by the best single predictor (high daring in London and lack of guilt in Pittsburgh) and by the multiple regressions (London: individual .36, childrearing .29, SES .25, parental .30; Pittsburgh: individual .35, childrearing .21, SES .31, parental .28). The best predictors were high daring, low school achievement, low nonverbal intelligence, and unpopularity in London; and lack of guilt, low achievement, and low anxiety in Pittsburgh.

The remaining three blocks of variables (childrearing, SES, and parental) were then tested one by one as predictors of the best single predictor of delinquency (high daring in London and lack of guilt in Pittsburgh). In both London and Pittsburgh, childrearing variables proved to be the best predictors of individual level variables, as measured both by the best single predictor (poor supervision in London and poor communication in Pittsburgh) and by the multiple regressions (London: childrearing .27, SES .22, parental .22; Pittsburgh: childrearing .33, SES .26, parental .25). Table 13.6 shows that the best predictors of high daring in London were poor supervision, harsh paternal discipline, and the boy spending leisure time outside the home, whereas the best predictors of lack of guilt in Pittsburgh were poor family communication, unhappy parents, and maternal physical punishment.

Table 13.5 shows that the most important independent childrearing predictors were harsh maternal discipline and authoritarian parental attitudes in London; and unhappy parents and poor supervision in Pittsburgh. These analyses suggest direct and indirect influences on delinquency. For example, in London, harsh maternal discipline and authoritarian parents had direct influences (independently of the individual variables), whereas poor supervision and harsh paternal discipline had indirect influences (because they influenced daring, which in turn influenced delinquency).

These results might be used to construct a path diagram of influences on delinquency. However, as blocks of variables are added, this path diagram becomes increasingly complex. For example, Table 13.6 shows that, both in London and Pittsburgh, the best predictors of the individual factor of low achievement were SES variables. Attending a high delinquency rate school (London) is a similar contextual variable to living in a bad neighborhood (Pittsburgh), and low family income (London) is comparable to welfare support (Pittsburgh).

Table 13.6 also shows the best predictors of the most important independent childrearing predictors of delinquency (in Table 13.5): harsh maternal discipline and authoritarian parents in London, and unhappy parents and poor supervision in Pittsburgh. The SES variables were the

TABLE 13.6
Hierarchical Regression Analyses for Intermediate Outcomes

London	F change	p	Pittsburgh	F change	p
High Daring			*Lacks Guilt*		
(Childrearing) (.27)			(Childrearing) (.33)		
Poor supervision	14.16	.0001	Poor communication	13.95	.0001
Harsh paternal discipline	3.03	.04	Unhappy parents	9.77	.001
Leisure outside home	2.22	.07	Maternal physical punishment	4.79	.01
Low Achievement			*Low Achievement*		
(SES) (.36)			(SES) (.29)		
Delinquent school	38.90	.0001	Family on welfare	11.67	.0004
Low family income	8.56	.002	Bad neighborhood (C)	4.19	.02
Mother at home	2.23	.07	Low SES	3.70	.03
			Poor housing	3.22	.04
Harsh Maternal Discipline			*Unhappy Parents*		
(Parental) (.16)			(Parental) (.34)		
Nervous mother	8.96	.002	Maternal stress	30.68	.0001
(SES) (.15)			Poorly educated mother	2.56	.06
Poor housing	8.06	.002			
Authoritarian Parents			*Poor Supervision*		
(SES) (.27)			(SES) (.24)		
Low family income	17.69	.0001	Family on welfare	15.85	.0001
Low SES	3.59	.03			
Separated From Parent			*Broken Family*		
(Parental) (.30)			(Parental) (.45)		
Convicted parent	28.16	.0001	Father behavior problems	46.78	.0001
Young mother	7.29	.004	Young mother	10.81	.0006
			Anxious parent	5.54	.01
			Family on Welfare		
			(Parental) (.44)		
			Young mother	26.65	.0001
			Poorly educated father	17.14	.0001
			Father behavior problems	8.35	.002
			Poorly educated mother	6.82	.005

Note. p values one-tailed; multiple R values in parentheses; C = Census.

best predictors of authoritarian parents and poor supervision, whereas the parental variables were the best predictors of unhappy parents. SES and parental variables were about equally important in predicting harsh maternal discipline. These empirical results were not clear-cut in supporting our theoretical position that SES variables were more proximate influences on childrearing than were parental variables.

Table 13.5 shows that, in London, separation from a parent predicted delinquency independently of individual and childrearing factors. Similarly, in Pittsburgh, a broken family was an independent predictor, as was the family on welfare. Table 13.6 shows that the best parental predictors of separation from a parent in London were a convicted parent and a young mother. Similarly, the best parental predictors of a broken family in Pittsburgh were the father's behavior problems and a young mother (as well as parental anxiety or depression). The best parental predictors of the family being on welfare in Pittsburgh were a young mother, the father's behavior problems, and a poorly educated mother and father.

Finally, Table 13.5 shows that, over and above the most important individual, childrearing and SES predictors, a convicted parent was an independent predictor of delinquency in London. Similarly, a poorly educated mother and father were independent predictors of delinquency in Pittsburgh. Also, African American ethnicity predicted delinquency independently of all other variables in Pittsburgh. However, the fact that this result was only just significant ($p = .04$; one-tailed), suggests that most of the linkage between African American ethnicity and delinquency operates through, and can be explained by, the other measured variables in this study.

These successive regression analyses suggest how causal influences on delinquency may operate. Both in London and Pittsburgh, the most important proximal influence is an individual factor reflecting low internal inhibition or self-control, and this individual factor is especially predicted by childrearing methods. Hence, these results agree with a theory attributing the development of delinquency primarily to the failure to build up internal inhibitions in a social learning process, because of inadequate childrearing methods.

However, the results also show that certain childrearing methods predict delinquency directly, independently of individual factors, as does the important SES factor of a broken family, and parental characteristics such as convictions and poor education. Other influences on delinquency operate indirectly through more proximal variables. For example, a young mother primarily predicts delinquency because it tends to be a precursor of a broken family, which in turn leads to delinquency. Hence, successive regression analyses empirically reveal patterns of causal influences.

In order to investigate whether the results would be any different using hierarchical logistic regression analyses, these are summarized in Table

TABLE 13.7
Logistic Regression Analyses for Juvenile Court Delinquency

London	LRCS change	p	Pittsburgh	LRCS change	p
Individual (n = 319)			Individual (n = 299)		
High daring	26.25	.0001	Lacks guilt	18.44	.0001
Unpopular	10.71	.0006	Low achievement	9.97	.0008
Not few friends	4.81	.014	Few friends	3.44	.03
Low achievement	2.39	.06	Low anxiety	3.53	.03
Childrearing (n = 226)			Childrearing (n = 231)		
Harsh maternal discipline	3.86	.025	Unhappy parents	3.93	.02
Authoritarian parents	3.14	.038	Not close to mother	3.02	.04
Socioeconomic (n = 244)			Socioeconomic (n = 178)		
Separated from parent	2.56	.055	Broken family	3.43	.03
			Bad neighborhood (C)	2.07	.07
			Low SES	2.15	.07
Parental (n = 256)			Parental (n = 212)		
Convicted parent	6.13	.007	Mother antisocial attitude	2.15	.07
			Poorly educated mother	1.82	.09
			Large family size	2.17	.07

Note. LRCS = likelihood ratio chi-squared; *p* values one-tailed; C = Census.

13.7. Generally, the most significant predictors in the OLS analyses were replicated in the logistic analyses. In London, the OLS results were closely replicated, despite the loss of cases. Seven of the eight significant predictors in the OLS analyses also emerged in the logistic analyses; the only difference was that low intelligence in the OLS analyses was replaced by not having few friends in the logistic analyses. In Pittsburgh, only 6 of the 10 significant predictors in the OLS analyses also emerged in the logistic analyses. Although having few friends seemed to be a protective factor in London, it was positively related to delinquency in Pittsburgh. However, as already explained, there was a severe loss of cases in the Pittsburgh logistic analyses; two thirds in one analysis (down to $n = 178$). For example, family on welfare was almost certainly insignificant in Pittsburgh because most of the families on welfare were missing from the analysis, because they had absent fathers. For all the reasons specified above, we believe that the results obtained in the OLS regressions are the most valid.

Cohen and Cohen (1983) argued that hierarchical multiple regression analysis should be carried out in the reverse order to the one we have used; that is, with the most distal variables entering the equation first and the most proximal last. The arguments advanced in favor of this ordering as as follows. The final equation in which all variables appear provides estimates of the direct effects of all variables in the model. Entering variables or variable sets in order from distal to proximal allows estimates of the total effect of each variable provided by its coefficient at the point at which it is added to the equation. Such an estimate will be independent of potential confounding common causes, if, for example, it is in part caused by an earlier entered variable. For example, if a variable had a significant and material effect when first entered into the equation predicting delinquency, but approached a zero value and nonsignificance in the equation when subsequent variables were added, this would indicate that its effect on delinquency was mediated through those other variables.

An alternative hypothesis is that the effect of the variable disappeared because it was intercorrelated with one of the other variables (i.e., both were essentially measuring the same underlying construct). Gordon (1968) showed how the weighting of any variable depends on the number of other similar variables in a multiple regression analysis. This is one of the reasons why we focused on *F* changes in stepwise regression rather than Beta values.

We investigated the effects of carrying out the hierarchical regression analyses in the reverse order, and the results are shown in Table 13.8. In London, two parental variables (a convicted parent and large family size) independently predicted delinquency. Similarly, three SES variables (separated from parent, high delinquency school, and low family income) independently predicted delinquency. When all these five parental and SES variables were then included in the equation, large family size and a high delinquency school were no longer independent predictors. There was no obvious tendency for the beta weights of the parental variables to decrease more than those of the SES variables. This either means that parental variables do not have indirect effects on delinquency via SES variables (as assumed in our model) or that effects of parenting mediated by socioeconomic circumstances are similar to confounding effects of parenting on socioeconomic variables.

When the four significant childrearing variables were added to the equation, only three variables were independently predictive, and again there were no obvious decreases in beta weights. Similarly, when the three significant individual variables were added, five variables were independently predictive of delinquency (a convicted parent, harsh maternal discipline, authoritarian parents, high daring, and low achievement). Comparing these results with those shown in Table 13.5, these were five of the seven most important variables in Table 13.5 (all except low intelligence and separation from a parent). Consequently, the results obtained with the reverse hierarchical regressions were similar to those obtained previously.

Similar conclusions can be drawn from the Pittsburgh analyses. Eight variables were independently important in the reverse hierarchical regressions (African American ethnicity, poorly educated father and mother,

TABLE 13.8
Alternative Hierarchical Regression Analyses

	Betas			
	Single	*P,S*	*P,S,C*	*P,S,C,I*
London				
Parental				
Convicted parent	.250	.230	.267	.217
Large family size	.112	—		
Socioeconomic				
Separated from parent	.120	.080	—	
High delinquency school	.120	—		
Low family income	.117	.107	—	
Childrearing				
Harsh maternal discipline	.168		.186	.151
Harsh paternal discipline	.117		—	
Authoritarian parents	.102		.115	.097
Leisure outside home	.096		—	
Individual				
High daring	.279			.225
Low achievement	.136			.115
Low intelligence	.118			—
Pittsburgh				
Parental				
African American	.233	.174	.158	.129
Poorly educated father	.133	.133	.122	.106
Poorly educated mother	.127	.108	.110	.121
Large family size	.094	.100	.093	—
Socioeconomic				
Family on welfare	.157	—		
Broken family	.148	.158	.168	.125
Low SES	.109	—		
Childrearing				
Unhappy parents	.150		.141	.112
Poor supervision	.124		—	
Individual				
Lacks guilt	.272			.197
Low achievement	.179			.104
Low anxiety	.095			.106

Note. Single = Single block of variables entered in regression. P = Parental, S = SES,
C = Childrearing, I = Individual. Beta values only shown if $p < .05$, one-tailed.

broken family, unhappy parents, lack of guilt, low achievement, and low
anxiety). These were 8 of the 10 most important variables in Table 13.5
(all except poor supervision and family on welfare). There was no obvious
tendency for the previous regression analyses to overestimate the importance of individual variables.

CONCLUSIONS

This is the first systematic comparison of the extent to which a large number of different risk factors are predictive of delinquency in two different countries. The definition and measurement of delinquency was similar in both countries. Several risk factors were identified as replicable predictors of delinquency over time and place (London in the early 1960s and Pittsburgh in the late 1980s). The most important were hyperactivity, impulsivity, and poor concentration; low school attainment; poor parental supervision; parental conflict; an antisocial parent; a young mother; large family size; low family income; and coming from a broken family. These effects must be quite robust to show up clearly in dichotomous data.

Several results were also replicated in regression analyses. The most important proximal predictors of delinquency were variables measuring low internal inhibition and low school attainment, and a broken family was an important independent predictor of delinquency in both London and Pittsburgh. Childrearing methods had the most important influences on low internal inhibition; and SES factors had the most important influences on low school attainment. A broken family was predicted by a young mother and an antisocial parent.

The differences between London and Pittsburgh can also be illuminating. Such differences could be attributable to many possible causes, including differences over time, differences between cultures, different operational definitions of theoretical constructs, different meanings of (theoretical constructs underlying) empirical variables, different causal mechanisms, and different samples. The use of the odds ratio meant that differences in strength of relationships could not be attributable to differences in prevalence. The major observed differences concerned maternal physical punishment, the boy spending leisure time outside the home, poor housing, a convicted parent (stronger predictors of delinquency in London) and low SES and a broken family (stronger predictors in Pittsburgh).

Maternal physical punishment was defined differently in London, because it included a cold, rejecting attitude. It is possible that physical punishment in Pittsburgh was sometimes given in the context of a loving relationship. There was no sign of any effect of physical punishment in Pittsburgh even when it was divided into three roughly equal categories (26.3%, 27.7%, and 30.3% delinquent, respectively). Similarly, the boy spending leisure time outside the home in London may be a different variable than the boy's low involvement in family activities in Pittsburgh. Spending leisure time outside the home may be conducive to peer influence, whereas low involvement in family activities may sometimes indicate a withdrawn personality.

Poor housing may have been a stronger predictor in London because housing conditions there in the early 1960s were objectively worse than in Pittsburgh in the late 1980s. Poor housing in London was an indicator of dilapidated slum housing, often earmarked for demolition in later slum clearance schemes.(For a graphic description of the London area, and changes in it since the 1960s, see Farrington & West, 1995.) Similarly, a convicted parent may have been a stronger predictor in London than the father's behavior problems in Pittsburgh because a conviction indicated a more antisocial individual.

Low SES may have been a stronger predictor of delinquency in Pittsburgh because it reflected parental education as well as occupation; a poorly educated father and mother were strong predictors of delinquency in Pittsburgh. Alternatively, the range of variability of SES may have been greater in Pittsburgh, because the sample was representative of the city rather than being drawn from one small area (as in London). A broken family may have been a stronger predictor in Pittsburgh than separation in London because a broken family indicated a permanent break, whereas separation included temporary breaks.

Comparisons over time and place highlight changes over time and place. For example, fathers were much more likely to be absent and mothers were more likely to be full-time workers in Pittsburgh in the late 1980s than in London in the early 1960s. Family size was greater in London, and the size of homes was less. It is interesting that most predictors were replicable despite these changes. An important theoretical issue is whether absolute or relative values of variables are important; for example, is it only family sizes greater than a certain absolute value that are criminogenic (e.g., because of the diffusion of the mother's attention over several children), or are relatively large families criminogenic irrespective of the absolute family size? The replicability of results suggests that relative values are most important. Systematic comparisons over time and place may be useful not only in establishing replicable results but also in throwing light on theoretical issues of this kind.

These results are not fully explainable by any existing theory of the development of delinquency. They are least compatible with classic theories that emphasize the importance of low social class (e.g., Cloward & Ohlin, 1960; Cohen, 1955) and criminal neighborhoods (e.g., Shaw & McKay, 1969), but this may be because of the restricted variability of these factors in inner-city samples. They are most compatible with classic theories that emphasize the importance of individual factors such as low self-control and impulsivity (e.g., Gottfredson & Hirschi, 1990; Wilson & Herrnstein, 1985), the importance of childrearing methods in building up internal inhibitions against offending (e.g., Patterson, Reid, & Dishion, 1992; Trasler, 1962), and the importance of attachment to and separation from parents (e.g., Bowlby,

1951). The challenge to criminologists is to devise more complex theories that can explain all the linkages between delinquency and the individual, childrearing, SES and parental factors included in more comprehensive longitudinal surveys such as the two described here.

REFERENCES

Achenbach, T. M., & Edelbrock, C. S. (1983). *Manual of the Child Behavior Checklist and Revised Child Behavior Profile*. Burlington: University of Vermont Department of Psychiatry.

Achenbach, T. M., Verhulst, F. C., Baron, G. D., & Althaus, M. (1987). A comparison of syndromes derived from the Child Behavior Checklist for American and Dutch boys aged 6–11 and 12–16. *Journal of Child Psychology and Psychiatry, 28*, 437–453.

Agresti, A. (1990). *Categorical data analysis*. New York: Wiley.

Akers, R. L. (1973). *Deviant behavior: A social learning approach*. Belmont, CA: Wadsworth.

Amdur, R. L. (1989). Testing causal models of delinquency: A methodological critique. *Criminal Justice and Behavior, 16*, 35–62.

Bell, R. Q. (1954). An experimental test of the accelerated longitudinal approach. *Child Development, 25*, 281–286.

Bowlby, J. (1951). *Maternal care and mental health*. Geneva, Switzerland: World Health Organization.

Caspi, A., Moffitt, T. E., Silva, P. A., Stouthamer-Loeber, M., Krueger, R. F., & Schmutte, P. S. (1994). Are some people crime prone? Replications of the personality–crime relationship across countries, genders, races and methods. *Criminology, 32*, 163–195.

Cleary, P. D., & Angel, R. (1984). The analysis of relationships involving dichotomous dependent variables. *Journal of Health and Social Behavior, 25*,334–348.

Cloward, R. A., & Ohlin, L. E. (1960). *Delinquency and opportunity*. New York: Free Press.

Cohen, A. K. (1955). *Delinquent boys*. Glencoe, IL: Free Press.

Cohen, J., & Cohen, P. (1983). *Applied multiple regression/correlation analysis for the behavioral sciences* (2nd ed.). Hillsdale, NJ: Lawrence Erlbaum Associates.

Costello, E. J., & Angold, A. (1988). Scales to assess child and adolescent depression: Checklists, screens and nets. *Journal of the American Academy of Child and Adolescent Psychiatry, 27*, 726–737.

Costello, E. J., Edelbrock, C. S., & Costello, A. J. (1985). The validity of the NIMH Diagnostic Interview Schedule for Children (DISC): A comparison between pediatric and psychiatric referrals. *Journal of Abnormal Child Psychology, 13*, 579–595.

Edelbrock, C. S., & Achenbach, T. M. (1984). The teacher version of the Child Behavior Profile: I. Boys aged six through eleven. *Journal of Consulting and Clinical Psychology, 52*, 207–217.

Elliott, D. S., Huizinga, D., & Ageton, S. S. (1985). *Explaining delinquency and drug use*. Beverly Hills, CA: Sage.

Eysenck, H. J. (1977). *Crime and personality* (3rd ed.). London: Routledge & Kegan Paul.

Farrington, D. P. (1983). Offending from 10 to 25 years of age. In K. T. Van Dusen & S. A. Mednick (Eds.), *Prospective studies of crime and delinquency* (pp. 17–37). Boston: Kluwer-Nijhoff.

Farrington, D. P. (1986). Age and crime. In M. Tonry & N. Morris (Eds.), *Crime and justice* (Vol. 7, pp. 189–250). Chicago: University of Chicago Press.

Farrington, D. P. (1991). Longitudinal research strategies: Advantages, problems and prospects. *Journal of the American Academy of Childand Adolescent Psychiatry, 30*, 369–374.

Farrington, D. P. (1992). Juvenile delinquency. In J. C. Coleman (Ed.), *The school years* (pp. 123–163). London: Routledge.

Farrington, D. P. (1993). Childhood origins of teenage antisocial behavior and adult social dysfunction. *Journal of the Royal Society of Medicine, 86,* 13–17.

Farrington, D. P. (1995). The development of offending and antisocial behavior from childhood: Key findings from the Cambridge Study in Delinquent Development. *Journal of Child Psychology and Psychiatry, 36,* 929–964.

Farrington, D. P., Barnes, G. C., & Lambert, S. (1996). The concentration of offending in families. *Legal and Criminological Psychology, 1,* 47–63.

Farrington, D. P., Biron, L., & LeBlanc, M. (1982). Personality and delinquency in London and Montreal. In J. Gunn & D. P. Farrington (Eds.), *Abnormal offenders, delinquency, and the criminal justice system* (pp. 153–201). Chichester, England: Wiley.

Farrington, D. P., Langan, P. A., & Wikström, P. H. (1994). Changes in crime and punishment in America, England and Sweden between the 1980s and the 1990s. *Studies on Crime and Crime Prevention, 3,* 104–131.

Farrington, D. P., Loeber, R., Stouthamer-Loeber, M., Van Kammen, W., & Schmidt, L. (1996). Self-reported delinquency and a combined delinquency seriousness scale based on boys, mothers and teachers: Concurrent and predictive validity for African Americans and Caucasians. *Criminology, 34,* 493–517.

Farrington, D. P., & West, D. J. (1990). The Cambridge Study in Delinquent Development: A long-term follow-up of 411 London males. In H.-J. Kerner & G. Kaiser (Eds.), *Kriminalitat: Personlichkeit, Lebensgeschichte und Verhalten* [Criminality: Personality, behavior and life history] (pp. 115–138). Berlin, Germany: Springer-Verlag.

Farrington, D. P., & West, D. J. (1995). Effects of marriage, separation and children on offending by adult males. In J. Hagan (Ed.), *Delinquency and disrepute in the life course* (pp. 249–281). Greenwich, CT: JAI Press.

Farrington, D. P., & Wikström, P. H. (1994). Criminal careers in London and Stockholm: A cross-national comparative study. In E. G. M. Weitekamp & H.-J. Kerner (Eds.), *Cross-national longitudinal research on human development and criminal behavior* (pp. 65–89). Dordrecht, Netherlands: Kluwer.

Fleiss, J. L. (1981). *Statistical methods for rates and proportions* (2nd ed.). New York: Wiley.

Gordon, R. A. (1968). Issues in multiple regression. *American Journal of Sociology, 73,* 592–616.

Gottfredson, D. C., McNeil, R. J., & Gottfredson, G. D. (1991). Social area influences on delinquency: A multi-level analysis. *Journal of Research on Crime and Delinquency, 28,* 197–226.

Gottfredson, M., & Hirsch, T. (1990). *A general theory of crime.* Stanford, CA: Stanford University Press.

Hawkins, J. D. (Ed.). (1996). *Delinquency and crime: Current theories.* New York: Cambridge University Press.

Hirschi, T. (1969). *Causes of delinquency.* Berkeley: University of California Press.

Hoffman, M. S. (Ed.). (1991). *The world almanac and book of facts, 1992.* New York: Pharos.

Hollingshead, A. B. (1975). *Four factor index of social status.* Unpublished manuscript.

Huizinga, D., Esbensen, F., & Weiher, A. W. (1991). Are there multiple paths to delinquency? *Journal of Criminal Law and Criminology, 82,* 83–118.

Janson, C. (1984). *Project Metropolitan: A presentation and progress report.* Stockholm: University of Stockholm Department of Sociology.

Junger-Tas, J., Terlouw, G., & Klein, M. W. (Eds.). (1994). *Delinquent behavior among young people in the western world.* Amsterdam, Netherlands: Kugler.

Larzelere, R. E., & Patterson, P. (1990). Parental management: Mediator of the effect of socio-economic status on early delinquency. *Criminology, 28,* 301–324.

Loeber, R., Farrington, D. P., Stouthamer-Loeber, M., & Van Kammen, W. B. (1998). *Antisocial behavior and mental health problems: Explanatory factors in childhood and adolescence.* Mahwah, NJ: Lawrence Erlbaum Associates.

Loeber, R., Stouthamer-Loeber, M., Van Kammen, W. B., & Farrington, D. P. (1989). Development of a new measure of self-reported antisocial behavior for young children:

13. DEVELOPMENT OF DELINQUENCY 329

Prevalence and reliability. In M. W. Klein (Ed.), *Cross-national research in self-reported crime and delinquency*. Dordrecht, Netherlands: Kluwer.

Loeber, R., Stouthamer-Loeber, M., Van Kammen, W. B., & Farrington, D. P. (1991). Initiation, escalation and desistance in juvenile offending and their correlates. *Journal of Criminal Law and Criminology, 82,* 36–82.

Moffitt, T. E. (1990). The neuropsychology of juvenile delinquency: A critical review. In M. Tonry & N. Morris (Eds.), *Crime and justice* (Vol. 12, pp. 99–169). Chicago: University of Chicago Press.

Moffitt, T. E., Capsi, A., Silva, P. A., & Stouthamer-Loeber, M. (1995). Individual differences in personality and intelligence are linked to crime: Cross-context evidence from nations, neighborhoods, genders, races and age-cohorts. In J. Hagan (Ed.), *Delinquency and disrepute in the life course* (pp. 1–34). Greenwich, CT: JAI Press.

Patterson, G. R. (1982). *Coercive family process.* Eugene, OR: Castalia.

Patterson, G. R., Reid, J. B., & Dishion, D. J. (1992). *Antisocial boys.* Eugene, OR: Castalia.

Pulkkinen, L. (1988). Delinquent development: Theoretical and empirical considerations. In M. Rutter (Ed.), *Studies of psychosocial risk* (pp. 184–199). Cambridge, England: Cambridge University Press.

Pulkkinen, L., & Tremblay, R. E. (1992). Patterns of boys' social adjustment in two cultures and at different ages: A longitudinal perspective. *International Journal of Behavioral Development, 15,* 527–553.

Robins, L. N. (1966). *Deviant children grown up.* Baltimore: Williams & Wilkins.

Rosenthal, R., & Rubin, D. B. (1982). A simple, general purpose display of magnitude of experimental effect. *Journal of Educational Psychology, 74,* 166–169.

Rutter, M. (1981). The city and the child. *American Journal of Orthopsychiatry, 51,* 610–625.

Schesselman, J. J. (1982). *Case-control studies.* New York: Oxford University Press.

Shaw, C. R., & McKay, H. D. (1969). *Juvenile delinquency and urban areas* (rev. ed.). Chicago: University of Chicago Press.

Simcha-Fagan, O., & Schwartz, J. E. (1986). Neighborhood and delinquency: An assessment of contextual effects. *Criminology, 24,* 667–703.

Stouthamer-Loeber, M., Loeber, R., Farrington, D. P., Zhang, Q., Van Kammen, W. B., & Maguin, E. (1993). The double edge of protective and risk factors for delinquency: Inter-relations and developmental patterns. *Development and Psychopathology, 5,* 683–701.

Stouthamer-Loeber, M., Loeber, R., & Thomas, C. (1992). Caretakers seeking help for boys with disruptive and delinquent behavior. *Comprehensive Mental Health Care, 2,* 159–178.

Sutherland, E. H., & Cressey, D. R. (1974).*Criminology* (9th ed.). Philadelphia: Lippincott.

Thornberry, T. P., Lizotte, A. J., Krohn, M. J., Farnworth, M., & Joon Jang, S. (1991). Testing interactional theory: An examination of reciprocal causal relationships among family, school and delinquency. *Journal of Criminal Law and Criminology, 82,* 3–35.

Trasler, G. B. (1962). *The explanation of criminality.* London: Routledge & Kegan Paul.

Van Kammen, W. B., Loeber, R., & Stouthamer-Loeber, M. (1991). Substance use and its relationship to conduct problems and delinquency in young boys. *Journal of Youth and Adolescence, 20,* 399–413.

West, D. J. (1969). *Present conduct and future delinquency.* London: Heinemann.

West, D. J. (1982). *Delinquency: Its roots, careers, and prospects.* London: Heinemann.

West, D. J., & Farrington, D. P. (1973). *Who becomes delinquent?* London: Heinemann.

West, D. J., & Farrington, D. P. (1977). *The delinquent way of life.* London: Heinemann.

Widom, C. S. (1989). The cycle of violence. *Science, 244,* 160–166.

Wikström, P. H. (1987). *Patterns of crime in a birth cohort.* Stockholm: University of Stockholm Department of Sociology.

Wilson, J. Q., & Herrnstein, R. J. (1985). *Crime and human nature.* New York: Simon & Schuster.

Chapter 14

The Maine and Vermont
Three-Decade Studies of
Serious Mental Illness:
Longitudinal Course Comparisons

Michael DeSisto
Outcomes, Inc., Farmingdale, ME

Courtenay M. Harding
University of Colorado School of Medicine

Rodney V. McCormick
Rod McCormick Research, Essex Junction, VT

Takamaru Ashikaga
College of Medicine, University of Vermont

George W. Brooks
College of Medicine, University of Vermont

Recent long-term studies have questioned the idea that schizophrenia becomes progressively worse over the long term (Harding, 1986; Harding, Zubin, & Strauss, 1987). Instead, outcome can vary along a continuum between complete recovery and total incapacity. Three studies, the Vermont Longitudinal Project (Harding, Brooks, Ashikaga, Strauss, & Breier, 1987) the Lausanne Investigations (Ciompi & Müller, 1976), and the Burghölzli Hospital Study (Bleuler, 1978) used hospitalization patterns to document individual course trajectories over many decades. Harding (1988) found both similarities and disparities among these studies in the percentage of subjects with various course types. However, all three groups displayed heterogeneity of course trajectories. The trajectories for Vermont subjects revealed a variety of individual course patterns (Harding, McCormick, Strauss, Ashikaga, & Brooks, 1989). The authors concluded that severe psychiatric disorder is not a unitary, linear process, but one that ebbs and flows at different rates across different areas of functioning.

This chapter compares the course trajectories of the Vermont cohort with a matched group from Maine. Vermont subjects participated in a pioneering rehabilitation program whereas Maine subjects received more traditional care. The characteristics of the Vermont program, the samples, methodology, and cross-sectional outcome comparisons were already presented (DeSisto, Harding, McCormick, Ashikaga, & Brooks, 1995a; Harding, Brooks, Ashikaga, Strauss, & Breier, 1987). Subject matching on age, gender, diagnosis, and length of hospitalization was used to control for possible subject and treatment era differences.[1] Rural Maine was selected using census and health department data to control for important social and cultural factors. The group in Maine was studied with the same protocols as used in Vermont. Reliability testing between states was also conducted. The evolution of developments in the systems of care in each state were documented (DeSisto, Harding, Howard, & Brooks, 1991) to account for policy and program events extraneous to the rehabilitation program. These events were then overlaid with the longitudinal course data for both groups to study the interplay between the natural history of individuals and the systems of care.

Social, Demographic, and Policy–Program Contexts

Maine and Vermont are poor, rural states. Vermont contains only one metropolitan area with 22% of its population (562,000) and more than 200 small towns. Maine, in contrast, has four metropolitan areas that contain 33% of its population (1.2 million). However, both states have similar distributions of age, gender, household size, per capita and household incomes, and low numbers of racial minorities (State Demographics, 1984; United States Bureau of the Census, 1950, 1960, 1972, 1982).

Mental Health Policy

Table 14.1 summarizes the major policy and program developments in Maine and Vermont between 1945 and 1980 (DeSisto, Harding, Howard, & Brooks, 1991; Chittick, Brooks, Irons, & Deane, 1961) and indicates that both state systems were influenced by national policy developments and cycles of reform in mental health care.

---

[1]Details of the methodology may be found in DeSisto, Harding, McCormick, et al. (1995a). Maine and Vermont subjects were first matched on *DSM–II* hospital diagnosis. *DSM–III* rediagnosis was performed by blinded psychiatrists using index hospitalization records from which all references to diagnosis were deleted. Kappa reliability for classification of cases as schizophrenia, schizoaffective disorder, affective disorder, or other for 40 randomly selected cases was 0.69 for Maine and 0.65 for Vermont. Kappa levels for classification of cases as schizophrenia or not schizophrenia were 0.69 for Maine and 0.78 for Vermont.

TABLE 14.1
Maine and Vermont Policy and Program Comparisons

Year	Maine	Vermont
1945		Vermont VR[a] appoints full-time counselor to serve mentally disabled persons.
1947	Work placement program finds jobs and housing for patients; 47 Maine subjects participate; 10 are also VR clients; 19 are alive at follow-up.	
1948	Night hospital program: Patients work at real community jobs during the day; 30 Maine subjects participate; 3 are also VR clients; 14 are alive at follow-up.	
1949–1951	Hospital social workers conduct community visits and community adjustment groups.	
1954		Phenothiazines introduced.
1955	Phenothiazines introduced.	
1956	Hospital social workers start patient support groups.	VR establishes first rehab house; jobs, work, and community adjustment for residents.
1957	U.S. Office of VR funds program to station one VR counselor at hospital; 30 Maine subjects are VR clients while in the hospital; 15 are alive at follow-up.	U.S. Office of VR funds Vermont Story Project; goals are self-sufficiency through rehabilitation and depopulation of the hospital; four rehab wards established; two VR counselors work at the hospital; VR counselors provide community case management; all 269 Vermont subjects are VR clients; 180 are alive at follow-up.
1958	Rehab ward established in the hospital.	Two more rehab houses established; 162 Vermont subjects are served by rehab houses.
1961	Hospital accepts voluntary admissions.	• *Vermont Story* published. • Vermont Dept. of Social Welfare places three workers at hospital to coordinate benefits and placement.
1962	"Operation Out" to depopulate elderly patients to boarding and nursing homes.	
1964		Nine psychiatric clinics organized as community mental health centers (CMHCs[b]).
1965	• Five CMHCs organized. • Title XIX (Medicaid) is available • Placement of elderly patients stopped due to problem with coordination of entitlements.	• 10-year follow-up of Vermont subjects conducted. • Title XIX (Medicaid) is available. • Vermont's second rehab/depopulation effort begins with Hospital Improvement (HIP) Grant for Educational Therapy.
1968		• Hospital accepts voluntary admissions. • Regionalization policy initiated. • Hospital organized by geographic units.
1970	CMHCs[a] provide screening and aftercare.	CMHCs vs. VR[b] now provide screening and aftercare.

TABLE 14.1
(Continued)

Year	Maine	Vermont
1971	• Maine's first depopulation and regionalization effort begins. • Hospital organized by geographic units.	• Vermont's third major depopulation begins; increased placements to boarding homes. • HIP Grant establishes program (IMPAC) to enhance life for boarding home residents with work and social opportunities.
1972	• First community halfway house opens. • Peak year of hospital depopulation.	HIP Grant for patient activity program.
1973	New involuntary commitment law includes dangerousness and enhances due process.	Civil suit establishes district court due process; involuntary commitment law rewritten.
1974	Supplemental Security Income (SSI) now available.	Supplemental Security Income (SSI) now available.
1975	Depopulation and regionalization derailed with new administration.	• Medicaid covers full range of community mental health services. • Continued depopulation; long-term patients discharged; two wards closed; $400,000 shifted to community programs.
1978	Hospital reorganized back to functional vs. geographic units.	Continued depopulation; geographic units reduced to two; plan to discharge another 185 patients over 2 years.
1979	Medicaid covers case management and outreach services.	$200,000 transferred to community programs.
1980	Community Support Program (CSP) enhances development of new residential programs.	Community Support Program (CSP) enhances development of new residential programs.

[a]CMHC = Community Mental Health Center. [b]VR = Vocational Rehabilitation.

Following World War II, psychosocial and work programs, and new pharmacological agents were introduced. In the 1960s, both states created centralized mental health agencies that were aggressive in the development of a statewide system of community mental health centers. In the 1970s, both states depopulated their mental hospitals and regionalized their systems of care.

Depopulation of institutions in Vermont began 16 years earlier than in Maine with the implementation of a model rehabilitation program in 1955. A second depopulation effort occurred in 1965 with a new Hospital Improvement Program (HIP) Educational Therapy Program in which hospital staff provided regional coordination. Regionalization was implemented in 1968. An acceleration in depopulation occurred in 1971 as more patients were placed in boarding homes, and again in the mid- and late 1970s as hospital patients were identified for placement (DeSisto, Harding, Howard, & Brooks, 1991).

Vocational Rehabilitation

Vermont's Rehabilitation Program was initiated in 1955, before the development of community centers and major entitlement programs. The program had a clear vision to reduce the number of patients in the hospital by training them to be self-sufficient and helping them with a job and a place to live. The program began in the hospital and had a marked impact on the social structure there, but the eventual focus would be the community. Vocational rehabilitation (VR) funds were used to build the elements of the community system.

Maine made some rehabilitation efforts in the late 1940s with night hospital, work placement, and outpatient clubs. These programs served significant numbers of patients, but were not as comprehensive as the Vermont program and did not result in significant changes in the social organization of the hospital. In 1957, the Maine VR agency initiated a modest program. One vocational counselor was stationed at the hospital 1 day per week to receive referrals for vocational assessment and other traditional services. Once federal support for this demonstration eroded, the program was all but terminated. By 1964, only two hospital patients were referred to VR (DeSisto, Harding, Howard, & Brooks, 1991).

Residential Programs

In Vermont, the rehabilitation program used halfway houses to help patients with the transition to community life. The first halfway house, financed by VR as adjustment training, was opened in 1956. VR counselors assessed capacity, provided training, and helped residents find work. Vermont hospital employees served as houseparents. Two more houses were established by 1958. A community-based residential program was not available in Maine until 1972 (DeSisto, Harding, Howard, & Brooks, 1991).

Entitlements

Throughout the period, both states used entitlement programs to place patients in boarding and nursing homes. In 1961, the Vermont state welfare agency actually placed two workers in the hospital to coordinate eligibility and placement. This resulted in a continuous use of boarding homes throughout the 1960s. Boarding home placements were accelerated in 1971 with a new push to depopulate the hospital. As the number of placements to boarding homes increased, so did the concern about the quality of life for persons residing in them. The Vermont hospital addressed this concern by establishing a program called Improvement in Alternate Care (IMPAC). This program trained boarding home operators in understanding mental illness and involved the residents in volunteer work and other community activities. In Maine, in 1965, the state welfare agency excluded persons with mental illness from eligibility. In 1971, with Maine's effort to depopulate its hospital, the boarding home was the major residential alternative (DeSisto, Harding, Howard, & Brooks, 1991).

In summary, between 1945 and 1980, both states introduced modern drug and psychosocial treatments, established mental health centers, and pursued a policy of depopulation and regionalization that reduced the populations of the hospitals. Yet there were also major differences in the systems. Vermont's model rehabilitation program was comprehensive and incorporated all known aspects of psychiatric treatment. Maine's rehabilitation efforts were not comprehensive, and there was no involvement by vocational rehabilitation in community case management, placement, and job finding. Community halfway houses were available 16 years earlier in Vermont than in Maine. Overall, the information suggests that there was more continuity and consistency of the policy of depopulation and regionalization in Vermont compared to Maine.

METHODS AND PROCEDURES

A modified version of the Meyer–Leighton Life Chart (Leighton & Leighton, 1949; Meyer, 1951) was used to retrospectively document the yearly course of several life domains. The entire instrument battery was described previously (Harding, Brooks, et al., 1987). The Life Chart documented cohort statuses over a 32-year period in Vermont and a 36-year period in Maine. Outcome domains included: work, source of income, residence, hospitalizations, medication, and community resources used. Life event domains included: presence of significant others, deaths, health, relationships, any legal entanglements, finances, and changes in family structure.

The trained clinician interviewer and the subject worked together over a 75- to 90-minute period to complete the Life Chart and other elements of the longitudinal questionnaire. A specific set of probes was asked for each year beginning with the most recent year and working back to earlier years. All data were verified by informants who knew the subject well. For deceased subjects, the Life Chart was completed with family members and significant others. Most subjects and families gave good accounts of their histories, a phenomenon noted earlier by others (Bleuler, 1978; Harding, 1986).

Interrater reliability trials resulted in an overall agreement (kappa) between Maine clinicians of .75 ($N = 48$ cases), between Vermont clinicians of .79 ($N = 36$ cases), and .65 ($N = 20$) between Maine and Vermont clinicians.

Data reduction of the Life Chart was conducted as follows:

Residence—Residence categories included hospital; independent living in a house, apartment, or rooming house; rehabilitation or halfway house; and boarding or nursing home. Residence was defined as the percentage of any year that a person resided in a category. For example, if in a particular year a subject spent 4 months in the hospital and 8 months living independently, both statuses would be recorded for that year, 33% for "hospital" and 67% for "independent living."

Work—The work domain had three categories: full time (30 hours of more with pay); part time or unpaid (combining housewife, volunteer part time, and volunteer full time); and unemployed. For a particular year, a subject was classified into one of these categories if it represented their status for more than 6 months.

Community Resources—Scores reflected receipt of services from any of these sources: community mental health center, vocational rehabilitation, private practitioner.

The status of the Maine and Vermont groups for each outcome domain was compared by determining the percentage of subjects that were in a particular status for each year from 1960 to 1980. These percentages were then plotted in a 21-year time series from 1960 to 1980. A Bonferroni adjusted chi-square comparison of proportions using an alpha of 0.0024 was performed to achieve a nominal 0.05 alpha overall for the 21-year period.

RESULTS

Due to mortality, the total number of Life Charts available from 1960 to 1980 for Maine and Vermont ranged from 224 to 143, and 243 to 173, respectively.

Figures 14.1 through 14.4 show the percentage of Maine and Vermont subjects for each year from 1960 to 1980 for the residence, work, primary income source, and community resources used.[2] Table 14.2 summarizes the temporal comparisons by domain.

---

[2]Note that for "Residence" (Fig. 14.1), data represent the average percentage of any year that the cohort was in a particular residential status, not the percentage of cases.

Percentages in Figs. 14.1 through 14.4 do not add to 100% because: (a) cases were not classified as unemployed if their primary residence was the hospital (Fig. 14.2), (b) income source was not classified as "Government" if a case's primary residence was the hospital (Fig. 14.3), (c) a case had to be residing in the community to be using community resources (Fig. 14.4). Therefore, many of the status changes for the cohorts across the various outcome domains parallel the changes in residential status. Missing data (not missing cases) for the Life Charts varied from 4% to 14% for any year across the 21-year period. These missing data do not impact the major conclusions.

Maine

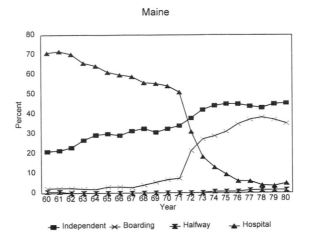

Vermont

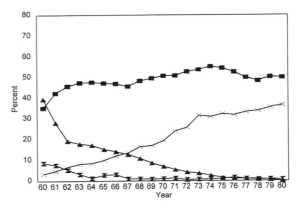

FIG. 14.1. Average % year in residence.

Residence

Maine subjects spent significantly more time in the hospital from 1960 through 1975 (50% vs. 13%) compared to Vermont subjects. The Vermont residential experience consisted of more independent living between 1960 and 1971, more residence in halfway houses between 1960 and 1963, and more use of boarding homes from 1963 to 1971.

Work and Income Source

A significantly greater percentage of Vermont subjects were employed full time between 1960 and 1975 (30.9% vs. 12.7%), and part-time or performing unpaid work in 1960 (7.9% vs. 1.8%). More Maine subjects were un-

Maine

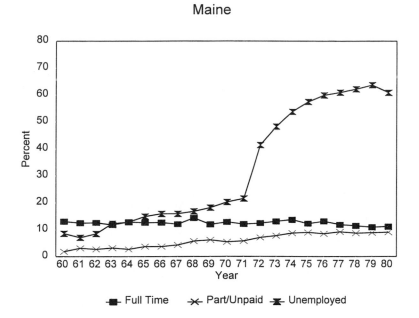

Vermont

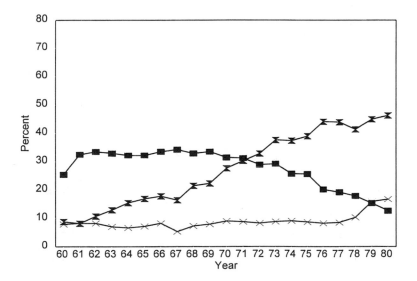

FIG. 14.2.   Primary work status.

Maine

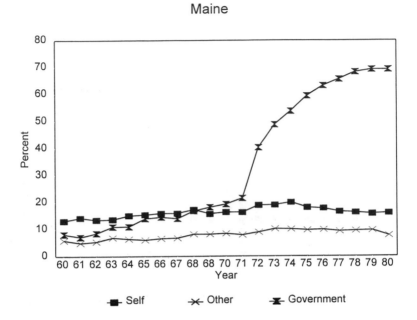

Vermont

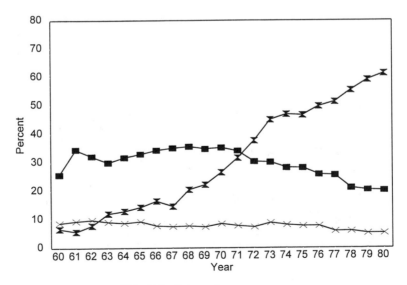

FIG. 14.3. Primary income source.

Maine

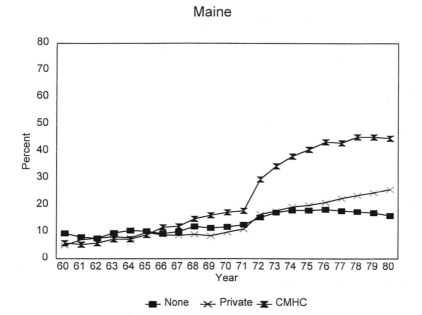

None ■ Private ✕ CMHC ◆

Vermont

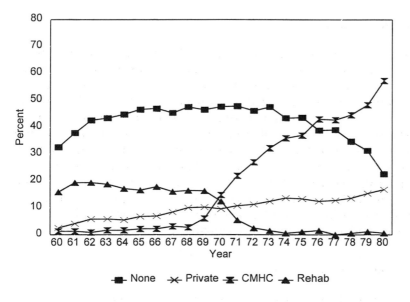

None ■ Private ✕ CMHC ◆ Rehab ▲

FIG. 14.4. Community resources used.

TABLE 14.2
Life Chart Course Comparisons Summary

Domain	Years[a]	Maine Percent[b]	Vermont Percent[b]
Residence:			
Hospital	60–75	50.0	13.0
Independent	60–71	25.6	46.4
Halfway house	60–63	0.3	6.2
Boarding home	63–71	3.9	14.4
Work:			
Full time	60–75	12.7	30.9
Part time	60	1.8	7.9
Unemployed	74,75,77–79	60.2	41.3
Community Resources Used:			
None	60–78	12.9	43.3
VR[c]	60–70	0.0	16.9
CMHC[d]	62,64–69	11.0	2.7

[a]Years for which significant differences between Maine and Vermont were observed. [b]Average percentage for years where significant differences were observed. [c]VR = Vocational Rehabilitation. [d]CMHC = Community Mental Health Center.

employed from 1974 to 1975, and 1977 through 1979 (60.2% vs. 41.3%). Naturally, the proportion of indivduals described as unemployed would tend to increase over time as individuals age.

Community Resources

Throughout most of the period (1960 to 1978; see Fig. 14.4), a significantly higher percentage of Vermont subjects were not making use of community programs at the same level as Maine subjects (43.3% vs. 12.9%). However, more Vermonters were enrolled in VR between 1960 and 1970 (16.9% vs. 0.0%). This can be contrasted with the higher percentage of Mainers enrolled in community mental health center programs in 1962 and between 1964 and 1969 (11.0% vs. 2.7%). Figure 14.4 shows that up until 1969, the major program for Vermonters was VR. However, the move to regionalize mental health services in 1968 made community mental health centers the primary referral and aftercare resource for Vermont patients. There was a gradual increase in the use of private resources by subjects in both states as private practitioners became more available in the service market.

DISCUSSION AND COMMENT

The illustrated longitudinal course comparisons demonstrate clearly that the Vermont program had a significant impact on the course for Vermont subjects compared to that of Maine subjects. Perhaps the most important aspect of the program was that it gave Vermont patients an earlier opportunity to adapt to life in the community. This opportunity, when combined with an array of residential, work, and social opportunities, resulted in a more diverse and favorable course compared to the Maine group across the domains studied.

Early differences in residential status can be attributed directly to the policy and program differences between the states. The Vermont program had both a rehabilitation goal and a depopulation goal. Not all Vermont subjects were prepared for independent living. Some needed the structure provided by a transitional facility or a boarding home. Therefore, these facilities were developed early in Vermont. The rehab houses served 162 Vermont subjects. Most of this number were served between 1955 and 1962. Length of stay was brief, and always less than 2 years. Facilitated by early cooperation between the mental health and human service agencies to coordinate entitlements and placement efforts by the VR counselors–case managers, boarding home development and placements in Vermont were early and continuous throughout the period. Funds for the program were modest. Therefore, clinicians' community integration efforts were directed toward finding natural supports and niches for people among churches and community organizations.

For Maine subjects, with depopulation in 1971, there was an abrupt decline in the percentage of time in hospital and an increase in the percentage of time in boarding homes and independent living (see Fig. 14.1). A community halfway house option was not available in Maine until 1972. Comparisons (Table 14.2) show that once Maine subjects were given the opportunity to live independently, significant differences in independent living disappeared.

Vermont policy regarding use of community resources shifted toward regionalization and resulted in an increase in the use of mental health centers by the cohort in the mid-1960s, a decline in VR involvement (see Fig. 14.4), and an increase in the release of lower functioning patients. Interestingly, there was not a corresponding decline in the percentage of the Vermont group that was not using community resources. Instead there is an increase, as more Vermonters were added to the rolls of those who had improved or recovered.

For Vermonters, policy of regionalization can be viewed as a paradigm shift for the system that served them, from a rehabilitation program that emphasized work and self-sufficiency to a treatment program that emphasized cure of illness through treatment by mental health centers (Kuhn, 1962). It could have been that the goals of work and self-sufficiency had already been achieved for all the subjects who were able. Perhaps a treatment emphasis was more appropriate for those remaining. Unfortunately, however, after this shift, the relationship between VR and mental health in vocational services would be less available to mentally disabled persons (DeSisto, Harding, Howard, & Brooks, 1991). With regionalization and more reliance on mental health centers and government entitlements for income, some of the continuity and comprehensiveness of the original Vermont rehabilitation program was lost.

In Maine, although 30 subjects were VR clients during index hospitalization, VR services were not provided after discharge. Instead, it was hospital social workers and then mental health centers which provided follow-up care in the community.

Over the entire 20-year period, the percentage of Vermonters engaged in some form of employment, either full-time or part-time paid work or volunteer work, ranged between 35% and 60%. Taking full-time work alone, the range was 25% to 35%. For Mainers, the range for some kind of employment was 12% to 30%, and for full-time work, 10% to 20%.

Employment base rates from short-term cross-sectional studies have ranged from 30% to 50% for any employment to 20% to 30% for full-time employment 1 year after discharge (Anthony, Buell, Sharratt, & Althoff, 1972). The longitudinal base rates obtained in this study suggest that the Vermonters fared better and that Mainers fared worse than patients in other studies. However, patients in other studies have typically been less chronic. This makes the employment outcome for Vermonters more remarkable. Although many Vermonters were involved successfully in some kind of industrial or work therapy prior to referral to the rehabilitation program, most literature does not support the idea that this form of work therapy has any impact on base rates for community work (Kunce, 1970). Instead, it may foster institutional dependency (Barbee, Berry, & Micek, 1969). Eighty-two percent of the 269 Maine subjects ($N = 228$) were also involved in hospital industrial work programs during index hospitalization. Thus participation in hospital work alone cannot account for these differences.

The Vermont rehabilitation program was a comprehensive and eclectic program that integrated the knowledge from social psychiatry, including principles of milieu therapy, therapeutic community, and interpersonal psychiatry, with the use of medicine and vocational rehabilitation (Chittick, Brooks, Irons, & Deane, 1961). The program created a comprehensive system of care prior to the two major mental health reform movements over the past 20 years: community mental health centers and community support (DeSisto, Harding, Howard, & Brooks, 1991; Morrissey & Goldman, 1984). These reforms increased the complexity of mental health systems and made service planning and continuity of care more difficult (Bachrach, 1986). In addition, the Vermont program relied on a collaboration with VR that is rare in most systems.

The Vermont legacy is not to be found, as Bachrach (1989) suggested, in the details of the program or the methods used, all of which were exemplary. Instead, its legacy is the values and principles which guided it. Students of model programs will find these values and principles very familiar. Perhaps the most important value was that the program had a pervasive attitude of hope and optimism about human potential, through the vision that, if given the opportunity, persons with mental illness could become self-sufficient. Anecdotal literature and personal accounts, in both the medical and psychiatric fields, directly support the notion that hope is an important factor in recovery (Cousins, 1979; Deane & Brooks, 1963; Lovejoy, 1984). With this hope and optimism, however, there were realistic expectations that not everyone would proceed at the same pace. There could be disappointments from which to learn and try again. There was the assumption that people are rare and unique, and the dignity and integrity of the person must be respected. This respect for the person was honored by asking sufferers about what they wanted, how things were going, whether the program was meeting their needs, and by involving them in program planning. Thus, collaboration was the hallmark of the program. There was a realization that the program was working with individual lives, not illnesses. Therefore, necessary services must be comprehensive and deal with all aspects of a life. They also had to be flexible because needs and situations changed over time. There was the recognition that long-term continuity and commitment across service settings was needed. Finally, there was a concern with outcome: what happened to people over the long-term and recognition of the need to keep in touch in order to find out.

Another notable characteristic of the Vermont program was its leadership. Leaders of the program were able to create a clear vision of economic self-sufficiency. They used the values outlined above to make both helpers and sufferers feel significant and to feel part of a community of learning that was special and exciting. The vision of self-sufficiency was an agenda that focused the attention of all participants as it was communicated in all the social activities of the program culture. The result was a transformation of the participants and the creation of a new culture. New values and beliefs were eventually taken for granted. Leaders who create visions which transform both the followers and the culture have been called *transformational leaders* (Bennis & Nanus, 1985; Burns, 1978). They make things happen by empowering others rather than by some kind of transaction of praise or reward. A testimonial to the quality of leadership was the adaptability and evolution of the Vermont program to changes brought on by the community mental health movement (DeSisto, Harding, Howard, & Brooks, 1991).

Both the Maine and Vermont cohorts became ill during a period when law and society allowed long periods of hospitalization. They were hospitalized prior to the availability of modern pharmacological treatment and changes in family structure and demography that occurred over the past 30 years.

Both the Individual Life Charts and cumulative course data of this study once again confirm the heterogeneity of long-term course in serious mental illness. In addition, the accumulated domain-specific courses in this report have demonstrated that the natural history of individuals and policy and program events affect the course of specific outcome domains.

ACKNOWLEDGMENTS

This work was supported by NIMH RO1-40032 to DeSisto and Harding, NIMH RO1–29575 and RO1–4067 to Harding and a Robert Wood Johnson Foundation Grant #190300 to Harding and DeSisto. The work was also supported by the State of Maine, Department of Mental Health and Mental Retardation, Robert Glover, Ph.D., Commissioner, and Medical Care Development, Inc., John A. LaCasse, Eng.Sc.D., President. Portions were read before the annual meeting of the American Psychiatric Association, New York, May 1990.

The authors would like to thank all those who contributed to various aspects of this work: Priscilla Ridgway, M.A., for her work on the matching subjects protocol and original application; Margaret Fuller, M.S.W., and Millard Howard, M.A., for abstracting Maine records and documenting Maine history; Alan McKelvy, M.S.W., and Christopher Salamone, M.S.W., for conducting the field interviews; Paul Landerl, M.S.W., from the Vermont team who trained Maine field workers; Janet Wakefield, Ph.D., from the Vermont team trained Maine record abstractors; Carmine Consalvo, Ph.D., from the Vermont team provided consultation to Maine interviewers; Alan Gelenberg, M.D., trained Maine field workers to assess abnormal movements. Further, Owen Buck, M.D., and Victor Pentlarge, M.D., conducted DSM–III rediagnosis of the Maine cohort; Walter Rohm, M.D., and the late William Schumacher, M.D., and Roy Ettlinger, M.H.A., provided Maine policy and program historical information; Dorothy Myer of the University of Vermont Department of Medical Biostatistics who supervised the data entry and coding; Walter Lowell, Ed.D., provided Maine Hospital data; John Pandiani, Ph.D., who provided Vermont Hospital data; John Pierce and Rodney Copeland, Ph.D., who provided Vermont policy information; Vasilio Bellini in Vermont and Ann DeWitt in Maine who provided social security historical data; Lois Frost located Maine records; Kevin Concannon, M.S.W., supported the initiation of the project; Robert Glover, Ph.D., and John LaCasse, Eng.Sc.D., supported its completion; Linda Clark who managed the project office and typed early drafts, and Eunice Reneyske, Micheline Morin Huggett, and Ellen Rector who typed the manuscript revisions; and finally, all the Maine and Vermont people who shared their lives with us.

REFERENCES

Anthony, W. A., Buell, G. J., Sharratt, S., & Althoff, M. E. (1972). Efficacy of psychiatric rehabilitation. *Psychological Bulletin, 78*(6), 447–456.

Bachrach, L. L. (1986). The challenge of service planning for chronic mental patients. *Community Mental Health Journal, 22,* 170–174.

Bachrach, L. L. (1989). The legacy of model programs. *Hospital and Community Psychiatry, 40*(3), 234–235.

Barbee, M. S., Berry, K. L., & Micek, L. A. (1969). Relationship of work therapy to psychiatric length of stay and readmission. *Journal of Consulting and Clinical Psychology, 33,* 735–738.

Bennis, W., & Nanus, B. (1985). *Leaders.* New York: Harper & Row.

Bleuler, M. (1978). *The schizophrenic disorders: Long-term patient and family studies* (S. M. Clemens, Trans.). New Haven: Yale University Press.

Burns, J. M. (1978). *Leadership.* New York: Harper & Row.

Chittick, R. A., Brooks, G. W., Irons, F. S., & Deane, W. N. (1961). *The Vermont story.* Waterbury, VT: The Vermont State Hospital.

Ciompi, L., & Müller, C. (1976). *Lebensweg und Alter der Schizophrenen: Eine Katanmestische Langzeitstudie bis ins Senium.* Berlin: Springer-Verlag.

Cousins, N. (1979). *The anatomy of an illness as perceived by the patient.* New York: Norton.

Deane, W. N., & Brooks, G. W. (1963). Chronic schizophrenics' view recovery. *Journal of Existential Psychiatry, 4*(14), 121–130.

DeSisto, M. J., Harding, C. M., Howard, M. A., & Brooks, G. W. (1991). *Perspectives on rural mental health: A comparison of mental health system policy and program development in Maine and Vermont.* Augusta, ME: Kennebec Press.

DeSisto, M. J., Harding, C. M., McCormick, R. V., Ashikaga, T., & Brooks, G. W. (1995a). The Maine and Vermont three decade studies of serious mental illness: I. Matched comparison of cross-sectional outcome. *British Journal of Psychiatry, 167,* 331–338.

DeSisto, M. J., Harding, C. M., McCormick, R. V., Ashikaga, T., & Brooks, G. W. (1995b). The Maine and Vermont three-decade studies of serious mental illness: II. Longitudinal course comparisons. *British Journal of Psychiatry, 167,* 338–342.

Harding, C. M. (1986). Speculations on the measurement of recovery from severe psychiatric disorder and the human condition. *Psychiatric Journal of the University of Ottawa, 11*(4), 199–204.

Harding, C. M. (1988). Course types in schizophrenia: An analysis of European and American studies. *Schizophrenia Bulletin, 14*(4), 633–643.

Harding, C. M., Brooks, G. W., Ashikaga, T., Strauss, J. S., & Breier, A. (1987). The Vermont longitudinal study of persons with severe mental illness: I. Methodology, study sample and overall status 32 years later. *American Journal of Psychiatry, 144*(6), 718–726.

Harding, C. M., McCormick, R. V., Strauss, J. S., Ashikaga, T., & Brooks, G. W. (1987). The Vermont longitudinal study: II. Long-term outcome for subjects who retrospectively met DSM–III criteria for schizophrenia. *American Journal of Psychiatry, 144*(6), 727–735.

Harding, C. M., McCormick, R. V., Strauss, J. S., Ashikaga, T., & Brooks, G. W. (1989). Investigating mediative factors in the long-term course of DSM–III schizophrenia with computerized Life Chart methods. *British Journal of Psychiatry, 155,* 100–106.

Harding, C. M., Zubin, J., & Strauss, J. S. (1987). Chronicity in schizophrenia: Fact, partial fact, or artifact? *Hospital and Community Psychiatry, 38*(5), 477–486.

Kuhn, T. S. (1962). *The structure of scientific revolutions.* Chicago: University of Chicago Press.

Kunce, J. T. (1970). Is work therapy really therapeutic? *Rehabilitation Literature, 31,* 297–299.

Leighton, A. H., & Leighton, D. C. (1949). *Gregorio, the hand trembler: A psychobiological personality study of a Navaho indian.* Peabody Museum Papers. Cambridge: Harvard University Press.

Lovejoy, M. (1984). Recovery from schizophrenia: A personal odyssey. *Hospital and Community Psychiatry, 35*(8), 809–813.

Meyer, A. (1951). The Life Chart and the obligation of specifying positive data in psycho-pathological diagnosis. In E. E. Winters (Ed.), *The collected papers of Adolf Meyer* (pp. 52–56). Baltimore, MD: The Johns Hopkins University Press.

Morrissey, J. P., & Goldman, H. H. (1984). Cycles of reform in care of the chronically mentally ill. *Hospital and Commmunity Psychiatry, 35*(8), 785–793.

State demographics: Population profile of the 50 states. (1984). Homewood, IL: Dow Jones-Irwin.

Strauss, J. S., & Carpenter, W. T. (1972). Prediction of outcome in schizophrenia: I. characteristics of outcome. *Archives of General Psychiatry, 27,* 739–746.

United States Bureau of the Census. (1950). *1950 United States census of population and housing.* Washington, DC: U.S. Department of Commerce, Bureau of Census.

United States Bureau of the Census. (1960). *1960 census of population. Detailed characteristics* (Maine and Vermont). Washington, DC: U.S. Department of Commerce, Bureau of Census.

United States Bureau of the Census. (1972). *1970 census of population. Detailed characteristics* (Maine and Vermont). Washington, DC: U.S. Department of Commerce, Bureau of Census.

United States Bureau of the Census. (1982). *1980 census of population. Chapter B. General population characteristics. Part 21 Maine; Part 47 Vermont.* Washington, DC: U.S. Department of Commerce, Bureau of Census.

Chapter 15

The Relation of Community and Family to Risk Among Urban-Poor Adolescents

Deborah Gorman-Smith
Patrick H. Tolan
David Henry
University of Illinois at Chicago

> *I don't even think about it anymore. I'll be walking through the neighborhood and see a group of about 30 boys walking toward me. They say "hey, how you doing?," I say "hey" back and the only thing I think is there's going to be some shooting, I better go make sure the kids are inside. Sad, isn't it?*

This is one young mother's description of walking from the corner grocery store to her home as she begins to offer her thoughts about raising young children while living in an inner-city community. This is the same community she lived in as a child, but the neighborhood has changed. There are fewer two-parent families, fewer adults are employed, fewer businesses are left in the community, and there has been a profound increase in the amount and seriousness of violence. She says she has become used to the violence, but the steps she has taken to ensure her family's safety and her desperation to move out of the neighborhood suggest otherwise. She does not fear that these young men will harm her or her children; they are friends of her children's father. However, she does want to keep her children away from these men. She does not want her son to end up in jail like his father. She does not want her children to grow up thinking it is "normal" to have shooting outside your house every night. She is not sure she will be able to protect them or keep them from becoming involved in criminal behavior. Others haven't. How can she be any better a parent in this community than others are?

In this chapter, we focus on how community context can influence risk and shape family impact on youth development. In particular, we focus on how characteristics of inner-city communities affect aspects of family functioning associated with risk for participation in delinquent and violent behavior. Despite extensive media attention on the effects of neighborhood violence and poverty, we have little empirical evidence from which to draw conclusions about how families negotiate and adapt to community influences or how these multiple levels of influence impact child behavioral and emotional development. The available evidence is often drawn from research that focuses on family functioning apart from context or on neighborhood analyses with limited consideration of family processes. As a result, information to guide public policy and inform community intervention and prevention is lacking. Decisions regarding public policy are often based on what is "believed" to be true rather than on empirical evidence. For example, the current demands for major reform of the welfare system are based on assumptions that the problems of poor urban communities are the consequence of inadequate social values, lack of work ethic, and the idea that receiving welfare is more attractive than working. However, there has been no research to conclusively demonstrate such contentions and existing empirical data do not support this view (Wilson, Aponte, Kirschenman, & Wacquant, 1988). The best evidence suggests a different perspective: that there have been long-term changes in the economic and social resources available in the inner city and this has had profound effects on the social organization of urban communities with severe detrimental impact on children and families living within these communities (Wilson, 1987). A careful set of analyses to examine how the social and economic organization of inner-city and other urban communities influences families' ability to manage the daily demands that are part of raising a child is needed.

PREDICTORS OF DELINQUENT BEHAVIOR

Two strains of research have dominated the literature on delinquent and violent behavior. Community-level research has evaluated structural characteristics of the community such as poverty, residential mobility, and economic and ethnic heterogeneity to explain variations in behavior and crime in different communities (Brooks-Gunn, Duncan, Klebanov, & Sealand, 1993; Bursik & Grasmick, 1993; Coulton & Pandey, 1992; Crane, 1991; Sampson, 1985, 1987). For example, community-level variations in population and housing density, family disruption (i.e., percent single-parent households), and residential mobility have been positively related to crime (Bursik, 1988; Byrne & Sampson, 1986). The focus of this research was differences in rates of crime or behavior in different communities, rather than understanding individual involvement in crime.

In contrast, a second strain of research has focused on individual differences in participation in delinquent and violent behavior. This research evaluated differences between delinquent and nondelinquent youth. A consistent finding in this literature is the importance of family influence on development (Gorman-Smith, Tolan, Zelli, & Huesmann, 1996; Loeber & Stouthamer-Loeber, 1986; McCord, 1991; Tolan & Loeber, 1993). In their review of predictors of delinquent behavior, Loeber and Dishion (1983) identified parenting practices and quality of family relationships as distinct and powerful predictors of delinquent behavior. Numerous studies found lack of parental monitoring and poor discipline to relate to participation in delinquent and violent behavior (Gorman-Smith et al., 1996; Patterson, Reid, & Dishion, 1992). Regardless of ethnic and socioeconomic group, it is important for parents to be involved, monitor their child's whereabouts, and use effective and consistent discipline. In addition to parenting practices, family relation characteristics such as cohesion or the emotional closeness experienced within the family, support, organization, and communication appear to be important indicators of risk for delinquent and violent behavior (Gorman-Smith et al., 1996; Henggeler, 1989; Tolan, 1988). Across various risk samples, low levels of parental warmth, acceptance and affection, low cohesion, and high conflict and hostility have been associated with delinquent behavior (Farrington, 1986; Henggeler, Melton, & Smith, 1992; Tolan & Lorion, 1988).

Although each of these areas of research provides important information about the relation of community characteristics to rates of crime and family influences on individual participation in delinquent behavior, there has been little integration of theories of these two levels of influence. Since Bronfenbrenner (1979) first articulated an ecological framework for understanding development, it has been recognized that a full contextual approach to understanding behavior would require analysis of multiple levels of contextual influence. However, the practical difficulties of such analyses and the need to develop adequate datasets has limited the number of studies that can evaluate multiple level influences. Most community-level research does not include individual level variables and research about individuals rarely includes measures of community (Sampson, 1991). If we are to understand the complexity of human development, we have to begin to integrate information from multiple contextual influences.

Nowhere does this need for a fuller evaluation seem more evident than in urban communities. Recent evidence suggests that inner-city communities may provide a qualitatively different environment in which children and families function (Brooks-Gunn et al., 1993; Crane, 1991; Mayer & Jencks, 1989). In this chapter, we present data from a longitudinal study of adolescent males and their families from Chicago to begin to bridge this gap in the literature by evaluating the interplay between community type, stress, and family functioning in predicting delinquent behavior.

THE FOCUS ON INNER-CITY AND URBAN-POOR
FAMILIES

This research focuses on families living in economically disadvantaged neighborhoods within the inner-city and urban-poor communities because it has become clear that children in these environments are at increased risk for most social and psychological problems (Children's Defense Fund, 1991). Although all children in these communities are at risk (Leadbeater & Bishop, 1994; Seidman, Allen, Aber, Mitchell, & Feinman, 1994), males have particularly elevated risk for academic, vocational, mental health, and social problems (Tolan, Henry, Guerra, Huesmann, VanAcker, & Eron, 1998). Characteristics of these communities linked to increased risk for depression, anxiety disorders, aggression, and delinquency include exposure to high rates of community violence (Bell & Jenkins, 1993; Gorman-Smith & Tolan, 1998; Reiss, 1993; Richters & Martinez, 1993), absence of economic and social resources (Sampson & Groves, 1989; Sampson & Laub, 1994; McLoyd, 1990), family disruption (e.g., percent female-headed households), economic heterogeneity (Brooks-Gunn et al., 1993), and lack of neighborhood support and involvement (Sampson & Groves, 1989; Simcha-Fagan & Schwartz, 1986). Although there is some evidence of bivariate effects for each of these characteristics, there has been little evaluation of how multiple characteristics of neighborhood and community affect risk and development. There also has been little investigation of how impact varies within inner-city and other urban-poor communities.

The distinctions between "ghetto" inner-city neighborhoods and otherwise poor urban communities have been clearly described (Crane, 1991; Wilson, 1987). *Inner-city neighborhoods* are characterized by high concentrations of families living in poverty, higher crime rates, less owner-occupied housing, and more public housing. They also have a higher proportion of single-headed households. *Urban-poor neighborhoods* are distinguished from inner-city neighborhoods by a population with a greater range of incomes and greater access to resources. Although less destitute overall than the inner-city communities, the urban-poor neighborhoods also have elevated rates of poverty, single-headed households, and they face significant economic and social impediments. Although both types of neighborhoods may carry some risk, it is likely that residence in inner-city neighborhoods may have more pronounced effects on children and families (Garbarino, Dubrow, Kostelny, & Pardo, 1992; Garbarino & Sherman, 1980; Rutter & Giller, 1983; Wilson, 1987), and it is likely that risk occurs for children living in inner-city neighborhoods irrespective of family functioning (Brooks-Gunn et al., 1993; Crane, 1991). For example, Tolan and colleagues (1997), using Wilson's criteria for inner city of 40% or more households below the poverty level, found that rates for all types of psychopathology among children living in inner-city neighborhoods were elevated above national rates, but were not elevated in "other urban-poor" neighborhoods. For example, aggression and delinquency rates were 2.5 and 2.8 times greater than the national rate in the inner-city communities. Crane (1991) reported a sharp increase in risk of school dropout and teenage pregnancy for adolescents living in inner-city neighborhoods. These findings suggest a particularly risky developmental trajectory attributable to inner-city residence. Thus, the emerging literature suggests that community characteristics can have a nonlinear effect, and that there may be pronounced differences among economically disadvantaged urban neighborhoods. That is, there may be direct effects on child development for those residing in the inner city.

STRESS AND URBAN COMMUNITIES

In addition to the specific stressors associated with living in the inner city, poor families living in urban environments are at increased risk of experiencing other life stressors such as the loss of a friend or family member, significant health problems in the family, or separation or loss of a parent. Women of lower socioeconomic status (SES) are more likely to experience the illness or death of children, the absence of husbands, and major losses in childhood that may make coping with new losses even more difficult (Belle, 1984; McLoyd, 1990; Reese, 1982). Even when income is controlled, families headed by single mothers are more likely than two-parent families to experience stressful life events such as unemployment, changes in income, job, residence, and household composition (McLanahan, 1983; McLoyd, 1990; Weinraub & Wolf, 1983). The experience of high levels of stress is associated with greater risk of anxiety, depression, and other health problems. Psychological distress associated with high levels of stress can undermine the quality of parenting and family relations (McLoyd, 1990). In addition, the number and chronicity of stressors limits parents' ability to consistently monitor and discipline their children (Patterson et al., 1992).

Children living in economically disadvantaged communities are exposed to significantly more stressful life events than children living in other settings. In fact, children in these communities were found to experience the same number of stressful events in 1 year as other children experience over their entire lifetime (Attar, Guerra, & Tolan, 1994). In addition to exposure to a greater frequency of stressful events, children living in urban settings are exposed to unique types of stressors such as community violence (Attar et al., 1994; Bell & Jenkins, 1993; Gorman-Smith & Tolan, 1998; Richters & Martinez, 1993). Exposure to violence was linked to increased risk for depression, anxiety disorders, aggression, and delinquency (Gorman-Smith & Tolan, 1998; Richters & Martinez, 1993). The greater number and types of stressors, combined with characteristics of urban environments, provide a particularly challenging set of circumstances under which families must manage the daily needs of their children.

COMMUNITIES, STRESS, AND FAMILY FUNCTIONING

The chronic environmental stress associated with living in urban environments and the increased vulnerability to the experience of other stressful life events creates a particularly pernicious environment in which families function. Much of the previous research on family influence on delinquent behavior failed to consider the important influence of this context on family functioning (Garbarino & Associates, 1992; Sampson, in press; Tolan & Gorman-Smith, 1997). For families living in the inner city, parenting is likely constrained by factors within the environment associated with poverty, such as lack of social and institutional resources and increased community violence (Garbarino, 1992; Guerra, Huesmann, Tolan, VanAcker, & Eron, 1994; Sampson, in press). Parenting in this context may look different than it does in the context of a relatively safe, economically and resource-rich neighborhood where concerns about safety from community violence are not as prevalent. What is good and effective parenting in an inner-city neighborhood may not be the same as what constitutes good parenting elsewhere. Also, characteristics of some communities may overwhelm the impact of even the highest functioning families (Garbarino & Kostelny, 1992). Inadequate attention to context may lead to erroneous conclusions, particularly about families living in poor urban communities.

How do stressful life events influence family functioning and child behavior among families living in urban environments? Can families protect their children from the effect of characteristics associated with life in urban communities? How are these factors related to participation in delinquent behavior? Previous research suggests that experience of multiple stressors is likely to have a profound effect on family relationship characteristics and parenting practices (Belsky & Vondra, 1989; Conger, Ge, Elder, Lorenz, & Simons, 1994; Elder & Caspi, 1988; Elder, Eccles, Ardelt, & Lord, 1993; McLoyd, 1990; McLoyd, Jayaratne, Ceballo, & Borquez, 1994; Sampson, in press; Simcha-Fagan & Schwartz, 1986). The number and chronicity of stressors experienced constrain parents' ability to consistently supervise and discipline their children (McLoyd, 1990). Patterson and colleagues argued that stressful life experiences have their impact on children through change in discipline and child management practices (Patterson, DeBaryshe, & Ramsey, 1989). Sampson and Laub (1994) found that discipline, monitoring, and parent–child attachment accounted for about two thirds of the impact of family poverty and other family structural variables (i.e., mobility, family size, maternal employment) on delinquency. Poverty appeared to inhibit informal social control within the family (i.e., discipline and monitoring as measured by parent–child attachment, maternal supervision, erratic harsh discipline), thus contributing to the development of delinquent behavior.

What has not occurred to date is an evaluation of how stress impacts family functioning among urban-poor communities. Previous research suggests that rather than simply being additive, the effects of exposure to multiple types of stressors are likely to be multiplicative (Garmezy, 1987). Studies consistently found that exposure to one stressor is not sufficient to lead to maladjustment; rather a combination of stressors account for the development of serious emotional or behavioral problems (Rutter, 1983; Seifer & Sameroff, 1987). The effects of exposure to multiple stressors are likely to be exacerbated in inner-city communities. Attar, Guerra, and Tolan (1994) found that children living in the most disadvantaged communities were most adversely affected by stressful events. Although little is known about the effects of multiple types of stressors on families, there may similarly be greater effects in more disadvantaged communities.

We present data from a longitudinal study of inner-city minority youth that assesses the relation between residence location, stress experienced, family functioning, and delinquent behavior of youth. This study tests a model that builds on the previous epidemiologic analysis that found psychopathology to be much elevated in inner-city children but not in other poor urban children (Tolan et al., 1997). This previous research suggests that living in inner-city communities carries with it a risk for delinquency that families may be unable to overcome. Thus, we propose that different models will hold for different types of urban environments. For families living in poor urban, but not inner-city communities, family relationships and parenting practices can temper the influence of stress on youth participation in delinquent behavior. However, for families living in inner-city communities (those with 40% of the population below the poverty level), family characteristics will have little ability to ameliorate the impact of stress on youth behavior.

THE CHICAGO YOUTH DEVELOPMENT STUDY

We have been conducting a longitudinal study of the development of serious delinquent behavior among minority adolescent males living in the inner-city and other urban-poor communities. The Chicago Youth Development Study (CYDS) began in 1990 and applies a multilevel, multiwave assessment to evaluate interactions between individual, family, peer, community, and social factors affecting boys' involvement in antisocial behavior. The CYDS focuses on the population most at risk for the development of delinquent and violent behavior, minority male adolescents living in the inner city. It attempts careful measurement of individual, family, neighborhood, and community characteristics.

Boys were recruited for the study when they were in fifth and seventh grades from 17 public schools in the poorest half of Chicago communities. After initial screening of 92% of the population of fifth- and seventh-grade boys, families were selected for participation in the longitudinal study based on boys' obtained scores on the Aggression Scale of the Teacher Rating Form (TRF; Achenbach, 1991). Subjects were chosen so that 50% of the boys selected were at high risk for involvement in delinquent behavior based on teacher ratings indicating that the boys were already participating in high levels of aggressive behavior. The remaining subjects were randomly selected from the remaining sample. Interviews were completed for 362 boys (75% of target) and their caregiver(s) during the first wave of the study. There were no differences between those who participated and those who did not on aggression or official records of delinquent behavior.

The subjects were African American (59%) and Latino (41%) boys and their caregiver(s) from economically disadvantaged inner-city neighborhoods in Chicago; 62% lived in single-parent homes; 47.6% of the families had a total income below $10,000 per year; and 73.5% had incomes below $20,000 per year. The families in this study live in the poorest half of Chicago neighborhoods. About 40% of the sample live in inner-city or "underclass" neighborhoods and 60% live in otherwise urban-poor neighborhoods.

Measures

Delinquent Behavior. This variable was measured by youth self-report and included the frequency of involvement in 38 criminal acts (including drug and alcohol use) using the Self-Report of Delinquency developed for the National Youth Survey (Elliott, Dunford, & Huizinga, 1987). The information was used to create categories as developed by Elliott et al. (1987):

1. nonoffending, no delinquent behaviors reported;
2. exploratory offenders—three or fewer minor misdemeanors and no serious misdemeanor or felony offenses;
3. nonserious unpatterned offenders—more than three minor misdemeanors but no serious offenses;
4. serious unpatterned offenders—one to three serious misdemeanors or felonies; and

5. serious patterned offenders—more than three serious misdemeanors or felonies.

Neighborhood Residence. This was determined by 1990 Census information discriminated between those residing in inner-city communities with 40% or more of the population below poverty and those residing in other poor urban communities.

Marital Status. Mothers were asked to report whether they were currently married or living with someone in a marriage-like arrangement. Responses were coded as 1 (*yes*) or 2 (*no*). Sixty-two percent reported living in single-parent homes.

Family Income. Mothers were asked to report total family income in the following categories:

1. less than $5,000,
2. more than $5,000, less than $10,000,
3. more than $10,000, less than $20,000,
4. more than $20,000, less than $30,000,
5. more than $30,000, less than $50,000. Forty-eight percent of the families had a total income below $10,000 per year and 73.5% had incomes below $20,000 per year.

Stressful Events. These were measured using the CYDS Stress and Coping scale (Tolan & Gorman-Smith, 1991). Mothers and sons were asked to report frequency of occurrence during their lifetime and within the past year for 35 potentially stressful events, including:

1. economic problems (e.g., quit or lost a job, had serious financial problems, been on public aid),
2. health (e.g., someone in family became seriously ill, someone in family had a major emotional problem),
3. loss (e.g., someone in family died, lost a good friend),
4. violence (e.g., seen someone shot, victim of violent crime, member of family robbed or attacked, witnessed a violent crime) and
5. other (e.g., gotten into trouble at work or with the authorities, had to move to a new home, new baby in the family).

Total stress occurring within the last year was used in these analyses.

Family Relationship Characteristics. The development of this measure is described in detail in previous papers (Gorman-Smith et al., 1996; Tolan, Gorman-Smith, Huesmann, & Zelli, 1997). The family measure used during the first year of data collection contained 92 items pooled from existing family relations measures. The measures selected were originally chosen because they tapped family processes that have previously been identified as relating to risk for antisocial and delinquent behavior (Loeber & Dishion, 1983; Tolan & Loeber, 1993). The caregiver(s) and boys were administered the same items. Factor analysis of the combined mother and child scores yielded six theoretically meaningful factors:

1. Family Beliefs (includes two scales: (a) beliefs about the importance of family relationships and (b) beliefs about development);
2. Emotional Cohesion;
3. Support;
4. Communication;
5. Shared Deviant Beliefs; and
6. Organization.

Comparison of higher order factor models indicated the best fit was a 3 factor structure of Cohesion, Beliefs, and Structure [$\chi^2(4) = 3.92$, $p >$ .41, RMS = .002, GFI = .98]. Beliefs represent expectations about the importance of family, purpose of the family, and expectations about child development. Cohesion represents the extent of emotional closeness and dependability, support and clear communication among families. Structure represents organization and support, and not tolerating antisocial values. The scale and factor structure of this measure was crossvalidated with a second sample that had greater ethnic diversity (26% White), younger children (Grades 1–6), and girls (Tolan et al., 1997). The higher order factors were found to relate to aggression, depression, and delinquent behavior (Gorman-Smith et al., 1996; Tolan et al., in press). The latent constructs of Cohesion, Beliefs, and Structure were used in these analyses.

Parenting Practices. Parenting practices were measured using questions from the Pittsburgh Youth Study (Loeber, Farrington, Stouthamer-Loeber, & van Kammen, 1998) which factor into four scales: Positive Parenting; Discipline Effectiveness; Avoidance of Discipline; and Extent of Monitoring–Involvement in the child's life. *Positive Parenting* refers to the use of positive rewards and encouragement of appropriate behavior. *Discipline Effectiveness* is a measure of how effective parental discipline is in controlling the son's behavior. *Avoidance of Discipline* refers to the parent's avoidance of providing consequences or disciplining for fear of the son's behavior escalating. *Extent of Involvement* is a measure of involvement in daily activity and routines and knowledge of son's whereabouts. Report of *Discipline Effectiveness* and *Avoidance of Discipline* is gathered from mother only. Estimates of *Positive Parenting* and *Extent of Monitoring–Involvement* is gathered from both mother and child. Internal consistency reliabilities of each of the subscales ranged from .68 to .81. Previous research had identified two underlying constructs of Discipline and Monitoring as important in understanding risk for antisocial and delinquent behavior (Patterson, Reid, & Dishion, 1992). Thus, confirmatory factor analyses were consistent with others in identifying two latent constructs of Discipline and Monitoring (Gorman-Smith et al., 1996). For the present study, scale scores for mother and child reports were standardized and combined using weightings from the LISREL-VII analyses to create scores on these two constructs.

RESULTS

Relation of Community and Family to Delinquent Behavior

We were interested in evaluating the effects of community (i.e., where the family lives) on youth outcome. The prevailing view regarding the association between urban residence and risk is that one cannot discriminate deleterious effects of the community ecology unless one controls for the possibility that the effects are merely the aggregate of individual risk. That is, it may be that the community effects are due to individual family differences such as low income, single-parenthood, and poor family functioning. Therefore, we first ran hierarchical multiple regression analyses in which these potential alternative explanations (i.e., marital status and family income) were tested. In addition, to test for possible differences in impact level of predictors (i.e., family, stress) we also included interaction terms in the initial test. The bivariate associations among delinquency, stress, family factors, and community are presented in Table 15.1. With the exception of stress, all relationships with delinquency were rather modest.

In initial regression analysis for the entire sample the interaction term for stress by community contributed significantly to the prediction of delinquent behavior. None of the family and community interaction terms were significant. Notably, single-parenthood and family income were not significantly related to delinquent behavior. Thus, these results suggest specific effects of community residence that are not attributable to individual family differences. These findings suggested to us a difference in the way stress impacted behavior in each of the two community types. To

TABLE 15.1

Correlation of Community, Stress, Family, and Delinquency

	Community	Stress	Discipline	Monitor	Beliefs	Cohesion	Structure	Marital Status	Family Income	Delinquency Level
Community	1.00									
Stress	-.07	1.00								
Discipline	.01	-.13*	1.00							
Monitor	-.11*	-.01	.16**	1.00						
Beliefs	-.07	-.01	-.08	.11*	1.00					
Cohesion	-.04	-.17**	.15**	.30**	.36**	1.00				
Structure	-.01	-.26**	.13**	.17**	.16**	.53**	1.00			
Marital status	-.04	.13*	-.09	-.00	-.13*	-.18**	-.08	1.00		
Family income	-.04	-.12	-.06	-.00	.09	.06	.10	-.44**	1.00	
Delinquency level	-.10	.21**	-.14*	-.10	.12*	-.11*	-.12*	.09	-.03	1.00

*$p < .05$. **$p < .01$.

evaluate these potential differences, we completed analyses separately for families living in inner-city and other urban-poor communities.

Differences by Community Type

Table 15.2 presents the results of the regression analyses completed for families living in inner-city and in other urban-poor communities. Only stress was a significant independent contributor to the prediction of delinquent behavior for youth living in inner-city communities. Family relationship characteristics and parenting practices did not significantly contribute to the prediction of delinquent behavior.

Table 15.2 also presents the results of the analyses completed for families living in other urban-poor communities. Stress was entered at the first step and was significantly related to delinquency [$F(1, 162) = 4.64$, $p < .05$]. However, when parenting characteristics were entered into the equation, stress was no longer significant and discipline was the only significant contributor. When family relation characteristics were entered cohesion and beliefs about family were significant contributors to the prediction of delinquency. The effect of discipline is not as strong at this step but remains close to significant ($p < .07$). These findings are consistent with the possibility that, in contrast to inner-city communities, family characteristics in

TABLE 15.2

Hierarchical Multiple Regression Analyses for Inner-City and Urban-Poor Communities Stress, Family Factors, and Delinquent Behavior

Variable	Delinquent Behavior			
	B	se_B	Beta	t
Inner-city commmunities ($N = 105$)				
Stress	.15	.05	.30	3.11**
Monitoring	−.15	.12	−.13	−1.22
Discipline	.10	.23	.04	.44
Beliefs	.05	.20	.03	.23
Structure	.13	.26	.06	.48
Cohesion	−.05	.18	−.04	−.25
$R^2 = .10$ $F(6, 99) = 1.91$				
Other urban-poor communities ($N = 163$)				
Stress	.04	.04	.08	1.01
Monitoring	−.03	.07	−.04	−.48
Discipline	−.21	.13	−.13	−1.64
Beliefs	.38	.14	.22	2.65**
Structure	−.16	.15	−.10	−1.09
Cohesion	−.20	.09	−.22	−2.20*
$R^2 = .15$ $F(6,155) = 4.46$**				

*$p < .05$. **$p < .01$.

TABLE 15.3
ANOVA Comparisons by Community

	Inner-City Communities		Other Urban-Poor Communities		
	M	SD	M	SD	F
Stress	4.59	2.74	4.07	2.64	2.68
Monitoring	.09	1.13	.01	1.33	.28
Discipline	.06	.59	−.02	.77	.94
Beliefs	−.10	.88	.10	.85	4.17*
Cohesion	−.08	1.17	.11	1.47	1.49
Structure	−.08	.70	.07	.88	2.75

*$p < .05$.

other poor urban communities may mediate the impact of stress on youth behavior. It should also be noted that the predictive models were not very strong in either set of neighborhoods, especially in the inner-city neighborhoods.

These analyses led to different predictive models for inner-city and other urban-poor communities. In inner-city communities, the amount of stress experienced appears to overwhelm the impact of family functioning. In urban-poor communities, the emotional closeness of the family, beliefs about the importance of family, and consistent and effective discipline appear to mediate the effects of stress experienced.

These results seemed to support our hypothesis that residence in inner-city communities exerted direct influence on risk for delinquent behavior and overwhelmed family factors. However, we also wanted to evaluate two other possible explanations. First, it may be that families in inner-city communities simply experience significantly more stressful life events than families living in other urban-poor communities. That is, the explanation may lie in the differences in the amount of stress experienced. A second possibility was that inner-city families' functioning was simply worse, and the reason families were overwhelmed was because they were functioning more poorly than families in other communities.

To test these hypotheses, two sets of ANOVAs were conducted to test differences in stress, and family relation characteristics including parenting practices between families living in inner-city and those living in other urban-poor communities. Table 15.3 presents the results of these analyses. The only significant difference we found between neighborhoods was in Beliefs About Family, with families living in urban-poor communities reporting significantly stronger beliefs about the importance of family [$F(1, 319) = 4.17$, $p < .05$]. There were no significant differences between any of the other family relation characteristics, discipline, monitoring, or amount of stress experienced.

Implications

In attempting to understand communities' effect on important family characteristics, we found that when we looked at our entire sample, community, stress, and family functioning each contributed bivariately to the prediction of youth participation in delinquent behavior. Importantly, individual family level variables such as family poverty or single-parenthood often thought to account for differences in risk and outcome among poor urban youth were not related to delinquency among this sample. Rather, characteristics of the community appear to have a direct impact on these youths' behavior. When we divided the sample by different types of communities, those living in inner-city or underclass communities (40% below poverty) and those living in poor but not as devastated communities, we found that different predictive models apply. In the inner-city communities, only stress experienced was significantly related to delinquent behavior. None of the family or parenting variables were related. However, in the other urban-poor communities, Cohesion and Beliefs About Family, and to some extent Discipline, mediated the impact of stress. These differences in predictive models are particularly noteworthy because there were no differences between groups on level of stress experienced, parenting practices, or family relation characteristics other than beliefs about the family.

These results are consistent with results of others who found a qualitative difference among poor urban neighborhoods (Brooks-Gunn et al., 1993). Crane (1991) found that as neighborhood quality decreased, there was a sharp increase in the probability that an individual would develop a social problem. This jump occurred at the bottom of the distribution of neighborhood quality. However, these results are somewhat inconsistent with previous research suggesting linear relations between poverty and parenting and aggression (Dodge, Pettit, & Bates, 1994). Differences in results may be explained by the failure of these investigators to consider other contextual factors, or they may arise from measurement methods or age differences. The current inner-city population may also be poorer than those populations sampled by other investigators.

Previous research consistently found higher levels of stress in inner-city than in urban-poor communities (Attar et al., 1994). However, our data show no differences in stress levels between communities. Rather, the results suggest that the relation between stress, delinquency, and community is more complex than implied in the literature. Stress and delinquency are related differently by community type, in that buffering effects of family are more apparent in "other urban" communities than in inner-city communities. One possible explanation for this finding is that there may be a qualitative difference in the types of stress experienced in each community. Although families may experience the same frequency of stressful life events, the nature of the events may be different depending on where one lives, a possibility that can be investigated in our data. It is also possible that the same stressor may have a very different impact on the family, depending on the level of chronic environmental stress. The family's ability to recover or to support the child during these acute stressors may be impeded by other factors within the community. The tasks faced by families living in inner-city communities are likely quite different than those faced by families living in other types of communities. Traditional interventions that focus on parenting practices such as discipline and monitoring may not be as effective with families living in the inner city as has been found with families living in other settings. It is not that these characteristics of families are not important. Rather, the task for families living in the inner city may be to maintain these characteristics in the face of stressors associated with living in an urban environment. The basic work for intervention and prevention efforts may be to help families learn to manage and cope with these stressors (Tolan & Gorman-Smith, 1997).

In noninner-city communities, as has been found in other types of communities, the impact of stress on children may be mediated by its negative impact on families. Within other than the most devastated inner-city communities, it may make sense to target those at risk and develop services aimed at providing consistent discipline and supervision and increasing support, communication, and organization within the family. In the inner city, a focus only on increasing family functioning is not likely to make a difference in child behavior. Risk in these communities is not necessarily related to family functioning. Rather, programs and policies aimed at reducing chronic strains and building social support and communication among families living in the neighborhood may be more effective in changing behavior in these communities. Increased support and social organization within the neighborhood may provide support to families to help negotiate and manage the demands of community stressors (Sampson, in press). Policies aimed at improving the quality of the neighborhood, those affecting the structural characteristics of the community such as the economic and social resources available, are likely to make the most significant changes for children and families in inner-city communities (Brooks-Gunn et al., 1993).

The current analyses are based on cross-sectional data. Therefore the direction of effects may not be that implied in our hierarchical models. It is possible that neighborhood differences reflect an entirely different process. That is, in the neighborhoods that are less than abjectly poor, families that are better functioning are better able to protect their children from exposure to high levels of stressful events. The current analyses in these areas are consistent with the possibility that stress exposure is related to delinquency only by virtue of their common origin in poor family functioning. In inner-city poverty areas stress experiences are relatively independent of family functioning because families are unable to protect their children from exposure.

REFERENCES

Achenbach, T. M. (1991). *Integrative guide for the 1991 CBCL/4-18, YSR, TRF profiles.* Burlington: University of Vermont, Department of Psychiatry.

Attar, B. K., Guerra, N. G., & Tolan, P. H. (1994). Neighborhood disadvantage, stressful life events, and adjustment in urban elementary-school children. *Journal of Clinical Child Psychology, 23,* 391–400.

Bell, C. C., & Jenkins, E. J. (1993). Community violence and children on Chicago's southside. *Psychiatry, 56,* 46–54.

Belle, D. (1984). Inequality and mental health: Low-income and minority women. In L. Walker (Ed.), *Women and mental health policy* (pp. 135–150). Beverly Hills, CA: Sage.

Belsky, J., & Vondra, J. (1989). Lessons from child abuse: The determinants of parenting. In D. Cicchetti & V. Carlson (Eds.), *Child maltreatment.* New York: Cambridge University Press.

Bronfenbrenner, U. (1979). *The ecology of human development: Experiments by nature and design.* Cambridge, MA: Harvard University Press.

Brooks-Gunn, J., Duncan, G. J., Klebanov, P. K., & Sealand, N. S. (1993). Do neighborhoods influence child and adolescent development? *American Journal of Sociology, 99*(2), 353–395.

Bursik, R. J. (1988). Social disorganization and theories of crime and delinquency: Problems and prospects. *Criminology, 26,* 519–552.

Bursik, R. J., & Grasmick, H. G. (1993). *Neighborhoods and crime.* New York: Lexington Books.

Byrne, J. M., & Sampson, R. J. (Eds.). (1986). *The social ecology of crime.* New York: Springer-Verlag.

Children's Defense Fund. (1991). *The adolescent and young adult fact book.* Washington, DC: Author.

Conger, R. D., Ge, X., Elder, G. H., Lorenz, F. O., & Simons, R. L. (1994). Economic stress, coercive family process, and developmental problems of adolescents. *Child Development, 65*(2), 541–561.

Coulton, C. J., & Pandey, S. (1992). Geographic concentration of poverty and risk to children in urban neighborhoods. *American Behavioral Scientist, 35,* 238–257.

Crane, J. (1991). The epidemic theory of ghettos and neighborhood effects on dropping out and teenage childbearing. *American Journal of Sociology, 96,* 1226–1259.

Dodge, K. A., Pettit, G. S., & Bates, J. E. (1994). Socialization mediators of the relation between socioeconomic status and child conduct problems. *Child Development, 65,* 649–665.

Elder, G. H., Jr., & Caspi, A. (1988). Economic stress in lives: Developmental perspectives. *Journal of Social Issues, 44,* 25–45.

Elder, G. H., Jr., Eccles, J., Ardelt, M., & Lord, S. (1993, March). *Inner city parents under economic pressure: Perspectives on the strategies of parenting.* Abstract presented at the 60th anniversary meeting of the Society for Research in Child Development, New Orleans.

Elliott, D. S., Dunford, F. W., & Huizinga, D. (1987). The identification and prediction of career offenders utilizing self-reported and official data. In J. D. Burchard & S. N. Burchard (Eds.), *Prevention of delinquent behavior* (pp. 90–121). Newbury Park, CA: Sage.

Farrington, D. P. (1986). Age and crime. In M. Tonry & N. Morris (Eds.), *Crime and delinquency: An annual review of research* (Vol. 7, pp. 189–250). Chicago: University of Chicago Press.

Garbarino, J. (1992). The meaning of poverty in the world of children. *American Behavioral Scientist, 35*(3), 220–237.

Garbarino, J., & Associates. (1992). *Children and families in the social environment* (2nd ed.). Hawthorne, NY: Aldine.

Garbarino, J., Dubrow, N., Kostelny, K., & Pardo, C. (1992). *Children in anger.* San Francisco: Jossey-Bass.

Garbarino, J., & Kostelny, K. (1992). Neighborhood and community influences on parenting. In T. Luster & L. Okagaki (Eds.), *Parenting: An ecological perspective.* Hillside, NJ: Lawrence Erlbaum Associates.

Garbarino, J., & Sherman, D. (1980). High-risk neighborhoods and high-risk families: The human ecology of child maltreatment. *Child Development, 51,* 188–198.

Garmezy, N. (1987). Stress, competence and development: Continuities in the study of schizophrenic adults, children vulnerable to psychopathology, and the search for stress-resistant children. *American Journal of Orthopsychiatry, 57,* 159–174.

Gorman-Smith, D., & Tolan, P. H. (1998). The role of exposure to community violence and developmental problems among inner-city youth. *Development and Psychopathology, 10,* 101–116.

Gorman-Smith, D., Tolan, P. H., Zelli, A., & Huesmann, L. R. (1996). The relation of family functioning to violence among inner-city minority youth. *Journal of Family Psychology, 10,* 115–129.

Guerra, N. G., Huesmann, L. R., Tolan, P. H., VanAcker, R., & Eron, L. (1995). Stressful events and individual beliefs as correlates of economic disadvantage among urban children. *Journal of Consulting and Clinical Psychology, 63,* 518–528.

Henggeler, S. W. (1989). *Delinquency in adolescence.* New York: Sage.

Henggeler, S. W., Melton, G. B., & Smith, L. A. (1992). Family preservation using multisystemic therapy: An effective alternative to incarcerating serious juvenile offenders. *Journal of Consulting and Clinical Psychology, 63*(4), 518–528.

Leadbeater, B. J., & Bishop, S. J. (1994). Predictors of behavior problems in preschool children of inner-city Afro-American and Puerto Rican adolescent mothers. *Child Development, 65,* 638–648.

Loeber, R., & Dishion, T. (1983). Early predictors of male delinquency: A review. *Psychological Bulletin, 94,* 68–99.

Loeber, R., Farrington, D. P., Stouthamer-Loeber, M., & van Kammen, W. B. (1998). *Antisocial behavior and mental health problems: Explanatory factors in childhood and adolescence.* Mahwah, NJ: Lawrence Erlbaum Associates.

Loeber, R., & Stouthamer-Loeber, M. (1986). Family factors as correlates and predictors of juvenile conduct problems and delinquency. In M. Tonry & N. Morris (Eds.), *Crime and justice: An annual review of research* (Vol. 7, pp. 29–149). Chicago: University of Chicago Press.

Mayer, S. E., & Jencks, C. (1989). Growing up in poor neighborhoods: How much does it matter? *Science, 243,* 1441–1445.

McLanahan, S. (1983). Family structure and stress: A longitudinal comparison of two-parent and female-headed families. *Journal of Marriage and the Family, 45,* 347–357.

McLoyd, V. C. (1990). The impact of economic hardship on black families and children: Psychological distress, parenting, and socioemotional development. *Child Development, 61,* 311–346.

McLoyd, V. C., Jayaratne, T. E., Ceballo, R., & Borquez, J. (1994). Unemployment and work interruption among African-American single mothers: Effects on parenting and adolescent socio-emotional functioning. *Child Development, 65*(2), 562–589.

Patterson, G. R., DeBaryshe, B. D., & Ramsey, E. (1989). A developmental perspective on antisocial behavior. *American Psychologist, 44,* 329–335.

Patterson, G. R., Reid, J. B., & Dishion, T. J. (1992). *Antisocial boys.* New York: Castalia.

Reese, M. (1982). Growing up: The impact of loss and change. In D. Belle (Ed.), *Lives in stress: Women and depression* (pp. 65–80). Beverly Hills, CA: Sage.

Reiss, D. (1993). Introduction: American violence and its children. *Psychiatry, 56*, 1–2.

Richters, J. E., & Martinez, P. E. (1993). Violent communities, family choices, and children's chances: An algorithm for improving the odds. *Development and Psychopathology, 5*, 609–627.

Rutter, M. (1983). Stress, coping and development: Some issues and some questions. In N. Garmezy & M. Rutter (Eds.), *Stress, coping and development in children* (pp. 1–42). New York: McGraw-Hill.

Rutter, M., & Giller, H. (1983). *Juvenile delinquency: Trends and perspectives*. New York: Guilford.

Sampson, R. J. (1985). Neighborhood and crime: Structural determinants of personal victimization. *Journal of Research in Crime and Delinquency, 22*, 7–40.

Sampson, R. J. (1987). Urban black violence: The effect of male joblessness and family disruption. *American Journal of Sociology, 93*, 348–382.

Sampson, R. J. (1991). Linking the micro- and macrolevel dimensions of community social organization. *Social Forces, 70*, 43–64.

Sampson, R. J. (in press). Crime and violence in the inner-city: Family and community contexts of childhood socialization. In J. McCord (Ed.), *Growing up violent: Contributions of inner-city life.*

Sampson, R. J., & Groves, W. B. (1989). Community structure and crime: Testing social-disorganization theory. *American Journal of Sociology, 94*, 774–802.

Sampson, R. J., & Laub, J. H. (1994). Urban poverty and the family context of delinquency: A new look at structure and process in a class study. *Child Development, 65*(2), 523–540.

Seidman, E., Allen, L., Aber, J. L., Mitchell, C., & Feinman, J. (1994). The impact of school transitions in early adolescence on the self-system and perceived social context of poor urban youth. *Child Development, 65*, 507–522.

Seifer, R., & Sameroff, A. J. (1987). Multiple determinants of risk and vulnerability. In E. J. Anthony & B. J. Cohler (Eds.), *The invulnerable child* (pp. 51–69). New York: Guilford.

Simcha-Fagan, O., & Schwartz, J. E. (1986). Neighborhood and delinquency: An assessment of contextual effects. *Criminology, 24*, 667–703.

Tolan, P. H. (1988). Socioeconomic, family and social stress correlates of adolescent antisocial and delinquent behavior. *Journal of Abnormal Child Psychology, 16*, 181–194.

Tolan, P. H., & Gorman-Smith, D. (1991). *The Chicago Stress and Coping Interview* (Tech. Rep.)

Tolan, P. H., & Gorman-Smith, D. (1997). Families and the development of urban children. In O. Reyes, H. Walberg, & R. Weissberg (Eds.), *Interdisciplinary perspectives on children and youth* (pp. 67–91). Newbury Park: Sage.

Tolan, P. H., Gorman-Smith, D., Huesmann, L. R., & Zelli, A. (1997). Assessing family processes to explain risk for antisocial behavior and depression among urban youth. *Psychological Assessment, 9*, 212–223.

Tolan, P. H., Henry, D., Guerra, N. G., Huesmann, L. R., VanAcker, R., & Eron, L. D. (1998). *Patterns of psychopathology among urban poor children: I. Community, age, ethnicity, and gender effects.* Manuscript submitted for publication.

Tolan, P. H., & Loeber, R. (1993). Antisocial behavior. In P. H. Tolan & B. J. Cohler (Eds.), *Handbook of clinical research and practice with adolescents* (pp. 1–2). New York: Wiley.

Tolan, P. H., & Lorion, R. P. (1988). Multivariate approaches to the identification of delinquency-proneness in males. *American Journal of Community Psychology, 16*, 547–561.

Weinraub, M., & Wolf, B. (1983). Effects of stress and social supports on mother–child interactions in single- and two-parent families. *Child Development, 54*, 1297–1311.

Wilson, W. J. (1987). *The truly disadvantaged.* Chicago: University of Chicago Press.

Wilson, W. J., Aponte, R., Kirschenman, J., & Wacquant, L. J. D. (1988). The ghetto underclass and the changing structure of urban poverty. In F. R. Harris & R. W. Wilkins (Eds.), *Quiet riots: Race and poverty in the United States* (pp. 123–151). New York: Pantheon Books.

Author Index

Subject Index

A

Adolescents
  antisocial behavior in, *see* Antisocial behavior
  suicidal, concomitant affective disorders in, 124
African Americans
  crimes rates among
    description of, 20–22, 26
    effects of urban isolation, 26–31
  violence against, 20–21, 26
Aggressive behavior
  in patients with major mental disorders, 66–67
  toward family members, relationship with poor parenting styles, 167
Alcohol use, relationship with antisocial personality disorder, 262–263, 268
Anti-Semitism, of early Nazis and neo-Nazis, 93–94, 97
Antisocial behavior
  conduct disorder and, 50–51
  major mental disorder development and, 76–77
  parenting practices and, 167, 194, 272
  studies of intergenerational continuity of
    analysis, 173
    behaviors that subject to, 164
    criticisms, 165–166
    definition of, 166
    description of, 163, 170–171
    discussion of findings, 181–182
    from first-generation dysfunction, 167–168
    limitations

measurement point, 184–185
    secular trends, 185
    mediating processes
      childrearing practices, 166–167, 178–182
      contextual continuity, 168–169, 171–172
      description of, 172, 177–178
      environmental circumstances, 168–169, 171–172
      first-generation deviance, 166–167
      psychological distress, 172–173, 179–182
    methodology
      description of, 164–166
      implications, 181
    methods, 171–173
    moderating processes, 169–170
    parenting practices that affect, 167–168, 178–181
    research implications, 186–187
    results, 174–181
Antisocial personality disorder
  cross-national studies of
    data analysis, 255–257
    methods, 251–257
    reasons for, 250–251
    relationship between adult antisocial behavior and childhood antisocial disorder, 265–274
    results
      age of onset, 263–265
      alcohol abuse or dependence, 262–263, 268
      gender predilection, 259t, 262
      in adults, 261t

studies in young adults
females
commonalities with young
males, 155–156
differences with young males,
156–157
stressors, 150–152
major depression diagnostic criteria,
144–145
males
commonalities with young females, 155–156
differences with young females,
156–157
stressors, 148–150
mental health services received for,
152–153, 158
method, 143–146
overview, 141–142
prevalence of, 146–147, 154–155
research implications, 157–158
stressors
career, 142–143, 155
description of, 142
failure to meet educational
goals, 143
interpersonal relationships, 143,
156
number of, 152, 157
types of, 145–146
treatment implications, 157–158
suicide and, 123–125
Depressive syndrome, definition of, 115
Disaster
past research, 218–221
psychological distress and
depression, 218
factors that influence
community characteristics,
240–241
gender, 220, 243–244
perceived control, 221, 227,
231–232, 244
post-traumatic stress disorder,
219, 222–224,
227–228, 235–238,
241–242
proximity to disaster, 219–222,
241
social support, 220–221, 227,
243
mediational models, 224, 238–239
past studies, 218–221
studies of
measures, 226–228

method, 225–228
results, 228–239
structural equation models,
235–239
substance use and
factors that affect
proximity to disaster, 219
social support, 220–221
studies of relationship between,
228, 234–235, 239,
242–243
Discipline, *see* Maternal discipline
Distress, *see* Psychological distress
Downward mobility
effect on rise of National Socialism in
Germany, 89
in early Nazis vs. neo-Nazis, 99

E

Ethnicity
conduct disorder and, 48
crime and, 20–22
Extremism, *see* Right-wing extremism

F

Family
and depression
in young adult females, 150
in young adult males, 148–150
divorce, effect on child delinquency,
321
effect on child development
description of, 279–280, 351
studies in American Indian and Appalachian communities
burden of risk, 294–295
family risk factors, 286–290
findings, 293–295
interviewing measures, 282–283
methods, 280–285
overview, 279–280
poverty, 290–295
procedures, 284–285
psychiatric disorders, 285–289,
287t–288t, 292–293
studies in inner-city and urban poor
families
Chicago Youth Development
Study, 355–364
description of, 352–353
environmental stress, 354–355
stressors, 353–354